Interactive Problem Solving Using LOGO

Heinz-Dieter Boecker
Hal Eden
Gerhard Fischer

LEA LAWRENCE ERLBAUM ASSOCIATES, PUBLISHERS
1991 Hillsdale, New Jersey   Hove and London

George Polya, *How to Solve It: A New Aspect of Mathematical Method.*
 Copyright 1945 Princeton University Press. © 1973 renewed by
Princeton University Press. Excerpt, pp. xvi-xvii reprinted with
permission of Princeton University Press.

UNIX is a trademark of AT&T

SCRABBLE is a trademark of Selchow and Righter

Lawrence Erlbaum Associates, Publishers
365 Broadway
Hillsdale, New Jersey 07642

Library of Congress Cataloging-in-Publication Data

Bocker, Heinz-Dieter, 1949-
 Interactive problem solving using LOGO / Heinz-Dieter Boecker, Hal
Eden, Gerhard Fischer.
  p. cm.
 Includes bibliographical references and index.
 ISBN 0-8058-0305-X (cloth) / 0-8058-0306-8 (paper)
 1. LOGO (Computer program language) 2. Interactive computer
systems. I. Eden, Hal. II. Fischer, Gerhard. III. Title.
QA76.73.L63B63 1990
005.26--dc20   90-43516
       70 5 7/   CIP

Printed in the United States of America
10 9 8 7 6 5 4 3 2 1

To Artur Fischer, a genuine problem solver and generous supporter

and

In memory of Dene and Gene Yoder

Table of Contents

Appendices

Interactive Problem Solving

—

Beyond Teaching Programming Languages

Problem Solving. Problem Solving is a ubiquitous human activity. If we want to do something but we do not know how, then we have a problem. The problem is the gap that separates us from where we want to be. In natural settings, problems are represented to us by the outside world. The sources for the problems may be derived from our own goals or they may be given to us by a teacher, a client, an advice seeker, etc. Problem solving often consists of two major activities: On the one hand we need to understand the problem; on the other hand we need to solve it. These two activities are not independent of each other: Attempting to solve a problem usually contributes to a better understanding of that problem, as well as to a better understanding of how to solve problems in general.

Problems may be represented in many different ways, influencing the difficulty substantially. The building blocks and tools that we have available to understand and solve problems influence our perception of them and our ability to solve them. These building blocks and tools can be either of a physical nature (e.g., a nail and a hammer) or they can be conceptual artifacts (e.g., musical notation or the "language" of mathematics). A powerful tool kit offering many interesting building blocks for problem solving that has emerged over the last few decades has been the computer and the developments surrounding it. Computers support problem-solving activities such as writing and using programs. They provide us with feedback to our solution attempts, serve as testbeds for our ideas, and thereby enhance our incremental understanding of problems.

Interactive Problem Solving with Computers. The computer, when used in an environment that supports interactive programming, can provide a rich opportunity to explore a variety of interesting subjects. The case studies presented here attempt to exploit this opportunity. They describe various *interest worlds* and provide an initial platform for investigation of related problems. The interest worlds documented in this book are: mathematics, computer science, artificial intelligence, linguistics, and games. The approach is by no means limited to these areas but serves as a model that can be applied to other fields of study as well. By providing and encouraging exploration into rich, open-ended problem domains aimed at capturing your interest and imagination, you will cultivate your cognitive talents in the areas of problem solving and formal thinking.

The computer, as one of the newest technological developments, holds a great attraction to many at first (especially when used for playing games, etc.). This enthusiasm soon vanishes when users grow tired of the available programs and realize that improving existing programs and creating new ones requires a nontrivial amount of learning and work. Using a computer-based interactive programming system as a learning environment offers many benefits. Here are some of the rewards you will experience if you master the "art of programming":

- You can be more independent, searching for your own problems and solutions.

- You can work on open problems, problems that are not completely specified, even some for which no known solution exists.

- The problems become your own rather than dull, rote exercises. This encourages intensive, active interaction with a problem over a longer period of time; days and weeks instead of hours.

- You get feedback about the flaws in your own thinking and where the errors are.

- Complex programming tasks allow an opportunity to work in groups, if desired, cultivating another important skill.

We hope that this book is useful for personal study as well as in more formal learning situations.

What is LOGO and Why Did We Choose LOGO?

While looking for an appropriate computer language for our work, we wanted one that supported the process of *problem solving* and *model formation*. The design criteria that led to the development of LOGO share these goals. The original developers of LOGO [Feurzeig et al. 69] articulated the following goals for their design. The language should:

- represent a usable metalanguage to support many aspects of problem solving processes (e.g., the description of heuristics, the representation of the relationship between global plans and the specifics of a detailed solution),

- support a precise description of problems,

- be especially suited for the solution of nonnumerical problems,

- represent a closed system,

- allow a modular style of programming (construction kit principle).

From the beginning LOGO built on the basic assumption that plenty of computational power at the hardware level will eventually be available, and the real limitation of successful use of the computer will be our ability to find an answer to the question "What can we do with it?" This book is an attempt to stretch these limits of our imaginations a bit.

From our perspective, misunderstandings and limited views about LOGO developed over the years. LOGO is not just Turtle geometry [Abelson, diSessa 80], and it is not just a specific programming language. The LOGO philosophy, as developed and articulated primarily by Seymour Papert [Papert 80], represents a new approach towards using computers in education and creating new views and contexts for exploration in education, psychology, and epistemology.

LOGO—The Programming Language. We do not want to promote the "religious" beliefs held by some people that "LOGO as a programming language" is something unique. In any case, the uniqueness of a programming language does not derive from its formal properties, because all programming languages are equivalent in a formal sense: Whatever one can do with language X one can also do with language Y.

But this formal equivalence has little to do with what people can do *in reality*. In using computers, we are in general not limited in our problem-solving activities by the limits of *objective computability* (i.e., that something cannot be done in principle) but by the limits of *subjective computability* (i.e., that something cannot be done because we do not understand the problem, we do not know how to solve it, or we do not have or do not want to spend the large amount of cognitive resources that its solution requires). LOGO has many important features to increase subjective computability in a variety of interest worlds:

- It provides us with an interactive programming environment including several powerful primitives to manipulate that environment, and it is run interpretively, which simplifies testing and debugging of evolving programs.

- It is based on nonnumeric, dynamic data structures (i.e., lists), which makes it well suited for symbolic computing in the interest worlds described in this book.

- It is centered around the procedure concept that allows the breakdown of complex problems into manageable pieces. After being defined, user-defined procedures become indistinguishable from system-defined procedures.

- The syntax of LOGO programs supports the equivalence of programs and data; this feature together with the availability of a Run command makes the creation of programs that manipulate other programs feasible, contributing to the extensibility of the language.

- Recursion is a powerful concept in the language. Again, it is not just the existence of recursion as a control structure, but its linkage with recursively defined data structures (such as lists and trees) and the creation of adequate models in the LOGO culture to understand recursion.

- Turtle geometry [Abelson, diSessa 80] , providing the foundation for one interesting interest-world, has shown the tailorability for a specific use of the language.

LOGO as a programming language has been in existence for 20 years now; but only over the last 10 years, a growing number of books have appeared that describe LOGO as a programming language and its use in solving problems (examples of such books are: [Abelson 82; Watt 83; Harvey 85; Harvey 86; Harvey 87a; Friendly 88]). LOGO as a programming language should not be evaluated along traditional desiderata such as formal simplicity, efficiency, verifiability, or uniformity, but along criteria such as understandability and support for common, directly useful abstractions. Simple problems should be simple and complex problems should be doable. The language should support interactive problem-solving and human-computer communication in a cooperative problem-solving setting. LOGO as a programming language is closely related to LISP with a few important differences that all contribute to the cognitive efficiency of LOGO: It uses names that are more meaningful for many of its built-in procedures (e.g., `First` and `ButFirst` versus `car` and `cdr`), it distinguishes clearly between operations and commands, and it restricts predicates to having either `True` or `False` as their output), etc.

LOGO—A New Approach to Using Computers in Education. Computer literacy in today's world means more than just using existing programs. It means being able to make the computer "do our bidding." This idea was much more revolutionary in the late 1960s, when the prime and almost exclusive use of computers in education was seen in "Computer-Assisted Instruction (CAI)" [Wenger 87]. The LOGO philosophy departed from the ideas behind computer-assisted instruction: Instead of being programmed by the computer with its rote instruction, it pushed the idea that people of all ages should have control over the computer by programming it. It radically changed people's perspective on what computers can be good for by putting students "in the driver's seat" of their interaction with computers. Instead of just playing games on the computer, students could now design and build their *own* games. Whereas courseware in a CAI environment imposed a specific curriculum on students, LOGO and other computational tools (such as word processor, spreadsheets, etc.) provide open, partially structured learning environments, in which many ideas can be explored. This perspective of an open learning environment embodies the idea of interest worlds such as turtle geometry [Abelson, diSessa 80], language [Goldenberg, Feurzeig 87], physics [Hurley 85], or the ones described in this book.

LOGO—A New Approach for Education, Psychology, and Epistemology. At a third level, the culture and ideas that were developed around LOGO provide new approaches, new opportunities, and new interesting questions and challenges for education, psychology, and epistemology [Papert 80; Papert 86; Falbel 89]. It enables researchers and educational theorists to study "Piagetian learning" or "learning without being taught." It allows the development of constructivist theories of psychology in which learning is seen as reconstruction rather than as transmission of knowledge. From a design perspective, it has created challenges to develop the right kind of building blocks or the right kinds of objects to think with. It has shed some light on what the notion of a *convivial tool* [Illich 73; Fischer 81] might mean in our society. It has led to ideas about learning environments that have "no threshold and no ceiling," and it has provided environments to engage in *hands-on science*. It has illustrated the necessity of investigating not only purely cognitive issues but extracognitive objectives [Papert 86] such as affective, cultural and gender-related issues as well. It challenges the basic view of science as a completely rational enterprise and creates appreciation for the negotiable character of true science.

What has not Happened in the LOGO World. Looking back at a 20-year history of a culture, one might also ask what has not happened that people assumed would happen 20 years ago. Turtle geometry turned out to be a success model for many ideas of the LOGO culture, but the original expectation that dozens, maybe hundreds, of equally successful interest worlds would be created has not materialized. This book and several other recent books (e.g., [Goldenberg, Feurzeig 87; Friendly 88; Harvey 85; Harvey 86; Harvey 87a; Hurley 85] try to eliminate this shortcoming.

LOGO is now used in some form in one-third of the elementary schools of the United States and has been quite successful in other countries as well (e.g., Australia, Austria, Costa Rica, Germany—to name just a few). Unfortunately LOGO did not have as profound an effect on the nature of learning and schools as LOGO enthusiasts had hoped. There are several reasons for this (e.g., the effort was not driven enough by educational concerns, the teachers were inadequately educated, the resistance of large scale organizations to change, etc.); one reason among all those was the lack of educational material illustrating the approach. This book helps remedy this situation.

History of This Book

This book has a long history. At the University of California, Irvine, in 1972/73, one of the authors (Gerhard Fischer), in collaboration with John Seely Brown and Richard Burton, was involved in using this approach to teach graduate students in the social sciences about computing. This teaching effort emphasized the modeling of knowledge and the processing of language by computers rather than the computation of numbers—and LOGO was preferred to LISP because of its greater cognitive efficiency.

From 1973 till 1978, Heinz-Dieter Boecker and Gerhard Fischer worked at the national research project PROKOP (directed by Ulrich Kling) at the Center for Educational Technology in Darmstadt, W-Germany. It was during this time that the first prototypical versions of the case studies presented in this book were developed and tested in experimental courses. The material was published (in German) as technical reports and was widely distributed and used in German high schools and universities. The material was refined during several courses for continuing teacher education that were taught at the University of Stuttgart between 1978 and 1981.

In the early 1980s the interest in LOGO continued to grow and adequate computational environments became available on a broader scale in schools and colleges. This provided the motivation to publish the material as books in German [Boecker, Fischer, Plehnert 86; Boecker, Fischer, Schollwoeck 86a; Boecker, Fischer, Schollwoeck 86b; Boecker, Fischer, Schollwoeck 87; Boecker, Fischer, Plehnert 87]. The current English version is based on the German edition but has been revised extensively to take into account newer developments and the existence of other books.

Many previous LOGO books can be criticized for focusing on the grammar of the language while ignoring the "literature" developed around the language. By focusing on content areas and on problem-solving processes, and not on the programming language LOGO itself, we have tried to make a contribution to the "literature." We did *not* intend to write a reference book on LOGO (e.g., such as [Abelson 82]) but we tried to convey the art of problem solving using LOGO as a language with which to exercise this art. Part 1 is not part of this global goal but is included to provide some programming basics and to illustrate the concepts of the language used in the later parts of the book in the context of simple problems.

Rationale for This Book

The book is intended for high school and university students and teachers in different disciplines. It may be used for courses as well as for explorations in problem solving by individuals. It provides case studies that hopefully will serve as entry points to many exciting areas. For users who are interested in symbolic computing, it should provide a gentle introduction allowing them to move on to other, more advanced computational frameworks (e.g., LISP, SCHEME, etc.).

This book uses a different approach than other books: Using illustrative case studies, it stresses the importance of interactive problem solving in several interest worlds rather than focusing on the mastery of a programming language. The history of the material presented in this book as outlined in the previous section has demonstrated the usefulness of this approach in several different educational settings.

By studying and working with this book and not just reading it, students and teachers alike can explore ideas, hypotheses, and conjectures that can serve as starting points for more formal analysis in several different domains. You are exposed to general problem-solving techniques (e.g., as illustrated by [Polya 45]) as well as powerful programming techniques (e.g., creating complex data structures, paying attention to cognitive efficiency, etc.). The individual programs can be regarded either as "black boxes" being used without a need to understand them or as "glass boxes" where you can look inside, comprehend them as they document a problem solution, and modify them for your own use.

Reading Guide

This book is organized as follows: The Fundamentals of LOGO (Part 1) explains the main concepts of programming in LOGO. Parts 2 through 6 present case studies in mathematics, computer science, artificial intelligence, linguistics, and games. New developments in computers and education in the LOGO culture and beyond are described in Part 7.

Part 1 ("Fundamentals of LOGO") is organized to introduce concepts of LOGO in an incremental way and should therefore, unless the reader is already familiar with LOGO, be read sequentially. Part 1 is also a prerequisite of Parts 2 through 6. No specific order need be followed for Parts 2 through 6, and the material can be selected and studied according to the interests of the reader. We include pointers to related material of other sections. The classification scheme is not unique. Certain problems (e.g., pattern matching) could have appeared in computer science, linguistics, or artificial intelligence—an indication that interest worlds are not totally disjoint from each other and that ideas cross-fertilize each other among different domains.

Acknowledgments

Over the years, many people have contributed to and have fostered environments for the research effort that led to this book.

John Seely Brown stimulated our thinking about these problems and Seymour Papert inspired us with his enthusiasm for the ideas explored in the LOGO culture. We are grateful that we had the opportunity to spend extended periods in the MIT LOGO Lab where we had many interesting discussions, especially with Hal Abelson and Andy diSessa. Wally Feurzeig from BBN has provided insights that have helped us gain a deeper understanding of our own work. Important to our current perspective was an invitation by Alan Kay to work with him and his colleagues in the Smalltalk/Dynabook environment in 1978 at Xerox Parc.

The German Ministry of Research and Technology provided the research funds for the PROKOP project, and Ulrich Kling envisioned the right future directions for computers and education in PROKOP, namely emphasizing interactive programming instead of computer-assisted instruction. Michael Plehnert and Ulrich Schollwoeck deserve credit for working together with us in publishing the German edition of our material. Numerous remarks and feedback were provided by students and teachers using the original versions of our documents.

A very special "Thank You" goes to Artur Fischer, the inventor of the Fischer-Technik Construction Kits, who has supported our research work over the last 10 years with great sympathy and has shared his insights and enthusiasm into the future of education with us.

Mitchel Resnick and Michael Friendly provided very valuable comments to earlier drafts of the book. The collaboration with Julia Hough and Hollis Heimbouch from Lawrence Erlbaum was enjoyable and productive. Pat and Jennell Breitenstein made their home available as a sanctuary from interruption. Laszlo Nemeth helped us make sure that the programs worked as printed and Roseanna Eden provided important feedback from the perspective of an educator as well as that of a LOGO-novice. Andreas Girgensohn gave us useful feedback on the object-oriented chapter. The BOXER figure in chapter 39 was graciously provided by Andy diSessa.

Part 1:
Fundamentals of LOGO

Introduction

Although the primary goal of our book is to provide a variety of interest worlds for you to investigate, some introduction to the fundamentals of programming using LOGO may be necessary. That is the goal of this part. However, given the diversity represented by the various versions of LOGO, we cannot present this material in a form that applies to all these systems. We advise you to use the user's manual for your LOGO system as a companion to this section as we do not discuss how to

- start up LOGO

- edit LOGO programs

- use special purpose keys or the mouse to perform special functions such as interrupting, positioning the cursor, or deleting characters

- save or load LOGO programs from disk.

There may also be variations on exactly how the LOGO programs are written; we discuss some of these differences in Appendix I but, again, you should study your user's manual to understand the details of your LOGO system.

We cover the basics that we feel are necessary to help you explore the topics presented in the rest of the book. In doing so, we hope to avoid an emphasis on minute details of LOGO as a programming language. We try to motivate and situate the various language constructs but, in some cases, this is not possible until you apply LOGO to the problems presented later and problems of your own.

Chapter 1:
Your First Encounters with LOGO

Every computer language has a set of primitive (built-in) objects. These can be classified into two sets: the set of procedures, or things that the language knows how to do, and the set of data types, or the types of things the language knows how to do things to. These two sets are tightly interrelated, since it is difficult to describe an action in a way that is completely independent from what is being acted on. This chapter presents some of the primitive LOGO objects and the actions that operate on them.

1.1. Words and Lists

Early programming languages emphasized the numerical capabilities of computers by providing numbers (integer and floating-point) as the primary fuel for the computational engine. The need to operate on groups of numbers repetitively and efficiently led to the addition of arrays (sets of numbers stored contiguously that could be accessed by providing an offset into their storage). More recently languages have also acknowledged the ability of the computer to process more than just numbers by introducing characters (letters represented by number codes) and strings (arrays of characters). In LOGO the emphasis is upon *symbolic computation*, operating on words and lists of words.

Words

LOGO (whose name is derived from the Greek word *logos*, which means "word") takes a different approach. The basic *data* building blocks in LOGO are *words*. Here are some examples of words:

```
word
this
1234
abc123
2.0
2e3
```

These words can be used for different things: They can be commands to tell LOGO to do something, they can be names for information we want to remember, or they can be the actual data (numbers, strings of letters) that we want to work with.

In order to treat a word as actual data, in general we precede it with a double quote character,"""". The word is then composed of all characters until some "white space" (space, tab, end-of-line, etc) is found.

Let's see what the computer "thinks" about this:

```
Welcome to Logo
? "word
You don't say what to do with "word.
```

This raises the next question: Now that we know about this simple data type, what can we (have the computer) do with it? This leads us to our first Logo operation, the Print command:

```
? Print "word
word
```

Lists and Sentences

The next primitive data type is the list. A list is simply a sequence of elements that are words, or other lists. We write lists in a special *syntax* or "way of writing things"; here is an example:

```
[this is a list]
```

The "open bracket" character, "[," is used to indicate the beginning of a list, and the "close bracket," "]," is used to indicate its end. Words that are part of a list do not have "'"'s in front of them. Lists that contain only words are called *sentences*. Since we use them often and their simple structure is similar to a sentence in regular language, it is useful to give them a special name.

As just mentioned, a list can also contain elements that are other lists. These are called *nested* lists.

```
[[this] [is a] [list of lists]]
[this is [a list] of words [and lists]]
```

Lists may be Printed as well:

```
? Print [this [is] [a list]]
this [is] [a list]
```

Note that the outermost set of brackets is left off when the list is printed. Sometimes it is useful to see the whole representation: To do this we can use the Show command. This is just like the Print command for words, but for lists, the outer brackets are printed when using Show:

```
? Show [this [is] [a list]]
[this [is] [a list]]
```

In general, we use the Print command, but when it is useful to show the entire structure (particularly in this chapter), we use the Show command.

Primitive Operations on Words and Lists

So far, all we can do with these basic data objects is to Print them out. Much of the work done in Logo requires us to put words, and lists together and to take them apart.

Here are some of the basic operations that allow this to be done.

- **First** extracts the first element of a word or a list:

  ```
  ? Show First "abc
  a
  ? Show First [ab cd ef]
  ab
  ```

- **ButFirst** gives back the word or list with the first element taken away:

  ```
  ? Show ButFirst "abc
  bc
  ? Show ButFirst [ab cd ef]
  [cd ef]
  ```

- **Last** extracts the last element of a word or list:

  ```
  ? Show Last "abc
  c
  ? Show Last [ab cd ef]
  ef
  ```

- **ButLast** returns the word or list with the last element taken away.

  ```
  ? Show ButLast "abc
  ab
  ? Show ButLast [ab cd ef]
  [ab cd]
  ```

Now that we know how to take things apart, how do we put them back together? Let's say we wanted to take the list [ab cd], break it into its first and last parts, and put them together in the opposite order.

We could try this:

```
? Show [Last [ab cd] First [ab cd]]
[Last [ab cd] First [ab cd]]
```

Hmmmm. This is not what we wanted! What we need are operations that can "reassemble the pieces." Here are the basic ones:

- **Word** assembles words together to form a new word:

  ```
  ? Show Word "abc "xyz
  abcxyz
  ```

- **List** assembles words and lists together to form a new list:

  ```
  ? Show List "a [b]
  [a [b]]
  ```

- **Sentence** assembles words and/or sentences together to form a new sentence:

  ```
  ? Show Sentence "This [is a sentence.]
  [This is a sentence.]
  ? Show Sentence [This is] [a sentence.]
  [This is a sentence.]
  ```

It is also useful (as we see better later) to be able to have the computer check various properties of data items.

- WordP tests whether the item is a word:

    ```
    ? Print WordP "abc
    True
    ? Print WordP [abc]
    False
    ```

- ListP tests whether the item is a list:

    ```
    ? Print ListP "abc
    False
    ? Print ListP [abc]
    True
    ```

- EqualP test whether two data items are equal:

    ```
    ? Print EqualP "a First "abc
    True
    ```

The Empty Word and the Empty List

The words and lists we have shown so far all shared the characteristic that they contained one or more elements. There are special cases where words or lists are needed that contain no elements. These are called the empty word and the empty list, respectively. These can be generated, for example, using the ButFirst command.

- The Empty List:

    ```
    ? Show ButFirst [a]
    [ ]
    ?
    ```

- The Empty Word:

    ```
    ? Show ButFirst "a

    ?
    ```

Now, don't squint or rub your eyes looking for some output that is missing on the last Show command; there is nothing there! The empty word prints out as nothing (as does the empty list when we Print it).

There are times the empty word or list needs to be typed into LOGO. Here is how they are typed:

- The Empty List:

    ```
    [ ]
    ```

- The Empty Word:

    ```
    "
    ```

Some examples:

```
? Print EqualP ButFirst [a] []
True
? Print EqualP ButFirst "a "
True
```

In addition, the predicate EmptyP is provided to determine whether an input is either the empty word or the empty list.

```
? Print EmptyP "
True
? Print EmptyP []
True
```

FPut and LPut

Sometimes it is useful to put an element at the beginning or end of a sequence. Although this could be done with the Word, List, or Sentence, this sort of operation is needed often enough that it is useful to introduce it here.[1] FPut (which stands for First Put) takes an element and a sequence as inputs, and returns a new sequence, with the element as its first element, and the sequence as the rest of the sequence:

```
? Show FPut "a [b c d e f]
[a b c d e f]
? Show FPut "a "bcdef
abcdef
? Show FPut [a b c] [d e f]
[[a b c] d e f]
```

LPut (which stands for Last Put) operates in a similar manner, except that the element is made the last element of the new sequence:

```
? Show LPut "a [b c d e f]
[b c d e f a]
```

Exercises

Enough of our words; a language is best learned by speaking it. So, go "speak" some LOGO to your computer!

What answers do you get from the following examples? Try to figure out the answer yourself; then compare your result with that of the computer!

(1) Show Last "mouse

(2) Show Last [mouse]

(3) Show ButLast "mousehole

(4) Show ButLast [there is the mouse]

---

[1]Also, since one of the versions of LOGO doesn't allow Word, List, or Sentence to have a single input (e.g., (List "a)), we sometimes need to use FPut for that purpose: FPut "a []

```
(5)  Print ListP Last [hello logo]
(6)  Print EqualP Last [man cat] ButLast [cat man]
(7)  Print EqualP ButFirst [man cat] ButLast [cat man]
(8)  Show First "a
(9)  Show Last "a
(10) Show ButFirst "a
(11) Print ListP = "false
(12) Print ListP ButLast ButFirst [the sun shines]
(13) Print EqualP First "b Last "b
(14) Print EqualP ButFirst "b ButFirst [a]
(15) Print EmptyP Last [a]
(16) Print EmptyP ButFirst [a]
(17) EqualP Sentence "this [is a sentence] Sentence [this
     is] [a sentence]
(18) Print EqualP [] "
```

1.2. Logo Arithmetic

Although the basic data types in LOGO are words and lists, this does not mean that LOGO does not understand *numbers*.

Numbers

Integer numbers are represented as words made up of only digits ("0" through "9") or digits preceded by a minus sign ("-").

```
"1234
"-12
```

Since it is unnatural for us to write numbers with a beginning quote ("""), numbers may be written without it.

```
1234
-12
```

The important point is that numbers are still words! We can use them with the operations that work on words:

```
? Print First 1234
1
? Print ButFirst -12
12
```

Another type of number is what is known as a *floating-point* number. One form of these are similar to what we generally call decimal numbers:

```
10.53
1234.5678
```

This can be extended in a manner similar to what is often called *scientific notation*, where the number has two parts; the first part looks just like what we have seen so far, while the second part represents a power-of-10 multiplier and is preceded by the letter "e."

in scientific notation:

6.023×10^{23}

in LOGO notation:

```
6.023e23
```

Different implementations handle equality of numbers differently, so you need to study your user's manual to find out how this is handled.[2] For example:

```
? Print EqualP 100 100.0
??????? ← implementation dependent
? Print EqualP 100 1e2
??????? ← implementation dependent
```

Number Operations

The basic operators of arithmetic are also available:

```
? Print 1+2
3
? Print 4/2
2
? Print 3*4
12
? Print 5-2
3
```

It is probably better style to put spaces around the operators, but, as this shows, it is not necessary. The results of these operations are numbers and are therefore words, as well:

```
? Print First 12 * 7
8
```

Depending on the implementation, these arithmetic operations may be handled differently if the inputs are written as floating-point numbers. Division is almost always handled differently:

```
? Print 2 / 3
0  ← integer division
? Print 2.0 / 3.0
0.66667 ← floating-point division
```

Whereas other operations may be handled in the same way:

```
? Print 2.0 * 3
6 or 6.0? ← depends on the implementation
```

But, if there is a fractional part, there should be no confusion:

```
? Print 2.2 * 3
6.6
```

---

[2]Implementation dependencies are discussed in greater detail in Appendix I.

The example 2 / 3 representing integer division (whole number division, no fractions) raises the question about how the *remainder* of the integer division can be calculated, the `Remainder` operator (infix "\") does this:

```
? Print 9 / 5
1
? Print 9 \ 5
4
```

Most systems require that the inputs to `Remainder` be integers.

Number Predicates

There are also some basic predicates that operate on numbers. The first of these are the comparison operators:

```
? Print 1 = 2
false
? Print 1 > 2
false
? Print 1 < 2
true
```

Sometimes it is necessary to check whether a word is a number:

```
? Print NumberP 1
true
? Print NumberP "one
false
```

Infix versus Prefix Notation

The commands presented in the last chapter all used something called *prefix notation*, where the command or operation *precedes* the arguments. The operations on numbers just presented (except for *NumberP*) use what is known as *infix notation*, where the operation is *between* the arguments. Since this is how we write things in our world (outside the computer), it is convenient to write things that way here, too. However, there can be some complications that arise from this notation; this is discussed later in this chapter. You should be aware that there is an equivalent prefix notation for these operators:

infix operator	equivalent prefix operation
+	Sum
-	Difference
*	Product
/	Quotient
\	Remainder
=	EqualP
>	GreaterP
<	LessP

For example:

```
? Print Sum 3 5
8
```

If you run into problems with the infix notation, you can try the equivalent prefix notation to get around the problem.

The Random Procedure

Suppose we want to program a game that has an element of chance, such as MONOPOLY. We need to be able to "roll the dice" in our program. The problem is that all the programming elements we have introduced so far have the property that they are extremely predictable (think of the mess we would have if they weren't!). What we need is a way to introduce a degree of uncertainty into our programs. This can be done using the Random procedure. For a given input :N, Random returns a number that is between 0 and :N - 1, inclusive. Subsequent calls to Random may return a different number:

```
? Print Random 10
3
? Print Random 10
0
? Print Random 10
8
```

To be honest with you, Random is not really random but is called a *pseudorandom* number generator. It uses an extremely complex formula to come up with its output and, because we can't see the "method to its maddness," it appears to be a random number. On page 77 you can investigate how "good" a job it does.

Since Random returns a number that is always between 0 and one less than the number specified, you usually need to adjust things a little bit, if what you really want is a number between 1 and some number.

```
? Print Sentence [The die rolls:] Add 1 Random 6
The die rolls: 4
```

Exercises

Here are some more phrases for you to speak to your computer (if you run into errors, don't panic. Just try to understand where the error is, and go on.):

```
(1)  Print 12 - First 345
(2)  Print ButLast "1A + 2
(3)  Print Word 12 + 5 Word ButFirst "dog 9 - 5
(4)  Print ButFirst 2 - ButFirst ButLast "X17Y
(5)  Print Word "- 4 + 4
(6)  Print "-4 = Word "- 4
(7)  Print First "A
(8)  Print Last "A
(9)  Print ButFirst "A
(10) Print 04 = 4
(11) Print 00 = 0
```

```
(12)  Print 04 - 4 = 0
(13)  Print 0 = []
(14)  Print 0 = "
(15)  Print 1.2 * 3.5
(16)  Print 1 / 5
(17)  Print 1.0 / 5
(18)  Print 13 \ 5
(19)  Print 13.0 \ 5
(20)  Print Word 5 ButFirst 3.15 / 2
(21)  Print Random 100 (do this one several times)
```

1.3. Techniques for Understanding the Structure of a LOGO Command

Given a LOGO instruction (i.e., a line of LOGO code) with various interrelated procedure calls, such as:

```
Print Word First ButFirst "House Word "w "ls
```

there are several ways to understand its structure (how the parts are related).

(1) **Use of parentheses:**

```
(Print (Word (First (ButFirst "House )) (Word "w "ls )))
```

Parentheses are placed around each procedure and its inputs to clarify how the parts of the instruction are related. Note that this may also be used as valid input to LOGO. Also, some commands (such as Word, List, and Sentence) can take a variable number of inputs by surrounding the entire command and its arguments with parentheses.

```
? Print (Word "a "b "c )
abc
? Print Word "a "b "c
There's something extra on the line.
Print takes only one input.
```

Word normally takes only two inputs, but by using the parentheses in the first example, Word takes "a, "b, and "c as its inputs. If we use explicit parentheses to clarify the structure of the second example, it looks like this:

```
? (Print (Word "a "b ) ) "c
```

which makes the error message a little clearer, the "c is the "something extra on the line."

(2) **Nested rectangles**

This representation is similar to the use of parentheses, but it makes visualization of the nesting easier. Here are the steps to follow to generate this representation:

a) Enclose all elements that begin with '"'', all numbers, and all lists in rectangles.

```
Print Word First ButFirst "House    Word  "w    "1s
```

Under each procedure, write how many inputs it has. If a procedure has an opening parenthesis in front of it, this number is not needed.

```
Print Word First ButFirst "House    Word  "w    "1s
  1    2     1      1                  2
```

b) For each procedure that has exactly the required number of rectangles to its right, draw a rectangle that surrounds the procedure and its associated rectangles.[3] If a procedure has an open parenthesis in front of it, draw a box that surrounds it and any arguments after it up to and including the matching close parenthesis. It is easier to work from the innermost set of parenthesis outward, but this is not required.

```
Print Word First ButFirst "House    Word  "w    "1s
  1    2     1      1                  2
```

c) Repeat this process, until the whole line is surrounded by a rectangle.

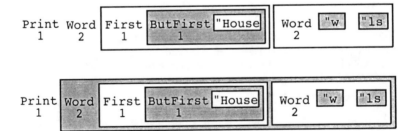

---

[3]It may be simpler for you to scan from right to left when doing this, but if you always ensure that the procedure has the correct number of **boxes** to its right, this will always work. If an element doesn't yet have a box around it, then you can't group it in a larger box.

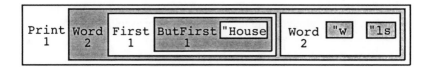

Here is an example with parens:

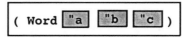

(3) Boxes in a tree structure

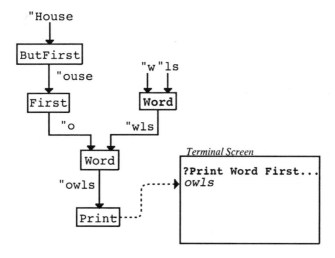

This kind of diagram is constructed as follows: The LOGO line is read from left to right and the diagram is built simultaneously from *bottom to top*. The lowest box in the diagram (corresponding to the leftmost procedure name) as a result will always contain the name of a procedure that has no output.

Infix operators present a small problem because they introduce *ambiguity*: Whereas it is unambiguous what Add Difference 5 3 2 means, what about 5 − 3 + 2? Does this mean that we should subtract 3 from 5 and then add 2 to the result, or add 3 and 2 and subtract the result from 5. As with usual mathematical notation, we can make this clearer by two methods:

(1) *Precedence rules:*

    a) Operators of higher precedence are evaluated first, where the operators are grouped into levels of precedence as follows:

Precedence Level	Operations
High	*, /, \
Medium	+, -
Low	=, <, >

    So, `4 - 3 * 2` means `Difference 4 Product 3 2`.

    b) Operators of the same level of precedence are evaluated left to right, so that `5 - 3 + 2` means `Sum Difference 5 3 2`.

(2) *Use of parentheses*: Just as we used parentheses to show the structure of the Logo command, they can also be used to make the order of evaluation explicit, or even to change the normal order of evaluation: `(5 - (3 + 2))` would mean `Difference 5 Sum 3 2`.

One area that often causes problems is the interaction between the normal prefix notation and the use of infix notation. It seems that it would be straightforward to write:

```
First "word = "w
```

if we wanted to compare the first element of a word to a particular letter. If we try this we get:

```
? Print First "word = "w
f
```

The problem is that prefix notation has the lowest precedence of all. If we use parentheses to make the order of evaluation explicit, this would be:

```
(First ("word = "w))
```

which explains the result we saw, since `First` is being applied to `"false`, which is the result of comparing `"word` to `"w`. To get what we really wanted, we could write:

```
? Print (First "word) = "w
true
```

Exercises

(1) Represent the exercises on page 10 as nested rectangles. How do you handle the infix operators?

(2) Represent the exercises on page 10 as tree structures.

Chapter 2:
Extending LOGO

2.1. Procedures

Suppose we want to extract the third letter (word, element) from a word (sentence, list), for example:

```
"House  →  "u  or
[Tomorrow it will rain]  →  "will
```

In LOGO there is no primitive operation available to do this; however, it is possible to assemble several operations together, for instance:

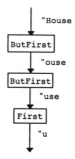

or as it would be typed in:

?Print First ButFirst ButFirst "House

LOGO allows us to construct new boxes and give them names. With these names, the boxes that we have constructed can be used exactly as the original LOGO primitives. For our example, this would appear as follows:

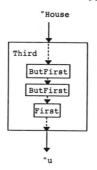

Let's build the outer box and call it Third. We should be able to use it, for instance, in this way:

```
?Print Third "House
u
```

How can we make LOGO understand what we want here? The following steps are necessary:

(1) We must specify the name of the box.

(2) We need to specify what should go into the box (e.g., how many inputs).

(3) We should understand what we plan to have come out of the box.

(4) The operations that are to be contained in the box must be given.

The finished product looks like this:

```
To Third :Input
    Output First ButFirst ButFirst :Input
End
```

Specifically, this says:

(1) The command To tells LOGO that we want to specify a new procedure or operation. LOGO switches into a version specific edit or define mode; that is, the commands that are given are saved up to be executed later rather than being executed immediately. Following the To the name that we have chosen for the procedure or operation is given.

(2) Because we want to be able to extract the third element from *any* word or list, we need a way to have something that "stands for" the item whose third element we want to extract. This is done by specifying the so-called *place holders* after the name of the procedure. These are always names that begin with a colon (":"). When Third is executed, this is "filled in" with the input to the procedure and any reference to this place holder in reality refers to the input to the procedure. These *place holders* are also called the *parameters* of the procedure.

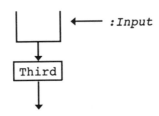

(3) Then the various operations that must be executed to achieve the desired result are given.

(4) The final result needs to be made available for use after the execution of the procedure. To do this, the `Output`-box is used; the input to this box represents the output value of the entire procedure.

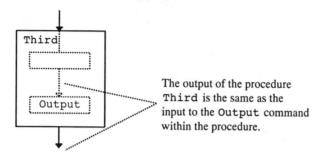

The output of the procedure `Third` is the same as the input to the `Output` command within the procedure.

(5) The end of a procedure specification is signaled to LOGO with the word **End** .

Further examples:

(1) Let's write a procedure that adds the number 1 to a specified number. An example of how this would be used (in box notation) would look like:

or in LOGO notation:

```
? Print Add1 7
8
```

And here is how we would define it:

```
To Add1 :Number
   Output Sum :Number 1
End
```

(2) Now let's try a procedure that constructs one word from three. Again a use of this procedure would look like this in box notation:

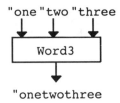

```
"one "two "three
```

"onetwothree

or in LOGO notation:

```
? Print Word3 "one "two "three
onetwothree
```

One possible definition looks like this:

```
To Word3 :First :Second :Third
   Output Word :First Word :Second :Third
End
```

The same result can be achieved with the LOGO procedure Word directly, by grouping procedure name and the three arguments with parentheses.

To summarize, in our discussion so far we have used three different elements:

(1) Words that have no beginning delimiters (such as Word, Add1) and always indicate the *name* of a box (procedure). In some versions of LOGO, the name of the procedure may be a number (composed of nothing but digits).

(2) Words that have a beginning colon delimiter (such as *:Number* in the line To Add1 *:Number*) are called place holders. At the time of definition of a procedure they reserve a place that takes on a certain value when the procedure is executed. That is, in Print Add1 9 the place holder *:Number* is bound to the value 9 whereas in Print Add1 27 the value 27 is bound to *:Number*.

(3) Elements that represent a *concrete value* such as words that begin with a double quotation-mark, numbers, or lists surrounded by brackets. These represent specific, literal values instead of something that is computed by using LOGO procedures.

Exercises

(1) Write a procedure `Alphabet` that furnishes the alphabet as result.

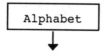

[A B C D E F G H I J K L M N O P Q R S T U V W X Y Z]

(2) Write a procedure that prints a certain dollar amount in cents.

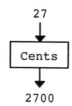

(3) Write a procedure that has two words as input, and outputs one word that is constructed from the two inputs with the second word first.

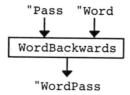

(4) Write a procedure

    a) `Random15to24`, which returns a random number between 15 and 24 (inclusive).

    b) `Lottery`, which simulates a lottery drawing (with numbers between 1 and 49)

(5) Write a procedure `Twist` with one word as input. The output should be the same word, except that the first and the last letter are swapped.

(6) Write a procedure `Join` that takes one sentence containing exactly 3 words as input. The procedure should join the three words into a single word as output.

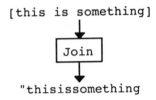

(7) Write a procedure `Square` that squares its input (a number).

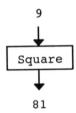

2.2. Conditionals

With what we have presented so far, we can't make the execution of LOGO commands dependent on certain conditions. To allow writing procedures that are flexible and able to react differently to different inputs, there must be a mechanism to choose between alternatives.

In LOGO the procedure `Test` (which takes exactly one input) exists for this purpose. Its input, which can, for example, result as the output of a predicate, must be either `"True` or `"False`. `Test` has *no* output, but an effect, which can be described as follows: An observer holds a flag and places it in either the `"True` or the `"False` position, depending on the input to the `Test` procedure (see Figure 2-1).

Two additional LOGO commands, `IfTrue` and `IfFalse`, exist to check whether the observer's flag is set to `"True` or `"False`. With the `IfTrue` command, the list of commands that is the input to `IfTrue` is executed only if the flag shows `"True`, otherwise nothing happens (similarly with `IfFalse`). Now let's examine an example: Suppose we want to construct a procedure `Abs` that has one input (a number) and will output the magnitude (absolute value) of the number:

```
? Print Abs 4
4
? Print Abs -47
47
```

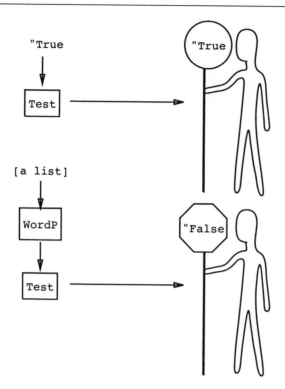

Figure 2-1: The Flag Model

One possible version of Abs is:

```
To Abs :Number
   Test (First :Number) = "-
   IfTrue [Output ButFirst :Number]
   IfFalse [Output :Number]
End
```

Similar to Test, IfTrue, and IfFalse, there are also the constructs well known from other programming languages: If and IfElse. The model for execution is similar for other conditionals, but everything "happens at once." Instead of the model with a flag person, it is better to think of these commands as if there were a person operating a train switch as is shown in figures 2-2 and 2-3.

For both commands, the "switch operator" evaluates the first argument, which should return either "True or "False. For the If command, if the value returned was "True, the operator switches the "train of command execution" onto a special siding where the special list of commands (the second argument)

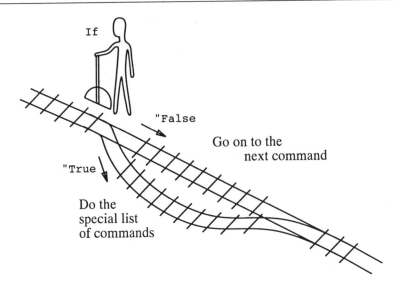

If

"False

Go on to the
next command

"True

Do the
special list
of commands

Figure 2–2: The Switch-Operator Model for If

is executed then goes back onto the "main track" and executes the next command, if there is one. If the value evaluated by the switch operator was "False, the "train" just goes straight ahead and executes next command, if there is one.

The IfElse command operates much the same way, except that if the value evaluated by the switch operator is "False, a second list of commands (the third input) is executed before the train goes on its way.

Making More Complex Conditions

The input to Test, as well as the first input to If and IfElse, must be one of the the values "True or "False. One way to generate this can be by using a predicate, such as WordP or = (EqualP). Often it is useful to combine several predicates together into what is known as a *logical expression*. The primitives Or, And, and Not can be used for this purpose.

Not simply outputs a value that is the opposite of its input:

```
? Print Not "True
false
? Print Not "False
true
```

Or outputs "True if at least one of its inputs is "True:

```
? Print Or "True "True
true
```

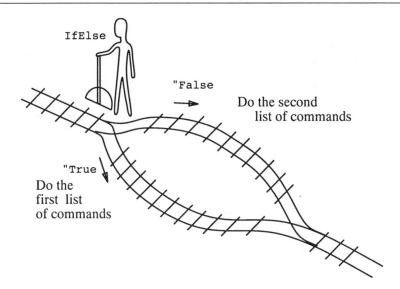

Figure 2–3: The Switch-Operator Model for IfElse

```
? Print Or "True "False
true
? Print Or "False "False
false
```

whereas And outputs "True if (and only if) *both* of its inputs are true:

```
? Print And "True "True
true
? Print And "True "False
false
```

With these primitives we can build up complex logical expressions:

```
If Not
    Or
       WordP :Input1
       And First :Input2 = "a Last :Input3 = [ ]
    [Do Something]
```

but you shouldn't get too carried away, since extremely complex expressions can be difficult to understand.

Exercises

(1) Write a procedure `NegativeP` that determines whether or not a number is less than zero.

```
? Print NegativeP -473
true
? Print NegativeP 68
false
```

(2) Simplify the `Test` line in `Abs`, using the predicate `NegativeP`, which tests whether a number is negative or not.

(3) Write a procedure `Greet` that can respond appropriately to different greetings as illustrated below:

```
? Print Greet [Hello]
Hi
? Print Greet [How are you?]
Fine. How are you?
? Print Greet [G'day]
G'day, mate!
? Print Greet [Bonjour]
Bonjour
? Print Greet [Good morning]
What's so good about it?
```

(So who says computers can't be grouchy, too?)

(4) Write a procedure `Coin` that randomly returns the word `"Heads` or the word `"Tails`.

```
? Print Coin
Heads
? Print Coin
Tails
? Print Coin
Tails
```

(5) Write a procedure `MaxThree` that determines the largest of three numbers:

```
? Print MaxThree 1 2 3
3
? Print MaxThree 2 3 1
3
? Print MaxThree 3 1 2
3
```

(6) Write a procedure `Longest` that returns the longer of its two inputs. Hint: there is a LOGO primitive `Count` that determines the number of words in a list or the number of characters in a word.

```
? Print Longest [Short list] [A long list]
A long list
```

(7) Write a procedure that does the same job as the primitive `EmptyP`.

(8) Write a procedure `InRangeP` that takes three inputs and checks to see if the first is in the range specified by the last two.

```
? Print InRangeP 5 1 10
true
? Print InRangeP 20 4 16
false
```

(9) Write a procedure `VowelP` that tests whether a letter is a vowel.

```
? Print VowelP "U
true
? Print VowelP "H
false
```

2.3. Various Classes Of Procedures

Graphically representing LOGO procedures as boxes, where arrows show the inputs and outputs, gives the additional advantage that the number of inputs and outputs is explicitly represented.

Examples:

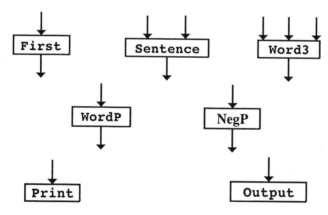

The first examples share the characteristic that exactly one arrow comes out of the box, whereas the latter two procedures have no output arrow.[4] This property may be used to place LOGO procedures into two categories:

* *Operations*: Procedures with outputs

* *Commands*: Procedures without outputs

---

[4]The lack of an arrow coming out of the `Output` box may seem a little confusing, at first. However, the `Output` command does not have any output (e.g., you cannot do a `Print Output ...`), but it is a *command* that causes **the procedure that it is in** to exit and output the specified value.

Operations can be used as input to other procedures, for example:

```
? Print Word "a "b
ab
```

However, `Word` `Print` `"a` `"b` is quickly recognized as incorrect input because a command cannot provide an input to an operation. After `Print` `"a` is executed, LOGO continues with the error message

Some primitive didn't get a value.

In general *commands* can never be used as input to another procedure. *Commands* have no result; instead they cause so called *side effects*. `Print`, for example, prints its input on the terminal screen. Another command that we have already seen is `To`. With `To` a procedure is defined as a side effect.

The example procedures whose names end with the letter ''P'' are special operations,[5] since the only possible values they can return are `"True` or `"False`. *Predicates* are operations, whose output can be only the value `"True` or `"False`. The Figure 2–4 shows the association graphically as a Venn diagram.

This classification is valid for LOGO's predefined procedures as well as for user defined procedures.

Exercises

Rewrite the operations defined in the exercises in chapter 2.1 as commands, which print out the computed result immediately; that is, they should behave as follows:

```
? Cents 27
2700
? WordBackwards "Pass "Word
WordPass
? RandomNumber15to24
22
? Lottery
6
```

---

[5]This convention is used by the version of LOGO we are using. We follow it as well since the name of the procedure helps remind us that the operation returns `"True` or `"False` and can be used as an input to `Test`, for example. Some versions of LOGO use a ''?'' instead of a ''P.''

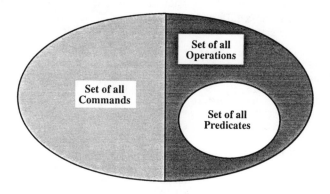

Figure 2–4: Commands, Operations, and Predicates

```
? Swap "House
eousH
? Join [This is something]
Thisissomething
```

2.4. The Stop Command

So far we have learned only one command to end the execution of a procedure: the Output command. Alternatively, a procedure may simply run out of things to do as was indicated by saying "End" when the procedure was defined.

Example of ending execution with the Output command:

```
To Abs :Number
   Test (First :Number) = "-
   IfTrue [Output ButFirst :Number]
   IfFalse [Output :Number]
End
```

Example of simply running out of things to do:

```
To SumProd :First :Second
   Print :First + :Second
   Print :First * :Second
End
```

The Output command is used if the procedure being defined is to output a value, that is, if it belongs to the class of operations. If the procedure simply runs out of things to do, it is a command. However, suppose that we want to write a command that has a branch arising from a `Test` or `If` command. On one branch of the conditional, we want to do one set of things; on the other branch we want to do a different set of things. We can certainly do this by "protecting" each statement with the appropriate `If`-construct:

```
To Whatever :This :That
Test :This = :That
IfTrue [Do1 :This
        Do2 :That]
IFFalse [DoOther1 :That
         DoOther2 :This
         DoOther3 :This :That]
```

Another way to think about this is that in one case we want to do one set of things and then stop; otherwise we want to do the other set of things. The `Stop` command allows us to formulate the problem in this way. Instead of "just falling off the end" we can explicitly stop the procedure.

So, our fake example could be written like this:

```
To Whatever :This :That
Test :This = :That
IfTrue [Do1 :This
        Do2 :That
        Stop]
DoOther1 :That
DoOther2 :This
DoOther3 :This :That
```

Example:

Suppose we want to write a command that prints out some information about a family. If there are no children in the family, we want to print out the word "couple" and the peoples names, but if there are children then we want to print out "parents" on one line, followed by the parents names on the next line, and then "children" followed by the childrens names on separate lines:

```
To PrintFamily :Parents :Children
  If :Children = []
    [Print (Sentence "Couple: :Parents)
     Stop]
  Print "Parents:
  Print :Parents
  Print "Children:
  Print :Children
End
```

In general it is not a good idea to have `Output` and `Stop` commands appear in the same procedure. Although it certainly can be done, using such a procedure would require you to understand how it works inside every time you use it:

Let's see, is this procedure going to output something, or is it going to act like a command this time?

Generally, you want to be able to use a procedure by treating it more or less as a *black box*.

2.5. The `TopLevel` Command

Sometimes, we find ourselves in a position where there is no way out of a problem; for example, if we are writing an operation that divides two numbers but checks first to see if the divisor is zero. If this is the case, what should we do? If we return some value, it will be incorrect. One possibility is to use the `TopLevel` command.[6] `TopLevel` returns control to the top level command interpreter, aborting the program:

```
To CheckAndDivide :Dividend :Divisor
  If :Divisor = 0 [TopLevel]
    Output Quotient :Dividend :Divisor
End
```

The main point here is that it is always good to check for bad inputs, even at the lowest level, even though higher levels should check as well since they have more information about how to deal with the problem. If you write some utility procedure and do not check for special conditions, such as the attempt to divide by zero in our example, and someone who uses your utility does not check for those special conditions, their program may continue to run with erroneous values, which could be very difficult to debug (see the discussion about `Factorial` in chapter 5). Some more recent versions of LoGo also provide `Throw` and `Catch` mechanisms to set up error recovery mechanisms; we consider these features to be beyond the scope of this book and refer you to your users manual if you wish to pursue this.

Exercise

Write a command `DebugMessage` that takes two inputs, the first, an error level, which can be either `"Note`, `"Warning`, or `"FatalError`. The second input is a message to print out. If the error level is `"Note`, the level and message are printed out. If the error level is `"Warning`, the global variable `:NumberOfWarnings` is incremented and the level and message are printed out. If the error level is `"FatalError`, the level and message are printed out and the program is aborted.

---

[6]This is very similar to what the `Quotient` operation actually does, so there is no reason to write this new operation. This is just to show the idea of `TopLevel`.

Chapter 3:
Recursive Procedures

Before we deal with recursive procedures in LOGO, let's examine the process of looking up an unknown word in a dictionary. For example, we might find the word *syntax* explained as follows: "the branch of *grammar* dealing with the formation of *phrases* and *sentences*." [American Heritage Dictionary 82]

Before we have read the explanation to the end, we come across further unknown words and we face the same problem as at the start. At *grammar* we might find: "the study of a *language* as a systematically composed body of words that exhibit discernible regularity of structure ..." [American Heritage Dictionary 82]

And again the same question presents itself: Find an explanation for the word *language* (among others, perhaps).

By now, we should begin to wonder: How will we ever reach our goal and find the explanation for the original word *syntax*? This can only be achieved if one assumes that certain *atomic concepts* exist, which need not be further explained. When we reach this point, that part of the process is finished and we can continue to work on the original word. A similar method can be used in LOGO when we attempt to solve the following problem.

Write a procedure `Mirror`, which reverses the order of the letters of a word. Example:

```
? Print Mirror "animal
lamina
? Print Mirror "cow
woc
```

This procedure can be written in many different ways. However, we want to examine this task from a perspective that is particularly suited for LOGO.

We use a powerful problem-solving technique called "wishful thinking." We split off the last letter and then assume for a moment that we have the remaining part (the part without the last letter) already turned around. There only remains the task of making a word out of these two parts, with the last letter placed at the beginning. With the unfinished portion of the word, we successively go through the same operation. When does this chain of events end? When we have reached the "trivial" case, where the word is "empty" (i.e., contains no letters)!

A solution in LOGO might look like this:

```
To Mirror :Word
   Test :Word = "
   IfTrue [Output "]
   Output Word (Last :Word) (Mirror ButLast :Word)
End
```

Representing this procedure using boxes is not possible; therefore, we would like to introduce a new illustrative metaphor: the *Theory of the Little People*. These people look all the same from the outside, but they live in separate worlds, and things that have the same names have different meanings. Furthermore, each one insists on a fair division of labor; that is to say, each of them works on only one part of the problem.

Let's say we ask `Print Mirror "cow`. The first `Mirror`-person, in whose world `:Word` has the meaning `"cow`, carries on as the preceding definition describes: The test in the first line fails and the next line is not executed. In the line after that she looks for the inputs to the `Word` operation. The second input is `First :Word ("c`), but she doesn't figure out the first input herself. Instead she calls another little person to help. This person, called with `Mirror "ow`, understands `:Word` to have the meaning `"ow`.

The process continues like this until finally a person is called with `Mirror "` (i.e., with the *empty* word). When this happens, the test in his first line succeeds and he does not need to call yet another person to help him. Instead, he gives back the `empty` word to the person who asked him as specified in his second line, and this person can complete the job of building a word from the value returned by the last person and `First :Word`.

In this same way all the other people finish up their work until the first person who was called puts the desired value together and gives it back to the `Print` command. Figure 3–1 represents this concept graphically.

The LOGO system itself offers an excellent aid, `Trace`, with which the user can observe the recursive procedure in action. `Trace`[7] has the following effect: When each procedure is entered, the name of the procedure as well as the values that are associated with each place holder are printed out with appropriate indentation indicating the level of recursion. When a procedure completes, the name of the procedure and its output value are printed out with the same level of indentation as the information printed when that instance of the procedure was invoked.

```
Execution of Mirror "cow
   Execution of Mirror "ow
      Execution of Mirror "w
         Execution of Mirror "
```

---

[7]Implementations of LOGO differ with respect to the `Trace` command. See appendix I for a discussion of this.

Figure 3-1: A Graphic Illustration For Recursive Procedures Using the Mirror Example

```
        Mirror outputs  "
      Mirror outputs  "w
    Mirror outputs  "wo
  Mirror outputs  "woc
  woc
```

Repeated execution of a set of commands (known as iteration) is also available in LOGO with the Repeat command (described in appendix I.3). In LOGO recursion is a more natural solution and should only be replaced by iteration if memory limitations are a concern.

Exercises

(1) Write a predicate `MemberP` that tests if its first input (a single letter word) is contained in its second input (a word).

```
? Print MemberP  "u "chimney
false
? Print MemberP  "i "chimney
true
```

How would this procedure look if it were supposed to test whether a word appears in a sentence instead?

(2) Write a procedure that counts the number of letters in a word. This may be a primitive in your version of LOGO; if it is, give your procedure a different name for the purpose of this exercise.

```
? Print Count "household
9
```

(3) Write a predicate `PalindromeP`, which determines whether a word is a Palindrome (i.e., reads the same forwards as it does backwards).

```
? Print PalindromeP "street
false
? Print PalindromeP "madam
true
? Print PalindromeP 85344358
true
```

Do this exercise two ways:

a) Reusing the `Mirror` procedure

b) Without using the `Mirror` procedure

(4) Write a predicate `VowelP`, which tests whether a letter is a vowel.

```
? Print VowelP "u
true
? Print VowelP "v
false
```

(5) Write a predicate `ConsonantP`. Consider, whether `VowelP` can be used to write this function.

(6) Write a procedure `Pack`, which compresses a sentence into a word.

```
? Print Pack [madam im adam]
madamimadam
```

(7) Write a procedure Nth. This procedure has two inputs, a word and a number. The number specifies the position of the letter (from the beginning) that should be returned. Again, this may be a primitive in your version of LOGO; do the exercise using a different name for the procedure.

```
? Print Nth "rain 4
n
? Print Nth "yesterday 3
s
```

How must the procedure be modified to select a specific word out of a list? Also, generalize the procedure such that, when a negative number is given, it specifies a position from the end of the word.

(8) Write a procedure Mirror1, which uses the procedures Last and ButLast instead of First and ButFirst to mirror a word. Draw a picture similar to Figure 3–1 to illustrate what happens.

(9) Write a procedure CountAll, which counts the number of letters and symbols in a sentence.

```
? Print CountAll [write a procedure]
15
```

(10) Write a procedure Explode, which returns a list composed of each single letter of the original word.

```
? Show Explode "bomb
[b o m b]
```

(11) Write two procedures FirstN and ButFirstN, which are similar to First and ButFirst, but instead of operating on (returning or taking away) only the first element, they operate on a specified number of elements. For example:

```
? Show FirstN 5 [s w a n l a k e]
[s w a n l]
? Show ButFirstN 5 [s w a n l a k e]
[a k e]
```

(12) Write a procedure UpToLetter, which returns all the elements of a sentence up to a certain letter or word. If that letter/word does not exist, return the entire sequence.

```
? Show UpToLetter "f [g o n e f i s h i n g]
[g o n e]
```

(13) Write a predicate AllNumbersP, which checks whether a sentence contains only numbers.

```
? Print AllNumbersP [4 2 5 7 1 3]
true
? Print AllNumbersP [4 2 5 text 7 1 3]
false
```

(14) Write a procedure `RemoveWord`, which removes each occurrence of a specific word from a sentence.

> `? Show RemoveWord "this [this and this and this]`
> `[and and]`

(15) Write a procedure `ReplaceWord`, which replaces each occurrence of a specific word with another.

> `? Show ReplaceWord "this "that [this and this]`
> `[that and that]`

(16) Write a procedure `Mix`, which merges two lists together, using the first element of the first list, then the first element of the second list, and so forth until both lists are exhausted. If the lists have different numbers of elements, `Mix` as many as possible, then include the rest of the longer list at the end.

> `? Show Mix [a b c d] [e f g h]`
> `[a e b f c g d h]`

(17) Write a procedure `Flatten`, which takes a nested list, and "flattens" it into a sentence.

> `? Show Flatten [a [b c] [d [e] [f g]] h [i]]`
> `[a b c d e f g h i]`

(18) Write a procedure `MirrorAll` which mirrors all levels of a nested list.

> `?Show MirrorAll [a [b c] [d e]]`
> `[[e d] [c b] a]`

Chapter 4:
Recommendations and Principles for Writing Procedures

Generally, it is helpful when writing a procedure (or proceeding towards any systematic goal) to follow these steps:

Step 1: Determine what the procedure should do.

Prepare a concise statement consisting of one or two English sentences, describing what the procedure should do, what the purpose of the procedure should be.

Example:
> Write a procedure, which determines whether a given letter is a member of the set of letters that make up a given word.

Step 2: Choose a name for the procedure.

Select a name that describes as precisely as possible the function of the procedure and shows what procedure class it belongs to (e.g., all names of predicates should end with a P). Extremely short and excessively long names should be avoided.

Example:
> The procedure just described can be defined as a predicate and we choose MemberP as its name.

Step 3: Determine the number, name, and types of the inputs.

It is useful to represent the procedure in the graphical "Box" notation. This method expresses the preceding information explicitly. For names of the inputs (which we call *place holders*) the same guidelines as for procedures apply (i.e., they should be as indicative of the use of the input as possible).

Example:
> Figure 4-1 shows the box picture for the procedure MemberP.

Step 4: Determine whether the procedure should be an operation or a command.

This decision establishes whether the procedure uses the Output command or the Stop[8] command. A procedure should never contain both commands at

---

[8]Instead of a Stop command, the procedure may perform an *implicit* Stop by running out of statements to execute.

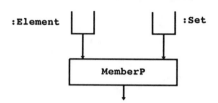

Figure 4-1: Box Notation for the Procedure MemberP

once. The box representation expresses this as well; if the procedure is an operation, an arrow comes out of the box, otherwise not.

Example:
> Because MemberP is a predicate, and predicates are a subset of operations, the definition will contain an Output command.

Step 5: Determine what side effects the procedure should produce.

Consider whether the procedure prints something, modifies a data structure (see chapter 8, Page 52), or requests information from the user (see chapter 7, Page 50).

Example:
> MemberP should have no side effects.

Step 6: Determine which previously defined procedures can be used.

It is not necessary for all procedures to be based directly on the elementary building blocks; instead, one should try to integrate other user defined procedures into the definition of a procedure in a reasonable way.

Example:
> MemberP is a simple building block, so it can be defined with LOGO building blocks.

Step 7: Write the text of the procedure.

This step, which deals with the *how* of the procedure, should come at the end, not at the beginning. This does not imply that this step cannot lead to changes in the results of the preceding steps.

No procedure should contain too many lines. As a rule of thumb, seven lines is sometimes considered to be an upper limit. Instead, all nonelementary operations should be defined with other procedures if possible.

Pertinent comments can be put in as further description of the procedure (if a line of the procedure contains a semicolon, the rest of the line is ignored by the system and can be used to put in comments).

Example:

```
To MemberP :Element :Set
  ;Tests whether :Element is contained in :Set
  Test :Set = "
  IfTrue [Output "False]
  Test :Element = First :Set
  IfTrue [Output "True]
  Output MemberP :Element ButFirst :Set
End
```

Step 8: Check (as much as is possible), whether the procedure is correct.

The following things can be checked:

- Are there syntactic errors?

- Are special cases such as empty words or lists, zero, negative numbers, and floating point numbers handled correctly?

- Can all possible results be achieved?

These checks can only be done as long as the procedure is of a reasonable length.

Example:

In MemberP one could check whether both the value "True as well as the value "False are output, whether the recursion always completes, whether it works with the empty list, and whether letters are found when they are at the beginning or end of the word.

The guidelines presented in this chapter should not be taken as "hard-and-fast rules." There are times when it is better to proceed in a less formal manner, especially when the problem is not well understood and exploration is necessary to come to terms with the problem.

Chapter 5:
Debugging

The importance of debugging as a general cognitive skill is best articulated by Seymour Papert [Papert 80]:

> Many children are held back in their learning because they have a model of learning in which you either "got it" or "got it wrong." But when you learn to program a computer you almost never get it right the first time. Learning to be a master programmer is learning to become highly skilled at isolating and correcting "bugs," the parts that keep the program from working. The question to ask about the program is not whether it is right or wrong, but if it is fixable. If this way of looking at intellectual products were generalized to how the larger culture thinks about knowledge and its acquisition, we all might be less intimidated by our fears of being wrong.

From this perspective, "bugs" should not be seen as terrible things that should be avoided by all means, but as an intrinsic part of the learning process providing us with opportunities to learn new things. Just as a person who never falls down while skiing will not become a better skier, a programmer who never encounters any bugs will miss many learning opportunities. But bugs should have no catastrophical consequences (this is why safety bindings for skis were developed), and the system should provide feedback to help us understand what went wrong. The elimination of errors should be considered a cooperative endeavor between you and the system, where your task is not to find fault or to assign blame but rather to create mutual understanding and to get a task done. Systems for educational computing should be based on a view that errors are interpreted as misunderstandings.

Classification of Errors

Errors can be classified in the following way (see Figure 5-1):

(1) **Implementation errors:** You know the right thing to do, but you make an error in communicating your design ideas to the computer (e.g., you make a typing error, leave something out, or do not remember how to formulate something in LOGO). When typing commands interactively, some of these errors are signalled immediately. Depending on the sophistication of your LOGO implementation, when these errors are in the body of a procedure, they may not be discovered until the program actually runs into them.

(2) **Design errors:** These errors yield a result that does not correspond to your intentions. These types of errors occur because you think about the problem in the wrong way. LOGO will not complain about these errors; it will just execute these programs. Without the capability to compare the program to the your intentions, LOGO just does what you told it to do. These are the most difficult errors to eliminate.

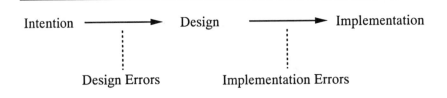

Figure 5-1: Design versus Implementation Errors

Debugging in LOGO

Most LOGO-Systems offer several important aids that can be helpful in tracking down errors:

- Error messages show the location and reasons for an error when it occurs.

- A tracing mechanism is available that shows which procedures are called and the value of the inputs for each procedure invocation.

- Because LOGO is an interactive system, changing procedures is simple.

Implementation Errors

Missing parentheses or quotation marks

```
? Print Sentence "House Door
Procedure Door unknown
```

The second input to Sentence is interpreted as a procedure name because it begins with a letter. The real problem here is that we meant to type "Door instead of Door, so this is really just a typographical error. The trick here is learning how to interpret the error messages. For example, the next error causes the same error message, for a different reason.

Use of undefined procedures.

```
? SpeakEnglish
Procedure SpeakEnglish unknown
```

These errors can have several causes: perhaps it is a simple error in typing or spelling, the function has simply not (yet) been defined, or we have forgotten to load it in from a file. So, debugging is always a matter of (1) finding the real cause for an error, and (2) knowing what needs to be done to fix the problem.

Things are made even more difficult because under certain circumstances an error may not even occur: Suppose that Door were a defined procedure returning a value in the Print Sentence "House Door example. No error message would have resulted even though the intention was to print HouseDoor!

Use of illegal procedure names

```
? To Word
Word is a LOGO Keyword
```

Some systems do not allow you to redefine the basic building blocks provided in the LOGO system, or to define procedures whose names begin with digits or consist entirely of digits

Incorrect types of inputs.

```
? Print Word [house] [door]
Word does not like [house] as input
? Test Remainder 48 7
Test does not like 6 as input,
requires either true or false
```

Incorrect number of inputs.

```
? SumProd 3 4 5
7
12
Too many inputs to SumProd
? Print SumProd 3
SumProd needs more inputs

? Print (Word "House "Door "No.47
Word needs more inputs
```

Here, the input to Word can only be completed with a closing parenthesis.

Use of commands as input.

```
? Print SumProd 4 5
9
20
No output from SumProd
```

Results of operations are not used.

```
To Exp :Basis :Power
  Test :Power = 0
  IfTrue [Output 1]
  Output :Basis * Exp :Basis :Power - 1
End

? Exp 3 4
You don't say what to do with 81
```

Errors in recursive procedures.

(1) A procedure produces an incorrect result:

```
To SumDigits :Number
  Test :Number = "
  IfTrue [Output "]
  Output Sum First :Number SumDigits Butfirst :Number
End
```

```
? Print SumDigits 2345
Sum doesn't like empty as input.
You were at line 3 in procedure sumdigits1
In call level 4 of SumDigits
```

The error message becomes clearer when you trace the function and discover that there is an empty word between *like* and *as*, which was returned by the fourth call to SumDigits. It is wrong to add an empty word to a number, so the second line of the program should be:

```
IfTrue [Output 0]
```

(2) Likewise, a procedure cannot sensibly contain both an Output and a Stop command.

```
To SumDigits :Number
   Test :Number = "
   IfTrue [Stop]
   Output Sum First :Number SumDigits ButFirst :Number
End
```

```
? Print SumDigits 2345
Your procedure doesn't have an output.
It can't be used as an input.
You were at line 3 in procedure sumdigits
In call level 4 of SumDigits
```

Design Errors

A Famous "Bug" in Turtle Geometry. Let us assume that we want to write a turtle program that draws an equilateral triangle. Knowing that the sum of the angles in a triangle is 180 degrees, we write the following program:

```
To EquilateralTriangle
   Repeat 3 [Forward 100 Left 60]
End
```

Running the program produces the following result—not quite in accordance with what the user had in mind:

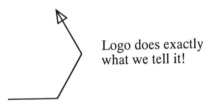

Logo does exactly what we tell it!

The reason for the discrepancy between our intentions and the figure drawn by the program is that 60 degrees is the inside angle in a equilateral triangle, whereas we need to specify the outside angle of 120 degrees for the turtle.

Other Examples of Specification Errors. In the preceding example from Turtle geometry, we can easily recognize the difference between what we had in mind and what we told the program to do. To determine this difference in other types of programs may be considerably more difficult. If you are trying to correct the fault that is being signaled, the information provided is not always sufficient to find the problem. Developing informative diagnostic systems is a big challenge for computer science research.

Incorrect Results.

The procedure `Factorial` should compute the product of all natural numbers between 1 and N:

```
To Factorial :N
   Test :N = 0
   IfTrue [Output 0]
   Output :N * Factorial :N - 1
End

? Print Factorial 3
0
```

The execution does not break but obviously the result is not correct, the factorial of 3 is : 1 * 2 * 3 = 6. Because an input of zero results in zero, and the factorial of zero is defined to be one, it is easy to find this error. This error would have been detected if extreme cases had been tried during testing.

```
To Factorial :N
   Test :N = 0
   IfTrue [Output 1]
   Output :N * Factorial :N - 1
End

? Print Factorial 3
6
```

Errors on Unanticipated Inputs.

Although the procedure `Factorial` is now error free, the following can happen (especially if `Factorial` is used by another procedure):

```
? Print Factorial -1
Stack overflow in line
Output :N * Factorial :N - 1
In call level 67 of Factorial
```

If you turn on tracing and call `Factorial` again with the input −1 or another negative number, you can quickly see why an error message rather than a result appears. The recursion in `Factorial` terminates when the value of the input is zero. By decreasing the value of the argument by one on each recursive call, this condition is sure to be reached eventually, *as long as the input value is greater than zero.* If this is not the case, the value becomes more and more negative but never is equal to zero. Factorial would continue to call itself recursively forever except that each step of the recursion uses up a little space on an internal data structure known as the "stack." Eventually the computer runs out of space resulting in an error message.

This problem with the procedure is easy to remedy:

```
To Factorial :N
   Test :N < 1
   IfTrue [Output 1]
   Output :N * Factorial :N - 1
End

? Print Factorial 3
6
? Print Factorial 12
479001600
? Print Factorial -1
1
```

Note, however, that the definition of Factorial no longer conforms to the mathematical definition.

Writing Programs to Support Users in Finding Bugs

You should write your programs by checking as much as possible for potential trouble spots. In real-life programs, this is an absolutely crucial activity—the parts of the program that try to detect and signal errors may be more elaborate and complicated than the part that does the actual computation.

Checking for Negative Inputs in the Factorial Function. In order to eliminate the problem that negative inputs to the Factorial function lead to infinite recursion, the program Factorial1 could be written:

```
To Factorial1 :N
   Test NegativeP :N
   IfTrue
      [Print [Factorial Undefined for Negative Numbers]
       TopLevel]
   Output Factorial :N
End
```

Checking for Nonintegers Inputs in the Factorial Function. The previous procedure will not behave properly if Factorial is called with a noninteger. An additional test including an informative error message needs to be added to handle this case:

```
To Factorial2 :N
   Test IntegerP :N
   IfFalse
      [Print [Factorial Undefined for Non-Integers]
       TopLevel]
   Test NegativeP :N
   IfTrue
      [Print [Factorial Undefined for Negative Numbers]
       TopLevel]
   Output Factorial :N
End
```

Strategies for Debugging. Debugging programs is a skill that needs to be learned—and modern computing systems often provide elaborate debugging facilities that are complicated systems in their own right. Here are a number of simple strategies to help you get started in developing debugging skills:

- Test the more primitive building blocks first (i.e., the ones that do not depend on other user-defined functions).

- Use the tracing facilities when dealing with a recursive procedure or a large number of functions calling each other.

- Design your own program so it can provide more assistance with problems that might arise when it is tested and used.

Chapter 6:
Analysis of a Program

In our daily lives, most of us must come to terms with systems (e.g., the library) and models (e.g., a city map) that we did not construct. We then have the task of inferring the underlying principles of these systems and models by:

- using descriptions available to us,
- observing them, and
- interacting with them.

Dealing with programs is a similar problem: a program is not only read by the computer, but by other people as well. They must work with or must tailor or augment the program to suit their needs. Frequently, we even find *ourselves* in the position of understanding a program *we* wrote a long time ago.

Therefore, the following things should concern us:

- *How do I write and document a program so that it can be understood, not only by the computer, but also by other people?*
- *What methods are available for analysis of a program that I did not write?*

For now, we want to deal with the second aspect by looking at a concrete example. Let's try to prove the following:

> Conjecture: All natural numbers (1; 2; 3; ....) are either symmetric (e.g., 14741) or can be made into a symmetric number like this: To the number x add its mirror image x′. If the result y is symmetric, then the process is complete. If not, repeat the process with y.

For example:

$$x = 57 \rightarrow x' = 75 \rightarrow x + x' = 132$$

$$y = 132 \rightarrow y' = 231 \rightarrow y + y' = 363$$

$$z = 363 = z' \rightarrow \textit{finished}$$

Let's consider the one possible solution to this problem:

```
To TestOverRange :Bottom :Top
   Test :Bottom > :Top
   IfTrue [Stop]
```

```
    Print
      (Sentence
        :Bottom
        "-->
        Stars Process :Bottom 0)
      Range :Bottom + 1 :Top
    End

To PrintStars :Number
      Test :Number = 0
      IfTrue [Output " ]
      Output Word "* PrintStars :Number - 1
    End

To TestOneNumber :Number :Again
      ; we set an arbitrary limit of 15 here
      ; in case the conjecture is not true
      ; and the process ends up going on too long
      Test :Again > 15
      IfTrue [Output 16]
      Test :Number = Mirror :Number
      IfTrue [Output :Again]
      Output
        TestOneNumber
          (:Number + Mirror :Number)
          (:Again + 1)
    End
```

Mirror is described in appendix III.

Here are some steps that can now be used to analyze this program:

(1) *Are building blocks (procedures) used that we already know?* This is true of PrintStars and Mirror. We still need to check whether the versions used correspond to our conception.

(2) *Can I figure out their purpose from the names of the procedures and their place holders?*

(3) *What is the structure of the program like?* Which procedures call/are called by what other procedures? In our case the program has the following underlying structure:

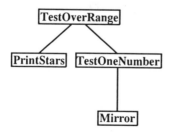

(4) *What does the results of a test run look like?*

```
? TestOverRange 80 90
80 --> *
81 --> *
82 --> **
83 --> *
84 --> **
85 --> **
86 --> ***
87 --> ****
88 -->
89 --> ***************
90 --> *
```

Now that we understand the program better, we can begin to study it to see if the results we get are the results we would expect from our understanding. As discussed in chapter 5 it is a good idea to test a program out using extreme values. So, we choose a series of numbers that should always generate a palindrome in one step: Numbers with a series of "1"s followed by some other digit less than "9," say "5."

Here is a little program to test the some of these numbers:

```
To OnesAndFive :MaxLevel
   OnesAndFive1 15 1 :MaxLevel
End

To OnesAndFive1 :Number :Level :MaxLevel
   If :Level > :MaxLevel [Stop]
   Print TestOneNumber :Number 0
   OnesAndFive1 Word 1 :Number :Level + 1 :MaxLevel
End

?OnesAndFive 20
1
1
1
1
1
1
1
1
Sum doesn't like "5705813791- as input.
You were at line 8 in procedure testonenumber
```

A trace of the number that causes the problem shows:

```
testonenumber of 1111111115 and 0
  testonenumber of 1927254930 and 1
    testonenumber of -1973185075 and 2
Sum doesn't like "5705813791- as input.
You were at line 8 in procedure testonenumber
```

As you can see, as the numbers produced by Mirror become larger than some system dependent value, the LOGO system may cut of any part that is larger than this value, the number may become a negative number, or the LOGO system may switch to another number representation (floating point representation). When this happens, the algorithm breaks down because rounding or truncation occurs or a different notation (using the letter E indicating the exponent, or a minus sign, as occurred in our example) is used. To attempt to avoid this, we can try using LongSum instead of the primitive infix operator "+." LongSum handles the addition of numbers and their mirror image in cases where the numbers become larger than arithmetic precision of your machine (some versions of LOGO handle this with the built in addition function).

The corresponding line of TestOneNumber then would look like this:

```
Output TestOneNumber
        ( LongSum :Number Mirror :Number )
        ( :Again + 1 )
```

Here is the definition of LongSum

```
To LongSum  :Summand1  :Summand2
   If :Summand1 = " [Output :Summand2]
   If :Summand2 = " [Output :Summand1]
   If (Last :Summand1) + (Last :Summand2) > 9
     [Output
        (Word
          (LongSum
            ButLast :Summand1
            LongSum ButLast :Summand2 "1)
            (Last (Last :Summand1) + (Last :Summand2))))]
   Output
     (Word
        (LongSum ButLast :Summand1 ButLast :Summand2)
        (Last :Summand1) + (Last :Summand2))
   End
```

The algorithm should now be constrained only by the space available in the computer for the recursive calls. If, however, your LOGO system automatically converts words consisting only of digits into an internal numerical representation, then this strategy will not work. A further extension, using something like "L1111111111111115 to represent our numbers, could be tried. LongSum could be then be adapted to use "L instead of " to signal the end of the recursion, and TestOneNumber would have to move the "L from the end of the long number to the beginning after it was Mirrored.

Chapter 7:
How Programs Communicate with the User

Until now, the ability of the program to communicate with the user has been one-way. The `Print` and `Show` commands allow the program to send messages to the user, but there has been no way for the program to receive information from the user, except for what is typed into the LOGO interpreter. The `ReadList` operation makes it possible to write a program that can receive information directly from the user. This is especially important for games, simulations, tutorial programs, and simple question and answer systems.

When a LOGO program encounters a `ReadList` operation while executing, it stops and waits for the user to type something in at the keyboard. The program resumes execution when the user at the keyboard completes the input with the Return-key (presumably after typing in a line of text). The `ReadList` operation outputs what the user typed in as a list. As such `ReadList` is an operation without inputs; one could say that it has roughly the opposite function of `Print`.

The following two examples should clarify the mechanism of the `ReadList` operation.

```
To TalkBack
  Print [Say something to me!]
  Print ReadList
  TalkBack
End
```

? TalkBack
Say something to me!
Hello
Hello
Say something to me!
Don't you know anything?
Don't you know anything?
Say something to me!
.
.
.

Because there is no termination condition for the recursive call to `TalkBack`, the procedure can only be stopped by interrupting LOGO from the keyboard.

Now for an example that makes a little more sense. The procedures that follow could be components of a teaching program on factorization:

```
To PromptAndRead :Prompt
   Type :Prompt
   Output ReadList
End
```

Here we also introduce the Type primitive, which is similar to Print except that it does not print a newline after printing its argument.

```
To RunGCD
   Print [I compute the GCD of two numbers!]
   Print
      (Sentence
        "GCD
        Euclid
          First PromptAndRead [First number:]
          First PromptAndRead [Second number:])
   End
```

In the procedure RunGCD two lines are read using ReadList, after appropriate prompts. The numbers are then taken from the first word of the respective list. These values are given to the procedure Euclid, which computes the Greatest Common Divisor (GCD) by a well-known algorithm. The procedure Euclid is presented in section 13.

```
? RunGCD
I compute the GCD of two numbers!
First number:456
Second number:678
GCD:6

? RunGCD
I compute the GCD of two numbers!
First number:2345
Second number:4567890
GCD:5
```

Chapter 8:
Names, Values, and Scope

In other programming languages (e.g., Pascal, BASIC, C, etc.) the assignment operator (as in `c:=sqrt(a*a+b*b)`) occupies a central role. In LOGO on the other hand, the procedure is the focus. However, there is an equivalent language construct in LOGO as well, in an even more general form, as we soon see.

Until now it was not possible for us to give "things" a name and later to call up these "things" using this name[9]. The introduction of the `Make` command should rectify the problem.

Example: The command

```
Make "Days [mo tu we th fr sa su]
```

has the effect, that the thing (or value) `[mo tu we th fr sa su]` is given the name `"Days`.

There are two ways to get the value of a name. Instead of giving the thing itself as the input to a command, for example:

```
? Print [mo tu we th fr sa su]
mo tu we th fr sa su
```

the following command could also be given:

```
? Print Thing "Days
mo tu we th fr sa su
```

that is, `Thing` is a operation with one input (the name) and it returns as output the thing (the value) associated with the given name.

```
Thing
```

---

[9]Of course, this assertion is not completely true, since we could use procedures, by having one return a constant value. We also used this technique in the exercises in section 2.1. A "days of the week" example would look like this:

```
To Days
   Output [MO TU WE TH FR SA SU]
End
```

Instead of the `Thing` operation, one can also use the shortened form by beginning the name with a ``:'' instead of a ``"''[10]:

```
? Print :Days
mo tu we th fr sa su
```

is equivalent to

```
? Print Thing "Days
mo tu we th fr sa su
```

In LOGO you must always differentiate between the *name* and its *value*.[11]; in BASIC, for instance, one would write `A = A + 1`, thus the *name* A that is to the left of the assignment operator is not syntactically distinguished from the *value* A that stands to the right of the assignment operator. To increase the value of the name `"X` by three and give the new value the name `"X` again, the following commands could be given.

```
Make "X Thing "X + 3
```

or

```
Make "X :X + 3
```

There is a difference, however, between `Thing "X` and `:X`. It is possible for the value of a name itself to be a name with no restrictions, for example:

```
? Make "USA "Colorado
? Make "Colorado "Boulder
? Make "Boulder "UCB
```

The `Thing` operation can be applied arbitrarily often, one after the other, whereas ``:'' cannot be nested (i.e.,

```
? Print Thing Thing "USA
Boulder
```

is possible, whereas

```
? Print ::USA
Name :USA unknown
```

is not allowed). For the previous example, we can now execute the following commands with the respective results:

```
? Print "USA
USA
? Print Thing "USA
Colorado
? Print Thing :USA
Boulder
? Print Thing Thing :USA
UCB
```

---

[10]The similarity between the notation of the parameters of a procedure and the association created by `Make` between a name and a value is obvious.

[11]This sharp distinction between the name and the value of a variable is not *syntactically* supported in most programming languages (e.g., BASIC and PASCAL)

```
? Print :Boulder
UCB
```

The data structure that was built up in this example can be depicted graphically as:

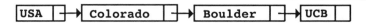

The command `PrintOutName Names` prints all the name-value bindings that exist in the workspace.

```
? PrintOutName Names
"Days is [mo tu we th fr sa su]
"USA is Colorado
"Colorado is Boulder
"Boulder is UCB
```

We can also make an *indirect assignment*, because the input to `Make` can also be a *variable*:

```
? Make :Boulder [we work here!]
? Print :UCB
we work here!
```

The ability to use *names of names of names of* ..., is a fundamental difference from most other programming languages (in Pascal, for example, there is no *name* data type). In LOGO, *names* and *values* are not completely disjoint sets; rather the set of all possible *names* is contained within the set of all *values*.

The concept of *names* is similar to the concept of *variables*; while *name* shifts the naming aspect into the foreground (a chessboard is a complex structure that is referenced with `:Chessboard`), the term *variable* expresses the idea that a place holder can take on different values ("vary").

8.1. Local and Global Variables—Scope of Variables

In the programming we have done so far, we have used the following property (perhaps without realizing it): Names (= variables) for the inputs (place holders) of a procedure, are not available except when that procedure is active. We use the term *scope* to refer to the availability, and we would say that the place holders of a procedure have *local scope* and are known as *local variables*.

Names that are created solely by the use of the `Make` command have what is known as *global scope* (i.e., they are available "everywhere in the world", to all procedures). These are known as *global variables*.

The meaning of the concepts *local* and *global* by and large correspond to their meaning in everyday language (e.g., local weather and global warming).

8.2. An Example: The Procedure Mirror

The following versions of the procedure Mirror serve as examples to demonstrate the issue of scope. Mirror is the procedure we have already examined as an example of a recursive procedure (chapter 3):

```
To Mirror :Word
   Test :Word = "
   IfTrue [Output "]
   Output Word (Last :Word) (Mirror ButLast :Word)
End
```

```
? Print Mirror "house
esuoh
? Print Mirror "cow
woc
```

Of course, this is not the only possible way to write a procedure to solve the problem of reversing the letters in a word. For example, one approach might be to change the last line of Mirror. Let's create a procedure MirrorV2.

```
To MirrorV2 :Sequence
   Test :Sequence = "
   IfTrue [Output "]
   Make "Begin First :Sequence
   Make "End ButFirst :Sequence
   Output Word MirrorV2 :End :Begin
End
```

When we run the procedure, we quickly discover that the results are not what we expected:

```
? Print MirrorV2 "house
eeeee
? Print MirrorV2 "cow
www
```

Even turning on tracing doesn't reveal why each call to MirrorV2 returns a word that is composed of all the same letter.

Let's examine what is going on with MirrorV2 from the standpoint of *scope*. In doing so, let's look at the model of the *little people* again. To distinguish between place holders and variables that were created with the Make command, we begin the latter with an "&" instead of a ":" in the following figures. In figure 8–1 on return from each branch of the recursion, the "world" of the appropriate person is restored and the place holders take the corresponding local values.

In figure 8–2 on returning from each branch of the recursion, the value of the global variable &Begin (created with the Make command) is used in the Word operation. This value doesn't change on return from the recursive call, instead, the name &Begin contains the value, which was last assigned to it, at the lowest level of recursion, where :List contains only a single (the last) letter "w.

Figure 8-1: Execution of Mirror

The difference can be described as follows: Local variables belong to each procedure as "private property"; that is, two local variables with the *same* name in *different* procedures are completely independent from one another. Global variables, on the other hand, have a fixed value, shared among *all* procedures, which can only be changed to a *new assigned value* with the Make command.

8.3. Scope of Names

The procedure call structure of an extensive program can be represented with the aid of a "tree" (see figure 8-3). The individual procedures are marked with P1 through P13 for brevity. The hierarchy shown by this tree represents the structure of the program in terms of "who calls whom."

Figure 8-2: Execution of `MirrorV2`

Let's use figure 8-3 to make some observations about the scope of variables[12].

(1) Global variables are known to *all* procedures unless hidden by some intermediate variable. `:&Global1` is available to all procedures in this program. `:Var` is not available in `P4`, `P9`, `P10`, `P11`, `P12`, and `P13` because the local variables "hide" it from view.

(2) The place holder `:PlaceHolder` in `P1` is visible to all the procedures in the figure.

(3) The local variable `:Local2` in `P6` is only known there.

(4) The local variable `:Local1` in `P2` is available to procedures `P2`, `P5`, and `P6` only.

_____

[12]This discussion is based on the concept of *dynamic* scope; another scoping scheme is used in some systems and is discussed in appendix I.3.

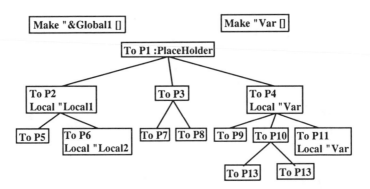

Figure 8–3: A Procedure Tree

(5) `:Var` is local variable of `P4`. It is only accessible from procedures `P4` and `P9 P13`. For procedures `P9`, `P10`, `P12`, and `P13`, this variable is also considered to be a *free* variable. It also "blocks" access to the global variable `:Var`.

(6) `:Var` is also the name of a local variable in `P11` that "blocks" access to the local variable `:Var` in `P4`.

In LOGO the value of variables is retrieved according to the following rules (note, that the *order* plays an important role):

(1) Is it the name of a place holder or local variable in the procedure in question?

(2) Is it the name of a place holder or local variable of a procedure that is higher in the call tree (a *free* variable)?

(3) Does a global variable exist with this name?

If the LOGO system can find no value, the error message

```
... has no value.
```

is printed.

8.4. Making Variables `Local`

One way to create local variables that has already been mentioned is to make a place holder. However this has the disadvantage that a extraneous input needs to be given when the procedure is invoked[13]:

---

[13]On older versions of LOGO, this is the only option

```
To Demo :Input1 :Input2 :LocalVar
  .
  .
End

? Demo "this "that "
```

A better way is available: The Local command designates the name given as
its input as a local variable.

```
To Demo :Input1 :Input2
Local "LocalVar
  .
  .
End

? Demo "this "that
```

8.5. Using the Make Command

The Make command does not always create a global variable; if the word given
to it to specify the name is already a name in some scope, then the value is
assigned to that name instead of creating a global name. This means that the
Make command can be used to:

- (re)assign values to *local* variables
- reassign values to place holders
- create *global* variables and assign values to them
- reassign values to *global* variables

A typical use of global variables is, for example, in game programs. Here,
global variables can be used to hold global data structures, such as the game
board in chess or the tableaus in solitaire. Aside from being used for
information that needs to be available to all procedures in a program and for
which a global scope is necessary, global variables should be avoided a much as
possible.

To show a reasonable use of the Make command, let's first give an example
that doesn't work:

```
To Dialogue
  Test MemberP ReadList [who where how when]
  IfTrue [Question]
  Test MemberP ReadList [forget find change]
  IfTrue [Command]
  Respond
End
```

The first line tests whether the line from the keyboard contains a question word.
If that is the case, then the procedure Question is called. Otherwise, the
same input line should be searched for a command word. However, the LOGO

system requests a new line of input from the user with each `ReadList`, and actually different sentences are searched, whereas we need to search the same sentence both times!

```
To Dialogue1
    Local "Sentence
    Make "Sentence ReadList
    Test MemberP :Sentence [who where how when]
    IfTrue [Question]
    Test MemberP :Sentence [forget find change]
    IfTrue [Command]
    Respond
End
```

This example still has the drawback that in order for `Question`, `Command`, and `Respond` to have access to `:Sentence`, they would need to contain *free* references to that name. This makes those procedures dependent on that name being defined in some other scope. It might be better to give `:Sentence` as an input to these procedures.

```
To Dialogue2
    Local "Sentence
    Make "Sentence ReadList
    Test MemberP :Sentence [who where how when]
    IfTrue [Question :Sentence]
    Test MemberP :Sentence [forget find change]
    IfTrue [Command :Sentence]
    Respond :Sentence
End
```

8.6. Advantages and Disadvantages of Local, Free, and Global Variables

Let's summarize what we have mentioned about the advantages and disadvantages of using global, free, and local variables.

Using global variables and free variables causes procedures to be dependent on one another, so that the complexity of the program is increased. One effect of this is that they cannot be tested separately.

On the other hand, it sometimes is cumbersome to pass all the information using place holders, since this can result in procedures with many place holders.

Global variables should only be used where data of a global nature needs to be named. If several people work on a project, then it should be determined beforehand what global variables should be used.

One last piece of advice: Use *meaningful names* for all variable names. It is sometimes a good idea to use special characters[14] in the names of global

---

[14]Some versions may restrict what special characters can be used in this way.

variables (e.g., :&Alphabet) so that name conflicts with place holders or free variables can be avoided as much as possible. Such a convention can also aid the readability of your program; if the reader is aware of your convention, then it will be easier to spot such global references.

Exercise

Assume that the following three procedures are in the workspace. Determine what information will be printed out if the Example procedure is called.

```
To Example
   Make "A [I have the overview]
   Make "B [So do I!!]
   World1 [I am input to world1!]
   World2
   (Print [A in example:] :A)
   Print [Show Names produces:]
   Show Names
End

To World1 :A
   (Print [A in world1:] :A)
   Print [Show Names produces:]
   Show Names
End

To World2
   (Print [A in World2:] :A)
   Print [Show Names produces:]
   Show Names
End
```

Chapter 9:
Data Structures

The way that many programs work can be viewed as follows:

Input Data ⟶ PROGRAM ⟶ **Output Data, Results**

That is, a program transforms the input data into output data in some desired manner.

Examples:

(1) `LongSum`

```
? Print LongSum 3 21
24
```

The input data are two numbers, and as a result, we get their sum.

(2) `RemoveVowels`

```
? Print RemoveVowels [This is a sentence]
Ths  s  sntnc
```

This procedure removes all the vowels from the input sentence.

(3) `Rectangle`

```
? Rectangle "* 2 5
*****
*****
```

The inputs are the character to be used, and the height and width of the rectangle. The result is a rectangle represented as rows of asterisks printed as a side effect of the procedure.

For simple problems, the data can be typed into the LOGO interpreter as input to a procedure. With large problem tasks, especially in non-numerical fields, the direct, explicit input of data is not possible or is at least much too troublesome. It is therefore necessary to find a suitable way to represent the data (analogous to the algorithm for procedures).

In the following paragraphs, we examine some general methods for shaping the structure of the data for a variety of problems. We do not look closely into the *formal* definitions of the individual data structures. Instead, the structures should be understood by forming *suitable abstractions from concrete problems*. We select problems that we have dealt with so far to serve as examples.

9.1. Lists

Lists can be formally defined as ordered sets, that is, there is a first, second, etc. element.

Some typical ways that we operate on lists are, for example:

- Insert a new element at a specific place,
- remove an element,
- join two lists into one, or
- determine the number of elements in a list.

Examples of Lists

(1) Lists of word classes:

For a project whose goal is "writing poems," the problem of choosing a single representative word from a class of words arises. The classes could be represented as lists:

A list of nouns → dog, house, coal, hat, ...
A list of verbs → go, count, think, call, ...

(2) Shopping List

It's your job to prepare your family's shopping list for the weekend. For that, you will need to write a list for each family member. For example:

Ingrid → flour, sugar, yeast, shampoo
Eva → milk, ketchup, eggs, hagendas, dr.pepper
Stephanie → bread, crackers, juice, yogurt

The individual list can then be joined into one single list. A list like this for a single family is still small enough that one can look at the whole thing, whereas this form of representation for a large hotel would be too large to look all at once. You could try to structure the list further:

a) Check whether elements appear more than once.

b) Separate the list into sublists that correspond to the shop where the items should be bought. That can be done either when the list is drawn up or later, by sorting the large list.

Baker → bread
Dairy → yeast, milk, yogurt
Supermarket → flour, ketchup, juice

c) Another extension would be to keep track of an amount along with each item:

Dairy → (yeast 1 package) (milk 3 qt.)
(Yogurt 1 lb.)

Naturally, the information about where the item should be purchased could be added with the item itself.

Shopping List → (bread 1 loaf baker)
(Yeast 1 package Dairy) ...

The structure of the list is then such that the elements of the main list are lists as well.

(3) List of reachable train stations:

When traveling it is important to know what other cities can be reached directly by train or other means of transportation.

Hamburg → Bremen, Hanover, Copenhagen
Rome → Milan, Palermo, Florence, Cairo

Here, too, more information could be incorporated:

• What is the distance?

• How long is the trip?

• What is the cost?

(4) Telephone Book

Even a telephone book is little more than a list of the telephone subscribers. It would certainly be of little use if the information contained in it were not structured according to certain criteria. Here are some criteria that are used.

• Dividing into sublists (separate localities)

• Ordering the sublist (alphabetically)

These or similar criteria could also be useful for the other lists we mentioned. Large lists that are only used to insert data randomly and then later to retrieve that information by searching sequentially, are of limited use. Additional information (such as ordering the data) or additional structure is needed to make them useful.

The previously mentioned LOGO data structure *list* lends itself well to the common use of the term in the previous examples and it can represent these problems without any difficulty. To illustrate, we write a program that generates "Poetry." The words for the "poems" are chosen randomly from lists.

```
To Data
  Make "&Article [the a this each one]
  Make
    "&Adjective
    [big silly sexy poor red colorful
     old difficult strong tiny]
  Make
    "&Noun
    [house teacher student girl rat car
     movie tree darling computer]
```

```
Make
  "&Verb
  [comes goes loves eats drinks thinks
   climbs visits believes communicates]
End

To RandomWord :List
  Output Nth 1 + Random Count :List :List
End
```

The procedure Nth, described in appendix III, is used to select a word from the sentence.

The procedure Verse0 then generates a verse by joining together the individual words.

```
To Verse0
  Output
    (Sentence
      RandomWord :&Article
      RandomWord :&Adjective
      RandomWord :&Noun
      RandomWord :&Verb)
End
```

9.2. Property Lists

Property lists are characterized as lists composed of property/value pairs. Using property lists, arbitrarily many of these property/value pairs can be associated with a single name:

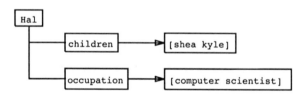

Figure 9-1: Property Lists

We can easily find further examples where this form of representation is appropriate:

(1) Personnel Data

Large companies as well as the government have available various data about interesting classes of people.

Companies:
age, tax classification, number of hours worked, hourly wage, overtime hours, ...

Government:
name of parents, birthdate and birthplace, profession, address, marital status, ...

All these properties or parameters have a specific value for each person. In addition to the data itself, there are also facilities for changing, retrieving, and organizing the data; this is called a (personnel) *data base* system.

(2) Records

School records are in general organized in this manner. The individual courses can be represented as properties, and the respective grades as the value associated with them. For this example, the values are primarily numbers (or can at least be represented as numbers), whereas other examples deal with various data types (words, sentences, numbers).

The procedures PutProp is used to associate a value with the property of a name:

```
? PutProp "hal "children [shea kyle]
? PutProp "hal "occupation [computer scientist]
```

and the operation GetProp is used to retrieve a value given the name and property:

```
? Print GetProp "hal "children
shea kyle
? Print GetProp "hal "occupation
computer scientist
```

If these are not available as primitives in your version of LOGO, see appendix III.

Exercises

(1) What is the difference between lists and property lists?

(2) What advantages and disadvantages do the two representations have?

9.3. Trees

Now, let's turn our attention to how other data structures can be used. Figure 9–2 shows the components and nomenclature of tree-structured information.

A tree is defined as follows: It is a node, which contains (zero or more) branches that are themselves trees. This is a recursive definition, since, to define the concept of a tree, we had to use the term *tree* itself. How does such a definition make sense? It is reasonable to assume that a tree has *finitely* many nodes. From that we see that each subtree as we step outwards from the root of the tree has fewer nodes until finally some subtrees have only one node (i.e., the node contains no branches; it is a *leaf* node), and the recursive process stops.

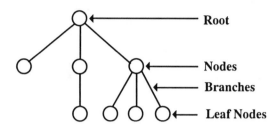

Figure 9–2: Trees

The terminology we use to talk about family trees (see figure 9–3) is also useful for describing tree data structures: Nodes of a tree can have parent nodes, child nodes, and sibling nodes[15].

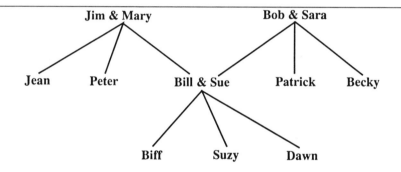

Figure 9–3: A Family Tree

Generally, in addition to the subtrees that make up a node, some kind of information is also stored at the node.

The following examples show that trees are well suited as data structures for diverse problems. The tree is a useful representation for tournament pairings where the corresponding losers are eliminated (i.e., a single-elimination tournament, the NCAA basketball tournament is an example; see figure 9–4). For round-robin or double-elimination tournaments, this representation is less useful.

For various games (e.g., chess, go), the plays that are possible from a certain

---

[15]The strictest definition of a tree requires that each subtree have only one parent tree, so the family tree in figure 9–3 is not a tree under that definition.

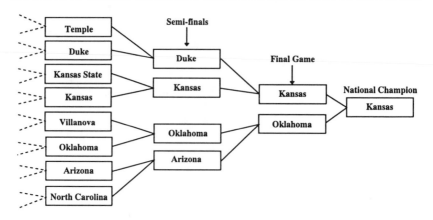

Figure 9-4: Pairings of a Sports Tournament

game position can be represented as a tree (see figure 9-5). Using this type of tree, a certain move can be evaluated in terms of its results as well as in terms of the possible responses of the opponent.

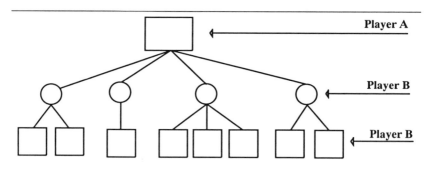

Figure 9-5: Game and Decision Trees

Further examples:

- The structure of a program, which includes several procedures (see figure 8-3)
  The structure of a book that is organized into chapters, sections, etc.

- Grammars, which characterize the sentences of a particular language.

- A LOGO command with nested procedure calls.

In general, every hierarchical classification system could be represented in a tree structure.

Binary Trees

An important subset of trees are *binary* trees, which have only two branches in each node (see figure 9–6). Binary trees are used extensively in computer algorithms.

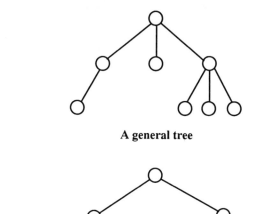

A general tree

A binary tree

Figure 9–6: Two Types of Trees

Here are some examples of how this type of tree could be used:

- Decision trees, where only yes and no answers are possible (see figure 9–7 and chapter 29).

- Trees representing binary operators (see figure 9–8); the tree representation makes the precedence of the operators explicit.

- Sorting trees: here, the nodes are organized so that only nodes "less than" a particular node are stored on one subtree of that node, and only nodes "greater than" that node are stored on the other. The concepts of "less than" and "greater than" are based on some ordering relationship defined on the information stored in each node (see figure 9–9). New nodes can be inserted into this tree by searching through the tree until a leaf node is found, then inserting the new information to the right or to the left as appropriate. This technique is used in chapter 18.

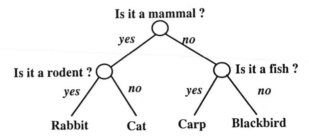

Figure 9-7: A Biological Classification System

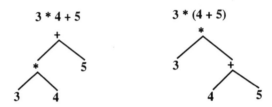

Figure 9-8: Binary Operators

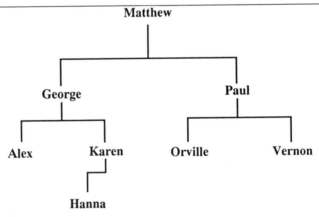

Figure 9-9: Alphabetical Sorting

Trees in LOGO

Let's look at a simple program to build binary trees in LOGO. Trees themselves are not available as a data structure in LOGO, thus we have the task (similar to our experience with procedures) of building complex elements from simpler ones.

We use the ability of nesting LOGO lists to represent the tree data structure, with empty lists representing an empty tree. Each node in the tree is a list of three elements: The first element represents the data stored at that node, the second and third elements represent the left and right subtrees, respectively. For example, a tree consisting of a single node containing the data "Root would look like this:

```
[root [] []]
```

whereas a tree consisting of node "a with the children "b and "c would look like this:

```
[a [b [] []] [c [] []]]
```

Now, here is a simple program to interactively construct a binary tree:

```
To BuildTree :Prompt
  Print :Prompt
  Local "Data
  Make "Data ReadList
  If EmptyP :Data [Output []]
  Output
    MakeTree
      :Data
      BuildTree
        Sentence [specify data for left child of]
          :Data
      BuildtRee
        Sentence [specify data for right child of]
          :Data
End

To MakeTree :Data :Left :Right
  Output (List :Data :Left :Right)
End
```

Notice that in comparison to a list, which is a linear structure and for which *one* recursive call suffices, with the branched structure of a binary tree, *two* recursive calls are necessary.

Using this program we can build, for example, a LOGO representation of one of the binary operator trees in figure 9–8.

```
? Make "Tree BuildTree [what is the data at the root?]
what is the data at the root?
+
specify data for left child of +
*
specify data for left child of *
3
specify data for left child of 3

specify data for right child of 3

specify data for right child of *
4
specify data for left child of 4
```

```
specify data for right child of 4
specify data for right child of +
5
specify data for left child of 5
specify data for right child of 5
? Show :Tree
[[+] [[*] [[3] [] []] [[4] [] []]] [[5] [] []]].
```

Traversing Binary Trees

Once we have created a tree structure, there are several ways to operate on that structure. One type of operation is to walk around the tree in some orderly fashion, doing something to each node of the tree. This is known as *traversing* the tree. We look at three types of traversals: *inorder, preorder,* and *postorder.* Each of these traversals performs the following operations on each node, although each in a different order.

- visit a node (and perform some operation on the contents of the node)

- work the left subtree.

- work the right subtree.

Inorder Traversals

If we do things in this order:

- work on left branch

- visit the node

- work on right branch

we call it an inorder traversal.

For our examples, to "visit" a node, we use the procedure Handle, which simply returns the value stored at the node:

```
To Handle :Node
  Output First :Node
End

To InOrderTraversal :Node
  Test EndP :Node
  IfTrue [Output []]
  Output
    (Sentence (InOrderTraversal LeftBranch :Node)
      (Handle :Node)
      (InOrderTraversal RightBranch :Node))
End
```

Running this on the result from the last section looks like this:

```
? Print InOrderTraversal :Tree
3 * 4 + 5
```

This corresponds to the infix notation for the expression represented by the tree.

Preorder Traversal

This takes its name from the fact that the operation is performed on the node
before it is performed on the children of that node:

- visit the node

- work on left branch

- work on right branch

```
To PreOrderTraversal :Node
   Test EndP :Node
   IfTrue [Output [ ]]
   Output
      (Sentence (Handle :Node)
         (PreOrderTraversal RightBranch :Node)
         (PreOrderTraversal LeftBranch :Node))
   End
```

Testing this on the expression tree

```
? Print PreOrderTraversal :Tree
+ 5 * 4 3
```

gives us the prefix notation of that expression.

Postorder Traversal

With this version the data of a node is operated on after the nodes of both
subtrees are visited:

- work on left branch

- work on right branch

- visit the node

```
To PostOrderTraversal :Node
   Test EndP :Node
   IfTrue [Output [ ]]
   Output
      (Sentence (PostOrderTraversal RightBranch :Node)
         (PostOrderTraversal LeftBranch :Node)
         (Handle :Node))
   End
```

This generates what is known as postfix notation:

```
? Print PostOrderTraversal :Tree
5 4 3 * +
```

Procedures to access the tree representation

We have written these examples in such a way that they use common procedures
to access the information used to represent the tree. This allows some flexiblity
in the representation of the tree: If we should decide that another representation

were somehow "better," we could change the representation by rewriting these procedures and the tree traversal procedures would still work. This is known as "data access using functions."

```
To LeftBranch :Node
   Output First ButFirst :Node
End

To RightBranch :Node
   Output Last :Node
End

To EndP :Node
   Output :Node = [ ]
End
```

Chapter 29, chapter 21, and the tree sort algorithm on page 156 pursue the use of tree data structures further. In chapter 28 we dicuss other characteristics of tree traversals.

9.4. Graphs

Graphs are the most general structure that we look at. A graph consists of a set of nodes, which are connected with lines. Lists and trees could be interpreted as special cases of graphs.

We examine two examples:

(1) Connected Graphs

A traveling salesperson, whose route covers several cities, uses the map represented in figure 9–10.

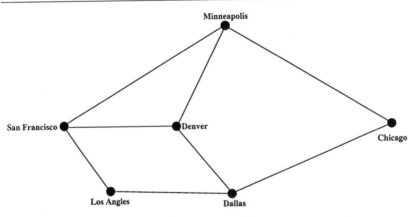

Figure 9–10: A Map

The following questions (among others) are of interest to the traveler:

- Can I reach all the cities?

- How can I lay out my trip route best, if I want to visit all the cities?

Similar questions would be raised for the electricity, water, and telephone networks (minimum material costs, adequate services for all subscribers, etc.).

(2) Directed Graphs

This subclass distinguishes itself in that the connecting lines have a direction. For example, set inclusion and the containment of elements in sets can be represented with directed graphs. Figure 9–11 gives some examples of directed graphs.

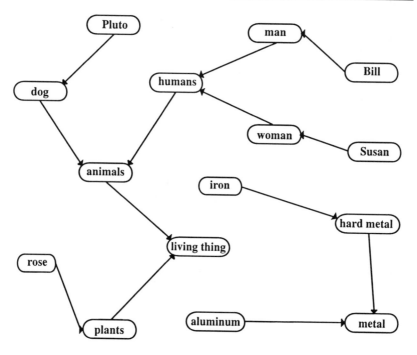

Figure 9–11: Examples of Directed Graphs

Graphs in Logo

Let's try to represent the map displayed in figure 9–12 in Logo. The places on the map are connected by one-way streets.

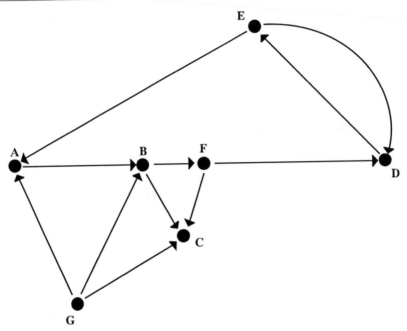

Figure 9–12: Connections between Places

The data base can be built up with the aid of suitable procedures.

```
? BuildMap
Specify starting point and reachable nodes:A B
Specify starting point and reachable nodes:B F C
Specify starting point and reachable nodes:F D C
Specify starting point and reachable nodes:E A D
Specify starting point and reachable nodes:D E
Specify starting point and reachable nodes:G A B C
Specify starting point and reachable nodes:

? PrintOutName Names
"A is [B]
"B is [F C]
"C is []
"D is [E]
"E is [A D]
"F is [D]
"G is [A B C]
```

The following procedures operate on this data structure, and determine whether one or more places are on the path to a specific destination.

```
To PathP :StartingPoint :Goal
   Test :StartingPoint = [ ]
   IfTrue [Output "False]
   Test :Goal = [ ]
   IfTrue [Output "False]
   Test MemberP First :Goal :StartingPoint
   IfTrue [Output "True]
   Output PathP Neighbor :StartingPoint :Goal
End

To Neighbor :Place
   Test :Place = [ ]
   IfTrue [Output [ ]]
   Output
      Sentence Thing First :Place ButFirst :Place
End

? Print PathP [G] [A]
true
? Print PathP [A] [D]
true
? Print PathP [C] [G]
false
```

9.5. Vectors and Matrices

Vectors and matrices are special cases of the class of data structures known as arrays. These data structures are used with problems whose data size and index range(s) (the number of the identically sized elements) can be determined in advance. Although some more recent versions of LOGO do include array data types, early versions left them out because LOGO focuses on recursive processing and the recursive list data type. Many discussions surrounding the use of arrays emphasize the straightforward mapping that exists between arrays and the linear addressablilty of computer memory which makes them ideal for fixed, repetitive structures with efficient, direct access to elements. However, our primary focus is on *cognitive efficiency* so we are interested in situations where the mapping between the problem and a solution is more natural using the abstract concept of arrays than it would be using lists.

Vectors

A vector is a *one-dimensional* array where a single value can be used to index an element.

As an example, let's use a vector to test whether a random number generator gives an even distribution. First, we need a result vector whose length is the same as the range of random numbers being generated. Each element stores the frequency of the result that matches the index of the element. The random number generated is used to index into the vector; the value stored in that element is incremented, and the process repeats a certain number of times. At the end of the test, each element of the vector should contain approximately the same value if the distribution is even.

Testing of the LOGO random number generator gives the following result.

```
? TestRandom
Test of the random number generator

Number of attempts: 100

Absolute Frequency
9 ***********************
8 ********************
7 ************************
6 ******************
5 *********************
4 ********************
3 ***********************
2 *****************
1 ******************
0 ***********************
```

For each component, a new LOGO name is generated. The data structure, then, looks like this:

```
? PrintOutName Names
"Number#9 is **********************
"Number#8 is ********************
"Number#7 is ***********************
"Number#6 is *****************
"Number#5 is ********************
"Number#4 is ********************
"Number#3 is **********************
"Number#2 is ****************
"Number#1 is *****************
"Number#0 is *********************
```

Matrices

A Matrix is a *two-dimensional* array. Two index values are needed to access a single element.

A chess board, for example, could be represented as a matrix-like construct, with two indices, where one is used for the rows and the other for the columns, the individual squares are completely determined (e.g., A3, B7).

Arrays with more dimensions are also possible. By using another index, elements in a three-dimensional space can be represented (necessary for three-dimensional tic-tac-toe, for example).

We use a maze as an example for matrices. We use a matrix to represent the maze in figure 9–13.

Figure 9-13: A Maze

One possible implementation is a list whose elements represent the individual rows of the matrix:

```
"Maze1 IS [WWWWWWW W.....W WWW.W.W
           WE..W.W WWW.W.W W...W.W WWWWWWW]
```

With a suitable procedure the maze can be printed in a more readable form:

```
? ShowMaze "Maze1
WWWWWWW
W.....W
WWW.W.W
WT..W.W
WWW.W.W
W...W.W
WWWWWWW
```

Mazes pose a list of varied problems; among others:

• Generating a pattern, that is, distributing the walls ("W") and pathways (".") into a matrix that is initially empty,

• placing of the treasure "T" in the generated pattern, and finally

• searching (more or less) skillfully for the treasure.

Chapter 10:
Data as Programs, Programs as Data

Data as Programs: The Run Command

The `Run` command represents one of the most powerful tools in the LOGO programming language. It has one input and it works as follows: The input text is viewed as a LOGO expression, and as such, is executed. The `Run` command is typical of an interpreted language; it corresponds to LISP's `Eval` function and the `Execute` operator of APL.

A simple Example:

```
? Run [Print 3]
3
? Run [Erase "Mirror]
? Print Run [First "house]
h
```

Here the commands in brackets could have been given directly, that is, using the `Run` command doesn't allow us to do more than we could already. This example does, however, point out a unique property of the `Run` command. Based on the classification given in section 2.3, it could be considered to be either an **operation** or a **command** depending on its input.

The `Run` command becomes important, when the parts of command to be executed needs to be put together first. Suppose, for example, you need to write a procedure that takes as its inputs a command and a list containing the inputs to that command, then executes the command with the inputs.

```
? RunCom "Print ["a]
a
? RunCom [Print Sum] [1 2]
3
```

A first attempt at this procedure might be something like:

```
To RunCom :Command :InputList
   :Command :InputList
End
```

However, this does not work, since the LOGO interpreter does not find a command name to execute. Instead, the `Run` primitive can be used:

```
To RunCom :Command :InputList
   Run Sentence :Command InputList
End
```

The `Run` command gives us the ability to have the final specification of individual parts of a procedure occur at run time, instead of when the procedure is written. This can be used as the foundation for several procedures that are able to change or create other procedures.

The Run command gives LOGO a real vitality, since it allows LOGO code to be created and executed at run-time.

With this, we can even write our own LOGO front-end that gives a different prompt and allows us to type any operation and have the result printed out:

```
To LogoLoop
  Type [yes master?:]
  Print Run ReadList
  LogoLoop
End

? LogoLoop
yes master?:1 + 2
3
yes master?:mirror "abc
cba
```

Programs as Data: the Text and Define Commands

There are two other predefined procedures that allow us to manipulate the text of programs as data: Text and Define.

Text   takes one input, the name of a procedure in the workspace. Its output is the text of the procedure as a list. The first element of the list is a list of the place holders, the second element is the text of the first procedure line (as a sentence), the third element contains the second line of the procedure text, etc.

```
? Print Text "RunCom
[:Command :InputList]
[Run Sentence :Command :InputList]
?
```

Define   is a command that does the inverse of Text; it takes two inputs, and as a side-effect, a procedure is defined by the name of the first input with the text of the second input. The second input must be of the same form as the output of Text

```
?Define "RunCom
       [[:Command :InputList]
        [Run Sentence :Command :InputList]]
?PrintOut "RunCom
To RunCom :Command :InputList
  Run Sentence :Command :InputList
End
```

These constructs allow procedures to be variable, just as names allow data to be variable.

10.1. Changing Procedures Automatically

The Problem: Suppose we want to replace one word with another in one (or several) procedure(s). For example, we might want to replace Node with Tree in the InOrderTraversal procedure from chapter 9.

```
? PrintOut "InOrderTraversal
To InOrderTraversal :Node
Test EndP :Node
IfTrue [Output []]
Output
  (Sentence
    (InOrderTraversal LeftBranch :Node )
    (Handle :Node )
    (InOrderTraversal RightBranch :Node ))
End
? Change "InOrderTraversal ":Node ":Tree
? PrintOut "InOrderTraversal
To InOrderTraversal :Tree
Test EndP :Tree
IfTrue [Output []]
Output
  (Sentence
    (InOrderTraversal LeftBranch :Tree )
    (Handle :Tree )
    (InOrderTraversal RightBranch :Tree ))
End
```

With the aid of Text and Define, we can write a LOGO program that automatically modifies procedures. Here is an example of such a program:

```
To Change :Pname :Old :New
  Define
    :Pname
    ModifyProcedure Text :Pname :Old :New
End

To ModifyProcedure :Text :Old :New
  Test :Text = []
  IfTrue [Output []]
  Output
    FPut
      ModifyLine First :Text :Old :New
      ModifyProcedure ButFirst :Text :Old :New
End

To ModifyLine :Line :Old :New
  Test :Line = []
  IfTrue [Output []]
  Test First :Line = :Old
  IfTrue
    [Output
      Fput
        :New
        ModifyLine ButFirst :Line :Old :New]
```

```
    IfFalse
      [Output
        Fput
          First :Line
          ModifyLine ButFirst :Line :Old :New]
    End
```

In both of these procedures the LOGO operation FPut appears for the first time. It requires two inputs (a word and a sentence) and outputs a new sentence with the given word in front of the old sentence. In ModifyProcedure, FPut creates the new text of the procedure by placing the modified first line in front of the rest of the modified text. In ModifyLine a new procedure line is constructed by placing the new word in front of the rest of the modified line if the old word appears at the beginning of the line.

10.2. Program Generator

Writing a program generator is certainly one of the most interesting problems that we can deal with. *Program generators* can be used when many similar programs are needed. The following LOGO program illustrates the principle.

With WriteProcedure

```
To WriteProcedure :Number
  Test :Number = 0
  IfTrue [Stop]
  Define
    (Word "Verse :Number)
    (List [] Sentence "Print Random 10)
  WriteProcedure :Number - 1
End
```

Programs like these are generated:

```
To Verse1               To Verse2
  Print 7                 Print 9
End                     End
```

The input to WriteProcedure specifies the number of procedures, that should be defined. The definition appears in the middle line of WriteProc. The name is derived from the word Verse and the current number of the definition; its text consists of a two-element list. The first element is the empty list, since the procedures have no inputs, while the second line consists of the command Print and a random number less than 10. The End of the procedures is provided by Define.

10.3. Program-Directed Selection of Programs

One programming project you could pursue is to write a program that generates "poetry," similar to what was done on page 65. In such a program it would be desirable to have different verse structures in a stanza. The Run command allows us to select easily between different verse structures at run time.

The procedures of the program:

```
To Stanza :Number
  Data
  Stanza1 :Number
End

To Stanza1 :Number
  Test :Number = 0
  IfTrue [Stop]
  Run Sentence "Print Word "Verse Random 2
  Stanza1 :Number - 1
End

To Data
  Make
    "&Article
    [the a this each one the a this each one]
  Make
    "&Adjective
    [big silly pretty poor red colorful
     old difficult strong tiny]
  Make
    "&Noun
    [house teacher student girl rat car
     movie tree darling computer]
  Make
    "&Verb
    [comes goes loves eats drinks thinks
     climbs visits believes communicates]
End

To Verse0
  Output
    (Sentence
      RandomElement :&Article
      RandomElement :&Adjective
      RandomElement :&Noun
      RandomElement :&Verb)
End
```

```
To Verse1
  Output
    (Sentence
      RandomElement  :&Article
      RandomElement  :&Adjective
      RandomElement  :&Noun
      RandomElement  :&Verb
      RandomElement  :&Article
      RandomElement  :&Adjective
      RandomElement  :&Noun)
  End
```

The program is initialized by a call to the Data procedure, which sets up the (global) data structures. Then, in the next to last line of Stanza1, one of the two procedures, Verse0 or Verse1, is called (randomly). This results in variations in the style of the "poem" lines.

A test run:

```
? Stanza 4
this big student communicates
this colorful movie climbs
a silly darling communicates
each pretty darling thinks each colorful tree
```

The first three lines were generated by Verse0, the last line by Verse1.

Exercise

Write a program that generates a table of values for an arbitrary arithmetic expression. A test run of such a program might appear as follows:

```
? Table [3 * Exp X 2 + 5 * X]  1  10
X     Y
1     8
2     22
3     42
4     68
5     100
6     138
7     182
8     232
9     288
10    350
```

Chapter 11:
Smaller Projects

On the following pages a few small projects are described. By a *project* we mean a problem whose solution requires more than one procedure.

The procedures needed for a given project depend heavily on one another. It is in your interest to follow the recommendations and guidelines discussed in chapter 4 to avoid being tangled in an incomprehensible mess. Only by working on a project whose solution is not readily apparent from the beginning can you understand the importance of recommendations and guidelines.

Arithmetic Procedures

Imagine that the following somewhat unpleasant story were to occur:

Last night a villain destroyed all the arithmetic operators ("+", "-", "*", and "/"). All that was left for you are two procedures Add1 and Sub1 that either add or subtract one from their input.

```
To Add1 :Number               To Sub1 :Number
    Output :Number + 1            Output :Number - 1
End                           End
```

You should repair the damage with the following steps:

(1) Write the procedures Sum and Prod that each take two inputs.

(2) Write Diff for two inputs.

(3) Write Exp that raises its first input to the power specified by the second input.

(4) Write Div that divides two numbers.

A Psycholinguistic Experiment

A psycholinguist has made the following assertion:

> Suppose that someone has removed all the vowels from all the words in a sentence. If that sentence contains more than seven words, we can reconstruct the original sentence.

Write a few LOGO procedures that remove all the vowels from an arbitrary length sentence.

```
? Print RemoveVowels [This is a sentence]
ths s  sntnc
```

Use this program to either support or refute the assertion of the psycholinguist. The following questions can also be investigated:

(1) Which words are especially difficult or simple to reconstruct?

(2) Modify the program so that it removes all the consonants instead of the vowels. Can a corresponding assertion be made?

(3) Write a procedure that determines how many vowels and how many consonants a sentence contains.

(4) Determine the average (mean) number of letters in a word and the average (mean) ratio of the number of vowels per word to the number of consonants per word.

(5) Compare English text with that of other languages.

This kind of problem is discussed along with some other linguistic games in chapter 33.

Terminal Screen Geometry

Write procedures that print geometric figures on the terminal screen. Some examples:

```
Rectangle 4 7    Triangle 4 7    Diamond 3

*******               *               *
*******              ***             ***
*******             *****           *****
*******            *******           ***
                                      *
```

```
House 4 5    OutlineRect 6 7

    *         *******
   ***        *     *
  *****       *     *
  *****       *     *
  *****       *     *
  *****       *******
```

Set Theory Lessons

Your younger brother or sister is having difficulty with set theory lessons in math class. To help, you write a few procedures that implement the suitable set operations:

- **Union**, which takes two sets and creates a set that contains the combined elements of those sets with duplicates removed:

  ? Show Union [a b d] [a c d]
  [a b c d]

- **Intersection**, which takes two sets and creates a set that contains only elements that are in both of those sets:

  ? Show Intersection [a b d] [a c d]
  [a d]

- **PowerSet**, which creates the set of all possible sets that can be made by combining zero or more elements of a given set:

  ```
  ? Show PowerSet [a b c]
  [[] [a] [b] [c] [a b] [a c] [b c] [a b c]]
  ```

- **SetDifference**, which generates the set of all elements in a first set that are not in a second set:

  ```
  ? Show SetDifference [a b d] [a c d]
  [b]
  ```

- **CartesianProduct**, which generates the set of all *pairs* of elements taking one from a first set and another from a second set. Using two-element lists to represent pairs, an example would look like this:

  ```
  ? Show CartesianProduct [a b d] [a c d]
  [[a a] [a c] [a d] [b a] [b c] [b d] [d a] [d c] [d d]]
  ```

A Mathematical Conjecture

Do you have a math teacher who pretends to know it all? Then ask whether the following assertion is true:

Take any arbitrary whole number, larger than one. If this number is even, let n' = n/2. If it is odd, then n' = 3*n+1. Then set n = n' and repeat the process. All numerical sequences generated this way reach the number one after a certain number of steps.

Example: Say, we choose the number 13; the following sequence is generated.

$$13 \rightarrow 40 \rightarrow 20 \rightarrow 10 \rightarrow 5 \rightarrow 16 \rightarrow 8 \rightarrow 4 \rightarrow 2 \rightarrow 1$$

Write LOGO procedures that you can use to test this assertion.

Can you find a number for which this assertion isn't true? Can you prove that this assertion holds for all natural numbers?

Random Numbers

Write a program that generates a specified number of large random numbers . The number of digits of these random numbers should be between 0 and 99.

Example:

```
? Print BigRandom 1
34943782
? Print BigRandom 3
290756
47352344375876987078956743652342432353464575687697958736236 5
85754634532424313152 61
```

Do you think that the generated numbers are really *random*? Can you check whether they are really random?

Launching a Space Rocket

Write a program that generates a specified number of launches of a space rocket. These launches should not always go off without a hitch.

Example for 3 launches:

```
? Launch 3
10 9 8 7 6 5 4 3 2 1 0 !!!
Successful launch!

10 9 8 7 6 ABORT LAUNCH! Leak in fuel tank!

10 9 8 7 6 5 4 3 2 1 0 !!!
Successful launch! -- WARNING:
There is a problem with the computer!
```

For further problem conditions, use your imagination!

Roman Numerals

Write a collection of procedures that convert back and forth between Roman and Arabic numerals and can perform basic arithmetic on Roman numerals. Some examples:

```
? Print Roman 6
VI
? Print Roman 27
XXVII
? Print Arabic "IX
9
? Print Arabic "IC
99
? Print RomanSum "II "IV
VI
? Print RomanSum "VI "LV
LXI
```

"Reading" Numbers

Write a program that can "say" arbitrary numbers. Some examples:

```
? Print Say 6
six
? Print Say 27
twenty-seven
? Print Say 66
sixty-six
? Print Say 713
seven hundred and thirteen
```

Balancing Your Checking Account

Write a program that can assist you with balancing your checking account. The program could:

• Ask you for the appropriate amounts from your checkbook and your checking account statement (ending balances, outstanding checks, outstanding deposits, etc.) and check to see if they balance.

- Allow you to keep track of the checks you have written and deposits you have made, then allow you to "check off" those checks and deposits that appear on your statement. This would allow the program to calculate the amounts of your outstanding checks and deposits.

- Have the program keep track of automatic deposits and withdrawals.

You could also take this project further by writing a similar, but more extensive program, that would handle the accounts for a whole bank. This program would need to:

- Post all transactions to the appropriate accounts (deposits, withdrawals, transfers).

- Check for overdrawn accounts.

- Calculate appropriate interest (simple, compound) on applicable accounts.

- Calculate service charges.

- Print statements.

You could also simulate an "automatic teller."

Part 2:
Mathematics

Introduction

In the early days of computing, computers were considered primarily as high-speed calculators. This view turned out to be at best only partly correct. Computers are general symbol-processing devices, capable of performing any well-defined process for the manipulation and transformation of information.

The impact of computers on mathematics was seen originally in their role as computing devices. Being able to compute correctly and efficiently with numbers is an important part of mathematics. However, the historical development led to a very one-sided view of the use of computers in mathematics. They were used as high-speed calculators and one of the prime tasks was correctly implementing existing algorithms. But computers can play a much more important role in understanding what mathematics is all about, namely the exploration of conjectures and hypotheses, not just the verification of given facts. By doing so, mathematicians follow the "scientific method:" they collect data, they notice regularities, they formulate algorithms and heuristics that account for the data, and they try to verify or reject their original conjectures and hypotheses.

Computational procedures need to be efficient—but advances in computer hardware have changed our perspective about what efficiency means. Often it is desirable to have procedures that are computationally less efficient, but conceptually easier to understand. These cognitively efficient representations can serve as *stepping stones* to understanding more complicated versions of an algorithm. These issues are illustrated by the first two case studies in this part. In chapter 14 we describe a general approach towards problem solving based on the work of Polya [Polya 45] in the context of a mathematical conjecture. We conclude this part by showing the recursive nature of algebraic operations and the conceptual simplicity of computing in different base systems.

Many books using computers are oriented towards mathematics. We hope that the few case studies documented in this part illustrate our different approach: finding ways of *doing mathematics—not just learning about mathematics* [Papert 80]. Computers can foster an approach towards mathematics allowing children to do what real mathematicians do: guess, investigate, refute, explore examples, explore counter examples, and prove theorems.

Chapter 12:
Prime Numbers

12.1. Testing for Prime Numbers

Definition 1: A prime number is a number that is not divisible by any number except for itself and 1.[16]

How can we write a program to help us find out if a given number is prime? A first approach is to write the procedure `NotDivisibleP` that divides the specified number by all numbers that are smaller than it is. If the remainder of any of these divisions is zero, the number is not a prime number.

```
To PrimeP :Number
  ; Determine whether a given number is prime.
  Output NotDivisibleP :Number (:Number - 1)
End

To NotDivisibleP :Number :Counter
  ; Divide a number by all smaller
  ; numbers, until a divisor is found
  Test :Counter = 1
  IfTrue [Output "True]
  Test (Remainder :Number :Counter) = 0
  IfTrue [Output "False]
  Output NotDivisibleP :Number (:Counter - 1)
End
```

Now, let's try out this procedure:

```
? Print PrimeP 34
False
? Print PrimeP 27
False
? Print PrimeP 71
True
```

Can we do better? Let's formulate the program a different way:

Instead of dividing the number by the larger numbers first, we can start with 2 and work our way up. When the number is prime, the program still tests the same number of potential factors. However, for large numbers that are divisible by small numbers, the result is found quickly.

---

[16]We revise this "definition" later.

```
To PrimeP1 :Number
   Output NotDivisibleP1 :Number 2
End

To TestP1 :Number :Counter
   Test :Number = :Counter
   IfTrue [Output "True]
   Test (Remainder :Number :Counter) = 0
   IfTrue [Output "False]
   Output TestP1 :Number (:Counter + 1)
End

? Print PrimeP1 45
False
? Print PrimeP1 173
True
? Print PrimeP1 342
False
```

Another approach uses *heuristics*. These are general problem-solving strategies similar to those that we use for finding solutions. The solutions we are searching for are the potential divisors of a number.

The heuristics presented here try to identify special cases that are easy for humans to recognize and decide. They are special "tricks" for determining that a number is "nonprime."

The heuristics that we present are, for the most part, representation dependent; they would not work if numbers were represented in some other number base system (e.g., in the base-7 system).

Here is the program extended to use heuristics. If none of the heuristics are applicable, the previously defined program, PrimeP1, is used. A few of the most useful heuristics have been chosen; however, the program can be easily extended as desired:

```
To PrimeP2 :Number
   ; This program models some of the
   ; heuristics which humans use to
   ; find the divisor of a number
   If (TwoP :Number)
      [Output [The number is divisible by two]]
   If (ThreeP :Number)
      [Output [The number is divisible by three]]
   If (FiveP :Number)
      [Output [The number is divisible by five]]
   Print [No heuristic applies]
   Output PrimeP1 :Number
End
```

Now, let's look at the individual heuristics:

```
To TwoP :Number
   ; The last number must be even
   Output MemberP (Last :Number) [0 2 4 6 8]
End
```

```
To ThreeP :Number
  ; The sum of the digits
  ; must be divisible by three
  Output (Remainder (SumDigits :Number) 3) = 0
End

To FiveP :Number
  ; The last digit must be either 0 or 5
  Output
     Or (Last :Number) = 0 (Last :Number) = 5
End

To SumDigits :Number
  Test :Number = "
  IfTrue [Output 0]
  Output
    (First :Number)
    +
    (SumDigits ButFirst :Number)
End
```

SumDigits is discussed further in chapter 14.

Let's write a procedure to test our heuristics over a certain range. The results of a test run show that these few heuristics suffice for most cases:

```
To TestOverRange :LowerLimit :UpperLimit
  Test :LowerLimit > :UpperLimit
  IfTrue [Stop]
  Print
    (Sentence
      "Given
      :LowerLimit
      "--->
      PrimeP2 :LowerLimit)
  Print "
  TestOverRange (:LowerLimit + 1) :UpperLimit
End
```

Here is a test run:

```
? TestOverRange 90 100
given: 90 ---> the number is divisible by two

no heuristic applies
given: 91 ---> false

given: 92 ---> the number is divisible by two

given: 93 ---> the number is divisible by three

given: 94 ---> the number is divisible by two

given: 95 ---> the number is divisible by five

given: 96 ---> the number is divisible by two

no heuristic applies
given: 97 ---> true

given: 98 ---> the number is divisible by two
```

```
given: 99 ---> the number is divisible by three
given: 100 ---> the number is divisible by two
```

12.2. Lists of Prime Numbers

The building blocks we have presented so far allow us to determine whether a certain number is prime. Using these, we can build a list of prime numbers by applying our predicate—our program `PrimeP`—to each number in a range. A number is placed in the list only if it "passes the test."

```
To PrimeNumberList :CurrentNumber :UpperLimit
   Test :CurrentNumber > :UpperLimit
   IfTrue [Output "]
   Test PrimeP :CurrentNumber
   IfTrue
      [Output
         Sentence
            :CurrentNumber
            (PrimeNumberList
               (:CurrentNumber + 1)
               :UpperLimit)]
   Output
      PrimeNumberList
         (:CurrentNumber + 1)
         :UpperLimit
End
```

A few test runs:

```
? Print PrimeNumberList 2 12
2 3 5 7 11
? Print PrimeNumberList 2 50
2 3 5 7 11 13 17 19 23 29 31 41 43 47
? Print PrimeNumberList 125 135
127 131
? Print PrimeNumberList 1000 1010
1009
? Print PrimeNumberList 1125 1135
1129
```

This program allows us to find the prime numbers within a given range of natural numbers. While using this program, you may have discovered that it is somewhat slow. Although our prime concern is representing problems in a cognitively efficient way, part of what we are doing is "experimental math," using the computer to explore the properties of large ranges of numbers. Since this would be difficult without the aid of the computer, there are times that speed and memory limitations do become valid concerns.

One limitation we have encountered comes from the programs excessive use of the recursive stack:

```
? PrimeP1 1087
Too many levels of recursion.
You were at line 5 in procedure NotDivisibleP1
```

Where this limitation appears depends on how large the stack is in your LOGO implementation.

Another limitation has its root in the way we formulated the definition of a prime number. Do we really need to test *every* *number* less than a certain number as a possible factor? If we can test fewer factor candidates, the program would allow us to test more numbers faster, right?

Let's look at new definition that will give us some insights into how we can lessen the impact of these limitations.

Definition 2: A prime number is a number that is not divisible by any *prime number* smaller than *its* *square root* other than 1.

Important features of this new definition:

(1) Restricting the factor candidates to prime numbers causes no real change in the meaning of a prime number; if the number were divisible by a nonprime number, then it would also be divisible by the prime factors of that nonprime number. However, this can give us the advantage that fewer numbers need to be tested against a prime candidate.

(2) Restricting the factors to numbers less than the square root works because, if one factor of a number is greater than its square root, then the product of the rest of the factors must be less than the square root of the number. This enables us to restrict how many numbers need to be checked even more.

To use the advantages that this new definition gives us, we change the program to generate and maintain a list of prime numbers. By building up and retaining the list of prime numbers incrementally, we can use the list to determine whether a certain number is prime. This is done by simply testing whether this number is divisible by one of the prime numbers in the list. Once all prime numbers less than or equal to the square root of the given number have been tested, we can stop.

The following program implements this algorithm:

```
To GeneratePrimes
  Print
    [Give the upper limit of the interval for which]
  Print [prime numbers should be calculated:]
  Make "PrimesList [2 3]
  PrimeNumbers 5 First ReadList
  Print :PrimesList
End

To PrimeNumbers :Number :UpperLimit
  Test :Number > :UpperLimit
  IfTrue [Stop]
  Make "PrimesList TestPrime :PrimesList :Number
  PrimeNumbers (:Number + 2) :UpperLimit
End
```

```
To TestPrime :List :Number
   Test (Square First :List) > :Number
   IfTrue [Output Sentence :PrimesList :Number]
   Test (Remainder :Number (First :List)) = 0
   IfTrue [Output :PrimesList]
   Output TestPrime (ButFirst :List) :Number
End

To Square :Number
   Output :Number * :Number
End
```

The prime numbers are stored in a global list shared by all procedures. Since even numbers are all divisible by 2, the program examines only the odd numbers by starting at 5 and adding 2 to :Number instead of 1.

Here are some results that can be produced with these routines:

```
? GeneratePrimes
Give the upper limit of the interval for which
prime numbers should be calculated:
70
2 3 5 7 11 13 17 19 23 29 31 37 41 43 47 53 59 61 67
? GeneratePrimes
Give the upper limit of the interval for which
prime numbers should be calculated:
500
2 3 5 7 11 13 17 19 23 29 31 37 41 43 47 53 59 61 67 71
73 79 83 89 97 101 103 107 109 113 127 131 137 139 149
151 157 163 167 173 179 181 191 193 197 199 211 223 227
229 233 239 241 251 257 263 269 271 277 281 283 293 307
311 313 317 331 337 347 349 353 359 367 373 379 383 389
397 401 409 419 421 431 433 439 443 449 457 461 463 467
479 487 491 499
? Make "PrimeNumbersTo500 :PrimesList[17]
```

Exercises

If a list like the one generated here is available, further properties of prime numbers can be investigated.

(1) **Prime Number Census:** We can use the LOGO primitive Count to determine the number of primes less than a certain number:

```
? Print Count :PrimeNumbersTo200
46
? Print Count :PrimeNumbersTo1000
168
```

---

[17]This is to save it for later use!

Write a program so that the census can be performed on specified ranges: One way this might work would look like this:

```
? Print PrimeCensus 100 200 :PrimesNumbersTo200
21
```

This idea could be taken further:

a) Rather than specify the list of prime numbers to perform the census with, have the program keep track of how far the numbers have been generated, and automatically extend the list as necessary.

b) Study how the number of primes less than n varies with respect to n.

(2) Which Numbers are Prime Number Twins?:

Prime number twins are prime numbers whose difference is exactly two. Write a procedure `PrimeNumberTwins` that computes all sets of prime number twins from a list of all known prime numbers.

A test run of this procedure might look like this:

```
? Print PrimeNumberTwins :PrimeNumbersTo500 []
(3 5) (5 7) (11 13) (17 19) (29 31) (41 43)
(59 61) (71 73) (101 103) (107 109) (137 139)
(149 151) (179 181) (191 193) (197 199)
(227 229) (239 241) (269 271) (281 283)
(311 313) (347 349) (419 421) (431 433) (461 463)
```

(3) Prime Number Triplets:

Write a procedure that can test whether (3 5 7) is the only prime number triplet. One approach is to view your solution as a sketch of a mathematical proof. This proof would need to show that for any set of prime number triplets one of the numbers must be divisible by 3.

(4) Distances between Prime Numbers:

Write a procedure that calculates the maximum distance between consecutive prime numbers over a given range.

Sample results:

```
? Print MaxDistance :PrimeNumbersTo200 0
14
? Print MaxDistance :PrimeNumbersTo1000 0
20
```

This leads to the question: How large can this maximum distance become? Is there a limit?

(5) Distribution of Prime Numbers:

a) Write a program that breaks a range into subranges and calculates the number of primes in each subrange.

b) Provide a visual representation (e.g., an histogram) of the distribution (perhaps something similar to what was done on page 77),

(6) Prime "Cousins":

A relative of the prime twins and triplets is the class of prime number pairs (n, n') such that n' = n * n + 1.

Write a procedure that finds all pairs of such prime numbers from a list of all known prime numbers.

Chapter 13:
The Greatest Common Divisor (GCD)

13.1. Decomposition of a Number Into Its Prime Factors

The ability to simplify fractions is necessary to master fraction arithmetic.

Suppose that we want to simplify the following fractions:

$$a)\ \frac{48}{72} \qquad b)\ \frac{342}{568} \qquad c)\ \frac{997}{1207}$$

For a) if it is not immediately clear that both the numerator and the denominator contain the number 24 (that is, it is their Greatest Common Divisor (GCD)), successive division by small prime numbers into both the numerator and denominator leads to this result:

$$\frac{48}{72} \to \frac{24 \times 2}{36 \times 2} \to \frac{12 \times 4}{18 \times 4} \to \frac{6 \times 8}{9 \times 8} \to \frac{2 \times 24}{3 \times 24}$$

For b) it is not readily apparent what the GCD of these two numbers is, so the only method remaining is division by prime numbers (the heuristics described in chapter 12 should be useful here):

$$\frac{342}{568} \to \frac{2 \times 171}{2 \times 284} \to \frac{2 \times 3 \times 57}{2 \times 2 \times 142} \to \frac{2 \times 3 \times 3 \times 19}{2 \times 2 \times 2 \times 71}$$

If one now knows that 19 and 71 are prime numbers, the process is complete; one can now cross out the matching factors in the numerator and denominator. In this example, only the 2 can be crossed out. The fraction can be represented in simplified form then as 171/284. If it is not known whether 19 and 71 are prime, this can be determined by one of the methods described in chapter 12.

For c) our known heuristics fail; the problem is only solved with considerable computational effort by decomposing the numbers into their prime factors.

The *canonic representation* of numbers gives us a mathematical foundation for the methods we have used. From the basics of number theory we know that each number can be represented in the following form:

$$n = 2^{n_2} \times 3^{n_3} \times 5^{n_5} \cdots = \prod_p p^{n_p}$$

$$m = 2^{m_2} \times 3^{m_3} \times 5^{m_5} \cdots = \prod_p p^{m_p}$$

where p stands for the prime numbers, $\prod$ means the product of all the numbers specified by the expression, and the exponents (n_2, n_3, ...) represent specific non-negative numbers, of which only finitely many are not equal to zero. Specifically, each number is then the product of a finite number of prime numbers (which may be raised to some power).

$$12 = 2 \times 2 \times 3 = 2^2 \times 3$$

The greatest common divisor (GCD) and the least common multiple (LCM) are defined then as follows (p stands for prime numbers):

$$GCD(m,n) = \prod_p p^{min(n_p, m_p)}$$

$$LCM(m,n) = \prod_p p^{max(n_p, m_p)}$$

The smaller (larger) exponent of each prime in the canonical representation of the numbers m and n is chosen as the exponent of the canonical representation of the GCD (LCM).

From these two relationships the following formula can be derived:

$$m \times n = GCD(m,n) \times LCM(m,n)$$

Next, a plan for converting the described procedures into a program needs to be developed. This contains the following steps:

(1) Generate a list of prime numbers (this is already available to us from section 12).

(2) Write a procedure that decomposes a number into its prime factors.

(3) Use this procedure on the numerator and denominator.

(4) Delete common factors from both lists (the GCD corresponds to the product of these common factors).

(5) Multiply the undeleted elements of the lists or divide the numerator and denominator by the GCD; these numbers correspond to the numerator and denominator of the simplified fraction.

The data for step 1:

```
? Print :PrimeNumbers
2   3   5   7   11  13  17  19  23  29  31  37  41  43  47  53  59  61  67  71
73  79  83  89  97  101 103 107 109 113 127 131 137 139 149
151 157 163 167 173 179 181 191 193 197 199 211 223 227
229 233 239 241 251 257 263 269 271 277 281 283 293 307
311 313 317 331 337 347 349 353 359 367 373 379 383 389
397 401 409 419 421 431 433 439 443 449 457 461 463 467
479 487 491 499
```

The program for step 2:

```
To PrimeFactors :Number
  ; Constructs a list of prime factors, which are
  ; contained in :Number.  The global variable
```

```
; :PrimeNumbers is a list of prime numbers to use
Output MakeList :Number :PrimeNumbers
End

To MakeList :Number :List
   If :Number = 1 [Output []]
   If (Square First :List) > :Number
   [Output (List :Number)]
   Test (Remainder :Number (First :List)) = 0
   IfTrue
      [Output
         Sentence (First :List)
            (MakeList Quotient :Number First :List :List)]
   Output MakeList :Number (ButFirst :List)
End
```

Some test results:

```
? Print PrimeFactors 365
5 73
? Print PrimeFactors 2468
2 2 617
? Print PrimeFactors 3072
2 2 2 2 2 2 2 2 2 3
? Print PrimeFactors 13579
37 367
```

The program for steps 3 and 4:

```
To CommonFactors :Number1 :Number2
; the common prime factors are removed
; from the lists of prime factors of two numbers
Output
   FindCommon
      (PrimeFactors :Number1)
      (PrimeFactors :Number2)
End

To FindCommon :List1 :List2
   If EmptyP :List1 [Output []]
   Test MemberP (First :List1) :List2
   IfTrue
      [Output
         Sentence (First :List1)
            (FindCommon
               (ButFirst :List1)
               (Remove (First :List1) :List2))]
   Output FindCommon (ButFirst :List1) :List2
End
```

The procedure Remove is described in appendix III.

A test run of CommonFactors with tracing turned on for FindCommon yields.

```
? Print CommonFactors 48 72
FindCommon of "2 2 2 2 3" and "2 2 2 3 3"
   FindCommon of "2 2 2 3" and "2 2 3 3"
```

```
FindCommon of "2 2 3" and "2 3 3"
  FindCommon of "2 3" and "3 3"
    FindCommon of "3" and "3 3"
      FindCommon of "" and "3"
      FindCommon outputs ""
    FindCommon outputs "3"
    FindCommon outputs "3"
  FindCommon outputs "2 3"
 FindCommon outputs "2 2 3"
FindCommon outputs "2 2 2 3"
2 2 2 3
```

The GCD is then simply the product of these factors:

```
To GCD :Number1 :Number2
  ; calculate the greatest common divisor by
  ; multiplying together the common factors
  Output MultiplyList CommonFactors :Number1 :Number2
End
```

```
To MultiplyList :List
  Test :List = [ ]
  IfTrue [Output 1]
  Output (First :List) * (MultiplyList ButFirst :List)
End
```

```
? Print GCD 45 68
1
? Print GCD 48 72
24
? Print GCD 342 568
2
? Print MultiplyList [2 2 2 3]
24
```

The program for step 5:

```
To SimplifyFraction :Numerator :Denominator
  ; Simplify a fraction using
  ; division by the GCD
  Output
    SimplifiedFraction
      :Numerator
      :Denominator
      (GCD :Numerator :Denominator)
End
```

```
To SimplifiedFraction :Numerator :Denominator :GCD
  Output
    (Word
      (Quotient :Numerator :GCD)
      "/
      (Quotient :Denominator :GCD))
End
```

```
? Print PrimeFactors 45
3 3 5
? Print PrimeFactors 342
2 3 3 19
```

```
? Print CommonFactors 342 568
2
? Print GCD 48 72
24
? Print SimplifyFraction 48 72
2/3
```

Furthermore, with the help of the formula describing the relationship between the LCM and the GCD, we can write a procedure to calculate the LCM.

```
To LCM :Number1 :Number2
; calculate the least common multiple
; of two numbers according to the formula:
; M*N = GCD(M,N) * LCM(M,N)
Output
   Quotient
      (:Number1 * :Number2)
      (GCD :Number1 :Number2)
End

? Print LCM 48 72
144
? Print LCM 342 568
97128
```

13.2. Is There a Better Way?

For large numbers (e.g., the number 1087) the decomposition into prime factors is a computationally intensive process because no procedure is known for finding the prime factors of a whole number quickly. Since this lack of speed limits our investigations, perhaps we can "kill two birds with one stone" by learning more about the properties of numbers and speeding up the program at the same time.

Another approach might be in order. Sometimes it is useful to look at the problem in a different way (see figure 14–1). Are there any other relationships between these numbers that may be useful?

Since the concept of the GCD is based on division, let's try looking at the integer quotient and remainders for these numbers and how they relate to the GCD. We can write a program that uses the GCD program we have written so far to tabulate the numbers, their GCD, their quotient, and the remainder of their division. We can leave out the cases where the GCD is 1 to save space.

```
To Investigate :LowerLimit1 :UpperLimit1
               :LowerLimit2 :UpperLimit2
   Print [Number1 Number2 GCD Quotient Remainder]
   Investigate0
      :LowerLimit1
      :UpperLimit1
      :LowerLimit2
      :UpperLimit2
End
```

```
To InvestigateO :LowerLimit1 :UpperLimit1
                :LowerLimit2 :UpperLimit2
   Test :LowerLimit1 > :UpperLimit1
   IfTrue [Stop]
   Investigate1 :Lowerlimit1 :LowerLimit2 :UpperLimit2
   InvestigateO
      (:LowerLimit1 + 1)
      :UpperLimit1
      :LowerLimit2
      :UpperLimit2
End

To Investigate1 :Number1 :LowerLimit2 :UpperLimit2
   Test :LowerLimit2 > :UpperLimit2
   IfTrue [Stop]
   Local "GCDResult
   Make "GCDResult GCD :Number1 :LowerLimit2
   If Not :GCDResult < 2
   [Print
        (Sentence PadRight 7 PadLeft 4 :Number1
         PadRight 8 PadLeft 4 :LowerLimit2 PadRight 4
         PadLeft 2 :GCDResult PadRight 9 PadLeft 6
         Quotient :Number1 :LowerLimit2 PadLeft 6
         Remainder :Number1 :LowerLimit2)]
   Investigate1
      :Number1
      (:LowerLimit2 + 1)
      :UpperLimit2
End
```

`? Investigate 60 65 25 30`

Number1	Number2	GCD	Quotient	Remainder
60	25	5	2	10
60	26	2	2	8
60	27	3	2	6
60	28	4	2	4
60	30	30	2	0
62	26	2	2	10
62	28	2	2	6
62	30	2	2	2
63	27	9	2	9
63	28	7	2	7
63	30	3	2	3
64	26	2	2	12
64	28	4	2	8
64	30	2	2	4
65	25	5	2	15
65	26	13	2	13
65	30	5	2	5

If you study the table you may make the rather interesting observation that all the remainders (the last column) are also multiples of the GCDs (the third column). Is this an accident for the particular numbers that we have chosen, or is it characteristic? If we were to run the program over other ranges of numbers, we would discover that the relationship seems to occur consistently.

Can we explain this? If we look at some of the properties of quotients and remainders, one place to start would be:

$$m = q \times n + r$$

where m, n, q, and r are the dividend, divisor, quotient, and remainder, respectively. Now, if g is the GCD of m and n, $Q_m = \frac{m}{g}$ and $Q_n = \frac{n}{g}$, then

$$(Q_m \times g) = (q \times Q_n \times g) + r \qquad (*)$$

Now, in general:

$$a \times x = b \times x + (a-b) \times x$$

since it could be written:

$$a \times x = b \times x + (a \times x - b \times x)$$

by distributivity.

So,

$$Q_m \times g = q \times Q_n \times g + (Q_m - q \times Q_n) \times g \qquad (**)$$

and by combining (*) and (**) and doing some manipulation we can show:

$$r = (Q_m - q \times Q_n) \times g$$

and since Q_m, Q_n, and q are all integers, r is always an integer multiple of g!

Before you go on to the next section, can you think how this might be applied to finding the GCD? Hint: Q_n is related to r in the same way that Q_m is related to Q_n. Also the remainder in this case is always smaller than r (assuming r was not zero!).

13.3. The Euclidian Algorithm

As the last section hinted, there is a procedure that allows the GCD to be calculated without decomposing the number into prime factors. This procedure is the *Euclidian algorithm*, which was discovered 2000 years ago. It is the grandfather of all algorithms, because it is the oldest nontrivial algorithm that has survived to the present. Around 1950 (when the use of the word "algorithm" was rarer than it is today), the concept "algorithm" was synonymous with the "Euclidean algorithm."

The Euclidian algorithm can be described as follows:

Let m and n be two positive whole numbers. To find the GCD of the two, proceed as follows:

Step 1: **Find the remainder:** divide m by n; let r be the remainder. (m = n * q + r)

Step 2: **Is remainder zero?** If r = 0, the algorithm is completed, the result is n.

Step 3: **Recursive step:** Perform this algorithm using n and r as the two number.

The mathematical proof is not difficult: building on the discussion in the last section you can show that the resulting number is a common factor of n and m, and that every other common factor is a factor of the result.

Here is the realization of this algorithm in a program:

```
To Euclid :Number1 :Number2
  ; calculate the GCD using
  ; Euclidian method
  Test :Number2 = 0
  IfTrue [Output :Number1]
  Output
    Euclid
      :Number2
      (Remainder :Number1 :Number2)
End
```

Some test results:

```
? Print Euclid 48 72
24
? Print Euclid 342 568
2
? Print Euclid 997 1207
1
? Print Euclid 123456789 987654321
9
```

A trace demonstrates the operation of this algorithm:

```
? Print Euclid 342 568
Euclid of 342 and 568
 Euclid of 568 and 342
  Euclid of 342 and 226
   Euclid of 226 and 116
    Euclid of 116 and 110
     Euclid of 110 and 6
      Euclid of 6 and 2
       Euclid of 2 and 0
       Euclid outputs 2
      Euclid outputs 2
     Euclid outputs 2
    Euclid outputs 2
   Euclid outputs 2
  Euclid outputs 2
 Euclid outputs 2
Euclid outputs 2
2
```

13.4. Finding One's Own Algorithms vs. Implementing Existing Algorithms

If you are presented with the problem of writing a program to simplify fractions, one of the following will probably occur:

Method 1: You already know the Euclidian Algorithm (e.g., from studying mathematics); then the problem is *only* another coding task, namely translating the algorithm from the notation of mathematics to the chosen programming language (certainly, the programming language should allow the algorithm to be represented as a program without major restrictions).

Method 2: You are not familiar with the Euclidian algorithm; it is not likely that you will find this algorithm on your own without coming to a deeper understanding of the problem. However, you will probably be in the position to assemble your knowledge about prime numbers, decomposition of numbers into prime factors, etc., and produce a program similar to the one in section 13.1. In this second case, a true problem-solving process takes place, in which you bring prior knowledge to bear in order to solve a problem and in the process deepen your understanding of the problem.

Method 3: After you apply what you already know and then step back and look around for other possibilities, studying the problem from different angles, looking for patterns in the results from your earlier efforts, you may *discover* the Euclidian algorithm.

This doesn't mean that we don't place a value on the first method; however, our focus in this book is more on problem solving and providing an environment for discovery.

You should be aware that the process of coding will probably not help:

- understand the Euclidean algorithm (if it was only partially understood prior to programming),

- prove it, or

- derive general principles that can contribute to finding one's own algorithms for solving other problems.

Chapter 14:
Problem Solving in Mathematics

Let's look at some general rules of problem solving as they appear in a schema from G. Polya [Polya 45](see figure 14–1). We can then try to see if any of these methods can be used to support the problem-solving and programming process.

14.1. The Problem

Almost everyone knows a simple trick that can be used to determine whether a number is divisible by three or not. Instead of testing whether the number itself is divisible by three, you can add together the digits of the number. If this sum is divisible by three, then the original number was also divisible by three. We used this trick in section 12.1 as one of the heuristics to weed out nonprime numbers.

Example:

$$471 \rightarrow 4 + 7 + 1 = 12$$
$$12 \div 3 = 4 \, remainder \, 0$$

thus 471 is divisible by 3

14.2. First: Do We Understand the Problem?

This should certainly be the first question we ask ourselves. Given some number, say 5647, we want to find out whether this number is divisible by 3. We can simply use the schema for long division that everyone learned in grade school.

```
    1882   ← the quotient
3 )5647
    3
    26
    24
    24
    24
     7
     6
     1   ← the remainder
```

(i.e., there is a remainder of 1 and the number is not divisible by three.)

UNDERSTANDING THE PROBLEM

First.

What is the unknown? What are the data? What is the condition?

You have to understand the problem.

Is it possible to satisfy the condition? Is the condition sufficient to determine the unknown? Or is it insufficient? Or redundant? Or contradictory?

Draw a figure! Introduce suitable notation.

Separate the various parts of the condition. Can you write them down?

DEVISING A PLAN

Second.

Have you seen it before? Or have you seen the same problem in a slightly different form?

Find the connection between the data and the unknown. You may be obliged to consider auxiliary problems if an immediate connection cannot be found. You should obtain eventually a *plan* of the solution.

Do you know a related problem? Do you know a theorem that could be useful?

Look at the unknown! And try to think of a familiar problem having the same or a similar unknown.

Here is a problem related to yours and solved before. Could you use it? Could you use its result? Could you use its method? Should you introduce some auxiliary element to make its use possible?

Could you restate the problem? Could you restate it still differently? Go back to definitions.

If you cannot solve the proposed problem, try to solve first some related problem. Could you imagine a more accessible related problem? A more general problem? A more special problem? An analogous problem? Could you solve a part of the problem? Keep only part of the condition, drop the other part: How far is the unknown then determined, how can it vary? Could you derive something useful from the data? Could you think of other data appropriate to determine the unknown? Could you change the unknown or the data, or both if necessary, so that the new unknown and the new data are nearer to each other?

Did you use all the data? Did you use the whole condition? Have you taken into account all essential notions involved in the problem?

CARRYING OUT THE PLAN

Third.

Carry out your plan.

Carrying out your plan of solution, *check each step.* Can you see clearly that the step is correct? Can you prove that it is correct?

LOOKING BACK

Fourth.

Examine the solution obtained

Can you *check the result?* Can you check the argument?

Can you derive the result differently? Can you see it at a glance?

Can you use the result, or the method, for some other problem?

Figure 14–1: Polya's Schema

Things would have been much simpler if we used our previously cited rule

$$5647 \rightarrow 5 + 6 + 4 + 7 = 22$$
$$22 \div 3 = 7 \; remainder \; 1$$

This method leads to the same result.

Note that our rule may be used in both directions; that is, if the sum of the digits is divisible by 3, then the original number is divisible by 3, **and** if the sum of the digits is **not** divisible by 3, then the original number is **not** divisible by 3. This is called an *if and only if* relationship in mathematics.

We should now try to classify our problem further. If we classify things as either proofs (which is what Polya deals with primarily) or analysis problems, this certainly falls into the class of proofs.

We can thus bring these general methods for proofs to bear on the solution of this problem.

> <u>Conjecture 1</u>: A number is divisible by 3 if and only if the sum of its digits is divisible by three.

14.3. Second: Devise a Plan

For many, it is not simple to prove that the given rule is correct. To begin with, we want to get a clearer picture, so we test the assertion on several examples. Perhaps we will be able to find a *counterexample*; then we are done and we can discard this rule.

To do this, we can use the computer in a way that is well suited to its abilities. The machine is capable of repetitive tasks, so we can use it to test this assertion over a large range of numbers.

To approach this programming task, we should try to specify suitable parts of a program. We need a predicate `CompareP` that compares the result from normal division with the result computed from summing the digits. We call the procedures that test divisibility by 3 in the two different ways `NormDivby3P` and `SpecDivby3P`. The procedure, which checks the assertion on some range of numbers, we call `TestConjecture`. It calls `CompareP`, which tests the assertion for one number.

14.4. Third: Carry Out the Plan

The procedures conceptualized in section 14.3 should now be written.

```
To TestConjecture :Bottom :Top
   Test :Bottom > :Top
   IfTrue [Output [Hypothesis appears to be correct]]
   Test CompareP :Bottom
   IfFalse [Output [Hypothesis is false]]
```

```
      Output TestConjecture :Bottom + 1 :Top
End
```

If the comparison in the fourth line (`Test CompareP :Bottom`) is ever `False`, the next line is executed, and our assertion is known to be false. Otherwise, after the whole range of numbers is tested, the correctness of our assertion over that range of numbers is established.

```
To CompareP :Number
   Output
      EqualP SpecDivBy3P :Number NormDivBy3P :Number
End

To NormDivBy3P :Number
   Output (Remainder :Number 3) = 0
End

To SpecDivBy3P :Number
   Output NormDivBy3P (SumDigits :Number)
End

To SumDigits :Number
   Test :Number = "
   IfTrue [Output "]
   Output Sum First :Number SumDigits ButFirst :Number
End
```

Having written procedures for all the subproblems specified in section 14.3, we do not need to create any further subproblems if all procedures can be described with either predefined LOGO procedures or procedures that we have already defined. Another note on method: We solved our problem with the aid of *top down* design, that is, it did not disturb us that while defining, for example, `CompareP`, we used two procedures, namely `NormDivBy3P` and `SpecDivBy3P`, which were themselves not yet defined. This *wishful thinking*, pretending that you already have the solution to a subproblem, is one of the most important methods for solving large complex problems.

We have not yet followed another piece of advice: *Check each step.* Let's rectify that oversight and check whether our little building blocks do what we wanted them to.

```
? Print SumDigits 2345
Sum doesn't like empty as input.
You were at line 3 in procedure sumdigits1
in call level 4 of SumDigits.
? Trace
Trace running
? Print SumDigits 2345
Execution of SumDigits  2345
   Execution of SumDigits  345
      Execution of SumDigits  45
         Execution of SumDigits  5
            Execution of SumDigits  "
            SumDigits outputs  "
Sum doesn't like empty as input.
You were at line 3 in procedure sumdigits1
in call level 4 of SumDigits.
```

By changing the second line of `SumDigits` the errors can be eliminated.

```
To SumDigits :Number
   Test :Number = "
   IfTrue [Output 0]
   Output Sum First :Number SumDigits ButFirst :Number
End
```

Similarly, the other procedures should be tested, working from bottom to top, from the simple to the more extensive procedure; *bottom-up*.

14.5. Fourth: Check the Solution

Do we have a mathematical proof?   The answer to this question is certainly "no." We do know that the assertion is true for a large range. However, even if we had tested a billion or more numbers, there are always more numbers (infinitely many) that we haven't touched. A reason that mathematicians conduct proofs is that they want to make assertions about structures with infinitely many elements.

Let's try a short sketch of a mathematical proof of our hypothesis:

(1) Every number can be represented(using base 10) as follows:

$$5647 = (5 \times 10^3) + (6 \times 10^2) + (4 \times 10^1) + (7 \times 10^0)$$

or, in general:

$$a_n \times 10^n + a_{n-1} \times 10^{n-1} + ... + a_1 \times 10^1 + a_0 \times 10^0 \qquad (*)$$

(2) When we sum the digits, we do away with the powers of ten

$$a_n + a_{n-1} + ... + a_1 + a_0$$

or, as in the example

$$5 + 6 + 4 + 7 \qquad (**)$$

We need a few rules that deal with remainders. We use the following notation.

$a = 10 \bmod 3$ means: a is the remainder, if 10 is divided by 3.

The following rules then apply:

a) $10 \bmod 3 = 1$

b) $(10 \times 10) \bmod 3 = (10 \bmod 3) \times (10 \bmod 3)$
$\qquad\qquad\qquad = 1 \times 1 = 1$

c) $(a + b) \bmod 3 = (a \bmod 3) + (b \bmod 3)$

If we then apply these rules to (*), we can make the following transformations:

$$(a_n \times 10^n + ... + a_0) \bmod 3$$

$$= (a_n \times 10^n) \bmod 3 + ... + (a_0 \times 10^0) \bmod 3$$

$$= (a_n \bmod 3) \times (10^n \bmod 3) + ... + (a_0 \bmod 3) \times (10^0 \bmod 3)$$

$$= (a_n \bmod 3) \times 1 + ... + (a_0 \bmod 3) \times 1 \qquad (***)$$

The rules applied to (**) gives:

$$(a_n + a_{n-1} + ... + a_1 + a_0) \bmod 3$$

$$= (a^n \bmod 3) + (a^{n-1} \bmod 3) + ... + (a^1 \bmod 3) + (a^0 \bmod 3) \qquad (****)$$

Since (**) agrees with (****), we have proved that our hypothesis is true for any arbitrary number.

An Extension of the Problem. Let's say that we completed the proof in the last section and now know that our assertion about divisibility by three is correct. However, the programming language that was available to us did not have a Remainder procedure. Could we have written a program to test our assertion?

An extension to our hypothesis (which may have been obvious to those for whom recursive thinking has become natural) can help us out. Our rule can again be applied to the number that is generated by summing the digits; that is, we can sum the digits of this new number. This process can be carried out until we reach a number that has only a single digit. For these ten possible numbers, we can explicitly specify which of them are divisible by 3, namely 0, 3, 6, and 9. The corresponding LOGO procedure would look like this:

```
To MemberDivBy3P :Number
   Test (ButFirst :Number) = "
   IfTrue [Output MemberP :Number [0 3 6 9]]
   Output MemberDivBy3P SumDigits :Number
End
```

Using the Method on a Similar Problem. The following rules for determining whether a number is divisible by 9 can be given.

(1) Add up the digits and reduce the intermediate sums to the remainder (modulo 9). Example: 43785 gives 4+3=7 → 7+7=14 reduced gives 5 → 5+8=13 reduced gives 4 → 4+5=9 reduced gives 0.

(2) If the last remaining result is zero, then the original number is divisible by 9, otherwise not.

14.6. On the Role of Proofs and Using Computers to Carry Them Out

This problem and the one presented in chapter 6 raise some interesting questions. For example:

- Can a mathematical questions such as these be "proved" with a computer?
- Why do we prove propositions in mathematics?
- What is the role of computers in mathematics?

Our discussion so far has shown that there are problems that cannot be proved by enumeration—calculating through a sequence of cases—using a computer.

This certainly does not mean that for many problems a proof will not be found and automated eventually.

Even though the conjecture cannot be *proved* with the aid of a program, the results can provide us with counterexamples or important indications of what portions of a proof might be tricky.

For example, with the conjecture from chapter 6, we can take a close look at the number 196. Here we use a version of the procedure `TestOneNumber` from that chapter that doesn't limit how many times the system will attempt to make a palindrome. It also prints out each number that it generates.

```
? TestOneNumber 196
196
887
1675
7436
13783
52514
94039
187088
1067869
10755470
18211171
35322452
60744805
111589511
227574622
454050344
897100798
1794102596
8746117567
16403234045
70446464506
130992928913
450822227944
900544455998
1800098901007
8801197801088
17602285712176
84724043932847
159547977975595
755127757721546
1400255515443103
4413700670963144
  .
  .
```

(Portions were left out to save a tree)

```
  .
143014864788892364119189890633647855247088090910463298897467410044
583162512777816004310098698058923531860807791002509628777215151385
116631402555564290951029640612737064811704681015910247554430412770
193845437011306310461216047731197802027751601175002713109634549381
377790873912623511032322205451406593165492213339016316220369097772
655581836935237121965643500012802197319994436569131642439747195545
120117358486948325393126899992659340552999987313825337497938538 1101
```

```
2213009424664216782245058999181637361829998494531777224664239092122
4425918749328444553600007998463274723649996999954653349328488095244
8851827597567878118200004997926549447298994000018207797567966290488
1769275429522585514630000999685399890359698800004632658522 5923572076
8472028724748441751030009896638498883946697800041048243748 5169301747
1594306834059578459117001869328788777878339670007120538859 5944750449 5
                        .
                        .
                        .
```

(We stop here and perhaps save a forest!)

As you can see, the number 196 certainly deserves close attention; [Yarbrough 76] indicates that after 80000 iterations, 196 yielded a number that contained 31000 digits without generating a palindrome. The following observation is also interesting: If there is *one* number that is not symmetric, then there are infinitely many similar numbers; all those that were generated by the `MirrorAndAdd` process. This raises another question:

- Is conjecture from chapter 6 disproved by the result obtained from the number 196?

14.7. Another Problem

Does the following process always stop?

Conjecture 2: (The Collatz Algorithm) Let n be a natural number.

- If n is even, let n' = n/2.
- If n is odd, let n' = 3*n+1.
- Set n = n' and repeat the process.

After finitely many steps, the number 1 is reached, and the process stops.

This conjecture can be turned into a program with little difficulty.

```
To MultOrDiv :Number
  ; This procedure tests the assertion that each
  ; sequence using (n even --> n/2, n odd --> 3n+1)
  ; converges to 1.
  Type :Number
  Test :Number = 1
  IfTrue [Print "
          Stop]
  Type "-->
  Test MemberP (Last :Number) [0 2 4 6 8]
  IfTrue [MultOrDiv (Quotient :Number 2)]
  IfFalse
     [MultOrDiv (Sum (Product :Number 3) 1)]
End
```

Now small and large numbers can be tested to see whether the conjecture holds or not.

```
? MultOrDiv 34
34 --> 17 --> 52 --> 26 --> 13 --> 40 --> 20 --> 10 --> 5
--> 16  --> 8 --> 4 --> 2 --> 1
```

```
? MultOrDiv 67
67 --> 202 --> 101 --> 304 --> 152 --> 76 --> 38 --> 19
--> 58 --> 29 --> 88 --> 44 --> 22 --> 11 --> 34 --> 17
--> 52 --> 26 --> 13 --> 40 --> 20 --> 10 --> 5 --> 16
--> 8 --> 4 --> 2 --> 1
? MultOrDiv 58253
58253 --> 174760 --> 87380 --> 43690 --> 21845 --> 65536
--> 32768 --> 16384 --> 8192 --> 4096 --> 2048 --> 1024
--> 512 --> 256 --> 128 --> 64 --> 32 --> 16 --> 8 --> 4
--> 2 --> 1
?
```

With the aid of this test run, we can make the following observations (among others), which could be confirmed by further test runs:

• With small numbers only a few steps are usually necessary.

• Large numbers in general require more steps; however, the number of steps is not directly proportional to the size of the number (as the example 58253 shows).

• Often large numbers reach the same number early; with 123456789 and 987654321, this is 232006. This means that after this number, the same sequence of numbers will follow.

Exercises

Conjecture 2 and the conjecture from chapter 6 are *unproved* assertions in number theory, whereas conjecture 1 is proved without difficulty.

Even though some problems do not yield a solution, the use of an interactive programming environment such as LOGO allows you to explore patterns in numbers and pursue new ideas. Who knows, maybe you will be able to solve an *open* problem, one that confounded generations of mathematicians before you. Here are some you might want to tackle:

(1) Goldbach's conjecture: Any even number may be written as the sum of 2 prime numbers (e.g., 8 = 5 + 3). Some numbers can be written in several ways (e.g., 48 = 7 + 41 = 11 + 37 = 17 + 31 = 19 + 29). Prove or disprove this conjecture.

(2) From [Gardner 83, chapter 18]: Spell out the name of any number (in English). Replace the name of the number with the number of digits in the name and repeat the process. The number (name) should loop at 4 (four).

(3) Apply the conjecture from the last problem to other languages.

(4) For further unsolved problems in number theory, see [Ulam 64; Guy 81].

Chapter 15:
Recursive Expansion of Arithmetic Operations

The material in this chapter is closely related to the material in chapter 17, which shows how the basic number operations can be built up with the aid of the successor concept. Similarly, this chapter shows how, with the help of recursion, arithmetic operations may be built on top of each other.

In addition, we attempt to improve and deepen your understanding of exponential growth. Using recursive formulations, we show how processes can be described, which cannot be calculated (at least not in realistic time frames) on even the biggest computer ever available.

15.1. Exponentiation

One difficulty for projects in mathematics arises because some versions of LOGO do not provide a predefined exponential function. In general, we assume that you have the following understanding of exponentiation:

$$m^n = \underbrace{m * m * \ldots * m}_{\text{n-times}}$$

The recursive nature of this formula is expressed by rewriting it as follows:

$$m^n = m * \underbrace{(m * \ldots * m)}_{\text{n-1 times}} = m * m^{n-1}$$

This description can be expressed directly in a LOGO program:

```
To Exponent :Base :Power
  ; raises the :Base to the :Power
  ; by repeated multiplication
  Test :Power = 0
  IfTrue [Output 1]
  Output Product :Base (Exponent :Base (:Power - 1))
End

? Print Exponent 3 4
81
? Print Exponent 3 9
19683
? Print Exponent 3 90
872796356808771242589139747947672734004449
```

Whereas the preceding results can be calculated on our system, it is easy to generate an arithmetic expression that would bring any existing computer to its knees:

```
? Print Exponent 24 24
1333735776850284124449081472843776
? Print Exponent 24 Exponent 24 24
. . . . .
```

Although the first expression is calculated without any difficulty, the second overwhelms the machine. Calculating the second would multiply 24 by itself as many times as the result of the first expression shows.

15.2. Superexponentiation

With the aid of recursion we can also define the operation `SuperExponent`, which is defined as:

$$m \uparrow n = \underbrace{m^{m^{m^{\cdots}}}}_{n \text{ times}}$$

written recursively:

$$m \uparrow n = \underbrace{m^{m^{\cdots}}}_{n-1 \text{ times}} = m^{m \uparrow (n-1)}$$

Or, as a LOGO procedure:

```
To SuperExponent :Base :SuperPower
  Test :SuperPower = 0
  IfTrue [Output 1]
  Output
    Exponent
      :Base
      (SuperExponent :Base (:SuperPower - 1))
End
```

Some test runs:

```
? Print SuperExponent 2 2
4
? Print SuperExponent 2 3
16
? Print SuperExponent 2 4
65536
? Print SuperExponent 7 1
7
? Print SuperExponent 7 2
823543
```

`SuperExponent 2 5` and `SuperExponent 7 3` both cannot be calculated; they require over 60000 (respectively 800000) recursive calls. As the following comparison shows, the results of **SuperExponent** correspond to the nested call to **Exponent**:

```
? Print Exponent 24 24
1333735776850284124449081472843776
? Print SuperExponent 24 2
1333735776850284124449081472843776
```

15.3. Hyperexponentiation

Although the next recursive function, **HyperExponent**, can certainly be defined without difficulty, it may only be calculated for the smallest of values.

$$\text{m} \otimes \text{n} \;=\; \underbrace{\text{m} \curlyvee \text{m} \curlyvee \ldots \curlyvee \text{m}}_{\textbf{n-times}}$$

Or, written recursively:

$$\text{m} \otimes \text{n} \;=\; \text{m} \curlyvee \underbrace{(\; \text{m} \curlyvee \ldots \curlyvee \text{m} \;)}_{\textbf{n-1 times}} \;=\; \text{m} \curlyvee (\; \text{m} \otimes \text{n-1})$$

```
To HyperExponent :Base :Power
  Test :Power = 0
  IfTrue [Output 1]
  Output
    SuperExponent
      :Base
      HyperExponent :Base (:Power - 1)
End
```

The following test results are more or less all that can be computed:

```
? Print HyperExponent 2 1
2
? Print HyperExponent 2 2
4
? Print HyperExponent 2 3
65536
? Print HyperExponent 3 1
3
? Print HyperExponent 3 2[18]
7625597484987
```

---

[18]This one will probably not work unless your version of LOGO uses arbitrary precision integer arithmetic.

We should give some indication about why it makes no sense to calculate the value of `HyperExponent 2 4`; it makes the following call in the last line:

```
SuperExponent 2 HyperExponent 2 3
```

65536 (see earlier)

From this it follows that this is the same as making the call:

```
SuperExponent 2 65536
```

Since we have already determined that

```
SuperExponent 2 5
```

could no longer be computed, and the latter is the same as

```
Exponent 2 65536
```

or 2^{65536}.

15.4. Logarithms and Superlogarithms

Whole number division, which is implemented as the primitive function `Div`, can be defined with the aid of subtraction:

```
To Divide :M :N
; Divides the number M by N, using
; repeated subtraction. The result is the same
; as the whole number Quotient (without remainder)
Test :N > :M
IfTrue [Output 0]
Output 1 + Divide (:M - :N) :N
End
```

A trace:

```
? Print Divide 48 9
Divide of "48" and "9"
  Divide of "39" and "9"
    Divide of "30" and "9"
      Divide of "21" and "9"
        Divide of "12" and "9"
          Divide of "3" and "9"
          Divide outputs "0"
        Divide outputs "1"
      Divide outputs "2"
    Divide outputs "3"
  Divide outputs "4"
Divide outputs "5"
5
```

Exercises

(1) The recursive extension of Divide would be SuperDivide. Consider the following: Just as multiplication is the inverse of division and exponentiation is the recursive extension of multiplication, SuperDivide would calculate the logarithm function, which is the inverse of the exponential function.

Write a procedure that implements the logarithm function.

(2) Just as we defined SuperExponent as the recursive extension to Exponent, SuperLogarithm can be defined such that the two are inverse functions of each other.

Write a procedure that implements the superlogarithm function.

(3) Test your newly defined SuperLogarithm by trying:

? **SuperLogarithm SuperExponent 5 6 5**

What is the problem?

Chapter 16:
Representing Numbers in Different Base Systems

What is a number base system? How are number bases constructed?

Our culture as well as most others uses the decimal number system. By investigating these questions and others, we hope that you discover that the use of the decimal number system is not based on some mathematical law. Instead, it can be traced back to a convention that is based on the human having ten digits; the use of ten numerals (number symbols) is therefore well suited for human manipulation. Other base systems are not as well suited: Number representations in the binary system contain too many digits, while a base sixty system (which the Babylonians used, for example) requires a very large number of symbols.

We want to teach you some aspects of the importance of representation by presenting the abstract concept it in a concrete form. Representation is a central theme of many of the sciences (and especially of computer science). People deal not only directly with the reality of a subject (here, the abstract concept of *numbers*), but also on the level of manipulating symbols (in this case *numerals*) that *represent* reality in a certain way. The advantages and disadvantages of various representations can be contrasted with each other.

16.1. The Structure of a Number Base System

In this chapter we try to place some emphasis on the ideas of the construction kit model of programming (i.e., we attempt to present new building blocks in a stepwise fashion). As an introduction, several building blocks are shown that illustrate the structure of a number base system. The procedure ExpandNumber gives a detailed representation of a given number in a specified base:

```
To ExpandNumber :Number :Base
  ; give an expanded representation
  ; of a number in a base system
  Output
    ButFirst
      ButFirst
        Expand :Number :Base (Count :Number) - 1
End

To Expand :Number :Base :Exponent
  Test :Number = "
  IfTrue [Output "]
```

```
        Word
          (Term First :Number :Base :Exponent)
          (Expand ButFirst :Number :Base :Exponent - 1)
      End
```

```
      To Term :Digit :Base :Exponent
      Output
        (Word " + :Digit "* ("** :Base :Exponent "))
      End
```

Some test runs:

```
      ? Print ExpandNumber 345 10
      3*(10**2) + 4*(10**1) + 5*(10**0)
      ? Print ExpandNumber 234 7
      2*(7**2) + 3*(7**1) + 4*(7**0)
      ? Print ExpandNumber 10101 2
      1*(2**4) + 0*(2**3) + 1*(2**2) + 0*(2**1) + 1*(2**0)
```

With tracing on:

```
      ? Print ExpandNumber 123 10
      ExpandNumber of 123 and 10
       Expand of 123 and 10 and 2
        Term of 1 and 10 and 2
        Term outputs  " + 1*(10**2)
        Expand of 23 and 10 and 1
         Term of 2 and 10 and 1
         Term outputs  " + 2*(10**1)
         Expand of 3 and 10 and 0
          Term of 3 and 10 and 0
          Term outputs  " + 3*(10**0)
          Expand of empty and 10 and -1
          Expand outputs empty
         Expand outputs  " + 3*(10**0)
        Expand outputs  " + 2*(10**1) + 3*(10**0)
       Expand outputs  " + 1*(10**2) + 2*(10**1) + 3*(10**0)
      Expandnumber outputs  " 1*(10**2) + 2*(10**1) + 3*(10**0)
      1*(10**2) + 2*(10**1) + 3*(10**0).
```

This can also be formulated mathematically. Number representations in an arbitrary number base system b have the following form:

$$a_{n-1} a_{n-2} \cdots a_0$$
$$= a_{n-1} b^{n-1} + \ldots + a_0 b^0$$

or, in recursive form:

$$= F_0$$
where
$$F_{n-1} = a_{n-1} b$$
and for $i < n-1$
$$F_i = (F_{i+1} + a_i) b$$

16.2. Conversion of Numbers from the Base Ten (Decimal) System to the Base Two (Binary) System

A simple technique for converting from decimal to binary that is often taught is:

(1) Divide the decimal number by 2; the remainder is the next most significant digit of the binary number.

(2) If the quotient from step 1 is greater than zero, repeat this process using the quotient as the number.

For example, starting with the decimal number 123:

```
1<-+   3<-+   7<-+   15<-+   30<-+   61<-+ 123 <--start here
+  |   +  |   +  |   +   |   +   |   +   |  +
2  |   2  |   2  |   2   |   2   |   2   |  2
=  |   =  |   =  |   =   |   =   |   =   |  =
0  +- 1 +- 3 +- 7  +- 15  +- 30  +- 61
r      r      r      r       r       r       r

1      1      1      1       0       1       1 <-- binary result
```

yields the binary result 1111011.

The following procedure DecimalToBinary performs this conversion:

```
To DecimalToBinary :Number
; Convert number from Base Ten to Base Two
Test :Number = 0
IfTrue [Output "]
Output
    Word
        (DecimalToBinary Quotient :Number 2)
        (Remainder :Number 2)
End
```

The algorithm is formed recursively: It joins the remainder of the division by 2 with the result of the operation DecimalToBinary on the quotient of the number and 2. Because of the placement of the recursive call, the number will be built from the "bottom up," similar to working "right-to-left" in the preceding example. Note that the non-numeric operation Word is used on numeric data.

```
? Print DecimalToBinary 123
1111011
? Print DecimalToBinary 45
101101
? Print DecimalToBinary 1024
10000000000
```

A trace illustrates the generation of the result:

```
? Print DecimalToBinary 68
DecimalToBinary of "68"
  DecimalToBinary of "34"
    DecimalToBinary of "17"
      DecimalToBinary of "8"
        DecimalToBinary of "4"
          DecimalToBinary of "2"
            DecimalToBinary of "1"
              DecimalToBinary of "0"
              DecimalToBinary outputs ""
            DecimalToBinary outputs "1"
          DecimalToBinary outputs "10"
        DecimalToBinary outputs "100"
      DecimalToBinary outputs "1000"
    DecimalToBinary outputs "10001"
  DecimalToBinary outputs "100010"
DecimalToBinary outputs "1000100"
1000100
```

16.3. Conversion from the Decimal System into an Arbitrary Base System

A natural generalization of the building block `DecimalToBinary` is that the constant 2 can be replaced by an input, which allows the number to be converted into any number base (less than or equal to ten).

```
To DecimalToBase :Number :Base
  ; Convert a number to
  ; an arbitrary base (<11)
  Test :Number = 0
  IfTrue [Output "]
  Output
    Word
      (DecimalToBase
        (Quotient :Number :Base)
        :Base)
      (Remainder :Number :Base)
End

? Print DecimalToBase 10000 2
10011100010000
? Print DecimalToBase 45 3
1200
? Print DecimalToBase 24 8
30
```

16.4. Conversion of Numbers from Arbitrary System into Decimal

```
To BaseToDecimal :Number :Base
; convert number from other base
; to decimal system
Test :Number = "
IfTrue [Output 0]
Output
    Sum
        Last :Number
        Product
            :Base
            BaseToDecimal ButLast :Number :Base
End
```

```
? Print BaseToDecimal 34 7
25
? Print BaseToDecimal "210120210210 3
424866
```

A test run with tracing turned on:

```
? Print BaseToDecimal 345 9
BaseToDecimal of "345" and "9"
  BaseToDecimal of "45" and "9"
    BaseToDecimal of "5" and "9"
      BaseToDecimal of "" and "9"
      BaseToDecimal outputs "0"
    BaseToDecimal outputs "5"
  BaseToDecimal outputs "41"
BaseToDecimal outputs "284"
284
```

16.5. Conversion Between Two Arbitrary Bases Less Than Ten

If the available building blocks are assembled in the right way, a procedure can be defined that converts back and forth between arbitrary number bases. In doing so, the decimal representation is used as an intermediate form:

```
To ConvertBases :Number :OldBase :NewBase
; Convert between two arbitrary bases (<= 10)
Output
    DecimalToBase
        (BaseToDecimal :Number :OldBase 0)
        :NewBase
End
```

:Number is the number to be converted, :OldBase is the base of :Number, and :NewBase is the base to convert :Number to. The result is the representation of the number in the new base.

```
? Print ConvertBases 24 10 2
11000
```

```
? Print ConvertBases 45 7 3
1020
? Print ConvertBases 7654321 8 9
3771034
```

Exercises

(1) Multiple Conversions at Once

Write a procedure that converts a number to all positive number bases less than or equal to a specified base.

```
? ConvertToBases 24 9
24        9=System        26
24        8=System        30
24        7=System        33
24        6=System        40
24        5=System        44
24        4=System        120
24        3=System        220
24        2=System        11000
```

(2) Extension to Number Bases Larger than Ten

Extend the procedures from this chapter to handle numbers ≤ sixteen. This should require only minor modifications to the building blocks DecimalToBase and BaseToDecimal. You should use the usual convention in which the numbers ten to fifteen are represented by the letters A to F.

(3) Basic Arithmetic Operations in Arbitrary Number Bases

Write procedures to implement the basic arithmetic operations in bases less than or equal to sixteen. One line procedures (with the aforementioned building blocks) should suffice to define the basic arithmetic operations for arbitrary number base systems. One strategy that could be used here is based on first converting the number into base 10. The result can then be calculated using the system functions and then converted back into the corresponding base.

A couple of examples:

```
? Print NewSum "3 "6 8
11
? Print NewDifference "F "A 16
5
```

The operations can naturally be nested:

```
? Print NewMult (NewSum "3 "4 5)
                (NewDifference "D "3 15) 16
B4
? Print NewMult (NewSum "3 "7 9)
                (NewDifference "12 "23 4) 9
121
```

(4) Negative Base Systems

With minor extensions, the proper procedures can be rearranged so that negative bases can be used (have you ever thought about negative bases before?).

These systems have some interesting properties. For instance, both positive and negative numbers can be represented in these systems *without* a sign digit.

Modify the procedures presented earlier to allow for negative base systems.

The "first" 32 numbers in the negative binary base system have the following representation in the binary and decimal base system:

(-2) System	2 System	10 System
1	1	1
10	-10	-2
11	-1	-1
100	100	4
101	101	5
110	10	2
111	11	3
1000	-1000	-8
1001	-111	-7
1010	-1010	-10
1011	-1001	-9
1100	-100	-4
1101	-11	-3
1110	-110	-6
1111	-101	-5
10000	10000	16
10001	10001	17
10010	1110	14
10011	1111	15
10100	10100	20
10101	10101	21
10110	10010	18
10111	10011	19
11000	1000	8
11001	1001	9
11010	110	6
11011	111	7
11100	1100	12
11101	1101	13
11110	1010	10
11111	1011	11
100000	-100000	-32

(5) Heuristics of Chapter 12 Revisited

Which of the heuristics used to identify nonprime numbers (page 93) are still valid for the base 2 or base -2 systems? Can you invent new heuristics?

Chapter 17:
Basic Rules of Arithmetic

In this chapter we hope to demonstrate how the basic rules of arithmetic can be built up from simple, elementary number operations. This form of constructive mathematics can give us some further insights into how a system of mathematics is put together. Our goal with this chapter is to develop a set of procedures that implement these basic rules without the use of the built-in LOGO primitives for arithmetic.

17.1. Construction of the Rules of Arithmetic

As we discussed in chapter 15 exponentiation is not available in some versions of LOGO as a system defined primitive; however, it is not difficult to define by treating exponentiation as repeated multiplication:

```
To Exp :A :N
   Test :N = 0
   IfTrue [Output 1]
   Output Product1 :A Exp :A Sub1 :N
End
```

The procedures Product1 and Sub1 are defined shortly.

Some examples:

```
? Print Exp 2 15
32768
? Print Exp 4 2
16
```

The procedure Exp was reduced to repeated multiplication, yet it can still be viewed as a primitive when used in the definition of a procedure SuperExponent, as was shown in section 15.2.

Working in the "opposite direction," multiplication can be reduced to repeated addition (Sum1 is similar to the LOGO function "+"):

```
To Product1 :N :M
   Test :M = 0
   IfTrue [Output 0]
   Output Sum1 :N Product1 :N Sub1 :M
End
```

Examples:

```
? Print Product1 3 4
12
? Print Product1 5 2
10
```

This example also shows how a procedure can represent the "main procedure" from one point of view, while it acts as a primitive function from another. By again changing the level of perspective so that we no longer view Sum1 as a primitive, we can reduce it to the application of the primitive functions Add1 and Sub1.

```
To Sum1 :N :M
   Test :M = 0
   IfTrue [Output :N]
   Output Add1 Sum1 :N Sub1 :M
End
```

Example:

```
? Print Sum1 3 4
7
```

Since the functions Add1 and Sub1 are taken to be primitive with respect to Sum1, we need to define them:

```
To Add1 :N
   Output :N + 1
End

To Sub1 :N
   Output :N - 1
End
```

With this, we have based the simple arithmetic operations such as addition, multiplication, and even exponentiation on the elementary successor functions Add1 and Sub1, generating more powerful building blocks that can then be used to build even more powerful ones.

We have not yet reached our goal of independence from the built-in LOGO arithmetic, but we pick that up in a moment.

It is typical that defined procedures always "stand on the shoulders of its direct predecessor" (Sum1 "stands atop" Add1, Product1 "stands atop" Sum1, etc.). It is also possible, for example, to formulate multiplication in terms of its "conceptual grandfathers," Sub1 and Add1.

```
To Product1A :N :M
   Output Produ :N :M :M
End

To Produ :N :M :Copy
   Test :N = 0
   IfTrue [Output 0]
   Test :M = 0
   IfTrue [Output Produ Sub1 :N :Copy :Copy]
```

```
    Output Add1 Produ :N Sub1 :M :Copy
End
```

Examples:

```
? Print Product1A 4 5
20
? Print Product1A 2 3
6
```

These procedures are certainly somewhat unwieldy and opaque, since they are built directly on the primitive functions Sub1 and Add1, instead of being built using the function Sum1. This does not take full advantage of the conceptual hierarchy.

17.2. Reduction of Add1 to Elementary Functions

One could view the problems excerpted here as closed in the sense that addition, multiplication, etc. are defined for the domain of natural numbers with Add1 and Sub1 as elemental language elements.

We now proceed towards our goal of independence from LOGO arithmetic by raising Add1 from its role as an elementary function.

The function Add1, as it is defined in the program described previously, refers to the function "+", which is part of LOGO's basic vocabulary. We show that (and how) one can base a second version of Add1 (Add1V2) on elementary functions, which can be viewed as general symbol manipulation processes.

First we need to make clear what symbols Add1V2 will operate on; they are numbers (strings, list of characters) that are composed of digits (symbols, elements) according to certain rules. What constitutes a permissible digit (element) is usually specified as an alphabet; permissible digits are characters, which are contained in that alphabet. In LOGO, we implement this with a global variable :Alphabet.

```
? Make "Alphabet [0 1 2 3 4 5 6 7 8 9]
```

If a string is interpreted as a number, the function Add1V2 can be defined as follows, using the predefined ordering of the alphabet:

```
To Add1V2 :Number
  Test :Number = "
  IfTrue [Output First ButFirst :Alphabet]
  Test (Last :Number) = Last :Alphabet
  IfTrue
    [Output
      Word
        (Add1V2 ButLast :Number)
        (First :Alphabet)]
```

```
Output
  Word
    (ButLast :Number)
    (Successor Last :Number :Alphabet)
End

To Successor :Character :Alphabet
  Test :Character = First :Alphabet
  IfTrue [Output First ButFirst :Alphabet]
  Output Successor :Character
End
```

Examples:

```
? Print Add1V2 1
2
? Print Add1V2 9
10
? Print Add1V2 0
1
? Print Add1V2 99899
99900
```

In addition to Add1v2 an elementary predecessor function Sub1 has often been used, which refers back to the LOGO function "-". To get rid of this "impurity," one of two things can be done:

(1) A new version of Sub1, Sub1V1, can be based on elementary processes as Add1v2 was:[19]

```
To Sub1V2 :Number
  Output RemoveZero SU1 :Number
End

To RemoveZero :Number
  If And (First :Number) = 0 (Count :Number) > 1
    [Output RemoveZero ButFirst :Number]
  Output :Number
End

To Su1 :Number
  Test :Number = First :Alphabet
  IfTrue
    [Type [Sub1 of first element]
     Print [of alphabet is undefined]
     TopLevel]
  Test (Last :Number) = First :Alphabet
  IfTrue
    [Output
        Word (Su1 ButLast :Number) (Last :Alphabet)]
```

---

[19]The procedure Mirror used in Predecessor is not the one defined in section 8–1, but the more general one defined in appendix<utilities>.

```
        Output
          Word
            (ButLast :Number)
            (Predecessor Last :Number :Alphabet)
        End

        To Predecessor :Number :Alphabet
          Output Successor :Number Mirror :Alphabet
        End
```

Examples:

```
    ? Print Sub1V2 7
    6
    ? Print Sub1V2 100
    99
    ? Print Sub1V2 37
    36
    ? Print Sub1V2 0
    Sub1 of first element of alphabet is undefined
```

(2) The individual basic functions can be redefined, such that they only contain Add1v2 as the elementary successor function (together with the comparison operator "="); for example, with addition:

```
    To Sum2 :N :M
      Output Summ :N :M First :Alphabet
    End

    To Summ :N :M :Counter
      Test :M = :Counter
      IfTrue [Output :N]
      Output Add1 Summ :N :M Add1 :Counter
    End
```

Examples:

```
    ? Print Sum2 3 4
    7
    ? Print Sum2 12 9
    21
    ? Print Sum2 9 19
    28
```

17.3. Extension to Other Number Place Systems

It would be easy to check that the given function Add1v2 could perform calculations in the hexadecimal system with a suitable definition of the alphabet.

```
    ? Make "Alphabet [0 1 2 3 4 5 6 7 8 9 A B C D E F]
```

Examples:

```
? Print Add1v2 "9
A
? Print Add1v2 "FF
100
? Print Add1v2 "123FDFF
123FE00
```

With this (and a few minor changes to Sum1 and Product1), the basic functions of this number base are defined:

```
To Sum16 :N :M
   Test (First :Alphabet) = :M
   IfTrue [Output :N]
   Output Add1v2 Sum16 :N Sub1v2 :M
End

To Product16 :N :M
   Test :M = First :Alphabet
   IfTrue [Output First :Alphabet]
   Output Sum16 :N Product16 :N Sub1 :M
End
```

Examples:

```
? Print Sum16 "A "B
15
? Print Product16 3 4
C
```

We have provided functions that offer the basic arithmetic operations of addition and multiplication. Arbitrary number bases can be used by simply changing the underlying alphabet.

Some further examples:

```
? Make "Alphabet [0 1 2 3]
? Print Sum16 12 12
30
? Print Sum16 1212 1212
3030
? Print Product16 3 3
21
? Print Product16 10 10
100

? Make "Alphabet [0 1]
? Print Sum16 1010 1010
10100
? Print Product16 111 111
110001
```

17.4. Extension to Nonplace Number Systems

We could also decide, instead of limiting our representations to place systems, to allow the arbitrary number systems, such as a dot notation or the Roman numeral system, to be used.

1	.	I
2	..	II
3	...	III
4	....	IV
5	.....	V
6	......	VI
7	....	VII
8	....	VIII
9	....	IX
10	....	X

To be able to calculate in these different base systems, we need to define all the higher mathematical operations (addition, multiplication, division, etc.) in a representation-independent manner. The definition of the sum, product, and exponentiation could look like this:

```
To GeneralSum :A :B
  Test :B = ZeroElementOfAddition
  IfTrue [Output :A]
  Output Add1 GeneralSum :A Sub1 :B
End

To GeneralProduct :A :B
  Test :B = ZeroElementOfAddition
  IfTrue [Output ZeroElementOfAddition]
  Output GeneralSum :A GeneralProduct :A Sub1 :B
End

To GeneralExp :A :N
  Test :N = ZeroElementOfAddition
  IfTrue [Output OneElementOfMultiplication]
  Output GeneralProduct :A GeneralExp :A Sub1 :N
End
```

Then, for each representation the functions `Add1`, `Sub1`, `ZeroElement-OfAddition`, and `UnitElementOfMultiplication` need to be defined. For our usual decimal system these definitions are trivial; `Add1` and `Sub1` are as already presented, the other two look like this:

```
To ZeroElementOfAddition
  Output 0
End

To UnitElementOfMultiplication
  Output 1
End
```

Exercises

(1) Dot Notation

The dot notation depicted earlier is a *unary* number system. Write the four procedures `Add1`, `Sub1`, `ZeroElementOfAddition`, and `UnitElementOfMultiplication` for this number system.

A few sample runs of your system should look something like this:

```
? Print GeneralSum "... ".....
........
? Print GeneralProduct ".... ".....
..................
? Print GeneralExp "... "...
.......................
```

Roman Numerals

Calculation with Roman numerals is more complicated, so we provide some hints to get you started: `Add1` can attach an extra "I" to the number to be incremented. This action usually produces suitable and correct results. However, Numbers like "IIII" and "IXI" are produced (III + I → IIII, IX + I → IXI), and the incorrect results must be corrected (simplified) in a second step.

When subtracting 1 the exact opposite must happen: If the last element of the representation is not a "I," the number representation must first be "expanded" (e.g., V → IIIII), then shortened (the last element removed), then finally simplified:

Some sample runs:

```
? Print GeneralSum "III "IV
VII
? Print GeneralProduct "II "IX
XVIII
? Print GeneralExp "III "III
XXVII
```

(2) Nonprime Heuristics—One More Time

Looking back at the heuristics for finding nonprime numbers presented in chapter 12 again, can you invent some heuristics for Roman Numerals?

Part 3:
Computer Science

Introduction

Problem solving in computer science also forms an important interest world. As computers are used more and more in our society, many questions that did not receive much attention before now become significant. Although the problems presented in the mathematics and linguistics parts existed long before computers were invented, the problems in this section have only emerged or received more exact treatment since then.

Although there are many aspects of computer science that could be expressed as elements of a "pure science," we prefer to view computer science more as a *methodological science*. From this perspective, it is a science of programming (in the sense discussed in the preface) whose central concepts are *problem solving* and *model formation*. We focus on these concepts instead of a complete coverage of the subject.

Let's take sorting as an example: Rather than dealing with specific details, such as sorting procedures for specialized computing hardware or particular programming language features, the various problems illustrate *models* of sorting that are independent of any particular environment. This causes the criterion of *cognitive efficiency* of the specific programs to take precedence over *execution efficiency* most the time.

Because most the problems stem from actual work with students, a few further important aspects should be pointed out. The "great insights" of good programming practices, which are emphasized by computer science theorists (structured programming, "goto free programming"), can only be learned by:

• writing programs yourself and

• (eventually) building large, complex programs.

The first point is trivial, but enormously important. The *basic concepts of programming* cannot be learned by abstract analysis or by *coding* programs designed by someone else. Although we do give programs that illustrate the principles we are discussing, we view them more as a starting point for further work.

The second point is an important extension to the first. The techniques and insights of computer science only become important if complex, interesting problems need to be solved. If a problem is simple and does not require careful design of programs and data structures, then a sloppy solution in BASIC and a well-structured solution in PASCAL are in some sense equivalent. If a problem captures your interest, then you will pursue the methods and techniques rather than treat them as dull exercises. We observed that our students found the projects presented here useful for their own work and, as a result, they explored them to a greater extent than they would have otherwise.

[Harvey 85; Harvey 86; Harvey 87a] also provide an excellent study of computer science using LOGO.

Chapter 18:
Sorting

A great deal of theoretical and applied computer science research has dealt with sorting because its use in commercial data processing and many other types of information processing requires efficient processing methods.

We do not wish to present a systematic and exhaustive overview of all sorting methods known to computer science;[20] neither do we wish to concentrate on the problem faced frequently by commercial data processing of merging and sorting data that are stored on external media. Rather, the goals of this chapter are:

- To give you a first impression of the central role played by sorting methods and related problems in traditional computer science.

- To show that different methods are "good" in different ways, and that they can be evaluated according to different criteria.

- To demonstrate the principle of generalization through a concrete example.

Our approach to these goals will be to

- Write a program that places a list of numbers in increasing order.

- Explore various methods of sorting.

- Compare the methods with each other.

- Generalize the methods so that an arbitrary ordering relationship can be used to order the elements.

18.1. Sorting Methods

The problem of sorting consists of generating a sequence (a list) of numbers in nondecreasing order from a sequence (a list) of unsorted numbers. There are many different methods that have been used to solve this problem; let's look at a few of them.

---

[20]The interested reader is referred to [Knuth 69] in which nearly 400 pages are devoted to a detailed discussion of this topic.

Insertion Methods

We can represent the elements to be sorted as items written on little slips of paper lying randomly mixed together before us on the left side of the table:

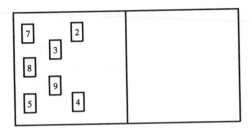

Figure 18-1: Initial Setup

The insertion method proceeds as follows: We take an *arbitrary* slip of paper (e.g., 5) from the set on the left and place it on the right side of the table:

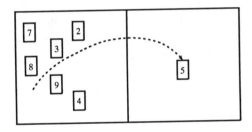

Figure 18-2: After One Step

Then we select another *arbitrary* item (this time, the 8) from the left side and lay it on the right side so that it forms a *non-decreasing* sequence:

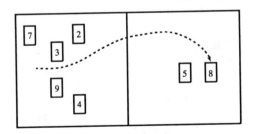

Figure 18-3: After Two Steps

Next we select the 7 and insert it in the already sorted list composed of 5 and 8 on the right:

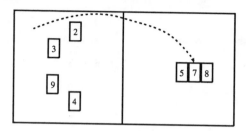

Figure 18–4: After Three Steps

Similarly, we continue with the remaining numbers 3, 4, 9, and 2 until we finally achieve the following result:

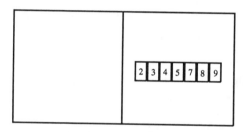

Figure 18–5: Final Results

The insertion process then consists of inserting each element of the unsorted list (the left side of the table) into an already sorted list (the right side of the table) in the proper location. The empty list (the empty right side of the table) in the beginning is a special case of an unsorted list (because there are no elements, none of them are "out of place").

It is important to note that the actual cost of sorting (namely the comparison of a particular element with the others) occurs at the moment when the element is placed in the new list; the removal of the element from the original set is trivial in comparison: Any element can be removed. The next method we discuss, the *selection sort*, reverses this process.

An Example of an Insertion Sort Program

```
To InsertionSort :List
  If :List = [] [Output []]
  Output
    Insert
      (First :List)
      (InsertionSort ButFirst :List)
End
```

This procedure sorts a list of numbers in increasing order. It inserts the first element of the list into an *already sorted* sublist until the list is exhausted. The actual comparison and insertion is done by the procedure Insert.

Some test runs:

```
? Print InsertionSort [7 3 4 8 9 5 2]
2 3 4 5 7 8 9
? Print InsertionSort [9 8 7 6 5 4 3 2 1 0]
0 1 2 3 4 5 6 7 8 9
? Print InsertionSort [1 2 3 4 4 3 2 1]
1 1 2 2 3 3 4 4
```

If we turn tracing on, we see how the program works:

```
? Print InsertionSort [4 2 3 1]
InsertionSort of [4 2 3 1]
  InsertionSort of [2 3 1]
    InsertionSort of [3 1]
      InsertionSort of [1]
        InsertionSort of []
        InsertionSort outputs []
      InsertionSort outputs [1]
    InsertionSort outputs [1 3]
  InsertionSort outputs [1 2 3]
InsertionSort outputs [1 2 3 4]
1 2 3 4
```

The procedure Insert looks like this:

```
To Insert :Element :List
  If :List = [] [Output Sentence :Element []]
  If GreaterP First :List :Element
    [Output Sentence :Element :List]
  Output
    Sentence
      First :List
      Insert :Element ButFirst :List
End
```

If the already sorted list is empty, :Element becomes the first element. Otherwise, the first element of :List that is larger than :Element is searched for and :Element is placed in front of it.

Selection Sort

We begin again with the numbered, unordered slips of paper on the table:

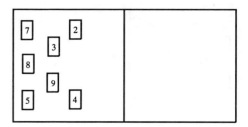

Figure 18-6: Initial Setup

From these numbers we search for the *smallest* and move it to the right side of the table:

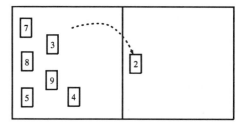

Figure 18-7: After One Step

We then search the remaining numbers again looking for the *smallest* element and move it to the right side of the table:

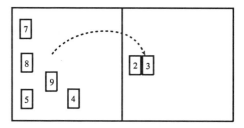

Figure 18-8: After Two Steps

We repeat this another time:

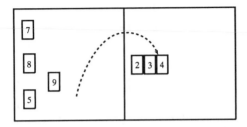

Figure 18-9: After Three Steps

At the end, we have the same picture as we did with the insertion process on page 143; all the numbers are sorted.

The essential difference from the insertion sort is that with the selection sort the real sorting cost occurs when the next element to be transferred is selected; the placement in the new list is trivial in contrast. The two sorting methods can then be compared based on when they manipulate the available information. Whereas the insertion sort makes the comparison at the time of insertion into the new list, this happens with the selection sort at the time of selection. This distinction corresponds to that between

• information processing at read-time

• information processing at question-time

This is a conceptual dual with a high degree of generality, which can be used to characterize many processes. Often in computer science we have to decide which of these two approaches will take precedence, or which viewpoint is given the greatest weight. In building information systems one must determine how strongly newly acquired information is connected with that which already exists. The computing costs of integrating new information with the existing must be weighed against the other possibility. Constructing the information system with an unstructured database (with small costs involved for integrating new data) will eventually require high computing costs to generate an answer.

The way people handle multiplication may be used as an illustration. There are two (extreme) positions that could be taken:

• All possible multiplications and their results could be "stored up" (which is impossible in reality) and retrieved when needed; this is comparable to "information processing at read-time."

• Each answer is computed when needed using a given algorithm; this corresponds to "information processing at question-time."

In reality, we have compromised: The results of simple, basic multiplications are "stored up" (the multiplication table!), whereas the results of complicated multiplications are computed based on the simpler, memorized values.

Generally it is recommended—as in the example—to do a certain amount of the information processing at read time. However extensive read-time processing can lead to storage problems; further discussion on these problems can be found in the artificial intelligence part in chapter 30.

An Example of a Selection Sort Program

This method chooses the smallest element of a list and prepends it to the result of recursively sorting the rest of the list (after the smallest element is removed).

```
To SelectionSort :List
  If :List = [] [Output []]
  Output
    Sentence
      Smallest :List
      SelectionSort Remove Smallest :List :List
  End
```

Sample runs:

```
? Print SelectionSort [7 3 4 8 9 5 2]
2 3 4 5 7 8 9
? Print SelectionSort [9 8 7 6 5 4 3 2 1 0]
0 1 2 3 4 5 6 7 8 9
? Print SelectionSort [4 3 2 1 1 2 3 4]
1 1 2 2 3 3 4 4
```

With tracing on:

```
? Print SelectionSort [4 2 3 1]
SelectionSort of [4 2 3 1]
  SelectionSort of [4 2 3]
    SelectionSort of [4 3]
      SelectionSort of [4]
        SelectionSort of []
        SelectionSort outputs []
      SelectionSort outputs [4]
    SelectionSort outputs [3 4]
  SelectionSort outputs [2 3 4]
SelectionSort outputs [1 2 3 4]
1 2 3 4
```

The procedure Smallest looks like this:

```
To Smallest :List
  If (ButFirst :List) = [] [Output First :List]
  Output
    MyMinimum
      First :List
      Smallest ButFirst :List
  End
```

The procedure Smallest locates the smallest element of the list with the help of the function Minimum; this element is then taken out of the list using the Remove function. Notice that the procedure Smallest has the expression ButFirst :List = []. This tests whether :List contains only one element without using a costly additional procedure to count the elements.

Remove, and Minimum are described in appendix III.

Exchange Sorts

Our set of numbers are placed in an arbitrary, unsorted sequence on the table; then we examine these numbers repeatedly from beginning to end. Whenever two elements are in the incorrect order, we exchange them. This continues until we can make no more exchanges. This is shown in the following example (the pairs to be exchanged are underlined):

```
 1st Step:   7   3   4   8   9   5   2
 2nd Step:   3   7   4   8   9   5   2
 3rd Step:   3   4   7   8   9   5   2
 4th Step:   3   4   7   8   5   9   2
 5th Step:   3   4   7   5   8   9   2
 6th Step:   3   4   5   7   8   9   2
 7th Step:   3   4   5   7   8   2   9
 8th Step:   3   4   5   7   2   8   9
 9th Step:   3   4   5   2   7   8   9
10th Step:   3   4   2   5   7   8   9
11th Step:   3   2   4   5   7   8   9
Result:      2   3   4   5   7   8   9
```

All the methods belonging to this family of sorting processes have in common some systematic way of exchanging pairs of elements (which are not always adjacent, as they were in our example), until no more such pairs exist.

The most well-known, simplest, but also least efficient method of this family is the bubble sort, which can be obtained by two minor changes to the basic algorithm. First, each pass goes through the entire list, even if an exchange has already been found. As can be seen using a simple example, the largest number is already in the rightmost position after the first pass. The part of the list remaining to be sorted can be shortened by successively ignoring the last element of the list that was the result of the previous pass, thereby saving comparisons and computation time; this method requires at most n passes to reach its goal where n is the number of elements in the list.

An Example of an Exchange Sort Program

```
To ExchangeSort :List
  If :List = [] [Output []]
  Output Exchange1 Sentence :List [] []
End

To Exchange1 :List :AlreadySorted
  If (ButFirst :List) = []
    [Output Sentence :AlreadySorted :List]
  If LessP First :List First ButFirst :List
    [Output
        Exchange1
          ButFirst :List
          Sentence :AlreadySorted First :List]
```

```
    Output
      Exchange1
        (Sentence :AlreadySorted First ButFirst :List
          First :List ButFirst ButFirst :List)
        []
End
```

This method appears somewhat more complex than the preceding two at first; a look at a trace of execution of this process will help to make things clearer:

```
? Print ExchangeSort [4 2 3 1]
ExchangeSort of [4 2 3 1]
  Exchange1 of [4 2 3 1] and []
    Exchange1 of [2 4 3 1] and []
      Exchange1 of [4 3 1] and [2]
        Exchange1 of [2 3 4 1] and []
          Exchange1 of [3 4 1] and [2]
            Exchange1 of [4 1] and [2 3]
              Exchange1 of [2 3 1 4] and []
                Exchange1 of [3 1 4] and [2]
                  Exchange1 of [2 1 3 4] and []
                    Exchange1 of [1 2 3 4] and []
                      Exchange1 of [2 3 4] and [1]
                        Exchange1 of [3 4] and [1 2]
                          Exchange1 of [4] and [1 2 3]
                          Exchange1 outputs [1 2 3 4]
                        Exchange1 outputs [1 2 3 4]
                      Exchange1 outputs [1 2 3 4]
                    Exchange1 outputs [1 2 3 4]
                  Exchange1 outputs [1 2 3 4]
                Exchange1 outputs [1 2 3 4]
              Exchange1 outputs [1 2 3 4]
            Exchange1 outputs [1 2 3 4]
          Exchange1 outputs [1 2 3 4]
        Exchange1 outputs [1 2 3 4]
      Exchange1 outputs [1 2 3 4]
    Exchange1 outputs [1 2 3 4]
  Exchange1 outputs [1 2 3 4]
ExchangeSort outputs [1 2 3 4]
1 2 3 4
```

As you can see, the real work happens in Exchange1, which takes two inputs. The second input (:Holder) serves as a temporary holding place for the already correctly ordered first part of the list (last line of Exchange1). Otherwise a pair of numbers that are out of order are found, these two are switched, and the entire list (:Holder, the exchanged pair, and the rest of the list) is reassembled and processed as if from the beginning by Exchange1. This goes on as long as the list is longer than one element; in other words until there are no more pairs of numbers that could be out of order.

Sorting by Merging

Another technique used in sorting is called *merging*, where two lists that are already sorted are combined, resulting in a single, sorted list. In each step of the process the smallest first element of the two lists (and therefore the smallest element of the two lists altogether, since they are in order) is taken as the next element of the combined list. This continues on until both of the initial lists are exhausted. Graphically:

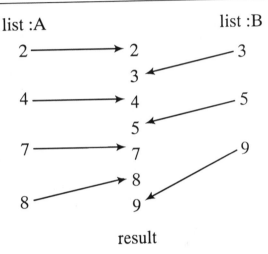

result

Figure 18-10: Merging Two Ordered Lists

Examples of Merge Sort Programs

The central procedure for the next two methods is Merge.

```
To Merge :A :B
  If :A = [] [Output :B]
  If :B = [] [Output :A]
  If GreaterP First :A First :B
    [Output
        Sentence First :B Merge :A ButFirst :B]
    Output Sentence First :A Merge ButFirst :A :B
End
```

Merge expects its two inputs to be lists that are already in nondescending order. These two inputs are combined into one list by Merge. To build sorting methods based on this procedure, it is necessary to provide it with sublists that have already been sorted by other procedures. Let's discuss a couple of different possible solutions.

Merging Method 1

One possible solution that can be based on the basic idea of merging is represented by the following procedures:

```
To MergeSort1 :Sentence
  If :Sentence = [] [Output []]
  Output
    Merge
      AlreadyOrderedPart :Sentence
      MergeSort1 ButAlreadyOrderedPart :Sentence
End

To AlreadyOrderedPart :Sentence
  if (ButFirst :Sentence) = []
    [Output :Sentence]
  if GreaterP
    First :Sentence
    First ButFirst :Sentence
    [Output Sentence First :Sentence []]
  Output
    Sentence
      First :Sentence
      AlreadyOrderedPart ButFirst :Sentence
End

To ButAlreadyOrderedPart :Sentence
  If (ButFirst :Sentence) = [] [Output []]
  If GreaterP
    First :Sentence
    First ButFirst :Sentence
    [Output ButFirst :Sentence]
  Output
    ButAlreadyOrderedPart ButFirst :Sentence
End
```

The procedure MergeSort1 divides the list into two parts: The first part is composed of any elements of the list that are already in the correct order (this may be just one element), and the second part is the rest of the list (from the point where the elements were out of order). After the second part is sorted by a recursive call to MergeSort1, the two parts are merged back together to obtain the desired result.

Examples:

```
? Print MergeSort1 [7 3 4 8 9 5 2]
2 3 4 5 7 8 9
? Print MergeSort1 [9 8 7 6 5 4 3 2 1]
1 2 3 4 5 6 7 8 9
```

With tracing turned on for MergeSort and Merge:

```
? Print MergeSort1 [1 2 1 2 4 3 8]
MergeSort1 of [1 2 1 2 4 3 8]
  MergeSort1 of [1 2 4 3 8]
```

```
    MergeSort1 of [3 8]
      MergeSort1 of []
      MergeSort1 outputs []
        Merge of [3 8] and []
        Merge outputs [3 8]
    MergeSort1 outputs [3 8]
    Merge of [1 2 4] and [3 8]
     Merge of [2 4] and [3 8]
      Merge of [4] and [3 8]
       Merge of [4] and [8]
        Merge of [] and [8]
        Merge outputs [8]
       Merge outputs [4 8]
      Merge outputs [3 4 8]
     Merge outputs [2 3 4 8]
    Merge outputs [1 2 3 4 8]
  MergeSort1 outputs [1 2 3 4 8]
  Merge of [1 2] and [1 2 3 4 8]
   Merge of [2] and [1 2 3 4 8]
    Merge of [2] and [2 3 4 8]
     Merge of [] and [2 3 4 8]
     Merge outputs [2 3 4 8]
    Merge outputs [2 2 3 4 8]
   Merge outputs [1 2 2 3 4 8]
  Merge outputs [1 1 2 2 3 4 8]
MergeSort1 outputs [1 1 2 2 3 4 8]
1 1 2 2 3 4 8
```

If MergeSort1 is used on a list of descending numbers, then this method operates the same way that InsertSort does as both of the following traces show:

```
? Print MergeSort1 [4 3 2 1]
MergeSort1 of [4 3 2 1]
  MergeSort1 of [3 2 1]
    MergeSort1 of [2 1]
      MergeSort1 of [1]
        MergeSort1 of []
        MergeSort1 outputs []
      MergeSort1 outputs [1]
     MergeSort1 outputs [1 2]
   MergeSort1 outputs [1 2 3]
MergeSort1 outputs [1 2 3 4]
1 2 3 4

? Print InsertSort [4 3 2 1]
  InsertSort of [4 3 2 1]
   InsertSort of [3 2 1]
    InsertSort of [2 1]
     InsertSort of [1]
      InsertSort of []
      InsertSort outputs []
     InsertSort outputs [1]
    InsertSort outputs [1 2]
   InsertSort outputs [1 2 3]
InsertSort outputs [1 2 3 4]
1 2 3 4
```

The `Insertion` of one element into a list corresponds to merging a single-element list with a multiple-element list.

Merging Method 2

A somewhat different solution based on `Merge` is as follows:

```
To MergeSort2 :List
  If :List = [] [Output []]
  If (ButFirst :List) = [] [Output :List]
  Output
    Merge
      MergeSort2 HalfList :List
      MergeSort2 SecondHalf :List
End
```

This method divides the list into two parts, recursively sorts these two parts, then merges the result back together. This recursive process proceeds until the lists to be merged contain only one element and the result can be constructed from "bottom up." The other procedures that are needed look like this:

```
To HalfList :List
  Test EmptyP :List
  IfTrue [Output []]
  Test EmptyP ButFirst :List
  IfTrue [Output :List]
  Output
    Sentence
      First :List
      HalfList ButFirst ButFirst :List
End

To SecondHalf :List
  Output HalfList ButFirst :List
End
```

The procedures `HalfList` and `SecondHalf` split the list up into two parts.

Some Examples:

```
? Print MergeSort2 [7 3 4 8 9 5 2]
2 3 4 5 7 8 9
? Print MergeSort2 [1 2 3 4 4 3 2 1]
1 1 2 2 3 3 4 4
```

Running this with tracing on serves to illustrate this process.

```
? Print MergeSort2 [7 3 4 8 9 5 2]
MergeSort2 of [7 3 4 8 9 5 2]
 MergeSort2 of [7 4 9 2]
  MergeSort2 of [7 9]
   MergeSort2 of [7]
   MergeSort2 outputs [7]
   MergeSort2 of [9]
   MergeSort2 outputs [9]
   Merge of [7] and [9]
    Merge of [] and [9]
```

```
   Merge outputs [9]
  Merge outputs [7 9]
 MergeSort2 outputs [7 9]
 MergeSort2 of [4 2]
  MergeSort2 of [4]
  MergeSort2 outputs [4]
  MergeSort2 of [2]
  MergeSort2 outputs [2]
  Merge of [4] and [2]
   Merge of [4] and []
   Merge outputs [4]
  Merge outputs [2 4]
 MergeSort2 outputs [2 4]
 Merge of [7 9] and [2 4]
  Merge of [7 9] and [4]
   Merge of [7 9] and []
   Merge outputs [7 9]
  Merge outputs [4 7 9]
 Merge outputs [2 4 7 9]
MergeSort2 outputs [2 4 7 9]
MergeSort2 of [3 8 5]
 MergeSort2 of [3 5]
  MergeSort2 of [3]
  MergeSort2 outputs [3]
  MergeSort2 of [5]
  MergeSort2 outputs [5]
  Merge of [3] and [5]
   Merge of [] and [5]
   Merge outputs [5]
  Merge outputs [3 5]
 MergeSort2 outputs [3 5]
 MergeSort2 of [8]
 MergeSort2 outputs [8]
 Merge of [3 5] and [8]
  Merge of [5] and [8]
   Merge of [] and [8]
   Merge outputs [8]
  Merge outputs [5 8]
 Merge outputs [3 5 8]
MergeSort2 outputs [3 5 8]
Merge of [2 4 7 9] and [3 5 8]
 Merge of [4 7 9] and [3 5 8]
  Merge of [4 7 9] and [5 8]
   Merge of [7 9] and [5 8]
    Merge of [7 9] and [8]
     Merge of [9] and [8]
      Merge of [9] and []
      Merge outputs [9]
     Merge outputs [8 9]
    Merge outputs [7 8 9]
   Merge outputs [5 7 8 9]
  Merge outputs [4 5 7 8 9]
 Merge outputs [3 4 5 7 8 9]
Merge outputs [2 3 4 5 7 8 9]
MergeSort2 outputs [2 3 4 5 7 8 9]
2 3 4 5 7 8 9
```

One could also describe this method as a process that traces out a tree structure as it executes (compare the structure of the procedure `MergeSort2` with the manipulation of binary trees described in section 9.3).

This tree structure needs to be illustrated using our last example. In the figure, the value that will be "passed down" is to the left of each node; the calculated result is found to the right of each node:

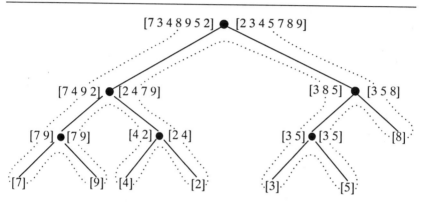

Figure 18–11: Tree Structure of `MergeSort2`

This sorting method as illustrated here bears some resemblance to one of the fastest methods known today, the quicksort. With quicksort, as with `MergeSort2`, a binary tree structure is traced out by the execution. In contrast to the previous method, the existing list is to some extent "presorted" before it is split apart, so that the lists can be directly joined from bottom up without needing to `Merge` them (this corresponds somewhat to the difference between insertion and selection sort).

The algorithm for quicksort can be described as follows:

- *Presorting:* From the list an arbitrary element is selected—this can be a particular element, say the middle one, it can be one selected using a random factor, or it can be the median of several values. Call this element m. Each element of the list is then classified into one of three groups; one group contains those elements less than m, the second contains all those values equal to m, and the third group contains all elements greater than m. This process can be done in many ways; some more efficiently than others. Since our goal here is *cognitive efficiency*, we simply scan the list, placing each item in one of three lists called `:Left` for those less than m, `:Middle` for those equal to m, and `:Right` for those greater than m.

- *Recursive Step:* Both the `:Left` and `:Right` sublists are recursively sorted until the recursive process receives a single-element list or an empty list. The resulting sorted sublists can be directly concatenated, with the `:Middle` list sandwiched between.

This algorithm can be converted into the corresponding procedures in a direct manner. We arbitrarily select the last element of the list as our element for comparison. The procedure `SplitUp` presorts the list for us and `QuickSort` handles the recursive step.

```
To QuickSort :List
  Local "SubLists
  If :List = [] [Output []]
  If (ButFirst :List) = [] [Output :List]
  Make
    "SubLists
    SplitUp :List Last :List [] [] []
  Output
    (Sentence
      QuickSort First :SubLists
      First ButFirst :SubLists
      QuickSort Last :SubLists)
End

To SplitUp :List :Element :Left :Middle :Right
  If :List = []
    [Output (List :Left :Middle :Right)]
  IfElse GreaterP :Element First :List
    [Make "Left Sentence First :List :Left]
    [IfElse GreaterP First :List :Element
       [Make "Right Sentence First :List :Right]
       [Make
          "Middle
          Sentence First :List :Middle]]
  Output
    SplitUp
      ButFirst :List
      :Element
      :Left
      :Middle
      :Right
End
```

The reader can now experiment with these procedures. To call this procedure the form:

```
QuickSort [list]
```

is used.

Sorting Using Tree Data Structures

While the methods described in the previous sections trace out a tree-like structure during their execution (as shown, for example, in figure 18–11), in this section we discuss methods that use an explicit tree data structure.

An example: We want to order the numbers "7 3 4 8 9" by increasing size. We start with 7, which we use as the root of a tree (branches that have not been filled in yet are shown as a "."):

Figure 18–12: Tree — Before Sorting

We insert the 3 into the tree (which to this point is a trivial tree) in order by starting at the root (next at the 7) and proceeding down the left branch, because 3 is smaller than 7. We obtain:

Figure 18–13: Tree — After One Insertion

Similarly, we insert the 4 into the tree, proceeding left from the 7 and *right* from the 3, because the 4 is greater than 3.

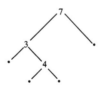

Figure 18–14: Tree — After Two Insertions

If we insert the rest of the numbers, we obtain the result:

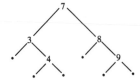

Figure 18-15: Tree — Final Form

With the following procedures, such a tree (or the data structures that represent the tree) can be built.

```
To ConstructTree :List :Tree
   If :List = [] [Output :Tree]
   Output
      ConstructTree
         ButFirst :List
         InsertNode First :List :Tree
End

To InsertNode :Element :Node
   If LeafP :Node [OutPut MakeNode :Element [] []]
   IfElse GreaterP :Element Data :Node
      [Output
         MakeNode
            Data :Node
            LeftBranch :Node
            InsertNode :Element RightBranch :Node]
      [Output
         MakeNode
            Data :Node
            InsertNode :Element LeftBranch :Node
            RightBranch :Node]
End

To MakeNode :Data :Left :Right
   Output (List :Data :Left :Right)
End

To Data :Node
   Output First :Node
End

To LeftBranch :Node
   Output First ButFirst :Node
End

To RightBranch :Node
   Output Last :Node
End
```

```
To LeafP :Node
  Output EmptyP :Node
End

To Leaf
  Output []
End
```

Here is a description of the individual procedures:

- ConstructTree traverses the list recursively giving the elements one at a time to InsertNode, to be inserted in their proper place in the tree.

- InsertNode determines whether the :Tree is a Leaf and if so, creates a new node using MakeNode with the :Element as the Data of the new node. If the tree is not a Leaf, then the element is recursively inserted into the RightBranch if it is greater than the Data in the :Tree. Otherwise the :Element is recursively inserted into the LeftBranch of the :Tree.

- The rest of the procedures have to do with the implementation of the tree data structure. MakeNode creates a new node that contains the :Data and has :Left and :Right as its subtrees. Data extracts the information stored at a node in the tree. RightBranch and LeftBranch return the respective subtrees. Leaf creates a leaf node; LeafP tells if a particular tree is a leaf node. These same procedures can be used when traversing the tree, which is described next.

The example shown in the figures would look like this:

```
? Show ConstructTree [7 3 4 8 9] Leaf
[7 [3 [] [4 [] []]] [8 [] [9 [] []]]]
```

If you examine these procedures, you see that they handle the case where values occur more than once in the list, since an element that is equal to the data at an existing node is treated the same as a node that is less than the data at an existing node.

```
? Show ConstructTree [5 2 2 3 3]
[5 [2 [2 [] []] [3 [3 [] []] []]] []]
```

When the sorting work is finished, all that is left is to gather the fruit of the ConstructTree's labor from the branches of the tree in the correct order. The following procedures do this:

```
To TraverseTree :Node
  If LeafP :Node [Output []]
  Output
    (Sentence TraverseTree LeftBranch :Node
      Data :node TraverseTree RightBranch :node)
End
```

If we put both parts (building the tree and "harvesting the fruit") together, we get the following sorting procedure:

```
To TreeSort :List
    Output TraverseTree ConstructTree :List Leaf
End
```

Examples:

```
? Print TreeSort [7 3 4 8 9 5 2]
2 3 4 5 7 8 9
? Print TreeSort [1 2 3 4 4 3 2 1]
1 1 2 2 3 3 4 4
```

With selective tracing on:

```
? Print TreeSort [4 3 2 1]
TreeSort of [4 3 2 1]
 ConstructTree of [4 3 2 1] and []
  InsertNode of 4 and []
  InsertNode outputs [4 [] []]
  ConstructTree of [3 2 1] and [4 [] []]
   InsertNode of 3 and [4 [] []]
    InsertNode of 3 and []
    InsertNode outputs [3 [] []]
   InsertNode outputs [4 [3 [] []] []]
   ConstructTree of [2 1] and [4 [3 [] []] []]
    InsertNode of 2 and [4 [3 [] []] []]
     InsertNode of 2 and [3 [] []]
      InsertNode of 2 and []
      InsertNode outputs [2 [] []]
     InsertNode outputs [3 [2 [] []] []]
    InsertNode outputs [4 [3 [2 [] []] []] []]
    ConstructTree of [1] and [4 [3 [2 [] []] []] []]
     InsertNode of 1 and [4 [3 [2 [] []] []] []]
      InsertNode of 1 and [3 [2 [] []] []]
       InsertNode of 1 and [2 [] []]
        InsertNode of 1 and []
        InsertNode outputs [1 [] []]
       InsertNode outputs [2 [1 [] []] []]
      InsertNode outputs [3 [2 [1 [] []] []] []]
     InsertNode outputs [4 [3 [2 [1 [] []] []] []] []]
     ConstructTree of [] and [4 [3 [2 [1 [] []] []] []] []]
     ConstructTree outputs [4 [3 [2 [1 [] []] []] []] []]
    ConstructTree outputs [4 [3 [2 [1 [] []] []] []] []]
   ConstructTree outputs [4 [3 [2 [1 [] []] []] []] []]
  ConstructTree outputs [4 [3 [2 [1 [] []] []] []] []]
 ConstructTree outputs [4 [3 [2 [1 [] []] []] []] []]
 TraverseTree of [4 [3 [2 [1 [] []] []] []] []]
  TraverseTree of [3 [2 [1 [] []] []] []]
   TraverseTree of [2 [1 [] []] []]
    TraverseTree of [1 [] []]
     TraverseTree of []
     TraverseTree outputs []
     TraverseTree of []
     TraverseTree outputs []
    TraverseTree outputs [1]
```

```
TraverseTree of []
 TraverseTree outputs []
 TraverseTree outputs [1 2]
 TraverseTree of []
 TraverseTree outputs []
 TraverseTree outputs [1 2 3]
 TraverseTree of []
 TraverseTree outputs []
 TraverseTree outputs [1 2 3 4]
TreeSort outputs [1 2 3 4]
1 2 3 4
```

18.2. Efficiency of the Methods

Computer scientists have investigated the machine efficiency of sorting methods because they have much practical importance and their simplicity makes reasonable candidates for study. All these investigations have the goal of determining the comparative length of time or amount of space the methods require. At this point we deal with only two aspects of these investigations:

(1) Selection of the sequences to be sorted. Many different sequences of various lengths can be devised as test sequences in determining the efficiency of the methods, of which the sequences

    1   2   3   4

and

    4   3   2   1

represent only two extreme examples. It could well be that one method would do well with one sequence, while another method would be faster or more efficient with the other. The degree of "presortedness" of a sequence may have much influence on the efficiency of a method.

(2) Another aspect concerns how the size of the sequence affects the speed of the method. It is possible that different sorting methods will be better for different sizes of sequences; while method A might be faster than any other on sequences up to size 100, method B may show better performance on long sequences. Which method to use depends on the length of the sequences that will normally be sorted.

The basic problems in determining the costs of the methods are:

- How often are the individual elements of the sequence *compared*?

- How often are the individual elements of the sequence *exchanged* or *moved*?

- How large is the average (or maximum) memory requirement?

As an example, let's look into the first question and test our method on several sequences. We solve the problem by defining a procedure MyGreaterP, which we substitute everywhere a GreaterP is used to compare two elements in the sequence:

```
To MyGreaterP :A :B
   Output :A > :B
End
```

If Minimum is a primitive in the LOGO being used, then MyMinimum also needs to be defined:

```
To MyMinimum :A :B
   IfElse MyGreaterP :A :B
     [Output :B]
     [Output :A]
End
```

In addition, we write a small program that provides a testing framework and a procedure to generate a list of random numbers:

```
To CompareMethods :Sequence :Methods
   If :Methods = [] [Stop]
   Make "CompareCount 0
   Make "Ignore Run (List First :Methods :Sequence)
   Type
     (Sentence First :Methods "compared :CompareCount
       "times)
   Print []
   CompareMethods :Sequence ButFirst :Methods
End

To TestSort :Sequence
   CompareMethods
     :Sequence
     [InsertionSort SelectionSort
      ExchangeSort MergeSort1
      MergeSort2 QuickSort TreeSort]
End

To RandomList :N :UpperLimit
   If :N = 0 [Output []]
   Output
     Sentence
       Random :UpperLimit
       RandomList :N - 1 :UpperLimit
End
```

The procedure `RandomList` provides a list of `:N` random numbers smaller than `:UpperLimit`. Let's test this on a few examples:

```
? TestSort [7 3 4 8 9 5 2]
InsertionSort compared 15 times
SelectionSort compared 42 times
ExchangeSort compared 42 times
MergeSort1 compared 22 times
MergeSort2 compared 13 times
QuickSort compared 34 times
TreeSort compared 11 times
? TestSort [1 2 3 4 4 3 2 1]
InsertionSort compared 19 times
SelectionSort compared 56 times
ExchangeSort compared 61 times
MergeSort1 compared 23 times
MergeSort2 compared 17 times
QuickSort compared 40 times
TreeSort compared 12 times
? TestSort [0 1 2 3 4 5 6 7 8 9]
InsertionSort compared 9 times
SelectionSort compared 90 times
ExchangeSort compared 9 times
MergeSort1 compared 18 times
MergeSort2 compared 25 times
QuickSort compared 83 times
TreeSort compared 45 times
? TestSort [9 8 7 6 5 4 3 2 1 0]
InsertionSort compared 36 times
SelectionSort compared 72 times
ExchangeSort compared 128 times
MergeSort1 compared 52 times
MergeSort2 compared 21 times
QuickSort compared 72 times
TreeSort compared 36 times
? TestSort RandomList 20 10
InsertionSort compared 125 times
SelectionSort compared 380 times
ExchangeSort compared 839 times
MergeSort1 compared 114 times
MergeSort2 compared 65 times
QuickSort compared 127 times
TreeSort compared 43 times
```

As can clearly be seen, the sequence to be sorted is a large factor. Although `ExchangeSort` performed badly in most of the tests, it was one of the best two in the third test; naturally, this is because the third sequence is already sorted and `ExchangeSort` discovers this more rapidly than the rest. `TreeSort`, on the other hand, which was the best overall in terms of the number of comparisons, performed worse on the third and fourth tests, because these already sorted sequences caused a completely-imbalanced, deep tree to be created.

This suggests that we should define a measurement that makes it possible to make some statement about the degree of "sortedness" of a list. It is desirable for this measurement to be informative as well as intuitive.

A first approach might be to compare the list (before it is sorted) to the list that results from sorting. In doing so, it can be noted how much each of the elements of the list are out of position. Generally, this value increases the farther the list is from being sorted. An example:

```
Before: 7   3   4   8   9   5   2
After:  2   3   4   5   7   8   9
Delta: -6   0   0  -2   4   2   2
```

The distances are given with respect to the sorted list. "Delta -6" means that in the original list the "2" is 6 positions to the left of where it should be (the minus sign is used to mean "to the left"). Because of the signs, these values cannot simply be added (they should always add up to 0). To get around this, the absolute value could be used, but we use the square as is customary in mathematics (e.g., variance):

```
SumOfSquares = 36+0+0+4+16+4+4 = 64
```

As is soon apparent, lists of differing length can hardly be compared, because longer lists automatically have greater distances to move. The value we use needs to be normalized. Usually, this is done so that an ordered list gives the maximum value,+1, and a list that is in reverse order yields the minimum value, -1.

`SumOfSquares`, in contrast, takes the minimum value 0 and the maximum value n*(n*n-1)/3, where n is the number of elements in the list (this formula can be derived easily). Using this result, we can define the following *correlation coefficient* ρ (rho)[21] that satisfies the normalization conditions.

$$\rho = 1 - \frac{6 \times SumOfSquares}{n \times (n \times n - 1)}$$

Here are the corresponding LOGO procedures:

```
To Rho :List
  Make "Sorted TreeSort :List
  Make "N Count :List
  Make "Pos 0
  Make "Chi :N * (:N * :N - 1)
  Make "SOS SumOfSquares :List :Sorted
  Output 1.0 - 6.0 * :SOS / :Chi
End

To SumOfSquares :List :Sorted
  If :List = [] [Output 0]
  Make "Pos :Pos + 1
  Make "D :Pos - Pos First :List :Sorted
```

---

[21]This coefficient is used in other disciplines as well; for example, in psychology it is known as the *Spearman* coefficient. When using this measurement, no element in the list can appear more than once.

```
    Output
       (SumOfSquares ButFirst :List :Sorted) + :D * :D
    End

    To Pos :Element :list
       If :Element = First :list [Output 1]
       Output 1 + Pos :Element ButFirst :list
    End
```

and some examples:

```
? Print Rho [7 3 4 8 9 5 2]
-.142857
? Print Rho [0 1 2 3 4 5 6 7 8 9]
1.
? Print Rho [9 8 7 6 5 4 3 2 1 0]
-1.
```

Now it is possible, with the help of the procedure TestSort, to investigate the efficiency of various methods and eventually represent the efficiency profile as it relates to ρ graphically. We leave this interesting exercise in "experimental" computer science for the reader. Other coefficients could also be defined to study other properties related to the efficiency of these methods.

18.3. Generalizing the Methods to Use Arbitrary Predicates

The procedures we have defined so far allow us only to sort numbers in increasing order; often, one would like to sort numbers in other than ascending order, such as in descending order, or in an order based on the magnitude. Furthermore, numbers are not the only elements that might need to be sorted. Other examples include:

• Letters in alphabetical order

• Words in alphabetical order

• Words according to their length

One can always sort sets of elements if an ordering relationship can be specified that takes two arbitrary elements and determines which of the two is first in the ordering.

To generalize our procedure for arbitrary predicates, we use the procedure Apply2 defined in section 23.1. It applies an arbitrary procedure to two arguments:

Example:

```
? Print Apply2 "Word "A "B
AB
```

In addition, we define some procedures, which order words (and thereby letters) according to the alphabet or according to their length.

```
To PredAlphaP :Word1 :Word2
  Output PrecedesP :Word1 :Word2 Alphabet
End

To PrecedesP :W1 :W2 :Alpha
  If :W1 = " [Output "True]
  If :W2 = " [Output "False]
  If (First :W1) = First :W2
    [Output
       PrecedesP
         ButFirst :W1
         ButFirst :W2
         :Alpha]
  If (First :W1) = First :Alpha [Output "True]
  If (First :W2) = First :Alpha [Output "False]
  Output PrecedesP :W1 :W2 ButFirst :Alpha
End

To Alphabet
  Output "ABCDEFGHIJKLMNOPQRSTUVWXYZ
End
```

We change our sorting procedures so that we allow an additional parameter and everywhere the ''>'' was used before, we use the procedure Apply2 with the additional parameter as the comparison function. Here is an example using MergeSort2

```
To MergeSort2V2 :List :Method
  If :List = [] [Output []]
  If (ButFirst :List) = [] [Output :List]
  Output
    MergeV2
      MergeSort2V2 HalfList :List :Method
      MergeSort2V2 SecondHalf :List :Method
      :Method
End

To MergeV2 :A :B :Predicate
  If :A = [] [Output :B]
  If :B = [] [Output :A]
  If Apply2 :Predicate First :A First :B
    [Output
       Sentence
         First :B
         MergeV2 :A ButFirst :B :Predicate]
  Output
    Sentence
      First :A
      MergeV2 ButFirst :A :B :Predicate
End
```

With this change we can use the procedure MergeSort2 for arbitrary predicates, for example:

```
? Print MergeSort2 [sorting is a boring job] "PredAlphaP
sorting is job boring a
```

we can even use ones that we may define after we have defined the sorting method:

```
To LongerP :A :B
   Output GreaterP Count :A Count :B
End
```

```
? Print  MergeSort2 [sorting is a boring job] "LongerP
a is job boring sorting
```

We can also redefine the alphabet that goes along with PredAlphaP:

```
To Alphabet2
   Output "0123456789ABCDEFGHIJKLMNOPQRSTUVWXYZ
End
```

```
? Print MergeSort2 [7 3 4 8 9 5 2 D G H] "PredAlphaP
H G D 9 8 7 5 4 3 2
```

Chapter 19:
Pattern Matching

In LOGO we have the ability to compare two lists to see if they are equal, no matter how they are constructed:

```
? Print EqualP [this [[is] [a]] [list]]
  (List "this [[is] [a]] [list])
true
```

Although this is a crude form of matching, what happens when we want to compare two objects that may not match exactly but may have certain salient characteristics in common? For instance, if we are looking in a large library database for a particular author, how can we be sure that the name we are looking for is the one that was used in the database?

Jerome David Salinger
Jerome Salinger
J. D. Salinger
J. Salinger

What we need is a more general matching facility, one that, instead of requiring each element to be specified exactly, allows us to specify a *pattern* that gives a general description of what we are looking for and can match several possible items. This is known as *pattern matching.*

We introduce the procedures in this chapter to extend LOGO to provide this capability. We start with simple methods of pattern matching and develop successively more complex algorithms.

These procedures are also interesting in a practical sense. On one hand, they lend themselves to a *glass-box-approach*, which allows you to study how they work by studying the code that is provided. On the other hand, you can use them for other tasks, as ready-made building blocks, without needing to understand exactly how they work (treating them as *black-boxes*).

19.1. The Methods

In all these methods, we need to deal with two types of expressions:

- The *pattern expression*, which describes, in a general form, what sorts of symbols should be matched;

- The *target expression*, a symbolic instance that we need to examine to see whether it matches the pattern.

In our LOGO implementation, these correspond to two sentences:

- The elements of the first sentence specify the *abstract* pattern using special notation.

- The second sentence is the *literal* expression to be tested.

Examples of Patterns: Examples of Targets:

```
[This is a pattern]          [This is a pattern]
[This .]                     [This too]
[? B ?]                      [There is a B here]
[?A + ?B]                    [3+4]
```

In all the examples, the target corresponds to the pattern directly to their left, the pattern *matches* the target. We discuss the exact meaning of the abstract pattern notation as we develop the various methods.

Simple Matching

Our first design decision is to use simple LOGO sentences for patterns and targets, so the simplest pattern-matching procedure that we can imagine is one that tests whether two sentences match identically:

```
To PatternMatch :Pattern :Target
  ; Version 1 - straightforward matching
  If And (:Pattern = []) (:Target = [])
    [Output "True]
  If :Pattern = [] [Output "False]
  If :Target = [] [Output "False]
  If (First :Pattern) = (First :Target)
    [Output
        PatternMatch
          ButFirst :Pattern
          ButFirst :Target]
  Output "False
End
```

This version of the Procedure `PatternMatch` tests whether the `:Pattern` agrees with the `:Target` element for element. If the program reaches a point where the next element in the `:Pattern` doesn't match the next element in the `:Target`, the result is `False`. Look at the programming techniques shown by interplay between the first line (`If And (:Pattern ...`) and next two lines. We output `False` in the second and third lines because the case where both the `:Pattern` and `:Target` were empty (and therefore equal) was handled in the first line. The procedure `PatternMatch` has the same effect as the built-in function "`=`," which can test the equality of two sentences.

Sample Runs:

```
? Print PatternMatch
      [This is an example] [This is an example]
  True
```

```
? Print PatternMatch
      [This is a pattern] [This is an expression]
False

? Print PatternMatch
      [The pattern is] [The pattern is too short]
False
```

Matching with Word Patterns

Our first extension to our trivial procedure `PatternMatch` includes the ability to match arbitrary single words denoted by a "." in the pattern.

Examples:

```
? Print PatternMatch [this . an .] [this is an example]
True
? Print PatternMatch [. . . .] [this is an example]
true
```

As the second example shows, in the extreme case the whole `:pattern` can consist of dots; the pattern in our example will "match" all sentences composed of four words.

With this method there no longer needs to be a perfect match between the `:Pattern` and the `:Target`; a "." in the `:Pattern` can match any element in the corresponding position in the `:Target`. This is done by changing the last condition (`If Or (First :Pattern ...`).

```
To PatternMatch :Pattern :Target
  ;Version 2 - matching word elements
  If And (:Pattern = []) (:Target = [])
    [Output "True]
  If :Pattern = [] [Output "False]
  If :Target = [] [Output "False]
  If Or
      (First :Pattern) = ".
      (First :Pattern) = (First :Target)
    [Output
        PatternMatch
          ButFirst :Pattern
          ButFirst :Target]
  Output "False
End
```

Multiple Word Patterns

The first two methods were restricted by having `:Pattern` and `:Target` the same length; every element of `:Pattern` corresponded to exactly one element of `:Target`. This restriction is lifted by this version since the `:Target` can contain more, or fewer, elements than `:Pattern`.

Examples:

```
? Print PatternMatch [? ?] [this works of course]
true
? Print PatternMatch [. .] [and this doesn't]
false
? Print PatternMatch
        [? any . ? be here]
        [any possibility could be here]
true
```

This version of the procedure `PatternMatch` is extended from the previous version in the following ways:

* Under the first condition: If the whole `:Pattern` has been reduced to a single question mark (which stands for 0 or more elements), the match succeeds.

* Under the next-to-last condition: If the first element of `:pattern` is a question mark, `TwoWayMatch` is called.

  The first line of `TwoWayMatch` assumes that the next element of `:Target` is not supposed to match with the question mark (or said another way, this is the case where the question mark matches zero words). If no successful match is found based on this assumption, the last line of `TwoWayMatch` comes into play. Here it is assumed that the first element of `:Target` can be "passed over" because it matches the question mark.

```
To PatternMatch :Pattern :Target
   ;Version 3 - multiple words
   If And (:Pattern = []) (:Target = [])
      [Output "True]
   If :Pattern = [] [Output "False]
   If (First :Pattern) = "?
      [Output QMarkMatch :Pattern :Target]
   If :Target = [] [Output "False]
   If Or
         (First :Pattern) = ".
         (First :Pattern) = (First :Target)
      [Output
         PatternMatch
            ButFirst :Pattern
            ButFirst :Target]
   Output "False
End

To QMarkMatch :Pattern :Target
   If :Pattern = [?] [Output "True]
   If :Target = [] [Output "False]
   Output TwoWayMatch :Pattern :Target
End

To TwoWayMatch :Pattern :Target
   If PatternMatch ButFirst :Pattern :Target
      [Output "True]
```

```
      Output PatternMatch :Pattern ButFirst :Target
End
```

An especially interesting aspect of this version and the capability provided by the "?" is shown by a selective trace of patternmatch:

```
? Print PatternMatch [? a b c ?] [a a b a b c]
PatternMatch of [? a b c ?] and [a a b a b c]
  TwoWayMatch of [? a b c ?] and [a a b a b c]
*   PatternMatch of [a b c ?] and [a a b a b c]
      PatternMatch of [b c ?] and [a b a b c]
      PatternMatch outputs false
    PatternMatch outputs false
    PatternMatch of [? a b c ?] and [a b a b c]
      TwoWayMatch of [? a b c ?] and [a b a b c]
*       PatternMatch of [a b c ?] and [a b a b c]
*         PatternMatch of [b c ?] and [b a b c]
            PatternMatch of [c ?] and [a b c]
backup      PatternMatch outputs false
backup      PatternMatch outputs false
backup  PatternMatch outputs false
try alternate
          PatternMatch of [? a b c ?] and [b a b c]
            TwoWayMatch of [? a b c ?] and [b a b c]
            PatternMatch of [a b c ?] and [b a b c]
            PatternMatch outputs false
            PatternMatch of [? a b c ?] and [a b c]
              TwoWayMatch of [? a b c ?] and [a b c]
                PatternMatch of [a b c ?] and [a b c]
                PatternMatch of [b c ?] and [b c]
                PatternMatch of [c ?] and [c]
                PatternMatch of [?] and []
                PatternMatch outputs true
              PatternMatch outputs true
            PatternMatch outputs true
          PatternMatch outputs true
          TwoWayMatch outputs true
        PatternMatch outputs true
      TwoWayMatch outputs true
    PatternMatch outputs true
  TwoWayMatch outputs true
PatternMatch outputs true
TwoWayMatch outputs true
PatternMatch outputs true
true
```

In an attempt to generate a match, sometimes the one possibility for the matching process continues successfully for awhile (see the *'s in the trace), then suddenly finds that the match fails. If this occurs, the process must backtrack to the last decision point and try out the second possibility. This backtracking (marked in the trace by backup) occurs in the second call to PatternMatch within TwoWayMatch and comes about as a result of the recursive structure of the program. TwoWayMatch can also be interpreted as using the first call to PatternMatch as a "test-call," and if it fails, a further attempt is made with different arguments.

Incidentally, `PatternMatch` can also be viewed as a generalization of the frequently used procedure `MemberP`, where:

```
PatternMatch [? word ?] :list
```

corresponds to:

```
MemberP "word :list
```

Remembering Simple Matches

The matching methods presented so far determine only whether a correspondence between `:Pattern` and `:Target` can be found; they provide no information about which elements of the `:Target` correspond to the "dots" and question marks when a successful match occurs.

So, next we add the capability to associate variable names with the special character ".". When a match is found for a special character, the element from the target that matches is assigned to the variable associated with that special character. If there are multiple occurrences of a variable in the pattern, they all have to match the same thing.

This is the syntax we use: If a pattern element begins with a dot or a question mark, the rest of the word (without the special character) is taken to be the name of the associated variable.

An example of how this would work:

```
? EraseName Names²²
? Print PatternMatch [.a plus .b is .c] [3 plus 4 is 7]
true
? PrintOutName Names
"a is 3
"b is 4
"c is 7
```

Because the match was successful, the name `:a`, `:b`, and `:c` have the values of the matching elements assigned to them.

The necessary changes and new procedures:

```
To PatternMatch :Pattern :Target
  ;Version 4 - remembering single word matches
  If And (:Pattern = []) (:Target = [])
    [Output "True]
  If :Pattern = [] [Output "False]
  If (First :Pattern) = "?
    [Output QMarkMatch :Pattern :Target]
  If :Target = [] [Output "False]
```

---

²²`EraseName` may be `Erase` or something else in your implementation. If your implementation does not have this facility at all, you can `Make "variable "`

```
    If Or
        (First :Pattern) = ".
        (First :Pattern) = (First :Target)
      [Output
          PatternMatch
            ButFirst :Pattern
            ButFirst :Target]
    If (First First :Pattern) = ".
      [Output DotVarMatch :Pattern :Target]
    Output "False
  End

  To DotVarMatch :Pattern :Target
    If Not NameP ButFirst First :Pattern
      [Make ButFirst First :Pattern "]
    If Not (Thing ButFirst First :Pattern) = "
      [Output CompareDotMatch :Pattern :Target]
    Make ButFirst First :Pattern First :Target
    If PatternMatch
        ButFirst :Pattern
        ButFirst :Target
      [Output "True]
    Make ButFirst First :Pattern "
    Output "False
  End

  To CompareDotMatch :Pattern :Target
    If EqualP
        Thing ButFirst First :Pattern
        First :Target
      [Output
          PatternMatch
            ButFirst :Pattern
            ButFirst :Target]
    Output "False
  End
```

In the third (logical) line of DotVarMatch, the variable specified in the pattern is provisionally assigned the first element of :Target.

This first couple of lines only come into play fully if the name associated with a special character has already been associated with a value during the matching process. The following example illustrates the problem:

```
? Print PatternMatch [.a .b .a] [here and here]
true
? Print PatternMatch [.a .b .a] [here and there]
false
```

In the first example, a is assigned the value "here and b is assigned the value "and. Because the first .a in the pattern would cause a to be assigned the first "here and then later the second .a would cause another value to be assigned to a, overwriting the first we need to check whether a variable already has a value assigned to it (other than the empty word). If this is the case, then CompareDotMatch is called to test whether the first element of :Target agrees with the value already assigned to the variable.

The second example shows that it is reasonable not to allow the value of a variable to be overwritten. Otherwise, the a would ''match'' different elements of :Target, in this example "here at one point and "there at another.

Also, we use the convention here that if a variable does not exist or if its value is the empty word, then it has not yet been used in the pattern-matching process. Thus, if we assign the empty word to a variable (see first and fifth lines of DotVarMatch), that is the same (from the point of view of this program) as erasing that variable. We do this because some implementations we have worked with did not have the ability to erase variables. The drawback of this approach is that targets that contain the empty word will not match properly:

```
? Print PatternMatch [.a .b .a] (Sentence " "this "that)
true
? Print :a
that
```

We do not feel that this will cause real problems in general use.

Further examples:

```
? EraseName Names
? Print PatternMatch [.x + .y] [a + b]
true
? EraseName Names
? If PatternMatch [compute the sum of .a and .b]
                  [compute the sum of 3 and 4]
    [Print :a + :b]
7
```

The last example already shows how the values assigned to variables might be used following a successful match.

One problem with this system occurs when the name of the pattern-matching variable is the same as the name of some input place holder in one of the active procedures. For example:

```
? Print PatternMatch [.pattern] [this]
false
? Print PatternMatch [.pat] [this]
true
```

When CompareDotMatch is called the place holder :pattern has the value [.pattern] so the variable that is accessed in the first line is pattern, and instead of Thing finding the value of the *global* variable, it finds the value of the place holder. The same problem exists for .target, as well as the name of any place holders and local variables for any active procedures.

Remembering Multiple Word Matches

The variables provided for in the last version can hold exactly one element of :Target. This restriction is removed by this version: A variable preceded by a question mark can be assigned a segment (i.e., arbitrarily many elements from :Target).

The new procedures:

```
To PatternMatch :Pattern :Target
   ;Version 5 : remembering multiple word matches
   If And :Pattern = [] :Target = [] [Output "True]
   If :Pattern = [] [Output "False]
   If (First :Pattern) = "?
     [Output QMarkMatch :Pattern :Target]
   If (First First :Pattern) = "?
     [Output
         QmarkVarMatch :Pattern :Target Count :Target]
   If :Target = [] [Output "False]
   If Or
       (First :Pattern) = ".
       (First :Pattern) = (First :Target)
     [Output
         PatternMatch
           ButFirst :Pattern
           ButFirst :Target]
   If (First First :Pattern) = ".
     [Output DotVarMatch :Pattern :Target]
   Output "False
End

To QMarkVarMatch :Pattern :Target :Length
   If :Length < 0 [Output "False]
   Local "VariableName
   Make "VariableName ButFirst First :Pattern
   If Not NameP :VariableName [Make :VariableName "]
   If Not (Thing :VariableName) = "
     [Output
         CompareQMarkMatch
           :Pattern
           :Target
           Count Thing :VariableName]
   Make :VariableName FirstN :Length :Target
   If PatternMatch
       ButFirst :Pattern
       ButFirstN :Length :Target
     [Output "True]
   Make :VariableName "
   Output QMarkVarMatch :Pattern :Target :Length - 1
End

To CompareQMarkMatch :Pattern :Target :Length
   If EqualP
       Thing ButFirst First :Pattern
       FirstN :Length :Target
     [Output
         PatternMatch
           ButFirst :Pattern
           ButFirstN :Length :Target]
   Output "False
End
```

Version 5 is extended with respect to version 4 in that if a ?-variable is found,
the procedure QMarkVarMatch is called.

QMarkVarMatch resembles the procedure DotVarMatch, which was introduced in the last section; it differs in that it has one additional argument. As in DotVarMatch, QMarkVarMatch provisionally assigns the first :Length elements of :Target to the appropriate variable. If the rest of the matching process (using the remaining portion of :Target) completes successfully, "True is returned and the variable keeps its value.

If the rest of matching process fails, then the variable is set to the empty word (which is used to indicate that no match has occurred for that variable, yet), and another attempt is made with the value of :Length reduced by 1. The procedure outputs "False if :Length is less than 0. If the variable matches 0 words, it contains the empty list, showing that the match was successful but that element matches no words.

CompareQMarkMatch is the same as CompareDotMatch except that it uses FirstN and ButFirstN instead of First and ButFirst.

In contrast to variables used by DotVarMatch, the variables used by QMarkVarMatch contain *lists* instead of *words*.

```
Examples:
? EraseName Names
? Print
    PatternMatch
      [( ?X ) * ( ?Y )]
      [( A + B ) * ( A - B )]
True
? Print :X
A + B
? Print :Y
A - B
```

In using the ?-variables, care should be taken that unambiguous patterns are formulated; the following example *is* ambiguous:

```
? Print PatternMatch [?A ?B] [( A + B )]
PatternMatch of [?A ?B] and [( A + B )]
  QMarkVarMatch of [?A ?B] and [( A + B )] and 5
    PatternMatch of [?B] and []
    PatternMatch outputs False
    QMarkVarMatch of [?A ?B] and [( A + B )] and 4
      PatternMatch of [?B] and [)]
        QMarkVarMatch of [?B] and [)] and 1
          PatternMatch of [] and []
          PatternMatch outputs True
        QMarkVarMatch outputs True
      PatternMatch outputs True
    QMarkVarMatch outputs True
  QMarkVarMatch outputs True
PatternMatch outputs True
True

? Print :A
( A + B
```

```
? Print :B
)
```

If ambiguous patterns are formulated, then the method (as it is defined) chooses the longest possible match for the first ?-variable. This is because QMarkVarMatch starts with the largest possible value of :Length (i.e., Count :Target).

A further example:

Here is a little procedure, which takes infix arithmetic expressions and produces prefix arithmetic expressions.

```
To Prefix :Infix
  Local "A
  Local "B
  If (ButFirst :Infix) = [] [Output :Infix]
  If PatternMatch [?A + ?B] :Infix
    [Output
        (Sentence "+ Prefix :A " " Prefix :B " ")]
  If PatternMatch [?A - ?B] :Infix
    [Output
        (Sentence "- Prefix :A " " Prefix :B " ")]
  If PatternMatch [?A * ?B] :Infix
    [Output
        (Sentence "* Prefix :A " " Prefix :B " ")]
  If PatternMatch [?A / ?B] :Infix
    [Output
        (Sentence "/ Prefix :A " " Prefix :B " ")]
  Print [Wrong syntax]
  TopLevel
End
```

The expressions that can be converted using this procedure are restricted to the four basic arithmetic operations with no parentheses.

Sample runs:

```
? Print Prefix [A + B]
+ A B
? Print Prefix [A + B * C / A - D]
+ A - * B / C A D
```

With tracing turned on:

```
? Print Prefix [A * A + B * B + C * C]
Prefix of [A * A + B * B + C * C]
  Prefix of [A * A + B * B]
    Prefix of [A * A]
      Prefix of [A]
      Prefix outputs [A]
      Prefix of [A]
      Prefix outputs [A]
    Prefix outputs [* A A]
```

```
      Prefix of [B * B]
        Prefix of [B]
        Prefix outputs [B]
        Prefix of [B]
        Prefix outputs [B]
      Prefix outputs [* B B]
    Prefix outputs [+ * A A * B B]
    Prefix of [C * C]
      Prefix of [C]
      Prefix outputs [C]
      Prefix of [C]
      Prefix outputs [C]
    Prefix outputs [* C C]
  Prefix outputs [+ + * A A * B B * C C]
  + + * A A * B B * C C
```

Matches That Use Predicates

Now we proceed to a type of pattern that is principally different from those we
have studied so far.   If we wanted to specify that the next element in the
:Target needs to meet some condition (for example, it must be a number) to
match, the methods presented so far do not give us a way to do this.   By
extending our "pattern-matching language" further, we can allow predicates to
be associated with pattern elements that specify conditions the matching
elements of :Target need to meet.

```
To PatternMatch :Pattern :Target
   ;Version 6 - using simple predicates
   If And :Pattern = [] :Target = [] [Output "True]
   If :Pattern = [] [Output "False]
   If (First :Pattern) = "?
      [Output QMarkMatch :Pattern :Target]
   If (First First :Pattern) = "?
      [Output
         QMarkVarMatch :Pattern :Target Count :Target]
   If :Target = [] [Output "False]
   If Or
         (First :Pattern) = ".
         (First :Pattern) = (First :Target)
      [Output
         PatternMatch
            ButFirst :Pattern
            ButFirst :Target]
   If (First First :Pattern) = ".
      [Output DotVarMatch :Pattern :Target]
   If (FirstN 2 First :Pattern) = "&.
      [Output MatchPred :Pattern :Target]
   Output "False
End
```

```
To DotPredMatch :Pattern :Target
   If Apply
      ButFirst ButFirst First :Pattern
      First :Target
   [Output
      PatternMatch
         ButFirst :Pattern
         ButFirst :Target]
   Output "False
End
```

The next to last line of this version allows for all pattern elements that begin with the character sequence ''&.'' to be treated as predicates that the element to be matched in :Target must fulfill. Whether the next element of :Target meets the condition is determined by MatchPred. To do so, the procedure Apply from section 23.1 is used, which applies an arbitrary procedure (which in our case is always a predicate) to an argument. The result of Apply is the result of this predicate being run with the second argument as its input.

Some Examples:

```
? Print
    PatternMatch
       [. &.NumberP . . .] [The 7 is a number]
True
? Print
    PatternMatch
       [&.WordP . . .] [Seven is a number]²³
True
```

Multiple Word Predicates

Just as we generalized version 2 to version 3 and version 4 to version 5 to allow multiple words instead of single words, we can extend version 6 to allow the predicate to be applied to several elements. We use the syntax &?<predicate-name> to specify predicates that can be applied to several elements from :Target (see the next to last line of this version of PatternMatch).

```
To PatternMatch :Pattern :Target
   ;Version 7 - multiple word predicates
   If And (:Pattern = []) (:Target = [])
   [Output "True]
   If :Pattern = [] [Output "False]
   If (First :Pattern) = "?
   [Output QMarkMatch :Pattern :Target]
   If (First First :Pattern) = "?
   [Output
      QMarkVarMatch :Pattern :Target Count :Target]
   If (FirstN 2 First :Pattern) = "&?
   [Output
      QMarkPredMatch :Pattern :Target Count :Target]
```

---

²³Note: The pattern matcher doesn't ''understand'' the sentences that it is matching; this example is *not* the same as NumberP "Seven!!

```
        If :Target = [] [Output "False]
        If Or
            (First :Pattern) = ".
            (First :Pattern) = (First :Target)
          [Output
             PatternMatch
               ButFirst :Pattern
               ButFirst :Target]
        If (First First :Pattern) = ".
          [Output DotVarMatch :Pattern :Target]
        If (FirstN 2 First :Pattern) = "&.
          [Output DotPredMatch :Pattern :Target]
        Output "False
      End

      To QMarkPredMatch :Pattern :Target :N
        If :N < 0 [Output "False]
        If Apply
           ButFirst ButFirst First :Pattern
           FirstN :N :Target
          [Output QMarkOrMatch :Pattern :Target :N]
        Output QMarkPredMatch :Pattern :Target :N - 1
      End

      To QMarkOrMatch :Pattern :Target :N
        If PatternMatch
           ButFirst :Pattern
           ButFirstN :N :Target
          [Output "True]
        Output QMarkPredMatch :Pattern :Target :N - 1
      End
```

QMarkPredMatch tests whether the predicate holds for the first :N elements of :Target (:N begins with the value Count :Target. If so, an attempt is made to find a match for the rest of the elements in the :Pattern (using QMarkOrMatch). If either the predicate or the continued match is not successful, this process is repeated with the value of :N reduced by one (the last line of QMarkPredMatch or QMarkOrMatch).

An example: We define a predicate that tests to see whether a symbolic expression is parenthesized:

```
To ParenExpressionP :Input
  Output PatternMatch [( ? )] :Input
End
```

This predicate can be used to recognize a particular form of expressions:

```
? Print PatternMatch
  [( &?ParenExpressionP * &?ParenExpressionP )]
  [( ( A + B ) * ( A - B ) )]
True
```

Combining Predicates and Variables

This version of `PatternMatch` in some sense combines the capabilities available in version 4 and version 6:

- A variable can be specified in the pattern element, which will have the matching element from `:Target` assigned to it.

- In addition, a predicate must hold for this element.

The syntax we use for this kind of pattern element is:

&<predicate>.<variable>

Some examples:

```
? EraseName Names
? Print PatternMatch
   [?A ?B &NumberP.C ?B ?A]  [1 2 3 4 5 6 3 4 5 1 2]
True
? Print :C
6
? EraseName Names
? Print PatternMatch
   [?A &NumberP.B ?A ?C]  [A B C D 777 A B C D E F G]
True

To PatternMatch :Pattern :Target
   ; Version 8 - combining predicates and variables
   If And :Pattern = [] :Target = [] [Output "True]
   If :Pattern = [] [Output "False]
   If (First :Pattern) = "?
     [Output QMarkMatch :Pattern :Target]
   If (First First :Pattern) = "?
     [Output
        QMarkVarMatch :Pattern :Target Count :Target]
   If (FirstN 2 First :Pattern) = "&?
     [Output
        QMarkPredMatch :Pattern :Target Count :Target]
   If :Target = [] [Output "False]
   If Or
       (First :Pattern) = ".
       (First :Pattern) = (First :Target)
     [Output
        PatternMatch
           ButFirst :Pattern
           ButFirst :Target]
   If (First First :Pattern) = ".
     [Output DotVarMatch :Pattern :Target]
   If (FirstN 2 First :Pattern) = "&.
     [Output DotPredMatch :Pattern :Target]
```

```
If And
    (First First :Pattern) = "&
    (MemberP ". ButFirst First :Pattern)
[Output
    PredVarDotMatch
        :Pattern
        :Target
        UpToChar ". ButFirst First :Pattern
        AfterChar ". First :Pattern]
Output "False
End

To PredVarDotMatch :Pattern :Target :Pred :Var
If Not Apply :Pred First :Target
    [Output "False]
If Not NameP :Var [Make :Var "]
If Not Thing :Var = "
    [Output
        CompareVarDotMatch :Pattern :Target :Var]
Make :Var First :Target
If PatternMatch
        ButFirst :Pattern
        ButFirst :Target
    [Output "True]
Make :Var "
Output "False
End

To CompareVarDotMatch :Pattern :Target :Var
If Thing :Var = First :Target
    [Output
        PatternMatch
            ButFirst :Pattern
            ButFirst :Target]
Output "False
End
```

This form of a pattern element is handled by the last line of this version of
PatternMatch, where the procedures UpToChar and AfterChar are
used to separate out the "predicate" and "variable" parts. These procedures are
defined in appendix III.

The first line of PredVarDotMatch determines whether the first element of
:Target fulfills the predicate. In the second line, if the variable already has a
value, CompareVarDotMatch is used to see if this value agrees with the
first value of :Target. The rest of the procedure corresponds to
DotVarMatch.

Putting It All Together

The last extension to our pattern matcher is to allow ?-variables whose matching
can be restricted by predicates. We use the following syntax for this type of
pattern.

&<predicate>?<variable>

This is how our final version looks:

```
To PatternMatch :Pattern :Target
; Version 9 - putting it all together
If And :Pattern = [] :Target = [] [Output "True]
If :Pattern = [] [Output "False]
If (First :Pattern) = "?
   [Output QMarkMatch :Pattern :Target]
If (First First :Pattern) = "?
   [Output
      QMarkVarMatch :Pattern :Target Count :Target]
If (FirstN 2 First :Pattern) = "&?
   [Output
      QMarkPredMatch :Pattern :Target Count :Target]
If And
      (First First :Pattern) = "&
      (MemberP "? ButFirst First :Pattern)
   [Output
      PredVarQmarkMatch
         :Pattern
         :Target
         UpToChar "? ButFirst First :Pattern
         AfterChar "? First :Pattern
         Count :Target]
If :Target = [] [Output "False]
If Or
      (First :Pattern) = ".
      (First :Pattern) = (First :Target)
   [Output
      PatternMatch
         ButFirst :Pattern
         ButFirst :Target]
If (First First :Pattern) = ".
   [Output DotVarMatch :Pattern :Target]
If (FirstN 2 First :Pattern) = "&.
   [Output DotPredMatch :Pattern :Target]
If And
      (First First :Pattern) = "&
      (MemberP ". ButFirst First :Pattern)
   [Output
      PredVarDotMatch
         :Pattern
         :Target
         UpToChar ". ButFirst First :Pattern
         AfterChar ". First :Pattern]
Output "False
End

To PredVarQMarkMatch :Pattern :Target :Pred :Var :N
If :N < 0 [Output "False]
If Not NameP :Var [Make :Var "]
```

```
      If Not (Thing :Var) = "
        [Output
            CompareQMarkPredMatch
              :Pattern
              :Target
              :Pred
              :Var
              Count Thing :Var]
      If Not Apply :Pred FirstN :N :Target
        [Output
            PredVarQMarkMatch
              :Pattern
              :Target
              :Pred
              :Var
              :N - 1]
      Make :Var FirstN :N :Target
      If PatternMatch
          ButFirst :Pattern
          ButFirstN :N :Target
        [Output "True]
      Make :Var "
      Output
        PredVarQMarkMatch
          :Pattern
          :Target
          :Pred
          :Var
          :N - 1
    End

    To CompareQMarkPredMatch :Pattern :Target :Pred :Var :N
      If And
          (Thing :Var) = FirstN :N :Target
          (Apply :Pred FirstN :N :Target)
        [Output
            PatternMatch
              ButFirst :Pattern
              ButFirstN :N :Target]
      Output "False
    End
```

It is not difficult to recognize that the procedures PredVarQMarkMatch
and CompareQMarkMatch are derived from QMarkVarMatch and
QMarkPredMatch

Some examples:

(1) Using the predicate LP3:

```
    To LP3 :S
      Output Count :S = 3
    End
```

```
? Print PatternMatch
      [&LP3?Y ? &LP3?X &LP3?Y]
      [A B C D E F G A B C]
True
? Show :x
[e f g]
? Show :y
[a b c]
```

(2) Using the predicate `ParenExpressionP`

```
To ParenExpressionP :Input
   Output PatternMatch [( ? )] :Input
End

? Print
  PatternMatch
    [( &ParenExpressionP?A * &ParenExpressionP?B )]
    [( ( a + b ) * ( a - b ) )]
true
? Show :A
[( a + b )]
? Show :B
[( a - b )]
```

Note that the name of the predicate itself may not contain a "?".

Perhaps it should be mentioned that the program presented here could be improved in terms of both size and speed. Some procedures are redundant and could be combined (e.g., `CompareDotMatch` and `CompareVarDot-Match`). However, what we have attempted to show is that a pattern matcher can be built up in a stepwise fashion. In an effort to make the building blocks as obvious as possible, we have not allowed efficiency to be a major concern, since it is not relevant to the goal at hand.

19.2. Summary of the Pattern Syntax

Here is a table that summarizes the pattern elements and examples of actual target sentences:

Constant	Constant
.	an arbitrary element.
?	arbitrarily many elements (0, 1, 2, ...).
.variable	an arbitrary element that is assigned to the global variable *variable*.
?variable	arbitrarily many elements (0, 1, 2, 3, ...) that will be assigned to the global variable *variable*. If several matches are possible, the longest match will be made.
&.predicate	an arbitrary element for which the predicate *predicate* must hold.

&?predicate   arbitrarily many elements for which the predicate *predicate* must hold collectively.

&predicate.variable

         an arbitrary element for which the predicate *predicate* must hold and that will be assigned to the global variable *variable*.

&predicate?variable

         arbitrarily many elements for which the predicate *predicate* must hold collectively and that will be assigned to the global variable *variable*.

19.3. Possible Extensions

Although the pattern-matching methods shown here are powerful and straightforward, there are certainly some further capabilities that could be added and improvements that could be made; here are few to think about:

- The external representation of the pattern elements could be improved, so that instead of using **&Pred?A**, something like **(Variable A, Condition Pred, arbitrarily many)**, or **A (Pred, ?)** could be used. This could be done using a preprocessor to convert it to an internal representation.

- For some patterns, there are several possibilities for a match; **PatternMatch [?A ?B] [A B C D]** could potentially represent the following relationship:

:A			:B		
A	B	C	D		
A	B		C	D	
A			B	C	D

Our methods only come up with *one* of these, namely the first. Perhaps some type of error checking to show that a pattern was ambiguous, or some means of returning the information for ambiguous matches could be developed.

- Often a match fails on only one or a few of the pattern elements. Each pattern matching method is useful, and partial information can be helpful, as well. It is sometimes desirable to make the successful portions of an unsuccessful match available.

- We could define a pattern element that allows the specification of predicates to hold for each element of an arbitrarily long segment. This could also be combined with a predicate that holds for the pattern as a whole.

19.4. Possible Uses

Pattern-matching methods are useful for recognizing and translating symbolic structures. One example of this was our program that transformed prefix notation to infix notation. Pattern matching could also be used to differentiate and integrate mathematical expressions symbolically. The work in section 20.2 could make further use of the translation capabilities of these pattern-matching methods to convert seminatural language into computer language. This could be used, for example, to make "front-ends," which would allow the dialog between the human and the computer to be somewhat more "user-friendly."

Exercise

A Doctor Program

The dialogue shown next occurred between a computer program named ELIZA [Weizenbaum 65] and a person (the sentences typed in by the person are **this font** with the ELIZA's answers in *this font*. You could imagine that this was a dialogue between a Psychiatrist and a patient. The following question can be studied with this program:

- What characteristics does the dialogue have? Why is it relatively simple to generate the responses in this dialogue with a computer program?

- Can we use the pattern-matching "language" developed in this chapter to implement such a program? How should one proceed? What problems might surface?

Men are all alike.
In what ways?
They're always bugging us about something or the other.
Can you think of a specific example?
well, my boyfriend made me come here!
My boyfriend made me come here?
He says that I am depressed much of the time
I'm sorry to hear that you are depressed.
It's true, I'm unhappy
Do you think that coming here will help you not to be unhappy?
I need some help, that much seems certain
What would it mean to you if you got some help?
Perhaps I could learn to get along with my mother
Tell me more about your family
My mother does everything for me
Who else in your family does everything for you?
My father
Your father.
You are a little like my father
What similarities do you see?
You are not very aggressive, but I think you don't like the fact that I noticed that.

What leads you to think that I am not very aggressive?
You don't argue with me
But why do you believe that I don't argue with you?
You are afraid of me
Does the thought of me being afraid of you amuse you?
My father was afraid of everything
What else comes to mind when you think of your father?
Bullies
*Does that have anything to do with the fact that your
    boyfriend made you come here?*
...

Chapter 20:

Formal Languages and Grammars

20.1. Introduction

The concept of formal languages and grammars plays a central role in linguistics, computer science, and mathematics. Working with grammars requires that we employ methods from all these fields. At the same time, this problem domain serves as a starting point for solutions to a multitude of problems in many diverse disciplines.

A formal language is a language that can be described by a formal grammar. An entire hierarchy of formal languages can be described, along with the types of theoretical machines that are required to recognize or generate them (see figure 20–1).

Type-0 Languages

= recursively enumerable languages

= languages accepted by finite state
machine with two stacks

∪

Recursive Languages

∪

Type-1 Languages

= context sensitive languages

∪

Type-2 Languages

= context free languages

= languages accepted by non-deterministic
finite state machines with one stack

∪

Type-3 Languages

= regular languages
= languages accepted by finite state
machines with no stacks

Figure 20–1: A Hierarchy of Formal Languages

In this chapter we address only two classes of languages: regular languages (section 20.2) and context-free languages (section 20.3).

In the first section we focus on the essential and leave out technical programming subtleties unless they are necessary for a basic understanding. In the second section, in addition to presenting alternate representations of languages in the computer, we also touch on a basic concept in computer science, the equivalence of programs and data.

In both sections we present a series of programs that deal with grammars:

- Interactive construction (definition) of a grammar,

- Generation of sentences of a grammar once it has been defined,

- Definition of some example grammars (for arithmetic expressions and Roman numerals) and extension of existing ones (incorporating classes of words)

- Recognition of sentences with respect to membership in a language defined by a grammar. (In section 20.3 we also show how pattern matching with a context-free grammar can be used to recognize sentences of a language.)

20.2. Regular Languages

Figure 20–1 shows that regular languages are those languages that are generated/recognized by a finite state machine. A finite state machine can be represented in different ways. One way is to draw a graph with nodes and arrows, where the arrows are labeled with elements of the language. These arrows correspond to transitions between states (nodes) that occur when the language element is seen. These are called transition graphs.

Another way to represent this information is by specifying:

- A set of states (these correspond to the nodes of the graph)

- A (set of) distinguished starting state(s) (marked with a "-" in the transition graph)

- A (set of) final, or accepting state(s) (marked with a "+" in the transition graph)

- A set of transition rules (these correspond to arrows in the transition graph)

Both of these formalisms have equivalent expressive power.

Interactive Construction of a Grammar

As an example, we first choose the transition graph shown in figure 20–2.

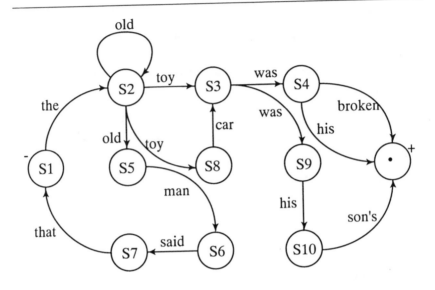

Figure 20–2: A Transition Graph for a Few English-like Phrases

The transition rules of finite state machines can also be represented using production rules as follows (brackets surround parts that are optional):

$$State_i \rightarrow Word\ State_j \ldots [Word\ State_1 \ldots]$$

Explanation: If a finite state machine finds itself in state S_i, the production rule for that state is triggered. This consists of at least two parts, a word, which will be added to the sentence being constructed, and the name of the next state S_j. It is possible for several of these pairs to be given.

The following two procedures allow the preceding grammar to be built:

```
To BuildAGrammar
   Print [Specify the next production rule :]
   GenerateDataStructure ReadList
   BuildAGrammar
End

To GenerateDataStructure :Input
   Make First :Input ButFirst :Input
End
```

```
? BuildAGrammar
Specify the next production rule:
S1 the S2
Specify the next production rule:
S2 old S2 toy S3 old S5 toy S8
Specify the next production rule:
S3 was S4 was S9
Specify the next production rule:
S4 broken . his .
Specify the next production rule:
S5 man S6
Specify the next production rule:
S6 said S7
Specify the next production rule:
S7 that S1
Specify the next production rule:
S8 car S3
Specify the next production rule:
S9 his S10
Specify the next production rule:
S10 son's .
```

A global data structure will be constructed internally, using LOGO names (one could also use property lists):

```
"S1 is [the S2]
"S2 is [old S2 toy S3 old S5 old S8]
```

and so forth.

Generating Sentences of the Grammar

Syntactically correct sentences, which are contained in the language defined by this grammar, may be generated by starting at the initial state S1 and running through the various states until a "." is found. If a production has several successor states, one of them will be chosen at random.

Examples:

```
? Repeat 3 [Print GenerateSentence "S1]
the old man said that the toy car was his
the toy was broken
the toy car was his
```

GenerateSentence generates one sentence by running through the states of the finite state machine:

```
To GenerateSentence :State
  Local "NextState
  Test EndStateP :State
  IfTrue [Output []]
  Make "NextState Choose NextRule :State
  Output
    Sentence
      First :NextState
      GenerateSentence Last :NextState
End
```

`PeriodP` defines the end condition.

```
To EndStateP :State
  Output :State = ".
End
```

`NextRule` gets the entire right-hand side of the production rule, given the left-hand side:

```
To NextRule :LeftHandSide
  Output Thing :LeftHandSide
End
```

`Choose` selects an element from the right-hand side of a rule. Each pair on the right-hand side of a rule is treated as a unit, such that `NthPair` extracts a pair based on the random number generated by `Random`.

```
? Print Thing "S2
old S2 toy S3 old S5 toy S8
? Print Choose Thing "S2
toy S8

To Choose :RightHandSide
  Output
    NthPair
      :RightHandSide
      Random (Count :RightHandSide) / 2
End

To NthPair :List :Number
  Test :Number = 0
  IfTrue
    [Output Sentence First :List First ButFirst :List]
  Output
    NthPair ButFirst ButFirst :List (:Number - 1)
End
```

Further Examples:

```
? Repeat 3 [Print GenerateSentence "S1]
the toy car was his son's
the old man said that the toy was his son's
the old toy car was his
```

Extension of Grammars: Inclusion of Word Categories

In moving from one state to the next in a finite state machine, it is not usually particular words that are of interest; instead, the class of the word is what is important (e.g., nouns, verbs, etc.). This suggests extending the system by building the finite state machine described in figure 20–3.

The corresponding grammar as data structures:

```
"S1 is [<article> S2 <name> S3]
"S2 is [<adjective> S2 <noun> S3]
"S3 is [<preposition> S4 <auxiliaryverb> S6
        <verb> S7 <verb> .]
"S4 is [<article> S5 <name> S3]
```

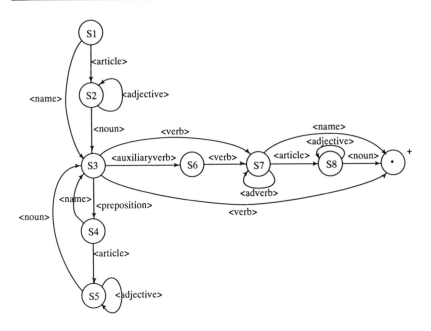

Figure 20–3: A More General Version of an English Grammar

```
"S5 is [<adjective> S5 <noun> S3]
"S6 is [<verb> S7]
"S7 is [<adverb> S7 <article> S8 <name> .]
"S8 is [<adjective> S8 <noun> .]
". is [**]
```

Furthermore, a simple dictionary for each of the categories is needed:

```
"<noun> is [man boy girl student house computer horse
                woman president]
"<name> is [John Angie Dieter George Hal]
"<article> is [a the this]
"<adjective> is [old nice smart crummy dark yellow]
"<adverb> is [tomorrow today yesterday slowly well]
"<preposition> is [in out with at on under of]
"<auxiliaryverb> is [has will should]
"<verb> is [talks looks writes likes plays is eats]
```

To generate sentences from this grammar, we need to make only a few minimal changes to the procedures in the previous section. In the last line of `GenerateSentence`, instead of simply using the first element of the right-hand side as the next word in the sentence, the word needs to be selected from the corresponding category (using `ChooseOne`):

```
To GenerateSentenceV2 :State
  Local "NextState
  Test PeriodP :State
  IfTrue [Output []]
  Make "NextState Choose NextRule :State
  Output
    Sentence
      ChooseOne First :NextState
      GenerateSentenceV2 ButFirst :NextState
End

To ChooseOne :Category
  Output
    NthElement
    (1 + Random Count Thing :Category)
    Thing :Category
End
```

Nth is described in appendix III.

A test run yields the following sentences:

```
? Repeat 3 [Print GenerateSentenceV2 "S1]
a crummy house looks the smart nice boy
the president has is well Angie
a horse talks
```

Obviously, a little more work is needed to be able to generate more acceptable sentences (in terms of correct syntax). The system needs to be more selective in the choice of words and needs to differentiate based on the case of a word. Among other things the system needs to:

- Ensure that the noun and verb are both singular or both plural.

- Use the present tense form of the verb (S3 → S7) or the infinitive form (after an auxiliary verb; S6 → S7).

- Select transitive (S3 → S7) versus intransitive (S3 → .) verbs.

The extension to distinguish the infinitive form from the present tense could look like this:

- Change the production rule:

    ```
    "S6 is [<infinitiveverb> S7]
    ```

- Add another category:

    ```
    "<infinitiveverb> is
      [talk look write like play be eat]
    ```

Examples:

```
? Repeat 3 [Print GenerateSentenceV2 "s1]
hal out a computer should look angie
george writes today the old horse
the computer will eat a horse
```

As this shows, there is still much work that is needed to avoid sentences that are incorrect in real english. Generation of sentences that would make sense would require a semantic component, as well. However, in this chapter we are more concerned with the general principles of grammars, which are used more for the specification of syntax than semantics.

One possibility that deviates from our present subject a little is to have a *morphology program* that takes the basic form of a word and generates the appropriate form based on case, tense, number, and so forth (see chapters 31 and 32).

An extension towards *augmented transition networks* [Woods 70] would be to introduce new states that represent complete subparts of a sentence. This allows more complex levels to be represented (these parallel levels of structure are characteristic of augmented transition networks). Figure 20–4 shows this in the context of our finite state machine:

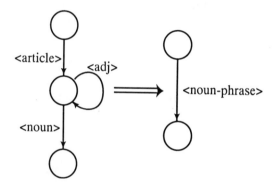

Figure 20–4: Combinations of Complex Structures

Some Examples of Application

Roman Numerals

As we have defined our `GenerateSentence` and our mechanism for storing the rules, there can be only one accepting state, which is represented by a ".". This is not really a limitation of finite state machines, so we can either rewrite our procedures or we can make use of a trick, which entails creating a "null transition," an artificial rule for a transition that can take place without generating any output. A small change still needs to be made to allow procedures to be evaluated that generate the symbols instead of looking them up in a variable.

The following grammar generates the roman numerals up to 200 with the aid of the (artificial) production rule `Nothing`, which moves from one state to another, without generating a character.

```
"S1 is [&C S1 &L S3 &X S2 &V S8 &I S7 &Nothing .]
"S2 Is [&C S6 &L S6 &X S5 &V S8 &I S7 &Nothing .]
"S3 Is [&X S4 &V S8 &I S7 &Nothing .]
"S4 Is [&X S5 &V S8 &I S7 &Nothing .]
"S5 Is [&X S6 &V S8 &I S7 &Nothing .]
"S6 Is [&V S8 &I S7 &Nothing .]
"S7 Is [&X S11 &V S11 &I S10 &Nothing .]
"S8 Is [&I S9 &Nothing .]
"S9 Is [&I S10 &Nothing .]
"S10 Is [&I S11 &Nothing .]
"S11 Is [Nothing .]
```

By modifying GenerateSentence again, we can add the ability to call a procedure whenever the element of the rule starts with the "&" character. With the following procedures syntactically correct roman numerals can be generated.

```
To GenerateSentenceV3 :State
  Local "NextState
  Test EndStateP :State
  IfTrue [Output []]
  Make "NextState Choose NextRule :State
  If (First First :NextState) = "&
    [Output
        Sentence Run ButFirst First :NextState
          GenerateSentenceV3 Last :NextState]
  Output
    Sentence ChooseOne First :NextState
      GenerateSentenceV3 Last :NextState
End

To C
  Output "C
End

To L
  Output "L
End

To X
  Output "X
End

To V
  Output "V
End

To I
  Output "I
End
```

Examples:

```
? Repeat 4 [GenerateSentenceV3 "S1]
X L
C X C V I I
C I X
L I V
```

Arithmetic Expressions

```
? Repeat 3 [GenerateSentence "S1]
64
( 30 * ( 94 * 32 ) )
23 + ( 98 )
```

This example requires care in generating the correct number of parentheses.

Analysis of Sentences

In contrast to generating sentences using a grammar, we now consider the opposite problem:

> Given an arbitrary sentence, does it belong to the language defined by a particular grammar?

To determine this, we use the following methods:

(1) We begin with state S1 and check whether the first word of the sentence matches the word A2 or belongs to the corresponding category.

Example: S1 → A2 S2 A3 S3 A4 S4 ...

(2) If this is the case, then the same process is performed using S2 and the rest of the original sentence.

(3) The sentence is contained in the language if the final state is reached at the same time as the whole input sentence is used up.

(4) If this is not successful (i.e., the next word of the sentence does not match with the word or category from the grammar), then the next production is used (in the previous example: S1 → A3 S3). This can also allow a return to an earlier decision point (*backtrack*): if the application of one production rule is not successful and the same word or category can lead to different states, the system can *backup* to the last point that it selected one of several possible productions, and try a different one.

Example: S1 → A2 S2 A3 S3 A2 S6

Here the word or category A2 can lead to either state S2 or state S6. Backtracking can also occur if a word falls into multiple categories. We might find a match between the next word in the sentence and A2 as well as a match between the next word and A3 (for example, light can be a noun, an adjective, or a verb).

(5) The sentence is *not* contained in the language if:

- A final state is reached, and there is still part of the original sentence remaining.

- No production can be used, because no symbol matches the next word in the sentence.

Examples (from the grammar defined on page 194):

```
? Print ParseP [the old smart student with the
                yellow horse likes Angie]
True
? Print ParseP [the president is well]
False
? Print ParseP [Hal eats the old crummy computer]
True
```

As this shows, our system decides that correct English sentences are not contained in the language described by our grammar because unexpected words or constructs were use.

The program:

```
To ParseP :Sentence
  Output Parse1P (NextRule "S1) :Sentence
End

To Parse1P :RuleList :Sentence
  Test And (EndP :RuleList) (:Sentence = [])
  IfTrue [Output "True]
  Test Or (EndP :RuleList) (:RuleList = [])
  IfTrue [Output "False]
  Test
    MatchP
      First :RuleList
      First Sentence :Sentence "*
  IfTrue
    [Test
       Parse1P
         NextRule First ButFirst :RuleList
         ButFirst :Sentence]
  IfTrue [Output "True]
  Output
    Parse1P
      ButFirst ButFirst :RuleList
      :Sentence
End

To NextRule :LeftHandSide
  Output Thing :LeftHandSide
End

To EndP :Rule
  Output :Rule = [**]
End

To MatchP :Category :Word
  Output MemberP :Word Thing :Category
End
```

A trace illustrates, how the input sentence "the boy is" is processed by this program (observe the backtracking that occurs):

```
? Print ParseP [the boy is]
Parse1P of [<article> S2 <name> S3] and [the boy is]
  Parse1P of [<adjective> S2 <noun> S3] and [boy is]
    Parse1P of [<noun> S3] and [boy is]
        Parse1P of [<preposition> S4 <helpingverb> S6
        <verb> S7 <verb> .] and [is]
         ParseIP of [<helpingverb> S6 <verb> S7
         <verb> .] and [is]
            ParseIP of [<verb> S7 <verb> .] and [is]
               ParseIP of [<adverb> S7 <article> S8
               <name> .] and []
                  ParseIP of [<article> S8 <noun> .] and []
                   ParseIP of [<noun> .] and []
                    ParseIP of [] and []
Backtrack           ParseIP outputs False
Backtrack           ParseIP outputs False
Backtrack          ParseIP outputs False
Backtrack         ParseIP outputs False
Try Alternate
                  ParseIP of [<verb> .] and [is]
                   ParseIP of ** and []
                   ParseIP outputs True
                  ParseIP outputs True
               ParseIP outputs True
            ParseIP outputs True
         ParseIP Outputs True
      ParseIP Outputs true
    ParseIP outputs True
ParseIP outputs True
True
```

20.3. Context-Free Languages

Figure 20–1 shows that a context-free grammar has the ability to describe a broader class of languages and, at the same time, requires a more powerful computational mechanism.

What is a Context-Free Grammar?

A context-free grammar consists of:

- A set of terminal symbols (these are the elements that actually appear in sentences of the language generated by the grammar),

- a set of non-terminal symbols (these are internal names that describe groupings or categories of terminal and nonterminal symbols,

- a "distinguished" symbol (called SS in some of the following examples) from the set of nonterminal symbols,

- a set of production rules (also called rewriting rules).

The terminal and nonterminal symbols together make up the *vocabulary*. The rules describe how the nonterminal symbols can be rewritten in terms of terminal (and other nonterminal) symbols.

Example:

```
<sentence> -> <subject> <verb> |
              <subject> is <adjective>
<subject> -> Fred | Barney
<verb> -> walks | runs | sleeps | writes | reads
<adjective> -> silly | big | tall | clever | small
```

Explanation:

- Non-terminal symbols (that is, symbols that do not appear in the language generated, but are only used in rewriting rules) are always shown between "<" and ">", for example <verb>.

- Terminal symbols are given directly, for example Barney.

- If one nonterminal symbol can lead to several, alternative possible expansions, these possibilities are separated by vertical bars ("|"). This signifies an "either-or" relationship (e.g. <subject> can be rewritten either Fred or Barney).

- If several elements on the right-hand side follow one after the other, this means that the left-hand side expands to both (this is a "and" relationship) in the order specified. So, for example, <sentence> expands to either <subject> followed by <verb> or to <subject> followed by is followed by <adjective>.

Examples of sentences from the language generated by this grammar.

```
Fred walks
Barney is tall
```

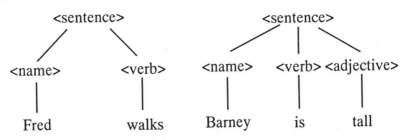

Figure 20–5: Tree Diagram Showing the Derivation of the Example Sentence

By a *language* we mean the set of all sequences of terminals symbols that can be derived using the rules by starting with the distinguished symbol (in the example, <sentence>.

A second example:

```
<SS> -> <S1> <S2>
<S1> -> 0 │ 0 <S1>
<S2> -> 1 │ 1 <S2>
```

This grammar can generate all sequences that begin with at least one "0" and end with at least one "1".

Example sequences from this language:

```
01
001
00011111
```

Generating Random Sentences from an Arbitrarily Defined Language

An implementation of the last example in LOGO for generating random sentences could look like this:

```
To SS
   Local "WhichOne
   Make "WhichOne Random 1
   If :WhichOne = 0 [Output (Word S1 S2)]
End

To S1
   Local "WhichOne
   Make "WhichOne Random 2
   If :WhichOne = 0 [Output 0]
   If :WhichOne = 1 [Output (Word 0 s1)]
End

To S2
   Local "WhichOne
   Make "WhichOne Random 2
   If :WhichOne = 0 [Output 1]
   If :WhichOne = 1 [Output (Word 1 S2)]
End
```

Examples:

```
? Print SS
0011111
? Print SS
001
? Print SS
00111
```

In this and other examples here, the production rules are represented as procedures instead of *lists* as they were in most of the last section. It would not be hard to put the rules in this section into a form that uses lists. This shows that the difference between *programs* and *data* is almost nonexistent, and that we can convert back and forth between the two. A procedure in data form can be manipulated by other procedures; the computer can even program itself, so to speak! This borders on *artificial intelligence*; problems of this type are dealt with in the artificial intelligence part, chapter 27.

To make the task of automatic programming easier, we need to give all the procedures a uniform appearance. To accomplish this, we have chosen the following format: The name of the procedure is the name of the nonterminal symbol. The first line is the same for each procedure and sets a local variable to the value of a random number less than the number of productions, which is then used to select the rule to use. Each rule is then written as an if statement, which will test to see if that rule is the one selected. Each rule tests against a different number starting at 0 for the first rule.[24]

Automatic Generation of Grammar Definitions

Since we have deliberately select a rigid form for our grammar definitions, we can easily automate the process of generation of the individual procedures that represent the production rules:

```
To DefineGrammar
  Print [Please specify the name of the class:]
  Make "ProcName Strip First ReadList
  Print [Please specify the rule:]
  Define
    :ProcName
    Fput [] GenerateDefinition ReadList
End

To GenerateDefinition :InputRules
  Local "RuleList
  Make "RuleList WriteRules 0 :InputRules
  Output
    FPut
      [Local "WhichOne ]
      FPut
        LPut
          (Count :RuleList)
          [Make "WhichOne Random ]
          :RuleList
End

To WriteRules :CaseNumber :InputRules
  If :InputRules = [] [Output []]
  Local "ThisRule
  Make "ThisRule ToSeparator :InputRules
  Make
    "RestOfRules
    WriteRules
      :CaseNumber + 1
      AfterSeparator :InputRules
```

---

[24] It would also have been possible to make the generated procedures use something like `Pick`, to select a sublist (one rule) from a nested list of rules. This would simply have allowed the list structures used in the last section to slip in through the back door. This is not meant to imply that the list structures are a bad form of representation; this section is only trying to illustrate an alternative representation and the interchangeability of data and programs.

```
      If (Count :ThisRule) = 1
        [Output
           FPut
             (List
               "If ":WhichOne "= :CaseNumber
               (FPut "Output WriteSimple :ThisRule))
             :RestOfRules]
     Output
       Fput
         (List
           "If ":WhichOne "= :CaseNumber
           (FPut
             "Output
             (FPut
               Word LeftParen "Word
               (LPut RightParen WriteSimple :ThisRule))))
         :RestOfRules
End

To WriteSimple :Sentence
   If :Sentence = [] [Output []]
   If (First First :Sentence) = "<
     [Output
        Sentence
          Strip First :Sentence
          WriteSimple ButFirst :Sentence]
   OutPut
     Sentence
       Quote First :Sentence
       WriteSimple ButFirst :Sentence
End

To CountElements :Input
   If :Input = [] [Output 1]
   If First :Input = VerticalBar
     [Output 1 + CountElements ButFirst :Input]
   Output CountElements ButFirst :Input
End

To Quote :Input
   If NumberP :Input [Output :Input]
   Output Word "\" :Input
End

To ToSeparator :Input
   If :Input = [] [Output []]
   If (First :Input) = VerticalBar [Output []]
   Output
     Sentence First :Input ToSeparator ButFirst :Input
End

To AfterSeparator :Input
   If :Input = [] [Output []]
   If (First :Input) = VerticalBar
     [Output ButFirst :Input]
   Output AfterSeparator ButFirst :Input
End
```

```
To VerticalBar
   Output Char 124
End

To LeftParen
   Output Char 40
End

To RightParen
   Output Char 41
End
```

The first procedure `DefineGrammar` defines a procedure using the built-in procedure `Define`. The content of the procedure is in the form of a list.

The name of the procedure (production rule) is contained in the variable `ProcName`; the nested list that becomes the body of the procedure is generated from the users input using `GenerateDefinition`.

In `GenerateDefinition`, the first line generated is always the same, except for the number given to `Random`, which depends on how many rules there are. The individual rules (which are separated by "|"'s in the user's input) are converted into program lines by `WriteRules`, with the appropriate `If` test as described previously in the prototype examples of `SS`, `S1`, and `S2`. Also, if the number of elements in a rule is only 1, then the `Word` construct is not needed. here>

Here is how the interaction would look while defining our 0-1 language:

```
? DefineGrammar
Please specify the name of the class:
<SS>
Please specify the rule:
<S1> <S2>
? DefineGrammar
Please specify the name of the class:
<S1>
Please specify the rule:
0 | 0 <S1>
? DefineGrammar
Please specify the name of the class:
<S2>
Please specify the rule:
1 | 1 <S2>
```

After these calls, the procedures that define the grammar (which were shown before) are available.

As a second example, let's define the following grammar:

```
? DefineGrammar
Please specify the name of the class:
<Number>
Please specify the rule:
<SignedNumber> | <DecimalNumber>
```

```
? DefineGrammar
Please specify the name of the class:
<SignedNumber>
Please specify the rule:
<WholeNumber> | + <WholeNumber> | - <WholeNumber>
? DefineGrammar
Please specify the name of the class:
<DecimalNumber>
Please specify the rule:
<SignedNumber> . <WholeNumber>
? DefineGrammar
Please specify the name of the class:
<WholeNumber>
Please specify the rule:
<Digit> | <Digit> <WholeNumber>
? DefineGrammar
Please specify the name of the class:
<Digit>
Please specify the rule:
1 | 2 | 3 | 4 | 5 | 6 | 7 | 8 | 9 | 0
```

Example Sentences from the language:

```
? Print Number
8
? Print Number
-622.07
? Print DecimalNumber
+774.8
? Print SignedNumber
-49
```

20.4. Recognition of Sentences in a Language

The programs presented so far allow us to define grammars automatically and generate sentences using those grammars.

The procedures we describe next (which can also be automatically generated) in some sense do the opposite: they determine whether a given sentence belongs to the language defined by a grammar.

We use our example of the 0-1 language again:

```
? Print ParseSS "001111
True
? Print ParseSS "10
False
```

Before we come to the description of the procedures SS, S1, and S2, we should explain the basic idea behind a simple, special purpose *pattern matcher*.

A Simple Pattern Matcher

The basic ideas about pattern matching were discussed in section 19. A pattern-matching program is a procedure with two inputs (see figure 20–6), which determines whether the structure of a :String corresponds to the structure specified by a :Pattern.

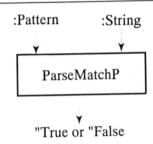

:Pattern   :String

ParseMatchP

"True or "False

Figure 20–6: Pattern-Matching Schema

For our language recognition, there are two types of pattern specifications we need:

(1) A pattern (syntactically: a LOGO list) can specify directly the terminal symbols that should make up the string. Example:

```
? Print ParseMatchP [1 2 3 4] [1234]
True
? Print ParseMatchP [A B C D] [ABCD]
True
```

(2) Individual elements of the pattern can be predicates that the elements of the string must satisfy. To distinguish these as predicates, they are surrounded by "<" and ">". Examples:

```
? Print
  ParseMatchP [A <NumberP> B <NumberP> C] [A123B456C]
True
? Print
  ParseMatchP [A <NumberP> B <NumberP> C] [AB12C]
False

To ArbitraryP :Input
  Output "True
End

? Print ParseMatchP
       [<ArbitraryP> A <ArbitraryP> B] [XZADF4B]
True
```

The definitions for the procedure ParseMatchP and its related procedures are given here; however, we do not discuss the methods used, as they are discussed in chapter 19.

```
To ParseMatchP :Pattern :Sentence
   Output PatMatchP :Pattern ListToWord :Sentence
End

To PatMatchP :Pat :Str
   If :Pat = [] [Output :Str = "]
   If PredicateP First :Pat
     [Output PredicateMatchP :Pat :Str Count :Str]
   If :Str = " [Output "False]
   IfElse (First :Str) = First :Pat
     [Output PatMatchP ButFirst :Pat ButFirst :Str]
     [Output "False]
End

To PredicateP :Input
   Output And (First :Input) = "< (Last :Input) = ">
End

To PredicateMatchP :Pat :Str :N
   If :N = 0 [Output "False]
   Test
     Apply Word "Parse Strip First :Pat FirstN :N :Str
   IfTrue
     [Test PatMatchP ButFirst :Pat ButFirstN :N :Str]
   IfTrue [Output "True]
   Output PredicateMatchP :Pat :Str :N - 1
End

To ListToWord :Input
   If WordP :Input [Output :Input]
   If ButFirst :Input = [] [Output First :Input]
   Output
     Word
       First :Input
       Word "' ListToWord ButFirst :Input
End
```

The Procedures ParseSS, ParseS1 and ParseS2:

```
To ParseSS :Input
   If ParseMatchP [<S1> <S2>] :Input [Output "True]
   Output "False
End

To ParseS1 :Input
   If ParseMatchP [0] :Input [Output "True]
   If ParseMatchP [0 <S1>] :Input [Output "True]
   Output "False
End

To ParseS2 :Input
   If ParseMatchP [1] :Input [Output "True]
   If ParseMatchP [1 <S2>] :Input [Output "True]
   Output "False
End
```

As the definitions of the procedures show, the use of a pattern matcher greatly simplifies checking the syntax of sentences: It becomes a trivial problem.

In ParseSS, for example, the only thing that needs to be done is to call ParseMatchP once, that is to say, ParseSS is really nothing more than ParseMatchP. It could be rewritten:

```
To ParseSS :Input
   Output ParseMatchP [<S1> <S2>] :Input
End
```

A somewhat complicated form was chosen, because SS, S1, and S2, were automatically generated, and it is simpler for the program that generated them to use a form that is the same for all productions.

To generate these procedures, the following procedures were used:

```
To DefineParserGrammar
   Print [Please specify the name of the class:]
   Make "ProcName Word "Parse Strip First ReadList
   Print [Please specify the rule:]
   Define
     :ProcName
     FPut [:Input] WriteParserRules ReadList
End

To WriteParserRules :Input
   If :Input = [] [Output [[Output "False]]]
   Output
     FPut
       (List
         "If
         "ParseMatchP
         ToSeparator :Input
         ":Input
         [Output "True])
       WriteParserRules AfterSeparator :Input
End
```

An example of use:

```
? DefineParserGrammar
Please specify the name of the class:
<SS>
Please specify the rule:
<S1> <S2>
? DefineParserGrammar
Please specify the name of the class:
<S1>
Please specify the rule:
0 | 0 <S1>
? DefineParserGrammar
Please specify the name of the class:
<S2>
Please specify the rule:
1 | 1 <S2>
```

If you compare the use and structure of DefineParserGrammar and DefineGrammar, you see that they are similar. The input form for the grammar is about the same for both.

As another example, we can use the grammar from the number example in the last section. Once the grammar is entered as it was before; the procedures can be used to test various numbers.

```
? Print Number 1
True
? Print Number "-2
True
? Print Number 3.55
True
```

Further Possibilities

One obvious extension is to combine the two procedures `DefineParserGrammar` and `DefineGrammar` so that the grammar only needs to be entered once. This combined procedure could build both the language-generating procedures and the language-recognizing procedures.

Exercise

Define a parser grammar for Roman numerals. As a first step you may want to limit yourself to numerals less than XX.

Chapter 21:
Tree Data Structures: Building a Dictionary

21.1. The Problem

We would like to create an information structure that is similar to a dictionary. A general characteristic of a dictionary is that in explaining one key-word, other key-words are used. Once this happens these other key-words need to be looked up as well. Our program should:

(1) Allow the interactive construction and extension of a dictionary:

```
? NewWord
Word:car
Definition:vehicle with motor and seats
Word:
```

(2) On request, the items contained in the dictionary should be printed out in one of several possible external representations. In doing so, this explanation should follow all references to other key-words until it reaches words that are atomic (i.e., the word is not further defined in the dictionary).

Here are three possible forms to be used for explanation:

a) Words in the explanation, which have dictionary entries of their own are marked with a preceding "=>", and the definition for these words appears below the current explanation.

```
? Explain "Toyota
Toyota : Japanese =>car manufacturer
car : vehicle with motor and seats
```

b) In the second form, the definition of a concept follows the word and is enclosed by parentheses; this process continues recursively:

```
? Print Explanation "Toyota
Toyota [Japanese car [vehicle with motor
and seats] manufacturer]
```

c) The third form uses a tree-like indented structure:

```
? ExplainAsTree "Toyota
Toyota
   .    Japanese car
   .    .    vehicle with motor and seats
   .    manufacturer
```

21.2. Objectives

To construct such a system, we must deal with the following problems:

- hierarchical, recursive construction of a concept system.

- stepwise reduction of complex concepts to atomic ones; however, the atomic concepts are not given *a priori* but are supplied by the author of the dictionary (compare this to the construction of your own procedures by reducing them step-by-step to the system provided procedures).

- generation of various external representation for an existing information structure.

Furthermore, we see how easily an information structure of this kind (i.e., one that is recursive in nature) can be realized using recursive procedures.

21.3. Construction of the Program

Data Structures

The program should not depend on the design of the internal data structures. Instead functions that provide the required *logical* access to the data should be provided. This way, if the internal representation needs to change later, only the data access functions need to be rewritten, instead of requiring a change everywhere in the program that the data is accessed.

We choose (for now) to represent the data using property lists, providing the functions PutDefinition and GetDefinition to the rest of the program.

```
To PutDefinition :Name :Def
   PutProp :Name "Definition :Def
End

To GetDefinition :Name
   Output GetProp :Name "Definition
End
```

If we needed to change the implementation of the dictionary later (if access is too slow, we need to put the information into files, or we wish to use an existing database system), we could still provide these functions, and the rest of the program would not need to change.

Interactive Construction of the Data Structures

The following procedure places new words and definitions into the dictionary:

```
To NewWord
   Local "Line
   Type [Word:]
   Make "Line ReadList
   If :Line = " [Stop]
```

```
    Type [Definition:]
    PutDefinition First :Line ReadList
    NewWord
End
```

Examples:

```
? NewWord
Word:vehicle
Definition:box with wheels
Word:motor
Definition:mechanical power source
Word:manufacturer
Definition:maker of goods
Word:
```

As an example, structures such as those in figure 21–1 can be represented:

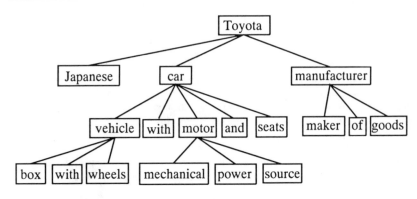

Figure 21–1: Dictionary - Tree Structure

Recursive Manipulation of the Data Structures

With the following three procedures we can produce explanations using a dictionary that has already been constructed.

```
To Explanation :Word
   Output Explanations (list :Word)
End

To Explanations :Sentence
   If :Sentence = [] [Output []]
   Test (GetDefinition First :Sentence) = []
   IfTrue
     [Output
        Sentence
           First :Sentence
           Explanations ButFirst :Sentence]
```

```
    Output
      (Sentence
        First :Sentence
        (List
          Explanations
            GetDefinition First :Sentence)
          Explanations ButFirst :Sentence)
    End
```

Example:

```
? Print Explanation "Toyota
Toyota [Japanese car [vehicle [box with
wheels] with motor [mechanical power source]
and seats] manufacturer [maker of goods]
```

The second line of Explanations checks to see whether the current word is an atomic concept (with respect to the current dictionary) or a concept for which further explanation exists in the dictionary. Depending on the result, the recursion continues in two different directions (with respect to the picture in figure 21–1):

- third (logical) program line: *horizontal*, to the sibling of the current node in the tree; this is found using ButFirst.

- fourth (logical) program line: *vertical*, to the child of the current node (and then later to the sibling); this is found using GetDefinition.

As you can see, the structure of the procedure Explanations is typical for manipulation of binary trees (see also section 9.3).

Alternate Forms of External Representation

The structure printed out in the last section is not all that readable for the human user. With a few procedures, the readability can be improved:

```
? ExplainAsTree "Toyota
Toyota
.    Japanese car
.    .    vehicle
.    .    .    box with wheels
.    .    with motor
.    .    .    mechanical power source
.    .    and seats
.    manufacturer
.    .    maker of goods
```

The procedures necessary for this are:

```
To ExplainAsTree :Word
  ExplTree (List :Word) 0
End

To ExplTree :Def :Depth
  If :Def = [] [Stop]
  InsertDotsPrint FirstPart :Def :Depth
```

```
      If DefinedP Last FirstPart :Def
        [ExplTree
            GetDefinition Last FirstPart :Def
            :Depth + 1]
      ExplTree RestPart :Def :Depth
    End

    To InsertDotsPrint :Stuff :N
      Print Sentence InsertDots :N :Stuff
    End

    To InsertDots :N
      If :N < 1 [Output []]
      Output (Sentence Period Spaces 3 InsertDots :N - 1)
    End

    To Period
      Output Char 46
    End

    To DefinedP :Word
      ;...Tests whether a definition exists for a word
      Output Not (GetDefinition :Word) = []
    End

    To FirstPart :Sentence
      If :Sentence = [] [Output []]
      If DefinedP First :Sentence
        [Output (List First :Sentence)]
      Output
        Sentence
          First :Sentence
          FirstPart ButFirst :Sentence
    End

    To RestPart :Sentence
      If :Sentence = [] [Output []]
      If DefinedP First :Sentence
        [Output ButFirst :Sentence]
      Output RestPart ButFirst :Sentence
    End
```

The structure of the most important procedure `ExplTree` is similar to the structure of `Explanations` because it also traverses the tree. The procedures `FirstPart` and `RestPart` are similar to `First` and `ButFirst`. `FirstPart` searches through the current definition for the part up to (and including) the first word that is defined further. `RestPart` gets the part that follows the first word that is further defined.

Examples:

```
? Print FirstPart [vehicle with motor and seats]
vehicle
? Print
  FirstPart RestPart [vehicle with motor and seats]
with motor
```

Another form, which is similar to the entries found in dictionaries implemented as books, is shown here:

```
? Explain "Toyota
Toyota : Japanese =>car =>manufacturer
car : =>vehicle with =>motor and seats
vehicle : box with wheels
motor : mechanical power source
manufacturer : maker of goods
```

The necessary procedures are left as an exercise for the reader.

21.4. Possible Extensions

These programs, as they were written, always carry the explanation to the lowest level. With a large dictionary, this can be overwhelming and redundant.

For further investigation modify the procedures so that:

• All explanations are made as simple as possible (avoid redundancy),

• Before any definition is expanded, the user is consulted,

• The depth of the explanation can be limited.

In every real dictionary you can find definitions that are circular (word A is explained using word B, word B is explained using word C, and word C is explained using word A again). How do these programs behave under such circumstances, and how can that behavior be modified? You may want to look at the discussion in section 23.2 for some ideas.

Chapter 22:

TOWERS OF HANOI

The TOWERS OF HANOI puzzle is a thought problem that allows us to study the use of conceptual models in understanding recursive problems. We can also use this concrete example to demonstrate the isomorphism between problems and programs.

22.1. Problem Description

The problem can be described as follows:

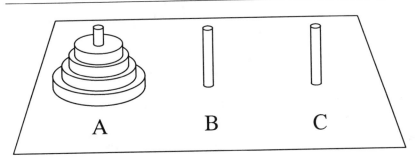

Figure 22–1: The TOWERS OF HANOI

A certain number of disks of different sizes are placed on peg A in order of size with the largest on the bottom. The disks are to be moved to peg C using peg B as an intermediate location when needed. The following rules need to be followed:

- Only one disk may be moved at a time,
- A larger disk may never be placed on a smaller disk.

This problem has been used as an example in countless articles about problem solving and programming. It has also been used in psychology to analyze how different groups of people solve a problem and whether they are able to generalize the problem from three disks to a larger number. In the artificial intelligence literature the problem is used as an example for the general method of problem decomposition.

22.2. A Simple Solution

The simple solution for N disks can be divided into three subproblems using stepwise refinement (see figure 22–2).

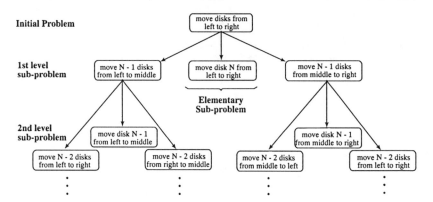

Figure 22–2: Breaking the Problem into Subproblems

In this case, the process of decomposition generates one elementary problem and two problems that may be further decomposed. This solution can be translated into the following recursive procedure:

```
To Hanoi :Number :From :Via :To
   If :Number = 0 [Stop]
   Hanoi :Number - 1 :From :to :Via
   Print
      (Sentence [Move disk] :Number "from :From "to :To
      "\!)
   Hanoi :Number - 1 :Via :From :to
End
```

The basic interaction can be performed by this procedure:

```
To HanoiDemo
   Print [How many disks should be used?]
   Hanoi First ReadList "Left "Middle "Right
   Print "
   Type "Again?
   If YesP [HanoiDemo]
End
```

The procedure YesP is described in appendix III.

A test run shows that the program generates the correct solution (e.g., for four disks):

```
? HanoiDemo
How many disks should be used? 4
Move disk 1 from left to middle !
Move disk 2 from left to right !
Move disk 1 from middle to right !
Move disk 3 from left to middle !
Move disk 1 from right to left !
Move disk 2 from right to middle !
Move disk 1 from left to middle !
Move disk 4 from left to right !
Move disk 1 from middle to right !
Move disk 2 from middle to left !
Move disk 1 from right to left !
Move disk 3 from middle to right !
Move disk 1 from left to middle !
Move disk 2 from left to right !
Move disk 1 from middle to right !

Again? no
```

This solution is short. But, is it understandable? Does it mirror what happens when the task is solved with the aid of a physical model? What if we interrupt the process at a particular point; could we determine how the disks are arranged on the three towers? Does the way we represent the physical process of moving a disk from one tower to another bear any relationship to the subproblems that are solved by that action?

The answer to all these questions is "no": No data structures exist that correspond to the physical structure of the problem. The flow of the process is controlled exchanging the arguments in the recursive calls, and this expresses the decomposition of the problem. It is the **only** thing that supports the isomorphism between problem representation and solution.

22.3. Extended Solution

This solution actually constructs a data structure that represents the physical structure of the problem. The recursive control structure will not be affected by this change. The towers will be represented as lists assigned to the global variables :Left, :Middle, and :Right. The disks will be represented as numbers that represent their size. NumberSequence generates such a list:

```
To NumberSequence :UpperLimit
  If :UpperLimit = 0 [Output [ ]]
  Output
    Sentence
      :UpperLimit
      NumberSequence :UpperLimit - 1
End

? Print NumberSequence 15
15 14 13 12 11 10 9 8 7 6 5 4 3 2 1
```

`Initialize` creates a global data structure to represent the problem, which can then be printed with `TellPosition`.

```
To Initialize :HowMany
  Make "Left (NumberSequence :HowMany)
  Make "Right []
  Make "Middle []
  Make "Move 0
  TellPositions 0
End
```

```
To TellPositions :Level
  Print
    (Sentence Spaces 3 * :Level [New configuration:])
  Print
    (Sentence Spaces 3 * :Level [Left Tower:] :Left)
  Print
    (Sentence Spaces 3 * :Level [Middle Tower:]
       :Middle)
  Print
    (Sentence Spaces 3 * :Level [Right Tower:] :right)
End
```

The procedure `Spaces` is defined in appendix III. The modified procedure `HanoiDemo2` calls the individual procedures in sequence.

```
To HanoiDemo2
  Print [How many disks should be used?]
  Initialize First ReadList
  SubProblem (Count :Left) "Left "Middle "Right 0
  Type "Again?
  If YesP [HanoiDemo2]
End
```

The call to `SubProblem` is called with arguments for the number of disks, the names of the towers, and the level in the recursion.

```
To SubProblem :HowMany :From :Via :To :Level
  If :HowMany = 0 [Stop]
  Print
    (Sentence Indent :Level "Level "# :Level
       [subproblem: move] NumberSequence :HowMany
       "from :From "to :to)
  SubProblem :HowMany - 1 :From :To :Via :Level + 1
  MakeAMove :HowMany :From :To :Level
  SubProblem :HowMany - 1 :Via :From :To :Level + 1
End
```

`SubProblem` corresponds structurally to the procedure `Hanoi` from page 219. The procedure `MakeAMove` modifies the indicated data structures. First, the appropriate disk is inserted into the list `:To`, then removed from `:From` list.

```
To MakeAMove :Number :From :To :Level
  Make :To (Sentence Thing :To Last Thing :From)
  Make :From ButLast Thing :From
```

```
   Make "Move :Move + 1
   Print (Sentence Indent :Level [Move #] :Move "is:)
   Print
     (Sentence Indent :Level "Move "disk :Number "from
       :From "to :To)
   TellPositions :Level
End
```

? HanoiDemo2
How many disks should be used?
3
 New configuration:
   Left Tower: 3 2 1
 Middle Tower:
 Right Tower:
Level # 0 subproblem: move 3 2 1 from Left to Right
   | Level # 1 subproblem: move 2 1 from Left to Middle
   | | Level # 2 subproblem: move 1 from Left to Right
   | | Move # 1 is:
   | | Move disk 1 from Left to Right
   | | New configuration:
   | | Left Tower: 3 2
   | | Middle Tower:
   | | Right Tower: 1
   | Move # 2 is:
   | Move disk 2 from Left to Middle
   | New configuration:
   | Left Tower: 3
   | Middle Tower: 2
   | Right Tower: 1
   | | Level #2 subproblem: move 1 from Right to Middle
   | | Move # 3 is:
   | | Move disk 1 from Right to Middle
   | | New configuration:
   | | Left Tower: 3
   | | Middle Tower: 2 1
   | | Right Tower:
Move # 4 is:
Move disk 3 from Left to Right
New configuration:
  Left Tower:
Middle Tower: 2 1
 Right Tower: 3
   | Level # 1 subproblem: move 2 1 from Middle to Right
   | | Level # 2 subproblem: move 1 from Middle to Left
   | | Move # 5 is:
   | | Move disk 1 from Middle to Left
   | | New configuration:
   | | Left Tower: 1
   | | Middle Tower: 2
   | | Right Tower: 3

```
| Move # 6 is:
| Move disk 2 from Middle to Right
| New configuration:
|   Left Tower: 1
| Middle Tower:
|   Right Tower: 3 2
|    | Level # 2 subproblem: move 1 from Left to Right
|    | Move # 7 is:
|    | Move disk 1 from Left to Right
|    | New configuration:
|    |   Left Tower:
|    | Middle Tower:
|    |   Right Tower: 3 2 1
Again? no
```

22.4. Models of Recursion

The solution given in section 22.2 is independent of a specific programming language. The algorithm can certainly be implemented without recursion; however, for this problem, only a programming language with recursive procedures allows an implementation that mirrors the structure of the algorithm. Non-recursive solutions are difficult, if not impossible, to understand.

Conceptual Model for Recursive Procedures

Suitable conceptual models and the terminology that correspond to them are central to the understanding of recursive procedures. For procedures with recursive calls (like the manipulation of a list), a tracing mechanism (as is available in LOGO, for example) is a valuable aid.

Experience shows that in procedures with two or more recursive calls are somewhat more difficult to understand. A representation such as the one shown in figure 22–3, is one way to help understand the recursive process (see also figures 8–1 and 8–2).

22.5. Isomorphisms

Definition

In mathematics, two structures (e.g., groups) are shown to be isomorphic, if a bijective (one-to-one and onto) mapping exists, which preserves the structure. In problem solving, two problems are shown to be isomorphic if, for example, the graphs of their representation in state space can be mapped onto one another in a definite manner. An isomorphic representation of a problem as a program means that the structure and the abstraction (with respect to data and operations) are carried over into the program. Stated simply, if our representation of the problem maps onto its implementation in a programming language in a straightforward way, then the program is isomorphic to our problem.

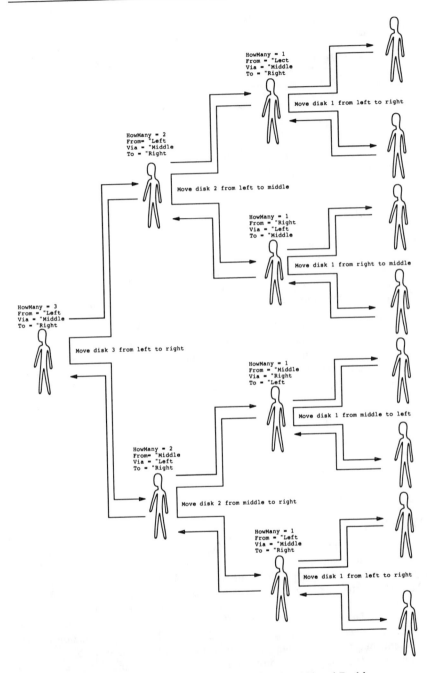

Figure 22–3: Tree Recursion in the Towers of Hanoi Problem

Isomorphic Problem Descriptions

A human rarely works "directly" on a specific problem, using instead some symbolic representation that is based on a particular understanding of the problem. This representation, which may be seen as a model, can be put into different forms: as neural connections in the human mind, as a picture, as a description in natural language, or in some mathematical formalism.

Finding a suitable representation for a particular problem is one of the most important components of the problem-solving process. Often it can be shown that some representations express the structure of a problem clearly and simplify the problem-solving process considerably while others hinder it. Therefore, to understand a problem well, not just any representation is sufficient. What is needed is the representation that is best adapted to the problem. This is basically what Polya's schema means when it says "Restate the problem" (see chapter 14). In this sense, searching for isomorphic problem descriptions is an important tool for solving problems.

Different Types of Isomorphisms

We can talk about solving a task at three levels:

(1) **The Problem Level:** On this level the problem is specified in a descriptive form (*what* needs to be done).

(2) **The Algorithmic Level:** This is the procedural description of a solution to the problem (*how* to solve it).

(3) **The Implementation Level:** The procedural description is implemented in a programming language (*how* to solve it in a particular language).

Isomorphic relationships can exist within a level (*horizontal isomorphisms*) and between two levels (*vertical isomorphisms*).

Examples of horizontal isomorphism at the problem level are described in chapter 34 between TIC-TAC-TOE and NUMBER SCRABBLE. In general, because different programming languages build on the same basic concepts, it is possible to implement programs isomorphically (that is, identically except for trivial syntactic differences). The result is that, for example, BASIC programs can be translated into PASCAL with few problems. In this chapter we have dealt with vertical isomorphism using a concrete example. In particular we have pursued the question of how a problem can be mapped isomorphically onto an algorithm. We have also briefly mentioned the basic concepts that need to be present in a programming language to support the mapping of this algorithm onto a program.

22.6. Names

How important a "good" choice of names can be for the understanding of a program is shown by the TOWERS OF HANOI. If we had used meaningless variable names, the program is much harder to understand.

```
To Hanoi :N :A :B :C
   If :N = 0 [Stop]
   Hanoi :N - 1 :A :C :B
   Print (Sentence [Move disk] :N "From :A "To :C ")
   Hanoi :N - 1 :B :A :C
End
```

This solution of the problem, as empirical studies show, does not lend itself as easily to an intuitive understanding. Even if the solution is already known, most "readers" have difficulty reconstructing it from memory.

If a naming schema is used that is oriented to the physical model of the puzzle, as is shown in the original Hanoi, then it is easier for someone to verify the correctness of program.

Chapter 23:
Software Tools for LOGO

The programs and projects presented in this chapter all in one way or another represent extensions to the LOGO language programming environment.

They are examples of how a programming environment (in this case LOGO) can be tailored to individual needs, wishes, or preferences. At the same time they are examples of how a language can be extended—without a specific problem or usage in mind. This viewpoint is compatible with the introduction of the *construction kit*[25] *model*; from such a construction kit programming language that contains certain basic elements (similar to the wheels, gears, motors, and blocks in a construction kit), newer, bigger modules can be assembled. Modules can even be built that create other modules as was done in chapter 27. The following small projects can also be viewed as "tool construction": new tools (building blocks) are made to be used in ways that the designer did not foresee.

Some of the following projects make up for weaknesses (deficiencies) in your LOGO programming environment. Some systems already contain some of these tools as primitives, but even so, having these versions available allows you to "look inside" the black-box of the LOGO primitive to see how it might appear if it were a glass-box. In any case, most of them show how easy these tools are to construct.

23.1. New Control Structures

The control structures presented in this section and their underlying concepts extend the LOGO in two directions. The procedures `Apply`, `Apply2`, `MapC`, `MapCar`, `PMapC`, `PMapCar`, and `MapCar2`, which are all similar to the corresponding functions in LISP, can be viewed as a LISP-like extension of LOGO. In contrast, the procedures `RepeatUntil`, `WhileDo` and `For` are extensions more in the direction of the control structures used in ALGOL, BASIC, or Pascal.

---

[25]Such as the classic, the Erector set, or more recently Lego, Lego Technic, and Fischer-Technik (see figure 23–1), to name a few.

A complex system can be built using simple, yet powerful, building blocks.

Figure 23–1: A Fischer-Technik Crane

Apply

Apply (which we used, for example, in `MatchPred` in chapter 19) takes a procedure (name) and a list containing as many elements as the procedure needs as inputs, and outputs the result of running the procedure with the elements of the list as inputs.

```
To Apply :Procedure :Inputs
   Run (Sentence "Output :Procedure " :Inputs)
End
```

Examples:

```
? Print Apply "NumberP 4
True
? Print Apply "WordP [this is a list]
False
```

MapC and MapCar

MapC and MapCar apply a command or, respectively, an operation (which must take one input) to each element of an input list.

```
To MapC :Command :InputList
   If :InputList = [] [Stop]
   Run Sentence :Command [First :InputList]
   MapC :Command ButFirst :InputList
End
```

Examples:

```
? MapC "Print [A B C D]
A
B
C
D

? MapC [Print 3 +] [10 20 30 40]
13
23
33
43
```

```
To MapCar :Operation :InputList
   If :InputList = [] [Output []]
   Output
     Sentence
       Apply :Operation First :InputList
       MapCar :Operation ButFirst :InputList
End
```

Examples:

```
? Print MapCar "NumberP [A 1 B 2 C 3]
False True False True False True
```

PMapC and PMapCar

The application of the procedure to the argument can also be made dependent on predicate. For each element of the input list, if the predicate is met, then the first command (respectively, the first operation) is applied to the element, otherwise the second command (respectively, the second operation) is applied to the element.

```
To PMapC :Predicate :Command1 :Command2 :InputList
   If :InputList = [] [Stop]
   Test Apply :Predicate First :InputList
   IfTrue
     [Run Sentence :Command1 [First :InputList]]
```

```
      IfFalse
        [Run Sentence :Command2 [First :InputList]]
      PMapC
        :Predicate
        :Command1
        :Command2
        ButFirst :InputList
  End
```

Example:

```
  ? PMapC "NumberP [Print 3 +] "Print [A 1 B 2 C 3]
  A
  4
  B
  5
  C
  6
```

```
  To PMapCar :Predicate :Operation1
                        :Operation2 :InputList
    If :InputList = [] [Output []]
    Test Apply :Predicate First :InputList
    IfTrue
      [Output
          Sentence
            Apply :Operation1 First :InputList
            PMapCar
              :Predicate
              :Operation1
              :Operation2
              ButFirst :InputList]
    Output
      Sentence
        Apply :Operation2 First :InputList
        PMapCar
          :Predicate
          :Operation1
          :Operation2
          ButFirst :InputList
  End
```

```
  ? Print PMapCar "ListP "ButFirst "NumberP [1 [1 2] B]
  True 2 False
```

Using the procedures PMapC and PMapCar provide programming structures that are reminiscent of predicate logic expressions: "For all x such that z is true, compute a(x), otherwise compute b(x)."

MapCar2 and Apply2

Procedures can also be defined that operate on two or more lists:

```
  To MapCar2 :Operation :InputList1 :InputList2
    If :InputList1 = [] [Output []]
```

```
    Output
      Sentence
        Apply2
          :Operation
          First :InputList1
          First :InputList2
        MapCar2
          :Operation
          ButFirst :InputList1
          ButFirst :InputList2
  End

To Apply2 :Operation :Argument1 :Argument2
  Run
    (Sentence
      "Output
      :Operation
      [:Argument1 :Argument2])
  End
```

Example:

```
? Print MapCar2 "Remainder [10 8 6 4 2] [3 3 3 3 3]
1
2
0
1
2
```

RepeatUntil, WhileDo, For, Loop

The control structure RepeatUntil repeats a command as long as a predicate returns the value True. The command is always done first and then the test is performed, so the command is always done at least once.

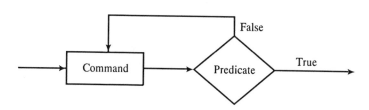

Figure 23–2: Flow Chart for RepeatUntil

```
To RepeatUntil :Command :Predicate
  Run :Command
  Run Sentence "Test :Predicate
  IfTrue [Stop]
  RepeatUntil :Command :Predicate
End
```

Example:

```
? Make "A "swanlake
? PrintOut "PrintAndCut
To PrintAndCut
 Print :A
 Make "A ButFirst :A
End

? RepeatUntil "PrintAndCut [:A = " ]
swanlake
wanlake
anlake
nlake
lake
ake
ke
e
```

In using the RepeatUntil control structure, as well as the other two that are yet to be described, the :Predicate asked for must refer to a global data structure, because the :Command needs to change the result of the :Predicate to allow the loop to stop. The only way this can happen is if the :Command has a side-effect on a global data structure, which the :Predicate uses for testing. Said another way, the use of RepeatUntil, WhileDo, and For implies a programming style that is based on side-effects.

The control structure WhileDo repeats a command as long as a condition is true. If the condition is not true at the outset, then the command will never be executed.

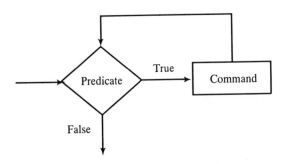

Figure 23–3: Flow Chart for WhileDo

```
To WhileDo :Predicate :Command
   Run Sentence "Test :Predicate
   IfFalse [Stop]
   Run :Command
```

```
     WhileDo :Predicate :Command
   End
```

Example:

```
? Make "A "swanlake
? PrintOut Command

To Command
 Print :A
 Make "A ButFirst :A
End

? WhileDo [Not :A = " ] "Command
swanlake
wanlake
anlake
nlake
lake
ake
ke
e
```

The For control structure repeats a command using the value of a variable that takes on successive values each time through the loop from a beginning value to an ending value in specified steps.

```
To For :Variable :From :Step :To :Command
   If :From > :To [Stop]
   Make :Variable :From
   Run :Command
   For :Variable :From + :Step :Step :To :Command
End
```

Example:

```
? For "I 0 2 10 [Print Sentence :I :I * :I]
0  0
2  4
4  16
6  36
8  64
10 100
```

Reverse stepping is not possible using this definition of For.

The Loop control structure works almost exactly like the For construct except that the step size is fixed at one.

```
To Loop :Var :From :UpTo :Instructions
   Make :Var :From
   Repeat
     (1 + :UpTo - :From)
     [Run :Instructions ! Make :Var (Thing :Var ) + 1]
End
```

Another, subtle problem with all the control structures defined in this chapter has to do with the scope of names, or the environment in which these names are evaluated. Since the evaluation is done using the Run command, if the expression given to the Run command has references to variables names that are the same as those used in the title line of the definition of the control structure, then the Run command uses the values of the variables in the control structure, which is probably not what the user had in mind. For example, if we use the `For` control structure defined earlier in the following procedure, we don't get the correct results.

```
To Print5TimesRIP :Person :from :To
   For "I 1 1 5
      [Print (Sentence :Person "Born: :from "Died: :To)]
End
```

The problem:

```
? Print5TimesRIP "Henry 1797 1856
```

```
Henry Born: 2 Died: 5
Henry Born: 3 Died: 5
Henry Born: 4 Died: 5
Henry Born: 5 Died: 5
```

That is, instead of printing *Henry Born: 1797 Died: 1856*, the values of the "internal" loop variables `:From` and `:To` are printed because they "happen" to have the same name as the inputs to `Print5TimesRIP`. This problem is particularly bad, because errors of this kind only appear when variable names are selected that are the same as those local to the control structure. Programs can function properly for years, until the variable names are changed and errors like this (that are difficult to track down) appear. One technique that can be used is to give the control structures unusual names that (we hope) no one else will use. `For` would look like this:

```
To For :&V.A&R.I&A.B&L.E&     :&F.R.O.M&
           :&S.T.E.P&    :&T.O&   :&C.O.M.M.A.N.D&
   If :&F.R.O.M& > :&T.O& [Stop]
   Make :&V.A&R.I&A.B&L.E& :&F.R.O.M&
   Run (Sentence :&C.O.M.M.A.N.D&)
   For
      :&V.A&R.I&A.B&L.E
      :&F.R.O.M& + :&S.T.E.P&
      :&T.O&
      :&C.O.M.M.A.N.D&
End
```

This method is not *guaranteed* to avoid the problem.[26]

---

[26]A correct solution to the problem uses macros, similar to those available in LISP.

23.2. A System to Show the Call Structure of Programs

Statement of the Problem

The structure of the programming language LOGO makes it possible to solve complex problems with the aid of many small, independent, and often universally applicable building-blocks, instead of by creating a single monolithic program. Intensive use of this programming technique makes it more difficult to remember how all the pieces interact. Using the `Trace` provided by the system to show the *dynamic* structure of the program is one possibility, but often (especially when applied to an entire program) it prints things out too quickly and produces so much information that it becomes more difficult to get an overview of the program this way, than with the original program text. Tracing is more useful for illustrating the workings of individual procedures or the interactions among a few procedures.

The system that is described here allows the user to generate a description of the *static* structure of a program; in particular the system provides the following information:

- Which procedures call which other procedures?

- Which procedures are called by which other procedures?

- What does the entire call structure (call tree) of the program look like?

Example:

You want to see what the call structure of a program that prints out the tree structure of a dictionary (see chapter 21). This program, which appears in all the following examples, consists of the following 8 procedures (we just show the title lines here).

```
To GetDefinition :Name
To DefinedP :Word
To InsertDots :N
To ExplainAsTree :Word
To ExplTree :Def :Depth
To InsertDotsPrint :Stuff :N
To FirstPart :Sentence
To RestPart :Sentence
```

`ProgramStructure` can be applied to these procedures:

```
? ProgramStructure
The program ProgramStructure should aid in the
understanding of complex Logo-programs.
It generates lists of procedures
1. Called by a specific procedure
2. Which call a specific procedure
as well as a call tree which has a
a specific procedure as its root
Available procedures:
```

(We will leave out the procedure listing to save space)

```
Which procedures should be examined?
(type "all" for all procedures): GetDefinition
DefinedP InsertDots ExplainAsTree ExplTree
InsertDotsPrint FirstPart RestPart
Do you want a list of procedures called
by specific procedures? yes
For which procedures?
(type "all" for all procedures):ExplTree
ExplTree uses InsertDotsPrint DefinedP GetDefinition
FirstPart ExplTree RestPart
Do you want a list of all procedures
which call specific procedures?yes
For which procedures?
(type "all" for all procedures):ExplTree
ExplTree is called by ExplainAsTree ExplTree
Do you want the tree printed out?yes
Legend:
 + this procedure's subtree
has already been shown
 * this procedure is recursive
What procedure should be the root?
ExplainAsTree
 ExplainAsTree
 . ExplTree *
 . . InsertDotsPrint
 . . . InsertDots *
 . . . . InsertDots * +
 . . FirstPart *
 . . . DefinedP
 . . . . GetDefinition
 . . . FirstPart * +
 . . DefinedP +
 . . FirstPart * +
 . . ExplTree * +
 . . GetDefinition +
 . . FirstPart * +
 . . ExplTree * +
 . . RestPart *
 . . . DefinedP +
 . . . RestPart * +
```

In contrast to `Trace`, this program details information about the *static* structure of a program; it does not contain, for example, any information about the values of the variables, because the program being studied is not ''active'' while it is being studied. The tree printed by `ProgramStructure` contains information solely about which procedures use other procedures and the order *in the program text* that they appear; the tree contains no information about what order or under what conditions the procedures are actually called.

For example, in our example program, `ExplTree`, the second line shows `InsertDotsPrint` before `FirstPart`; however, `FirstPart` is called before `InsertDotsPrint`. This dynamic property of the program is not expressed in the tree printed by `ProgramStructure`.

Objectives

(1) This program is an example of the ability of programs to be used as data. It shows that the distinction between the information structures in programs and data is always a distinction made by and defined in the system that interprets the information structure and is not an inherent property of the information structure itself. Whereas the procedures that are used as examples in this chapter were interpreted and explained as programs in chapter 21, our interest in the same procedure text in this chapter is *as data* for our program `ProgramStructure`.

(2) The program represents a good example of the *glass-box approach*. The program can be used as a tool as presented here; you don't have to understand its inner workings. However, if you are interested (now or later), you can study or modify the inner workings.

(3) We also use this program as an example of how the goal of *run-time efficiency* can be taken into account when designing a program, in contrast to most of the sections in this book, where *cognitive efficiency* was in the forefront. We show that the careful selection of suitable data structures can aid in this goal. Since this program is one that (we hope) will be useful to anyone programming in LOGO and may be used often, its *run-time efficiency* is even more desirable.

Underlying Difficulties

Direct and Indirect Recursion

While printing out the tree, if we were to simply print out all the procedures that are called by the current procedure, we could easily find ourselves in an infinite recursion. For example, in the case where procedure A calls procedure B and B also calls A, our tree would look like this:

```
A
. B
. . A
. . . B
```

etc.

We must proceed carefully to avoid this trap.

Procedures That Have Already Been Explained

It certainly makes sense while printing out the call tree to explain the call structure of any procedure only once and to refer to any previous explanation, should the need arise. Otherwise, the tree can quickly become too large to be read easily.

Run Lists and Functional Arguments

With the version of LOGO used here, which uses what is known as LCSI syntax, the arguments to commands such as `If`, `IfElse`, `IFTrue`, and `IfFalse` can be *run lists*, or lists made up of commands to be executed. On the surface it is difficult distinguish between literal lists that are data, and literal lists that are commands to be executed.

```
If :This = [] [Output First :Thing]
Print [Output First Thing]
```

This problem is made more difficult by the fact that these lists do not need to be literal lists, but they can also be constructed lists.

```
If :This = [] List :Command ":Variable
```

A related problems deal with what is known as the functional argument problem. Given the procedure:

```
To FuncArgDemo :A :B
   Run (Sentence "Print :A ":B)
End
```

When called, for example:

```
? FuncArgDemo "First "Test
T
```

Run is given the expression [`Print First :B`] to evaluate (i.e., within the procedure `FuncArgDemo` an explicit call to the interpreter using `Run` causes `First` to be called). In general, because the value associated with the input `:A` can be anything, it is not possible to show all the procedures that are "called by" `FuncArgDemo`. This is a dynamic property of the procedure and is not shown by the program `ProgramStructure`.

This program does not solve the latter problem, although it does attempt to solve the former one, by assuming that the `If` commands always use literal lists instead of constructed lists. If the program being examined does not do this, then some incorrect results may occur. Also, if the version of LOGO being used uses a "2-or-3-argument `If`," some information may be missed. A correct solution to this problem would require knowing how many arguments every procedure uses so that the proper alignment of words in the program text to program arguments could be made.

The Program

```
To ProgramStructure
   PrintProgramDescription
   Print Procedures
   Print []
   Print [Which procedures should be examined?]
   Type [(type "all" for all procedures):]
   Make "WorkingSet ReadList
   If :WorkingSet = [all]
      [Make "WorkingSet Procedures]
   MarkProc :WorkingSet
   MapC "TryProcNames :WorkingSet
   CalleesList
   CallersList
   Tree
End

To PrintProgramDescription
   Print
      [The program ProgramStructure should aid in the]
   Print [understanding of complex LOGO-programs.]
   Print [It generates lists of procedures]
   Print [1 - Called by a specific procedure]
   Print [2 - Which call a specific procedure]
   Print [as well as a call tree which has a]
   Print [specific procedure as its root]
   Print [Available procedures:]
End
```

After printing out all the procedures in the workspace, the names of the procedures that are of interest to the user are read in and assigned to the global variable WorkingSet.

The ability to restrict the work to a few procedures is reasonable, since it keeps the tree from becoming so large that it cannot be easily read. However, if all procedures should be examined, that is an option as well.

Efficiency Problems

As already mentioned briefly, in designing this program some problems arise regarding *run time efficiency*. In determining the names of all the procedures called by a particular procedure, the following basic methods could be considered: Each word of the procedure text is checked to see if it is contained in the list WorkingSet. In doing so, the list is searched from beginning to (more times than not) end, as many times as there are elements in the procedure text. Clearly, this sequential searching method is time consuming, especially when it is used on a large program (when it is the most useful!), that the program becomes unusable. So, we use another method.

```
To MarkProc :Names
   If :Names = [] [Stop]
   PutProp First :Names "ProcedureName "True
   MarkProc ButFirst :Names
End
```

MarkProc puts the value "True on the "ProcedureName property of the names of all the procedures in WorkingSet. Later (in procedure Filter), when the program needs to check a word from a procedure to see if it is the name of a procedure under investigation, this can be done quickly by just using GetProp.

The procedure MapC from section 23.1 does the actual search of the program text. The procedure MapC applies the procedure TryProcNames to each element of :WorkingSet.

```
To TryProcNames :ProcName
  Make
    :ProcName
    TryProcNames1 ButFirst Text :ProcName
End

To TryProcNames1 :List
  If :List = [] [Output []]
  Output
    Sentence (Filter First :list)
      TryProcNames1 ButFirst :List
End

To Filter :TextLine
  If :TextLine = [] [Output []]
  Local "NextWord
  Make "NextWord First :TextLine
  If ListP :NextWord
    [Output Filter ButFirst :TextLine]
  If (First :NextWord) = SemiColon [Output []]
  If MemberP First :NextWord [: " ]
    [Output Filter ButFirst :TextLine]
  If (First :NextWord) = LeftParen
    [Make "NextWord ButFirst :NextWord]
  If (Last :NextWord) = RightParen
    [Make "NextWord ButLast :NextWord]
  If NumberP :NextWord
    [Output Filter ButFirst :TextLine]
  If :NextWord = "If
    [Output
        (Sentence Filter ButFirst ButLast :TextLine
           Filter Last :TextLine)]
  If MemberP :NextWord [IfTrue IfFalse]
    [Output Filter Last :TextLine]
  If :NextWord = "IfElse
    [Output
        (Sentence
           Filter ButFirst ButLast ButLast :TextLine
           Filter Last ButLast :TextLine
           Filter Last :TextLine)]
  Local "ProcProp
  Make "ProcProp GetProp :NextWord "ProcedureName
  If EmptyP :ProcProp
    [Output Filter ButFirst :TextLine]
```

```
If :ProcProp
  [Output
      Sentence :NextWord Filter ButFirst :TextLine]
  Output Filter ButFirst :TextLine
End
```

We use this method of specifying these special characters since it is more likely to be portable:

```
To SemiColon
  Output Char 59
End

To LeftParen
  Output Char 40
End

To RightParen
  Output Char 41
End
```

In `TryProcNames` a global variable that contains all the names of other procedures that are called by that procedure is created with the same name as the procedure in question. `TryProcNames1` determines what those names are by going through the program text of the procedure line by line. `Filter` tests to see if names in a line are procedure names as described in the description of `MarkProc`; because comments, constants (words, numbers, and lists), and variable names may also be present in the program text and may look like procedure calls, these need to be ignored as well. `If`-constructs are detected and handled in a special fashion, and parentheses are removed.

After `MapC` has completed its work, the following global variables corresponding to the procedure names in `WorkingSet` have been created.

```
"GetDefinition is []
"DefinedP is [GetDefinition]
"InsertDots is [InsertDots]
"ExplainAsTree is [ExplTree]
"ExplTree is [InsertDotsPrint FirstPart DefinedP
FirstPart ExplTree GetDefinition FirstPart
ExplTree RestPart]
"InsertDotsPrint is [InsertDots]
"FirstPart is [DefinedP FirstPart]
"RestPart is [DefinedP RestPart]
```

After this the procedure `CalleesList` gives the user the opportunity to see what procedures are called by one or several of the procedures of interest.

```
To CalleesList
  Print []
  Print [Do you want a list of procedures called]
  Type [by specific procedures?]
  If Not YesP [Stop]
  Print [for which procedures?]
  Type [(type "all" for all procedures):]
  Local "WhichOnes
  Make "WhichOnes ReadList
```

```
    If :WhichOnes = [all] [Make "WhichOnes :WorkingSet]
    MapC "PrintSet :WhichOnes
End
```

`PrintSet` just removes duplicate elements using `Set`

```
To &PrintSet :ProcName
   Print
     (Sentence
        :ProcName
        "uses
        &Set Thing :ProcName)
End

To Set :L
   If :L = [] [Output []]
   If MemberP First :L ButFirst :L
     [Output Set ButFirst :L]
   Output Sentence First :L Set ButFirst :L
End
```

`CallersList` gives the user the opportunity to see all the procedures that call a specified procedure.

```
To CallersList
   Print []
   Print [Do you want a list of all procedures]
   Type [which call specific procedures?]
   If Not YesP [Stop]
   Print [for which procedures?]
   Type [(type "all" for all procedures):]
   Local "WhichOnes
   Make "WhichOnes ReadList
   If :WhichOnes = [all] [Make "WhichOnes :WorkingSet]
   MapC [Print SearchCallers] :WhichOnes
End

To SearchCallers :ProcName
   Output
     (Sentence :ProcName [is called by]
        FoldMapCar
          :WorkingSet
          [MemberP :ProcName Thing])
End

To FoldMapCar :List :Function
   If :List = [] [Output []]
   Test Run Sentence :Function [First :List]
   IfTrue
     [Output
        Sentence First :List
          FoldMapCar ButFirst :List :Function]
   IfFalse
     [Output FoldMapCar ButFirst :List :Function]
End
```

`CallersList` is similar in form to `CalleesList`, although the search for "Callers" is somewhat more difficult. All the global variables (which are contained in :WorkingSet) are searched using FoldMapCar and MemberP looking for the current procedure name; if it is found the variable being searched is the name of a procedure that calls the current procedure, and it is combined with others. FoldMapCar is similar to MapCar except that it leaves empty elements out of the result list.

In the last line of ProgramStructure the user is finally asked if a call tree printout is desired. This program is also similar to the other two.

```
To Tree
    Type [Do you want the tree printed out?:]
    If Not YesP [Stop]
    Print [Legend:]
    Print [+ this procedure's subtree]
    Print [has already been shown]
    Print [* this procedure is recursive]
    Print [What procedure should be the root?]
    TreePrint ReadList 0
End
```

First an explanation of the special notations is given. Then the real work is done by TreePrint:

```
To TreePrint :Procedures :Level
    If :Procedures = [] [Stop]
    Test OldP First :Procedures
    PrintIt First :Procedures :Level
    IfFalse
       [TreePrint Thing First :Procedures :Level + 1]
    TreePrint ButFirst :Procedures :Level
End
```

TreePrint's actual output is done using PrintIt, which prints out the procedure name preceded by as many dots as necessary to show its :Level in the hierarchy.

```
To PrintIt :ProcName :Level
    Print
       (Sentence Dots :Level :ProcName
          Recursive :ProcName Old :ProcName)
End

To Dots :HowMany
    If :HowMany = 0 [Output []]
    Output Sentence Char 46 Dots :HowMany - 1
End
```

The procedures Recursive and Old add a "+" or "*" as appropriate.

```
To Recursive :ProcName
    IfElse MemberP :ProcName Thing :ProcName
       [Output "*]
       [Output "]
End

To Old :ProcName
    If OldP :ProcName [Output "+]
```

```
    MakeOld :ProcName
    Output "
End
```

If a procedure whose structure has not yet been printed out is at hand, this is done in the fourth line of `TreePrint`; `TreePrint` is applied recursively to the "callees" of the procedure. Otherwise the process continues with the rest of the procedures at the current level.

To finish things up, here are `OldP` and `MakeOld`.

```
To OldP :Procedure
  If Not NameP Word "OldProc. :Procedure
    [Output "False]
  Output
    Thing Word "OldProc. :Procedure = [already done]
End

To MakeOld :Procedure
  Make Word "OldProc. :Procedure [already done]
End
```

With `MakeOld` it is noted that a procedure has been "explained" by assigning a value to the `OldProc` property of the name of the program. `OldP` checks to see if this has been done.

Possible Extensions

The program could be extended in several ways:

- Keep track of the callers in the same way we kept track of callees, so that it does not need to be computed by `CallersList`.

- The names of the parameters could be given with the printed tree.

- Information about the access to and scope of local and global variables could be shown.

- Some more general way of resolving (as much as is possible) functional arguments and command lists could be developed. A first approach to this would be to specify which inputss of which procedures are "functional" (e.g., the input to `Run`, the second input to `If`, the second and third inputs to `IfElse`, the first input to `MapC`, etc.) and treat them as being called by the program that calls the procedure with a functional argument. For example, for

```
To Example :List
  .
  .
  MapC "Procedure :List
  .
End
```

  the program could show both `MapC` and `Procedure` as being called by `Example`, perhaps with another special notation.

- Allow the system to be queried about whether procedure B is used either directly or indirectly by procedure A.

- Allow the user to choose the order in which the procedures are listed in the tree (alphabetically, order in program text (the current way), or according to the nesting (order of call)).

This program resembles the program that was used here as sample data (the dictionary program); both programs allow *hierarchical, tree-like* structures to be presented. This program is more general in that it handles *circular* (recursive) definitions.

Chapter 24:
Simulation of a Moving Camera

This chapter presents a project that allows the computer to be used in a reasonable *project-oriented* mathematical pursuit. The simulation of a camera (or a human eye) is an intuitive and concrete undertaking. Rather than simply using the computer as a "number cruncher" as is often done in mathematical examples, the computer uses mathematical manipulations to produce a *visible* result.

The function of the computer and programming are twofold:

- In programming the computer to simulate a camera (or the eye), you will come to understand a little better how your own sight works. This is similar to the example in the artificial intelligence part that simulates human thought and often requires some intensive self-observation.

- The program (as soon as it is built) represents an explicit, detailed theory (which may be false) in geometry and trigonometry. In that sense, we are not just interested in a running program, but also in the code of the individual procedures that are a description (in a specific language) of certain mathematical and physical laws.

The project is also interesting from the mathematical perspective because it brings together knowledge from several sub-disciplines: Analytical geometry, descriptive geometry, plane geometry, and trigonometry are all used in the solution of this problem and some of the extensions can lead into the areas of graph theory and matrix theory. In spite of this, it is still a small program.

24.1. The Problem

If we position a camera at an arbitrary point in three-dimensional space, directed towards a geometric solid, then the question arises: "How does this solid appear to the camera?" How does the view change, if we move the camera around (closer to the solid, or further from it)? Hows does the view change if we rotate the camera?

This projection of an object in space onto the film (focal plane) through the lens of a camera (in the simplest case: the hole in a pinhole camera) is called a *perspective projection*. This is generated by the same type of geometric methods used in a perspective drawing. When compared with other methods such as the *oblique parallel projection*, this produces a picture closer to what the human viewer would perceive.

The following program simulates a camera that can move about in space, and which is capable of *translations* as well as *rotations*. The picture that the camera perceives is drawn by the program on the screen. We see the "world" on the screen similar to the way that our imaginary camera sees it or as a (one-eyed!) human observer would see from the position of the camera.

We simplify the problem somewhat and assume that all objects are completely within the view of the camera.

24.2. Defining Objects in Three-Dimensional Space

There are many possible ways to define objects in three dimensions, each having its own characteristics in terms of generality, efficiency, and usability with respect to the kinds of operations that need to be performed. We use a representation that is general and is well suited to the projections that we need to perform. The representation that we have selected is a list of edges, each edge represented by two points.

The cube in figure 24–1 could be defined with the following list of edges (with each edge represented as two point, and each point represented by 3 Numbers, the x,y, and z coordinates of the point):

```
[[[2 1 2] [2 4 2]]
 [[2 4 2] [2 4 5]]
 [[2 4 5] [2 1 5]]
 [[2 1 5] [5 1 5]]
 [[5 1 5] [5 4 5]]
 [[5 4 5] [5 4 2]]
 [[5 4 2] [5 1 2]]
 [[5 1 2] [2 1 2]]
 [[2 1 2] [2 1 5]]
 [[2 4 5] [5 4 5]]
 [[2 4 2] [5 4 2]]
 [[5 1 2] [5 1 5]]
]
```

Complex pictures (such as concave bodies) can be defined and drawn with this representation. For our experiments, we use simple blocks and pyramids that all have rectangular bases parallel to the axes of the coordinate system.

We assume that the definitions of the line segments that make up all the objects are in a list that has been assigned to the global variable :World. We can generate a world with some objects in it using the following procedures:

```
To GenerateWorld
   Make "World []
   GeneratePyramid -3 0 20 5 4 3
   GenerateBlock 3 0 16 4 4 4
   GenerateBlock -3 0 12 4 4 5
End
```

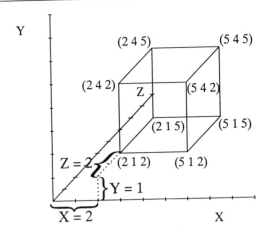

Figure 24–1: The Definition of a Solid by Coordinates

```
To GenerateBlock :X :Y :Z :DX :DY :DZ
  If Not NameP "World [Make "World [ ]]
  Make
    "World
    Sentence
      (List
        (List Add 0 0 0 Add 0 0 :DZ)
        (List Add 0 0 :DZ Add 0 :DY :DZ)
        (List Add 0 :Dy :Dz Add 0 :DY 0)
        (List Add 0 :DY 0 Add :DX :DY 0)
        (List Add :DX :DY 0 Add :DX :DY :DZ)
        (List Add :DX :DY :DZ Add :DX 0 :DZ)
        (List Add :DX 0 :DZ Add :DX 0 0)
        (List Add :DX 0 0 Add 0 0 0)
        (List Add 0 0 0 Add 0 :DY 0)
        (List Add 0 0 :DZ Add :DX 0 :DZ)
        (List Add 0 :DY :DZ Add :DX :DY :DZ)
        (List Add :DX 0 0 Add :DX :DY 0))
      :World
End

To GeneratePyramid :X :Y :Z :DX :DY :DZ
  If Not NameP "World [Make "World [ ]]
```

```
Make
  "World
  Sentence
    (List
       (List Add 0 0 0 Add 0 0 :DZ)
       (List Add 0 0 :DZ Add :DX 0 :DZ)
       (List Add :DX 0 :DZ Add :DX 0 0)
       (List Add :DX 0 0 Add 0 0 0)
       (List Add 0 0 0 Add (:DX / 2) :DY (:DZ / 2))
       (List Add (:DX / 2) :DY (:DZ / 2) Add 0 0 :DZ)
       (List
          Add :DX 0 :DZ
          Add (:DX / 2) :DY (:DZ / 2))
       (List Add (:DX / 2) :DY (:DZ / 2) Add :DX 0 0))
    :World
End

To Add :DiX :DiY :DiZ
  Output (list :X + :DiX :Y + :DiY :Z + :DiZ)
End
```

24.3. The Simulated Camera

For now, we assume that the lens of our camera is at the origin of the coordinate system and that it is looking along the z-axis (the z-axis and the camera's axis are the same) in the positive z direction. If we place the focal plane (the graphics screen!) parallel to the x–y plane, we can project points in space through the origin (the camera lens) onto it as long as the points have positive z coordinates. This situation is shown in figure 24–2.

By setting the film (our graphics screen) a specific distance (the focal length) from the lens, and using film that has a fixed size (the size of our screen), the viewing angle of our camera can be determined. If we move the film further back, the viewing angle is reduced; if we move the film closer, the viewing angle is increased.

To achieve a "normal" viewing angle of about 50 degrees, we use a focal length of 255 (assuming that our graphics screen is about 280 by 240, and using the smaller vertical dimension).

An arbitrary point (x y z) with a positive z-value can then be projected onto our film (figure 24–3). Using basic geometry and at the same time "inverting" the image, the x and y coordinates of the projection of a point onto the focal plane are given by:

$$y' = \frac{y \times 255}{z}$$

and

$$x' = \frac{x \times 255}{z}$$

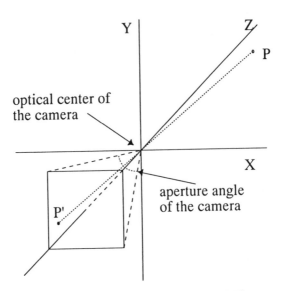

Figure 24-2: Projection onto the Focal Plane

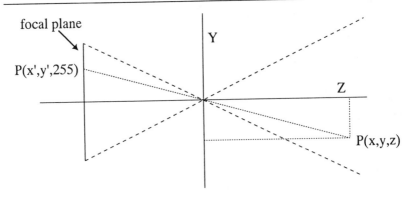

Figure 24-3: Projection—Continued

Both of these coordinates are calculated by the procedure `Projection` and are used to move the current x–y point (of the LOGO "turtle"):

```
To Projection :P
  SetXY
    255 * (First :P) / (Last :P)
    255 * (First ButFirst :P) / (Last :P)
End
```

To show the whole "world" on the film, this projection is performed on all points in the "world," by drawing each projected line segment on the graphics screen. With the "pen" up, the first point is moved to, then with the "pen" down, the second point is moved to. The procedure ShowWorld performs these operations:

```
To ShowWorld :World
  If :World = [] [Stop]
  PenUp
  Projection First First :World
  PenDown
  Projection Last First :World
  ShowWorld ButFirst :World
End
```

The procedure DemoCamera provides a simple way to run the experiment:

```
To DemoCamera
  ClearScreen
  ShowWorld :World
End

? DemoCamera
```

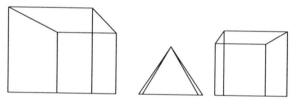

Figure 24–4: Initial View of the World

24.4. Moving the Camera Around the World

With what we have defined so far, it is possible to project objects that lie in view of the camera on the graphics screen. What is missing is the ability to move the camera around the room. We can differentiate between *translational* movements (those which change the location of the camera) and *rotational* movements (those which change the direction in which the camera "points"). There are three of each type.

Translations

x: The camera moves along the x-axis (i.e., to the right or to the left). It still looks straight ahead. If the camera moves to the right, image on the graphics screen moves to the left. This is done by the procedure &Right.

y: The camera moves along the y-axis (i.e., up or down). When the camera moves up, the image on the screen moves down. The procedure &Higher implements this.

z: The camera moves along the z-axis (i.e., forwards or backwards). When the camera moves forwards, the picture on the screen gets bigger; backwards, and it gets smaller. This corresponds to the procedure &Forwards.

This all can be done by a small change to the procedure Projection, and by using the global variables :CameraX, :CameraY, and CameraZ.

```
To Projection :P
  Local "PX
  Local "PY
  Local "PZ
  Make "PX (First :P) - :CameraX
  Make "PY (First ButFirst :P) - :CameraY
  Make "PZ (Last :P) - :CameraZ
  IfElse :PZ = 0
    [SetXY 0 0]
    [SetXY 255 * :PX / :PZ 255 * :PY / :PZ]
End
```

As the changes to Projection show, the translations are simply a matter of subtracting x, y, and z components of the position of the camera lens from the corresponding components of each point.

These procedures actually perform the translations:

```
To Forwards :Amount
  MoveCamera 0 0 :Amount
End

To Right :Amount
  MoveCamera :Amount 0 0
End

To Higher :Amount
  MoveCamera 0 :Amount 0
End

To MoveCamera :DX :DY :DZ
  Make "CameraX :CameraX + :DX
  Make "CameraY :CameraY + :DY
  Make "CameraZ :CameraZ + :DZ
End
```

Here is an example of moving the camera up 5 units using `Higher`:

```
? Higher 5
```

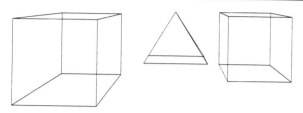

Figure 24–5: `Higher 5`

Rotations

There are also three different axes of rotation, around which the optical axis (the axis from the center of the lens to the center of the focal plane) can turn. These correspond to the three axes of the coordinate system.

x: If the optical axis is rotated around the x-axis, the z and y components of all points are changed, while the x component remains the same. The motion of the camera is similar to the rotations you perform with your head when you nod your head "yes." With a positive rotation, the camera tips downward, and with a negative rotation the camera points more upward. In nautical and aeronautical terminology, this is known as *pitch*, so we use this name for our procedure.

y: The camera is turned about the vertical (y) axis, similar to the rotation that your head makes when you shake your head "no." Positive motions move the line of sight of the camera to the left, negative ones to the right. All the y-components remain the same, while the x and z components change. This is known as *Yaw* in nautical and aeronautical terminology.

z: Here, the optical axis is rotated about the z-axis, which causes the camera to "tilt" to one side or the other. The z-components of all the points remain the same, while the x and y components all change. Positive motions tilt the camera to the right side; negative motions tilt it to the left. In nautical and aeronautical terminology, this is called *Roll*.

Another change to `Projection` allows us to implement these rotations. Some trigonometric and matrix multiplication "magic" as well as a new representation of the position of the camera called a transformation matrix does the real work here, but we simply provide the procedures that do these transformations for the sake of simplicity. Interested readers may wish to study [Foley, Dam 82].

```
To Projection :Point
  Local "NegateTM
  Make
    "NegateTM
    ListToArray (1 - 0)
  Local "TransPoint
  Make
    "TransPoint
    TMPointProduct
      :Point
      TMProduct :NegateTM :TransMatrix
  Local "X
  Local "Y
  Local "Z
  Make "X First :TransPoint
  Make "Y Nth 2 :TransPoint
  Make "Z Nth 3 :TransPoint
  IfElse :Z = 0
    [SetXY 0 0
     Stop]
    [SetXY 255 * :X / :Z 255 * :Y / :Z]
End

To TMPointProduct :Point :TM
  Local "PointX
  Local "PointY
  Local "PointZ
  Make "PointX First :Point
  Make "PointY Nth 2 :Point
  Make "PointZ Nth 3 :Point
  Output
    (List
      (Sum
        :PointX * (ArrayGet :TM 0)
        :PointY * (ArrayGet :TM 3)
        :PointZ * (ArrayGet :TM 6)
        (ArrayGet :TM 9))
      (Sum
        :PointX * (ArrayGet :TM 1)
        :PointY * (ArrayGet :TM 4)
        :PointZ * (ArrayGet :TM 7)
        (ArrayGet :TM 10))
      (Sum
        :PointX * (ArrayGet :TM 2)
        :PointY * (ArrayGet :TM 5)
        :PointZ * (ArrayGet :TM 8)
        (ArrayGet :TM 11)))
End
```

The translation matrix representation here uses the array facility available in OBJECTLOGO. We can then introduce the procedures Pitch, Yaw, and Roll to allow the camera angle to be changed:

```
To Pitch :DeltaAngle
  Make
    "TransMatrix
    RotateXTM :DeltaAngle :TransMatrix
End

To RotateXTM :Angle :TM
  Make
    "RotationMatrix
    ListToArray
      (List
        1 0               0
        0 Cos :Angle      Sin :Angle
        0 -1 * Sin :Angle Cos :Angle
        0 0               0)
  Output TMProduct :TM :RotationMatrix
End

To Yaw :DeltaAngle
  Make
    "TransMatrix
    RotateYTM :DeltaAngle :TransMatrix
End

To RotateYTM :Angle :TM
  Make
    "RotationMatrix
    ListToArray
      (List
        Cos :Angle 0  -1 * Sin :Angle
        0          1  0
        Sin :Angle 0  Cos :Angle
        0          0  0)
  Output TMProduct :TM :RotationMatrix
End

To Roll :DeltaAngle
  Make "TransAngle RotateZTM :DeltaAngle :TransAngle
End

To RotateZTM :Angle :TM
  Make
    "RotationMatrix
    ListToArray
      (List
        Cos :Angle      Sin :Angle 0
        -1 * Sin :Angle Cos :Angle 0
        0               0          1
        0               0          0)
  Output TMProduct :TM :RotationMatrix
End
```

```
To TMProduct :TM1 :TM2
  Output
    ListToArray
      (List
        (Sum
          (ArrayGet :TM1 0) * (ArrayGet :TM2 0)
          (ArrayGet :TM1 1) * (ArrayGet :TM2 3)
          (ArrayGet :TM1 2) * (ArrayGet :TM2 6))
        (Sum
          (ArrayGet :TM1 0) * (ArrayGet :TM2 1)
          (ArrayGet :TM1 1) * (ArrayGet :TM2 4)
          (ArrayGet :TM1 2) * (ArrayGet :TM2 7))
        (Sum
          (ArrayGet :TM1 0) * (ArrayGet :TM2 2)
          (ArrayGet :TM1 1) * (ArrayGet :TM2 5)
          (ArrayGet :TM1 2) * (ArrayGet :TM2 8))
        (Sum
          (ArrayGet :TM1 3) * (ArrayGet :TM2 0)
          (ArrayGet :TM1 4) * (ArrayGet :TM2 3)
          (ArrayGet :TM1 5) * (ArrayGet :TM2 6))
        (Sum
          (ArrayGet :TM1 3) * (ArrayGet :TM2 1)
          (ArrayGet :TM1 4) * (ArrayGet :TM2 4)
          (ArrayGet :TM1 5) * (ArrayGet :TM2 7))
        (Sum
          (ArrayGet :TM1 3) * (ArrayGet :TM2 2)
          (ArrayGet :TM1 4) * (ArrayGet :TM2 5)
          (ArrayGet :TM1 5) * (ArrayGet :TM2 8))
        (Sum
          (ArrayGet :TM1 6) * (ArrayGet :TM2 0)
          (ArrayGet :TM1 7) * (ArrayGet :TM2 3)
          (ArrayGet :TM1 8) * (ArrayGet :TM2 6))
        (Sum
          (ArrayGet :TM1 6) * (ArrayGet :TM2 1)
          (ArrayGet :TM1 7) * (ArrayGet :TM2 4)
          (ArrayGet :TM1 8) * (ArrayGet :TM2 7))
        (Sum
          (ArrayGet :TM1 6) * (ArrayGet :TM2 2)
          (ArrayGet :TM1 7) * (ArrayGet :TM2 5)
          (ArrayGet :TM1 8) * (ArrayGet :TM2 8))
        (Sum
          (ArrayGet :TM1 9) * (ArrayGet :TM2 0)
          (ArrayGet :TM1 10) * (ArrayGet :TM2 3)
          (ArrayGet :TM1 11) * (ArrayGet :TM2 6)
          (ArrayGet :TM2 9))
        (Sum
          (ArrayGet :TM1 9) * (ArrayGet :TM2 1)
          (ArrayGet :TM1 10) * (ArrayGet :TM2 4)
          (ArrayGet :TM1 11) * (ArrayGet :TM2 7)
          (ArrayGet :TM2 10))
        (Sum
          (ArrayGet :TM1 9) * (ArrayGet :TM2 2)
          (ArrayGet :TM1 10) * (ArrayGet :TM2 5)
          (ArrayGet :TM1 11) * (ArrayGet :TM2 8)
          (ArrayGet :TM2 11)))
  End
```

```
To ListToArray :List
   Output ListToArray1 :List array count :list 0
End

To ListToArray1 :List :Array :Index
   If EmptyP :List [Output :Array]
   ArrayPut :Array :Index First :List
   Output
       ListToArray1 ButFirst :List :Array :Index + 1
End
```

Translation procedures must also be changed to use the translation matrix representation.

```
To MoveCamera :DX :DY :DZ
   Make
       "TransMatrix
       TranslateTM :DX :DY :DZ :TransMatrix
End

To TranslateTM :X :Y :Z :TM
   Make
       "TranslationMatrix
       ListToArray (List 1  0  0
                         0  1  0
                         0  0  1
                        :X :Y :Z )
   Output TMProduct :TM :TranslationMatrix
End
```

If you want to view the scenery from the opposite side, this can be done with:

```
? Forwards 40
? Yaw 180
? DemoCamera
```

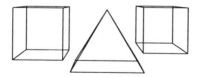

Figure 24-6: The World - from the Other Side

Note that sometimes an object does not appear on the screen and, instead, wild lines are splashed across the graphics screen. This can be caused by one of two things:

• The camera is too close to the object, so only part of the lines that make up its outline are visible. The rest of the points of the lines are "off the screen."

• The camera is close to the object again, but this time so that the endpoints of one of the lines lies at the focal point of the lens (at the origin in the initial state). `Projection` does not handle this case properly.

Both of these can be remedied by "moving the camera back."

24.5. Possible Extensions

If you want to study this problem further, here are some ideas:

- Different focal lengths could be allowed (telephoto lens, wide-angle lens).

- The camera could be placed in the midst of the objects such that some of the objects might be *behind* the camera and therefore should not be visible.

- A second picture could be generated that includes the camera in the world and observes it, as well.

- Study the efficiency of the representation used for the world and the objects. For example, instead of representing the objects as sets of individual line segments, with the program repeatedly raising the pen, moving to the first point, lowering the pen, moving to the second point, and then repeating the whole process for each line segment, are there other representations that could be used? You might try to apply some *graph theory* to investigate representing the objects as a set of lines such that each line can be drawn without lifting the pen.

- All objects could be represented individually and then moved around in space.

- Find a way to handle the problem that occurs when the endpoint of a line is at the focal point of the lens.

- Create animations of the motions of the camera.

    Calculating and generating individual scenes can be computationally intensive depending on the number of vectors that need to be drawn. It is sometimes difficult to actually simulate a "moving" camera. One way to get around this problem is to generate a series of scenes, saving each one, then displaying them rapidly, one after the other to create the animation.

    Your version of LOGO may provide some primitives to help you with this process.

- and many more...

Chapter 25:
The Game of LIFE

LIFE is not really a game in the sense that one player plays against another or against the computer. Instead it is a *simulation* of the death and growth behavior of a population. In another sense, it can be considered a "no-person"—as its inventor John H. Conway called it—game or a "pure" computer game. Since its introduction to the world at large in 1970 [Gardner 70] and with the proliferation of computers, which makes it easier to run many generations of the simulation, LIFE has enjoyed a great deal of popularity. It even had its own newsletter [Lifeline 73] for a while.

The game is defined as follows:

- The game is played on a checkerboard-like board of arbitrary size.

- An unlimited number of game pieces are used. These can be placed on the board in a random or systematic fashion at the beginning.

- After this initialization, the board is propagated through arbitrarily many generations using specific rules.

- Each member of the population can have between zero and eight neighbors (this is derived from the layout of the board).

- The members of the population are "born" and "die off" according to the following rules:

    - If a member has too few (<2) neighbors, it will "die" of "exposure."

    - If a member has too many (>3) neighbors, it will "die" of "overcrowding."

    - If a member has two or three neighbors (i.e., five or six of the neighboring spaces are unoccupied), it stays alive.

    - If a space is unoccupied, a new member is "born" in that space if it has exactly three neighbors.

    - The entire "next generation" is calculated at once, that is, all the "births" and "deaths" happen at the same time.

The following figures illustrate several generations of the game:

```
1st Generation  2nd Generation  3rd Generation
. . . . . . .    . . . . . . .    . . . . . . .
. . . . . . .    . . . . . . .    . . . X . . .
. . . X . . .    . . X X X . .    . . X . X . .
. . X X X . .    . . X . X . .    . X . . . X .
. . . X . . .    . . X X X . .    . . X . X . .
. . . . . . .    . . . . . . .    . . . X . . .
. . . . . . .    . . . . . . .    . . . . . . .

4th Generation  5th Generation  6th Generation
. . . . . . .    . . . . . . .    . . . X . . .
. . . X . . .    . . X X X . .    . . X X X . .
. . X X X . .    . X . . . X .    . X . X . X .
. X X . X X .    . X . . . X .    X X X . X X X
. . X X X . .    . X . . . X .    . X . X . X .
. . . X . . .    . . X X X . .    . . X X X . .
. . . . . . .    . . . . . . .    . . . X . . .

                7th Generation
                . . X X X . .
                . . . . . . .
                X . . . . . X
                X . . . . . X
                X . . . . . X
                . . . . . . .
                . . X X X . .
```

In each new generation some of the members "die," some new members are "born," and others remain from the previous generation.

25.1. Objectives

Implementing and playing the LIFE is interesting from several points of view:

- It illustrates the limitations of human conceptual power with respect to comprehension of dynamic, complex, strongly interdependent processes: Almost each generation is surprising.

- It is an excellent example for illustrating concepts of *systems* and *states* and can be used as an outstanding demonstration of the stable, instable, and cyclic behavior of systems.

- It can be used as an introduction into the theory of cellular automata.

- It illustrates utility and limitations (when dealing with cell-masses that wander in an unlimited fashion) of fixed, matrix-like data structures (see the second implementation in that regard).

- It is easy to implement and requires little programming knowledge.

25.2. Example

To save space, we always print the generations three-across even though they were printed one under the other in the original output.

```
? Life
How large should the square be? 8
. . . X . . . .    . . X X . . . .    . . X X . . . .
. . X X . . . .    . . X X . . . .    . X . . X . . .
. X . . . . . .    . X . X . . . .    . X . X X . . .
. X X . . X . .    . X X . . X . .    . X . X X . X .
. . . . X X X .    . X . . X . X .    . . . . . . X . .
. . . X . X . X    . . X X . X . X    . . X X X . . X
. . X X . . . .    . . . . . . . X    . . . . X . X .
. . X X . . X X    . . X X . . . .    . . . . . . . .
Quit?no             Quit?no            Quit?no

. . X X . . . .    . . . X X . . . .   . X X X . . . .
. X . . X . . .    X X . X . . . .    X . . X . . . .
X X . . . . . .    X X X . . . . .    X . X . . . . .
. . . X . . . .    . . . . . . . .    . X X . . . . .
. . . . . X X .    . . X . X X . .    . . . . X X X .
. . . X X . X .    . . . X . . X .    . . . X X . . X .
. . . . X X . .    . . . X X X . .    . . . X X X . .
. . . . . . . .    . . . . . . . .    . . . . . . X . . .
Quit?no             Quit?no            Quit? yes
```

25.3. Implementation

In the following sections, two implementations of the LIFE are described. Both are shown to demonstrate different approaches to the same problem, and how different assumptions and preconditions can affect the implementation of a program. The first implementation is based on an ALGOL-like implementation. This shows up primarily in the data structures that are used; the game board is a finite, fixed size square. As a result, the rules for the spaces along the edges are no longer appropriate, since, for example, a corner space can no longer "die" from overcrowding. It also becomes apparent, that some versions of LOGO are not particularly well suited for this type of implementation because they lack both a purely iterative control structure as well as an array data type. The second implementation attempts to create a version of the program that is better suited to the style of LOGO programming that we have used in this book and also better suited to the rules of the game. The static restriction on the playing board is removed and lists are used for the data structures.

Both versions have to deal with the basic task of generating successive generations of the game board. According to the rules, the makeup of one generation is dependent only on the makeup of the previous generation; whether a space is occupied in the n+1-st generation is dependent only on whether it and its eight neighbors were occupied in the n-th generation.

The Game Board as a Matrix

As was already suggested, it is possible to use a two-dimensional array—a matrix—to implement the playing board. However, since each transition from one generation to the next must take place "all at once," the old playing board must be available until the new playing board is completely generated and may not be even partially overwritten by the new information. This requires the use of two arrays; one to contain the n-th generation, and the other to contain the n+1-st generation.[27] We call these two fields &BDTrue and &BDFalse to be able to switch between the two boards by the logical negation of the variable &Board. In addition to the arrays and this logical variable, the variable &N contains the size of the playing board. Both boards are stored row-by-row (the index becomes part of the name) in &N-element lists. The For control structure (described in chapter 23) is useful for creating and accessing these variables.

```
? PrintOut Names
"&BDFalse0 is [0 0 0 0 0]        "&BDTrue0 is [0 0 0 0 0]
"&BDFalse1 is [0 0 0 0 0]        "&BDTrue1 is [0 0 0 0 0]
"&BDFalse2 is [0 0 0 0 0]        "&BDTrue2 is [0 0 0 0 0]
"&BDFalse3 is [0 0 0 0 0]        "&BDTrue3 is [0 0 0 0 0]
"&BDFalse4 is [0 0 0 1 1]        "&BDTrue4 is [0 0 0 1 1]
"&BDFalse5 is [0 0 0 1 1]        "&BDTrue5 is [0 0 0 1 1]
"&BDFalse6 is [0 0 0 0 0]        "&BDTrue6 is [0 0 0 0 0]
"&N is 5
```

In the procedure Life1 the data structures are initialized first, allowing the user to specify the size of the board.

```
To Life1
  Initialize
  LifeLoop1
End

To Initialize
  Type [Size of the Board?]
  Make "&N First ReadList
  Make "&Board "True
  DefineBoard :&Board :&N 0
  DefineBoard Not :&Board :&N 0
  ReadCoordinates Word "&BD :&Board
End

To LifeLoop1
  Local "I
  Local "J
```

---

[27]Alternatively, the old and new information could be coded in the number stored in the element of one array (e.g., 0 = unoccupied both generations, 1 = occupied nth - unoccupied n+1st, 10 = unoccupied nth - occupied n+1st, and 11 = occupied both generations). We could then generate the intermediate representation and afterwards make a second pass over the information and throw out the old information.

```
    For "I 1 1 :&N
      [For "J 1 1 :&N [PrintAndCalculate]
        Print " ]
    Type "Quit?
    IfElse YesP
      [Stop]
      [Print " ]
    Make "&Board Not :&Board
    LifeLoop1
End

To DefineBoard :Name :N
    Local "I
    For "I 1 1 :N
      [Make (Word "&BD :Name :I) RandomList :N 2]
    Make (Word "&BD :Name 0) ZeroList :N
    Make (Word "&BD :Name :N + 1) ZeroList :N
End
```

Both boards &BDTrue and &BDFalse (except for 0-th and n+1-st lines) are filled with random zeroes and ones by DefineBoard; &Board is initialized to "True.

The actual game loop is found in Step1. The user is asked if the game should end before another generation is calculated.

Printing the board and the calculation of the next generation takes place in the procedure PrintAndCalculate, which itself calls Calculate. The array access is handled by the procedures Get and Put.

```
To PrintAndCalculate
    Type XorDot Get Word "&BD :&Board :I :J
    Type "
    Put
      Word "&BD Not :&Board
      :I
      :J
      Calculate :I :J :&Board 0
End

To Calculate :I :J :WhichBoard :NumNeighbors
    Make "NumNeighbors CountNeighbors :I :J :WhichBoard
    If Or (:NumNeighbors > 3) (:NumNeighbors < 2)
      [Output 0]
    IfElse :NumNeighbors = 3
      [Output 1]
      [Output Get Word "&BD :WhichBoard :I :J]
End

To Get :Name :I :J
    Output Nth :J (Thing Word :Name :I)
End
```

```
To Put :Name :I :J :K
  Make
    Word :Name :I
    Replace (Thing Word :Name :I) :J :K
End

To Replace :LI :Index :new
  If :LI = [] [Output []]
  If :Index = 1 [Output FPut :New ButFirst :LI]
  Output
    FPut
      First :LI
      Replace ButFirst :LI :Index - 1 :New
End

To XorDot :IN
  IfElse :In = 0
    [Output ".]
    [Output "X]
End
```

In Calculate the coding of the rules about whether a member continues to exist, dies, or whether a new member is created are easy to understand; for each space on the board, the number of neighbors is calculated. Neighbor insures that the borders of the playing board are not overstepped.

```
To CountNeighbors :I :J :WhichBoard
  Output
    (Sum
      Neighbor :I - 1 :J - 1
      Neighbor :I     :J - 1
      Neighbor :I + 1 :J - 1
      Neighbor :I - 1 :J
      Neighbor :I + 1 :J
      Neighbor :I - 1 :J + 1
      Neighbor :I     :J + 1
      Neighbor :I + 1 :J + 1)
End

To Neighbor :I :J
  If (Or (:I < 1) (:J < 1) (:I > :&N) (:J > :&N))
    [Output 0]
  Output Get Word "&BD :WhichBoard :I :J
End
```

The procedure Nth is described in section III.

Using a List For Occupied Spaces

In the following implementation, the game board is stored as a list instead of as a two-dimensional array. One way would be for the list to contain all the spaces that are occupied. The spaces can be denoted by x–y pairs; the following figure shows a game board and its corresponding list representation.

```
X . . . X
. . . X X
. . . . .
X . X . X
X . . X .
```

```
:Board is [[1 1][1 5][2 4][2 5]
          [4 1][4 3][4 5][5 1][5 4]]
```

This representation allows the game board to grow as large as is needed in both positive and negative x and y directions. It does have the disadvantage that our most important operation (counting neighbors) would be inefficient to implement, since the entire list would have to be searched to see if a space is occupied. So, we try another representation, which better supports counting neighbors. This representation uses a list of pairs consisting of a row and a list of columns in that row that are occupied.

```
[row_i [columns] row_j [columns] ...]
```

This representation would look like this for the preceding example:

```
:Board is [1[1 5] 2 [4 5] 4 [1 3 5] 5 [1 4]]
```

This also has advantages in terms of the amount of space that is used. This list contains at most 2*(number of rows) elements (if all the spaces were occupied), whereas the other representation would have at most (rows * columns) elements. This becomes advantageous when at least three elements of a row are occupied but is even more important when the board becomes large. The advantage is small for our little example.

Using this representation, the procedure OccupiedP determines whether a space is occupied.

```
To OccupiedP :X :Y :Board
   Output
      MemberP
         :Y
         First
            ButFirst
               GetMember :X Sentence :Board list :X []
End

To GetMember :EL :LI
   If :LI = [] [Output []]
   If :EL = First :LI [Output :LI]
   Output GetMember :EL ButFirst :LI
End
```

The procedure MemberP is described in appendix III.

The last procedure dealing with this list representation is InsertSorted, which places elements into a list that already contains individuals.

```
To InsertSorted :X :Y :Board
   If :Board = [] [Output List :X (List :Y)]
   If (First :Board) > :X
     [Output FPut :X FPut (List :Y) :Board]
   If (First :Board) = :X
     [Output
        (FPut
          :X
          (FPut
             SortedInsert :Y First ButFirst :Board
             ButFirst ButFirst :Board))]
   Output
     (FPut
        First :Board
        (FPut
           First ButFirst :Board
           InsertSorted :X :Y ButFirst ButFirst :Board))
End

To SortedInsert :Y :L
   If :L = [] [Output :Y]
   If :Y = First :L [Output :L]
   IfElse :Y < First :L
     [Output FPut :Y :L]
     [Output
         Sentence First :L SortedInsert :Y ButFirst :L]
End
```

The rest of the procedures differ in small ways, but not in principal ways from the implementation described in section 25.3.

Life2 performs the necessary initialization and then starts the main part of the simulation (printing the fields, checking whether it should stop, calculating a new generation).

```
To Life2
   InitializeV2
   LifeLoop2
End

To LifeLoop2
   If EmptyP :Board
     [Print [Population depleted -- game over]
      Stop]
   PrintBoard
     First :Board
     Last ButLast :Board
     MinY ButFirst :Board
     MaxY ButFirst :Board
     0
   Type "Quit?
   If YesP [Stop]
```

```
      Make
        "Board
        NewGeneration
          (First :Board) - 1
          (Last ButLast :Board) + 1
          (MinY ButFirst :Board) - 1
          (MaxY ButFirst :Board) + 1
      LifeLoop2
    End

    To InitializeV2
      Local "I
      Local "J
      Type [Size of Initial Board?]
      Make "OX First ReadList
      Make "OY :OX
      Make "Board []
      For "I 1 1 :OX [For "J 1 1 :OY [InitSpace :I :J]]
    End

    To InitSpace :I :J
      If  0 = Random 2
        [Make "Board InsertSorted :I :J :Board]
    End
```

With this representation, it is necessary to know the maximum and minimum x
and y values, for example, to know how much of the conceptually infinite game
board to print out. The maximum and minimum x values are easily calculated
using First :Board and Last ButLast :Board; however, the
determination of the maximum and minimum y values take more effort.

```
    To MaxY :Board
      IfElse (ButFirst :Board) = []
        [Output Last First :Board]
        [Output
            Maxi
              Last First :Board
              MaxY ButFirst ButFirst :Board]
    End

    To MinY :Board
      IfElse (ButFirst :Board) = []
        [Output First First :Board]
        [Output
            Mini
              First First :Board
              MinY ButFirst ButFirst :Board]
    End

    To Maxi :A :B
      IfElse :A > :B
        [Output :A]
        [Output :B]
    End
```

```
To Mini :A :B
  IfElse :A < :B
    [Output :A]
    [Output :B]
End
```

These minimum and maximum x and y values are passed on to `PrintBoard`, which prints out the game board:

```
To PrintBoard :UX :OX :UY :OY :K
  Print "
  For "K :UX 1 :OX
    [Type Spaces 10 + 2 * :UY
     PrBD1 :UY :OY 0
     Print "]
  Print "
End

To PrBD1 :UY :OY :J
  For "J :UY 1 :OY
    [IfElse OccupiedP :K :J :Board
        [Type "X]
        [Type ".]]
End
```

`Spaces` is shown in appendix III.

The boundary values of x and y are also used by `NewGeneration`. This procedure generates the new game board in which all the points (x,y) where x is in the range $[x_{min}-1 ... x_{max}+1]$ and y is in the range $[y_{min}-1 ... y_{max}+1]$. The neighbors are counted using `CountNeighbors`, whose third input is a lists of constants that specify the (eight possible) neighbors.

```
To NewGeneration :UX :OX :UY :OY
  If :UX > :OX [Output []]
  Output
    Sentence
      NewGen :UX :UY :OY 0
      NewGeneration :UX + 1 :OX :UY :OY
End

To NewGen :UX :UY :OY :NumNeighbors
  If :UY > :OY [Output []]
  Make
    "NumNeighbors
    CountNeighborsV2
      :UX
      :UY
      [[1 1] [1 0] [1 -1] [0 -1]
       [-1 -1] [-1 0] [-1 1] [0 1]]
  If :NumNeighbors = 3
    [Output
       InsertSorted
         :UX
         :UY
         NewGen :UX :UY + 1 :OY :NumNeighbors]
```

```
        If :NumNeighbors = 2
          [If OccupiedP :UX :UY :Board
             [Output
                InsertSorted
                  :UX
                  :UY
                  NewGen :UX :UY + 1 :OY :NumNeighbors]]
        Output NewGen :UX :UY + 1 :OY :NumNeighbors
End

To CountNeighborsV2 :X :Y :Neighbors
   If :Neighbors = [] [Output 0]
   IfElse
       OccupiedP
       :X + First First :Neighbors
       :Y + Last First :Neighbors
       :Board
     [Output
        Sum
          1
          CountNeighborsV2 :X :Y ButFirst :Neighbors]
     [Output
        CountNeighborsV2 :X :Y ButFirst :Neighbors]
End
```

The advantage of the dynamically expandable game board can be shown by the
following test runs:

```
? Life2
Size of Initial Board? 7
                    X . . X . . X
                    X X . . X . X
                    . X X . X X .
                    . X X . X X .
                    . X . X . X X
                    X . X . X . .
                    X . . X X . .
Quit?
                    X X . . . X .
                    X . . . X . X
                    . . . . . . X
                    X . . . . . .
                    X . . . . . X
                    X . X . . . .
                    . X . X X . .
Quit?
```

Here it is 5 generations later:

```
                    . . X X . .
                    . X . X . .
                    X X . X . .
                    X X . X . .
                    X X . X X .
                    . . X . X .
                    . . . X X X
```

```
Quit?
```

And after 12 more generations:

```
. X X . . . . . . .
X . . . . . . . X .
X X . X X . . X . X
X X . X X . . X . X
. . X . . . . . X .
```

```
Quit? Yes
```

25.4. Possible Extensions

After some initial experience is gained from the program as described, it can be restructured so that an experiment with patterns of members is possible; to do so it must be possible to input the initial pattern. This can be done easily with a simple modification to Initialize.

```
To InitializeV1
   Type [Size of the Board?]
   Make "&N First ReadList
   Make "&Board "True
   DefineBoard :&Board :&N
   DefineBoard Not :&Board :&N
   ReadCoordinates Word "&BD :&Board
End

To ReadCoordinates :Name
   Print "
   Print [Input the occupied spaces]
   Print "
   Print [End with <RETURN>]
   Print "
   ReadCoord :Name []
End

To ReadCoord :Name :Input
   Type [coordinates (row column):]
   Make "Input ReadList
   If :Input = [] [Stop]
   If (And
       (First :Input) > 0
       (First :Input) < (:&N + 1)
       (Last :Input) > 0
       (Last :Input) < (:&N + 1))
     [Put :Name First :Input Last :Input 1]
   ReadCoord :Name []
End
```

Besides stable patterns (like the "beehive"), eventually periodic patterns (like the "blinker") and wandering patterns (like the "glider") result:

The Beehive:

```
. X X .        . X X .
X . . X   →    X . . X
. X X .        . X X .
```

The Blinker:

```
. X .     . . .       . X .      . . .
. X .  →  X X X  →    . X .  →   X X X
. X .     . . .       . X .      . . .
```

The Glider:

```
. X . .     . . . .      . . . .      . . . .       . . . .
. . X .  →  X . X .  →   . . X .  →   . X . .  →    . . X .
X X X .     . X X .      X . X .      . . X X       . . . X
. . . .     . X . .      . X X .      . X X .       . X X X
```

A basically different modification would be to experiment with different underlying rules, such as:

- Consider a different number of spaces to be neighbors (e.g., only those that are diagonal neighbors).

- Introduce different types of individuals, perhaps some that can take on different forms (white, grey, black) in addition to dying. These different types could also affect the birth and death conditions.

- The game could be played on a honeycomb-like game board, or with multi-dimensional structures.

You may also wish to experiment with alternate data structures or use this program to experiment with improving run-time efficiency. For example, the minimum and maximum indexes could be calculated when generating the new board instead of in a separate step.

25.5. Further Readings

[Berlekamp, Conway, Guy 82, chapter 25] discusses many types of configurations of LIFE, including building a computer using LIFE objects. [Poundstone 85] provides a good background and exploration of foundations of this game, including it's relation to self-reproducing (VonNeumann) machines. Reprints of [Lifeline 73], mentioned earlier, are available from the editor (there is a cost involved):

Lifeline
12 Longvue Avenue
New Rochelle, N.Y. 10804

Part 4:
Artificial Intelligence

Introduction

Artificial intelligence (AI) is a new area of study; although a unified definition for AI does not exist, the following statements give a general characterization:

(1) AI deals with how computers can be programmed so they can solve problems that, when solved by humans, require the use of certain cognitive capabilities that are generally characterized as *intelligence.*

(2) AI attempts to develop methods and principles, which when all taken together compose one component of a science of intelligent behavior and cognitive processes, independent from the underlying system (human or machine).

(3) One practical goal of AI is to make computers more *useful* and *usable.* Making solutions to a new class of problems available and building systems, both with the aim of improving and facilitating human-computer communication, are examples of pursuits based on this goal.

AI is often viewed as a subdomain of *cognitive science*, which more traditionally encompasses parts of computer science, psychology, linguistics, and pedagogy.

Problems from Artificial Intelligence

AI deals with problems, which open new dimensions in the use of computers.

- Knowledge representation (chapters 27, 28, 30)

- Solving classes of problems based on individual problems (chapter 26)

- Question-Answer systems (chapter 29)

- Simulation of general cognitive capabilities such as learning (chapter 29) deduction of implicitly represented knowledge (chapter 30), and inductive development of rules (chapter 27)

- Implementation of new formalisms (chapter 28) that can be used in solving the aforementioned problems. They are also significant as illustrations and implementation of psychological models.

Problems from the area of artificial intelligence are particularly well suited for our global objective, which is expressed in our title, "Interactive Problem Solving Using LOGO," for the following reasons:

- The user (as an intelligent information-processing system) has, in most cases, an intuitive understanding of the problems.

- The problems require an explicit description of human cognitive processes and encourage a better understanding of them.

- The examples illustrate that problems can have different complexities for humans and machines (part of the reason is that the human is equipped with sensors (eyes, ears), and the simulation of these sensors has been more difficult than the simulation of the thought processes of the central nervous system).

- They raise the question that subjectively elicits an eerie sensation: Can computers "think"?

AI Problems and AI Programming Languages

One of the most important insights that has come out of the last 30 years of study in AI is that intelligent behavior of systems (whether natural or artificial) can be traced back to a multitude of levels of abstraction built on simple information-manipulating processes and operations.

In attempting to develop adequate formalisms and programming languages for AI problems, a multitude of abstract representations and language concepts have been developed, which have become part of other programming languages in the mean time. In this regard, the fact that most programming languages are formally Turing machine equivalent (that is, all functions that are computable can be represented in them) is only of secondary importance for our purposes. We are more interested in what *conceptual* possibilities a programming language provides. This can be measured by how simply and isomorphically the solution of a problem can be represented as a program. Some of the basic characteristics and requirements of AI programming languages are summarized here:

- dynamic data structures,

- equivalence of data and programs,

- pattern matching and recursion,

- data driven program control,

- object-oriented programming,

- "*message passing*" as a universal control structure,

- suitable data types (arbitrary length strings, lists),

- procedural oriented programming, to support modular programming and the formulation of "*minilanguages*" adapted to a given problem,

- ease of representation of symbolic information in the existing data structures,

- integration of the language into a complete environment (with interactive "listener," editor, etc.).

Practical programming of AI problems requires a deeper understanding of the often repeated statement, "Computers can only do what they have been programmed to do." Having a concrete program available has the advantage that it can be executed and thereby the consequences and the validity of the assumptions that were made can be tested and evaluated.

The Scope of this Part

We illustrate some of the problems from AI that have been studied in the context of computers by the research community and discuss how they can be programmed. However, in presenting these case studies, we try to maintain an introductory flavor for those who are not versed in AI and its methods and techniques.

The material presented here should be of interest to computer scientists, linguists, and psychologists: students and educators alike.

To avoid any misconception, we would like to note specifically that this section should not be considered to be a textbook for AI. The whole area of AI is much broader than our case studies represent.

We have used our material for the most part with high-school and college students, who showed much interest in the subjects presented here. The extensibility and open-endedness of the problems often led to students being absorbed in the problems for weeks or months at a time.

Chapter 26:
Problem Solving Using LOGO

Many problems that are faced in *artificial intelligence* as well as in everyday life can be described as follows: One wants to proceed from an initial state (for example, the idea of writing this chapter about problem solving) to a particular final state (such as reaching page 297). The *initial state* can be transformed into certain *intermediate states* and finally to the *final state* according to a specific set of rules; the rules that lead from one state to another are called *transformation rules*. Some intermediate states in our example are:

- various completed parts of this chapter,
- the hand-written version of this chapter,
- the written programs,
- the version entered into the computer,
- the version translated from German to English,
- the proof-read version,
- etc.

We could come up with arbitrarily many intermediate states.

Possible transformation rules:

- translate the program ideas into programs,
- enter the hand-written text into the computer,
- improve the written text,
- translate the text from German into English,
- delete superfluous paragraphs,
- correct spelling and typographical errors.

The transformation rules can also be refined, for example, down to the pressing of individual keys on the keyboard, if that leads to a state change.

By the *solution* to a problem we mean the specification of the path used to proceed from the *initial state* using the *transformation rules* to the *goal* or *final state*.

26.1. The Problem

In this chapter we write a program that:

• can solve the problems formulated as states and transformations

• can be viewed as a model or simulation of a general problem-solving system (human or machine) for this class of problems.

This program allows the use of a single transformation rule; this is not really a restriction in principle, because this transformation rule can be arbitrarily complicated and can be applied to different circumstances. In addition, when a transformation rule is applied to a state, it should generate all possible successor states.

26.2. A Simple Example:

A problem that is certainly simpler than writing this chapter is counting change (as long as there is enough change available) or, more precisely, the order and selection of the individual coins (monetary units):

Suppose you are at the cash register of a store and need to pay 36 cents for a candy bar; we want to do this with the fewest number of coins possible. We lay our coins out one after the other on the counter, assuming that we have only quarters, dimes, nickels, and pennies, and that we have plenty of each kind.

In the beginning, 0 cents is on the counter, the initial state can simply be represented by the number 0. The transformation rule as we have said should generate all possible states from a given state. Now, it is certainly permissible to add 25 cents, 10 cents, 5 cents, or 1 cent to the amount of money already on the table. A LOGO procedure Pay generates a list of all possible successor states from the list :Amount, which represents the present state (see figure 26–1).

```
To Pay :Amount
   Output
      (List
         Add :Amount 25
         Add :Amount 10
         Add :Amount 5
         Add :Amount 1)
   End

To Add :A :B
   Output FPut (First :A) + :B []
   End
```

An example of how Pay transforms one state to another:

```
? Print Pay [36]
[61] [46] [41] [37]
```

Our problem now consists of generating successor states with the procedure

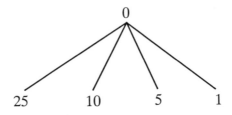

Figure 26–1: One State and Its Successor States

Pay until one of these successor states matches the given final state (see figure 26–2).

In general this type of problem solving consists of generating a tree using the respective transformation rules, until a leaf of this tree contains the desired final state; then "climbing" back from the final state to the initial state, giving a description of the path as a solution. In our example, the path is 0, 25, 35, and 36.

26.3. Construction of the Tree

There are several possible methods for constructing the tree.

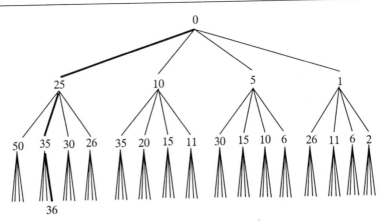

Figure 26–2: Program Generated Tree

Breadth First

This method consists of constructing the search tree by beginning a new level only after completing the current level. For a binary tree (which has only two successor states instead of the four in our example), the order in which the states are generated is illustrated in figure 26–3, where the number of the node is the order that state is generated.

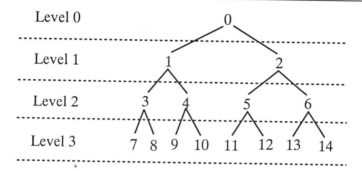

Figure 26–3: *Breadth First* Search

Depth First

In contrast to the previous method, this method attempts to find the solution first in the left (or right) half of the next level. So that the search is not endless, it is necessary to specify a maximum search depth. With a binary tree and a maximum search depth of 3, the order in which the states are searched is given in figure 26–4 (i.e., the search descends to the maximal depth, goes back up to a higher level, descends again, etc.).

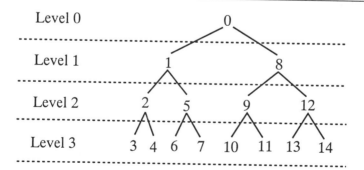

Figure 26–4: *Depth First* Search

The result of both methods is guaranteed because it searches the entire tree blindly but systematically for the desired final state. Both methods work in principle; however, with nontrivial problems, they fail hopelessly, because the generated tree becomes too large.

In each level of depth n there are (with binary trees) 2^n states. With our Pay example, each level has 4^n states; if we wanted to pay 39 cents, the solution would lie in the 6th level, which has $4^6 = 4096$ states altogether.

Heuristic Search

With practical problems it is necessary to drastically limit the portion of the tree to be searched. One simple method to do this is to only search further in a branch of the tree if it somehow shows promise. Usually, a *distance function* is used that gives an assessment of how "far" the current state is from the goal state. Also, in doing so, each state in the tree should only be generated once.

Functions that are used to pursue or abandon paths in a reasonable way, are called *heuristics*[28].

This could also be called a *best first* search, where what is "best" is determined by the heuristic distance function. Using figure 26-1 as an example, it is "better" to pursue the tree rooted at 25, because it is "closer" to the goal than 10, 5 or 1. If our goal were 24 instead of 36, this measure of "closer" would lead us away from our goal for a while, pursuing the trees rooted at 26, 30, and 35, until we get to the point that 10 is closer to 24 than any alternative.

The kind of path traced out by a heuristic search might look something like figure 26-5, where the numbers again show the order in which the nodes are visited.

One possible distance function for our example would be the absolute value of the difference of two amounts:

```
To Heuristic1 :A :B
  Output Abs (First :A) - (First :B)
End
```

Abs is described in appendix III.

In order to reduce the number of fruitless searches, we can modify our distance function like this:

```
To Heuristic2 :A :B
  IfElse (First :B) > (First :A)
    [Output 100000]
    [Output (First :A) - (First :B)]
End
```

---

[28]"Heuristic" comes from the Greek word *heuriskein*—"to find"; thus, an heuristic should be understood as a "searching method," just like a tree search.

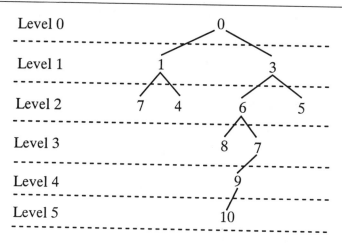

Figure 26–5: Search Using a Distance Function

This is better because, if too much has already been paid, there is no need to search this branch further; in our procedure, we return a "distance" that is large to indicate this.

26.4. Comparing the Methods

One way to find out how much these heuristics reduce the size of the tree to be searched is found by adding counters similar to those used in chapter 18. The following table shows how many nodes were visited by the program presented in section 26.5 on the Pay example.

| | Goal | | | | | |
Search Method	8	9	14	19	150	175
BreadthFirst	46	70	69	*29	71	*29
Heuristic1	7	10	9	15	7	8
Heuristic2	5	6	6	7	7	8

These measurements do not give the whole picture, since they do not measure any extra effort required to assess the heuristic distance or to order the nodes according to that assessment.

---

[29] ran out of memory!

As one would expect these statistics do show that `Heuristic1`, which was the simpler of the two heuristics, did not provide as good an improvement for the nodes on the "right-hand" side of the tree because it did not eliminate cases where the amount represented by the node were greater than, though closer to, the goal.

26.5. A General Problem Solving Program

```
To SolveProblem
  Type [Enter initial state:]
  Make "InitialState ReadList
  Type [Enter goal state:]
  Make "FinalState ReadList
  Type [Specify Transformation Rule :]
  Make "Rule ReadList
  Make "Heuristic []
  Type [Should a heuristic search be used?]
  If ReadList = [yes]
    [Print
        [What is the name of the heuristic function]
     Print [for computing the distance between a]
     Type [state and the final state?]
     Make "Heuristic ReadList]
  PrintSolution
      GeneratePath FPut list :InitialState [] [] []
End
```

We now write a program that solves the problem we have presented in the following way:

- an arbitrary *initial state* and an arbitrary *goal state* can be given;

- The *transformation rule*, which transforms an arbitrary state to its successor state(s), must be formulated as a LOGO procedure, and its name given to the program `SolveProblem`;

- If a heuristic formulated as a LOGO procedure exists, its name can be specified, otherwise a default search is performed;

- `PrintSolution` prints the solution ("the path through the tree") found by `GeneratePath`.

Examples:

```
? SolveProblem
Enter initial state: 0
Enter goal state: 14
Enter tranformation rule: Pay
Should a heuristic search be used?
Is there a special printing function,
and if so, what is its name?
Solution:
```

0
10
11
12
13
14
? SolveProblem
Enter initial state: **0**
Enter goal state: **14**
Enter tranformation rule: **Pay**
Should a heuristic search be used? **yes**
What is the name of the heuristic function
for computing the distance between a state
and the final state? **Heuristic1**
Is there a special printing function,
and if so, what is its name?
Solution:
0
10
11
12
13
14

Generating the Tree

The procedure GeneratePath finds the path from InitialState (or the initial states) to the FinalState if a solution exists.

```
To GeneratePath :ToDo :Completed
   If :ToDo = [] [Output []]
   If Equalp :FinalState First First :ToDo
      [Output FPut First :ToDo []]
   Run
      (Sentence
        [Make "New SetDifference]
        :Rule
        [First First :ToDo]
        (FPut :Completed []))
   Output
      BuildPath
        First :ToDo
        GeneratePath
          GenerateToDo :ToDo :New
          FPut First :ToDo :Completed
End
```

:ToDo is a list of the nodes (states) that have already been generated, but not yet searched; these correspond the leaves of the tree that have been generated so far.

:Completed is a list of the nodes, which have already been searched; these correspond to the internal nodes of the tree that have been generated so far.

Figure 26–6 illustrates these two types of nodes.

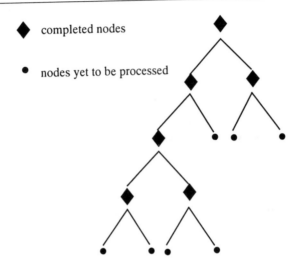

Figure 26-6: A Partially Generated Tree

Now, a close look at the procedure:

First line:
If the list of nodes :ToDo is empty, GeneratePath returns an empty list as the path from beginning to end, that is: there is no solution to the problem.

Second line:
The next node on the :ToDo list (i.e., the current node) is checked to see if it matches the goal state (for an explanation of why the second First is used, see section 26.5).

Third line:
The transformation :Rule is applied to the current node to generate all possible successor states. Any elements that are in this list and in the list :Completed are removed using SetDifference, so that nodes that have already been searched will not be searched again. The results of this set difference are placed in the global variable :New.

Fourth line:
The search for the path continues: the :New nodes are added to the :ToDo list by GenerateToDo. The current node is added to the :Completed list (FPut First :ToDo :Completed) and GeneratePath continues its work recursively. Later (when the recursion "unwinds"), BuildPath places the first element of :ToDo into the path that is being built from the bottom up. This represents the solution to the problem.

Specifying the Search Order

As we have already seen, there are different methods for generating/searching a tree (breadth first, etc.).

Because the procedure `GeneratePath` operates on the first element of the `:ToDo` list, the order in which the tree is generated and searched is the order in which they are listed in `:ToDo`; this happens in `GenerateToDo`:

```
To GenerateToDo :ToDo :New
   If Not :Heuristic = []
      [Output
         HeuristicOrder
            ButFirst :ToDo
            PairUp :New First First :ToDo]
   Output
      Union
         ButFirst :ToDo
         PairUp :New First First :ToDo
End
```

This version of the program allows two possibilities:

• Either a `:Heuristic` is used to search the tree, in which case the list is ordered according to the criterion represented by the `:Heuristic`, or

• A breadth first search is used, and the new list of `:ToDo` nodes is created by placing the newly generated nodes at the end of the list; the function `Union` is used instead of `Sentence` since we need to remove any duplicate entries.

If the newly generated states were placed at the *beginning* of the `:ToDo` list (i.e., if the order of the arguments to `Union` were switched), then a depth first search would be used (i.e., the children of the current node would be the next nodes to be visited).

Using an Heuristic

```
To HeuristicOrder :Old :New
   If :New = [] [Output :Old]
   Output
      HeuristicOrder
         HeurInsert First :New :Old
         ButFirst :New
End

To HeurInsert :New :Old
   If :Old = [] [Output FPut :New []]
   If (First First :Old) = (First :New) [Output :Old]
   If (Distance :New) > (Distance First :Old)
      [Output
         FPut First :Old HeurInsert :New ButFirst :Old]
   Output FPut :New :Old
End
```

```
To Distance :State
  Run
    (Sentence
      "Output
      :Heuristic
      [:FinalState First :State])
End
```

HeuristicOrder places the newly generated states into the list in order and assumes that the items in the list are already sorted according to the same criterion. The insertion of an individual node is performed by the procedure HeurInsert, which also eliminates duplicates. The criterion that is used to order items in the list is the distance of a state from the goal state; this distance is calculated by Distance using the global variable :Heuristic: The smaller (greater) the distance, the closer it is placed to the beginning (end) of the list.

Finding the Path

So far we have not completely dealt with how the path from the initial state to the goal state is generated once we have found a solution.

This problem is handled by the procedures PairUp and BuildPath.

PairUp generates a list of pairs from a arbitrarily sized list and a single element list:

Example:

```
? Print PairUp [[25] [10] [5] [1]] [0]
[[25] [0]] [[10] [0]] [[5] [0]] [[1] [0]]
```

PairUp is used in building the list :ToDo, so that in addition to keeping track of what states still need to be processed, information is maintained about what previous states led to a state.

```
To PairUp :List :Item
  IfElse :List = []
    [Output []]
    [Output
      FPut
        List First :List :Item
        PairUp ButFirst :List :Item]
End

To BuildPath :Front :Tail
  If :Tail = [] [Output []]
  IfElse (First :Front) = (Last First :Tail)
    [Output
      FPut
        :Front
        FPut First First :Tail ButFirst :Tail]
    [Output :Tail]
End
```

When the recursion "unwinds" after the :FinalState has been found,

BuildPath extracts information regarding the predecessor state that has been stored in this manner. If the node specified by :Front (which corresponds to First :ToDo in GeneratePath, i.e. the node that was being processed at that level of the recursion) is the predecessor specified by Last First :Tail, then First First :Tail is specified as a node in the solution path.

The following example with a trace of GeneratePath illustrates how the tree is generated, how the list :ToDo changes, and that the correct nodes (the ones that led to the solution) are included in the solution.

```
? SolveProblem
Enter initial state: 0
Enter goal state: 15
Enter tranformation rule: Pay
Should a heuristic search be used?
  GeneratePath of [[[0] []]] and []
    GeneratePath of
      [[[25] [0]] [[10] [0]] [[5] [0]] [[1] [0]]]
      and [[[0] []]]
      GeneratePath of
        [[[10] [0]] [[5] [0]] [[1] [0]] [[50] [25]]
        [[35] [25]] [[30] [25]] [[26] [25]]]
        and [[[25] [0]] [[0] []]]
        GeneratePath outputs [[[10] [0]] [15]]
      GeneratePath outputs [[[10] [0]] [15]]
    GeneratePath outputs [[[0] []] [10] [15]]
Is there a special printing function,
and if so, what is its name?
Solution:
0
10
15
```

Printing the Solution, Miscellaneous Procedures

Printing the solution is simple; however, because an arbitrary printing function can be specified for printing the result, things are a little more complicated. If a <Return> is entered in answer to the question, the standard Print procedure is used. Otherwise the name of the procedure to use is given. This printing function is applied to each element of the solution, with the first element receiving special treatment because it contains predecessor information (see section 26.5)

```
To PrintSolution :Solution
  If :Solution = [] [Stop]
  Print [Is there a special printing function,]
  Type [ and if so, what is its name?]
  Make "PrintingFunction ReadList
  If :PrintingFunction = []
    [Make "PrintingFunction [Print]]
  Print []
  Print [Solution:]
  Print []
```

```
Run
   Sentence
      :PrintingFunction
      [First First :Solution]
   PrintSol ButFirst :Solution
End

To PrintSol :Solution
   If :Solution = [] [Stop]
   Run Sentence :PrintingFunction [First :Solution]
   PrintSol ButFirst :Solution
End
```

26.6. Using the Problem Solver on Other Problems

The program is not restricted to the Pay problem but was designed to be used for a class of problems; here are some other examples.

River-Crossing Problem

A father (F) wants to cross a river with his two sons (A and B); all that they have available is a canoe (C) that will carry at most 200 pounds. He weighs 200 pounds and each of his sons weighs 100 pounds. How do they cross the river?

The transformation rule that describes this problem could be written as follows (the transformations are performed based on a single item that is a list of what elements of the problem remain on the original side of the river):

```
To CrossRiver :State
   If :State = [C A B F]
      [Output [[F] [B F] [A F] [A B]]]
   If :State = [C A B] [Output [[B] [A] [[]]]]
   If :State = [C A F] [Output [[F] [A]]]
   If :State = [C B F] [Output [[F] [B]]]
   If :State = [A] [Output [[C A B] [C A F]]]
   If :State = [B] [Output [[C A B] [C B F]]]
   If :State = [F]
      [Output [[C A F] [C B F] [C A B F]]]
   If :State = []
      [Output [[C A] [C B] [C A B] [C F]]]
   If :State = [A B] [Output [[C A B F]]]
   If :State = [A F] [Output [[C A B F]]]
   If :State = [B F] [Output [[C A B F]]]
   Output [[]]
End
```

We also define a printing function to make the solution more readable:

```
To PrintCrossRiver :State
   If MemberP "C :State [Type [Canoe]
      Type Spaces 1]
   If MemberP "A :State [Type [Son A]
      Type Spaces 1]
   If MemberP "B :State [Type [Son B]
      Type Spaces 1]
```

```
If MemberP "F :State [Type [Father]]
   Print []
End
```

Example:

```
? SolveProblem
Enter initial state: C A B F
Enter goal state: []
Enter tranformation rule: CrossRiver
Should a heuristic search be used?
Is there a special printing function,
and if so, what is its name?
? PrintCrossRiver
Solution:
Canoe Son A Son B Father
Father
Canoe Son A Father
Son A
Canoe Son A Son B
[]
```

The Eight Puzzle

An "Eight Puzzle" is a small toy that consists of 8 square, wood or plastic elements labeled with the numbers 1 to 8 mounted on a square rack. The ninth position, an empty space, allows the numbered pieces that are next to it to be moved, creating ("moving") the empty space where they were, offering new possible moves. The task for the player is usually to move the numbers around until they are all in order.

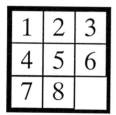

Figure 26–7: Eight Puzzle

Here are the procedures that can be used to represent this problem. We do not provide a detailed explanation, but the example at the end shows how one game situation can be transformed into a goal state.

```
To EightPuzzle :State
  Make "EmptPos EmptyPos :State
  Output NewBoards WhereTo :EmptPos :State :EmptPos
End

To EmptyPos :State
  IfElse (First :State) = "*
    [Output 1]
    [Output 1 + EmptyPos ButFirst :State]
End

To NewBoards :WhereTo :State :Empty
  If :WhereTo = [] [Output []]
  Output
    FPut
      Exchange :State First :WhereTo :Empty
      NewBoards ButFirst :WhereTo :State :Empty
End

To Exchange :State :P1 :P2
  Output
    Exch Minimum :P1 :P2 Maximum :P1 :P2 :State []
End

To Exch :P1 :P2 :Sentence :Temp
  ; If this is the second item, replace it with
  ; the first item, which is in :Temp
  If :P2 = 1
    [Output Sentence :Temp ButFirst :Sentence]
  ; If this is the first item replace it with
  ; the second item found by indexing into the list
  If :P1 = 1
    [Output
      Sentence
        Nth :P2 :Sentence
        Exch
          0
          :P2 - 1
          ButFirst :Sentence
          First :Sentence]
  ; Otherwise just copy the list
  Output
    Sentence
      First :Sentence
      Exch :P1 - 1 :P2 - 1 ButFirst :Sentence :Temp
End

To WhereTo :A
  Output
    Nth
      :A
      [[2 4] [1 3 5] [2 6] [1 5 6] [2 4 6 8]
       [3 5 9] [4 8] [7 5 9] [6 8]]
End
```

```
To PrintEightPuzzle :State
  If :State = [] [Stop]
  Print
    ButLast
      ButLast ButLast ButLast ButLast ButLast :State
  Print
    ButFirst
      ButFirst
        ButFirst ButLast ButLast ButLast :State
  Print
    ButFirst
      ButFirst
        ButFirst ButFirst ButFirst ButFirst :State
  Print []
End
```

The procedures Maximum and Minimum are described in appendix III.
Sample Runs:

```
? SolveProblem
Enter initial state: 1 2 3 4 * 5 6 7 8
Enter goal state: 1 2 3 4 5 8 6 * 7
Enter tranformation rule: EightPuzzle
Should a heuristic search be used?
Is there a special printing function,
and if so, what is its name?
? PrintEightPuzzle
Solution:
1 2 3
4 * 5
6 7 8

1 2 3
4 5 *
6 7 8

1 2 3
4 5 8
6 7 *

1 2 3
4 5 8
6 * 7
```

The Traveling Salesperson Problem

The problem that travelers who want to get from one place to another face can
also be handled by this system.

Given a list of places and information about the connections (highways, trains,
planes) between these places, the question arises, how to get from a starting
point to another (goal) location (by what means, what transfers need to be made,
etc.) This can be simplified so that all connections are considered to be the
same.

Example:

```
? Traveling
Enter the names of all of the cities : Cincinnati Miami
NewYork WashingtonDC Atlanta Chicago LosAngeles Denver
Seattle
Enter cities with connections to Cincinnati : Miami
NewYork
Enter cities with connections to Miami : NewYork
Cincinnati
Enter cities with connections to NewYork : WashingtonDC
Miami LosAngeles Cincinnati
Enter cities with connections to WashingtonDC : Atlanta
NewYork
Enter cities with connections to Atlanta : WashingtonDC
LosAngeles
Enter cities with connections to Chicago : Atlanta
WashingtonDC
Enter cities with connections to LosAngeles : Atlanta
Denver
Enter cities with connections to Denver : LosAngeles
Seattle
Enter cities with connections to Seattle : Denver
Enter initial state: Seattle
Enter goal state: NewYork
Enter tranformation rule: Thing First
Should a heuristic search be used?
Is there a special printing function,
and if so, what is its name?
Solution:
Seattle
Denver
LosAngeles
Atlanta
WashingtonDC
NewYork
```

Once the "structure of the map" (or the train connections) is initialized, this problem can be solved with SolveProblem:

```
? SolveProblem
Enter initial state: NewYork
Enter goal state: Seattle
Enter tranformation rule: Thing First
Should a heuristic search be used?
Is there a special printing function,
and if so, what is its name?
Solution:
NewYork
LosAngeles
Denver
Seattle
```

The procedures to initialize a global data structure:

```
To Traveling
   Print [Enter the names of all of the cities:]
   GetConnections ReadList
```

```
      SolveProblem
  End

To GetConnections :Cities
  If :Cities = [] [Stop]
  Type
    (Sentence
      [Enter cities with connections to]
      First :Cities
      ")
  Make First :Cities Listen ReadList
  GetConnections ButFirst :Cities
End

To Listen :list
  If :list = [] [Output []]
  Output
    FPut
      FPut First :list []
      Listen ButFirst :list
End
```

Because a state is always represented as a list with one element (the current place), the successor state is obtained by accessing the global data structure that is the same as the name of the city (`Thing First`).

The Elephant Problem

Six elephants meet on a small pathway in the jungle (3 on each side, see figure 26–8) and cannot pass each other, because the path is too narrow.

Figure 26–8: The Elephants Meet on the Pathway

As the drawing shows, both groups have become so close that there is only one elephant-length left between them. The problem now is how the elephants can get past each other. The situation is made even more difficult by the following conditions:

- No elephant can move backwards.

- An elephant can only climb over another elephant by climbing up its trunk, and then climbing right down its back. *It then cannot:*
    - climb over an elephant from the rear;
    - climb over two elephants at once; it must always return to the ground, otherwise it will lose its balance.

- The whole maneuver must take place within the seven spaces shown in the drawing.

Figure 26–9: The Elephants Made It!

How do the elephants need to move (either by moving forward one space or by climbing over one another), to get by each other?

We represent the states as simple lists:

Initial State: 1 1 1 0 2 2 2
Final State: 2 2 2 0 1 1 1

After establishing this representation, the transformation rule `Elephants` can be defined that calculates all possible states from an arbitrary state:

```
To Elephants :State
  Make "OneGroup ButFirst Member 0 Mirror :State
  Make "OtherGroup ButFirst Member 0 :State
  Output
    (Sentence
      Walk :OtherGroup :OneGroup 2
      Walk :OneGroup :OtherGroup 1
      ClimbOver :OneGroup :OtherGroup 2
      ClimbOver :OtherGroup :OneGroup 1)
End

To Walk :OneSide :OtherSide :WhichOne
  If :OneSide = [] [Output []]
  If Not (First :OneSide) = :WhichOne [Output []]
  If :WhichOne = 2
    [Output
      FPut
        Sentence
          Mirror :OtherSide
          Sentence [2 0] ButFirst :OneSide
        []]
  Output
    FPut
      Sentence
        Mirror ButFirst :OneSide
        Sentence [0 1] :OtherSide
      []
End

To ClimbOver :OneGroup :OtherGroup :WhichHerd
  If (Count :OtherGroup) < 2 [Output []]
```

```
            If :WhichHerd = 2
              [If [1 2] = FirstN 2 :OtherGroup
                 [Output
                    FPut
                      Sentence
                        Mirror :OneGroup
                        Sentence
                          [2 1 0]
                          ButFirstN 2 :OtherGroup
                      []]]
            If :WhichHerd = 1
              [If [2 1] = FirstN 2 :OtherGroup
                 [Output
                    FPut
                      Sentence
                        Mirror
                          Sentence
                            [1 2 0]
                              ButFirstN 2 :OtherGroup
                      :OneGroup
                      []]]
            Output []
          End

          To Glue :A :B
            if :A = [] [Output :B]
            Output Sentence Last :A Glue ButLast :A :B
          End
```

Sample runs:

```
? SolveProblem
Enter initial state: 1 1 1 0 2 2 2
Enter goal state: 2 2 2 0 1 1 1
Enter tranformation rule: Elephants
Should a heuristic search be used?
Is there a special printing function,
and if so, what is its name?
Solution:
1 1 1 0 2 2 2
1 1 0 1 2 2 2
1 1 2 1 0 2 2
1 1 2 1 2 0 2
1 1 2 0 2 1 2
1 0 2 1 2 1 2
0 1 2 1 2 1 2
2 1 0 1 2 1 2
2 1 2 1 0 1 2
2 1 2 1 2 1 0
2 1 2 1 2 0 1
2 1 2 0 2 1 1
2 0 2 1 2 1 1
2 2 0 1 2 1 1
2 2 2 1 0 1 1
2 2 2 0 1 1 1
```

This problem is also interesting since it can be proved on theoretical grounds that its solution, if one exists[30], lies at a depth of 15. The proof looks something like this:

- Each elephant must be moved exactly 4 spaces; the total distance covered by all the elephants is then 6 * 4 = 24 spaces.

- Each of the three left elephants must climb over the three right elephants (or vise versa); altogether then, 3 * 3 = 9 "climb overs" must be made. With each of these, two spaces are covered, so altogether 9 * 2 = 18 spaces are moved in this fashion.

- There are then 24 - 18 = 6 spaces that are moved by "walking" instead of by "climbing over": altogether there are 6 + 9 = 15 moves.

---

[30]If we do not restrict the proof in this way we could prove by the same line of reasoning that the 6 elephants could do the same trick in 9 moves on 6 spaces with no empty space between them.

Chapter 27:
The Equivalence between Programs and Data

27.1. General Observations

Normally, when working with computers, there is a sharp distinction drawn between programs and data. The programs specify how the data is to be processed. This distinction is not so clear, as the following study should illustrate. In some programming languages (e.g., LISP, to some degree LOGO) this distinction has been removed and exists only in a general interpretation of symbolic structures.

If one attempts to understand a software system (e.g. an information system) as a system in which the computer is the "expert" on the "knowledge" of the facts and interrelationships of a certain domain, then one can differentiate between two types of knowledge representation. All the knowledge in the system is either represented in **variables** (name-value pairs) or as **procedures** (algorithms, programs).

The arbitrariness of this distinction can be shown with an example:

The fact that $\pi = 3.1415926...$ can be represented either by a (preferably global) name:

```
Make "Pi 3.14159
```

or by a procedure

```
To Pi
   Output 3.14159
End
```

The difference between accessing the information stored in either way is minimal. For the version using the name, it is written as:

```
? Print Thing "Pi
3.14159
? Print :Pi
3.14159
```

whereas the procedural representation is used by writing:

```
? Print Pi
3.14159
```

In most other programming languages the difference is not recognizable externally.

Usually knowledge that is considered to be somehow *static* is stored as variables, whereas knowledge about dynamic processes is expressed as procedures (programs). Said another way: Knowledge that has already been computed can be represented by a simple operation that is similar to printing a book. In this book analogy, the text corresponds to the static information in the computer (*explicit knowledge*).

However, to be made available in an explicit form, it must first be generated using suitable methods known as algorithms (*implicit knowledge*).

This distinction can be found in many fields and is ancient: The ancient Babylonians, for example, put large amounts of their knowledge about the basic arithmetic operations and other simple arithmetic functions (for example, square root, reciprocals, etc.) into large tables; for simple algebraic equations, however, there were lists of rules to be used to obtain a result.

Both forms of explicitly and implicitly available knowledge are merged into the procedure `Pi`; the algorithm simply consists of giving the constant a name.

The differentiation between programs and data also parallels another pair of concepts that deal with when information processing occurs. As we discussed in chapter 18, there is a difference between *information processing at read time* and *information processing at question time*.

"Information processing at read time" is new, incoming information being stored or connected to other information as it comes in; this is generally a more storage-intensive method, though the information and its interactions with other information is readily available when it is needed (for example, the times table).

"Information processing at question time" corresponds to the explicit storage of information in procedural form. When the question is asked, then the manipulation (calculation) is begun. This method is more general, saves storage, but possibly requires a great amount of computational effort.

Whereas the ancient Babylonians depended on the table created by "information processing at read time" (which, admittedly, they had to carry around with them all the time) for multiplying two-digit numbers, we use more of an "information processing at question time" mechanism by knowing a simple algorithm for multiplying, and using it as needed. This corresponds to the transition in the last several years from extensive use of mathematical tables (read time) to using electronic calculators (question time).

27.2. Programs that Write Programs

If we decide to store our knowledge exclusively as procedures (programs), then it would seem useful to have available a procedure that takes simple pieces of knowledge and takes over the task of writing the procedure to contain this information; since this procedure does effectively the same thing as the LOGO command `Make` (associates a value with a name) we call the procedure `ProgMake`.

```
To ProgMake :Name :Value
   Define :Name List [] LPut :Value [Output]
End
```

This procedure `ProgMake` represents a simple example of a program that writes another program.

Figure 27–1: The Procedure `ProgMake`

```
? ProgMake "Pi "3.14159
? PrintOut "Pi
To Pi
 Output 3.14159
End
```

As a result of writing the procedure `ProgMake`, a piece of knowledge is recorded: This is the algorithm for writing this type of procedure, which represents a simple type of knowledge.

Procedures can therefore represent knowledge about other procedures, that is, they can produce other procedures as data. Procedures can also be written that modify knowledge represented in other procedures, or at least their form of representation; examples for this type of program can be found in section 20.3 on page 203.

These examples illustrate that the distinction between programs and data is not really arbitrary and determined apart from the context: *A procedure can be run as well as serve as data for another program; programs can be written that write or modify other procedures.*

Whereas in the preceding examples the programs more or less directly modify their procedures according to their input, what follows is an example to show how actual "automatic" programming can be presented as a process of concept formation, which the program presented here computes in a complicated manner.

27.3. Completing Letter Sequences

The Problem

Intelligence tests often contain problems that require you to specify what the next item in a sequence is, based on the pattern that is established by the initial part of the sequence. For example:

(1) A B A B A B ...
(2) A B G A B G ...
(3) A X D Z G ...

In this section we study techniques for writing a program that can discover these "hidden" rules or patterns by systematic analysis.

If you like, this program can be viewed as a simple simulation of human problem-solving methods for problems that require inductive reasoning; humans who can solve such problems (among other things) qualify as "intelligent."

The Basic Solution

Our program is based on the assumption that the letter sequence has some sort of regularity or periodicity.

The simplest form of periodicity would be something like:
A A A A A A .....

The length of this period is 1 and the next element in the series is the "0th successor in the alphabet" of the preceding element.

A somewhat more difficult problem:
A B A C A D .....

Here the period length is 2; the sequence can be broken down into two parts, one written over the other:

A B A C A D ... →
A A A ...
B C D ...

and it is easier to recognize that the first line always has the same letter (the 0th successor), and the second line always has successive letters of the alphabet (the 1st successor), so that the first element in each period of the sequence is always the same as the first element of the previous period and the second element of the period is always the letter that follows the second element of the previous period.

If the elements of the periods are allowed to be not only the "Nth successor" but also the "Nth predecessor," how could we describe the following sequence?
A Z B C X B E V B ...

After several tries, the following solution is found with a period length of 3:

A C E . . ← 2nd successor in the alphabet
Z X V . . ← 2nd predecessor in the alphabet
B B B . . ← 0th successor in the alphabet

Because these sequences are conceptually infinite, we use the concept of a cyclic ("wrap-around") alphabet, such that after "Z" we start again at "A" (similar to the way that 1 "follows" 12 on a clock).

The Program

The program Sequence represents its knowledge about letter sequences *as programs*. It makes sense to represent knowledge about these sequences as algorithms because:

- Humans use algorithms to generate these sequences, too.
- The length (the number of elements) is not restricted.

```
To Sequence :Seq :N :PrintProc
   Local "ProNam
   Make "ProNam Progname :Seq
   If Not MemberP :ProNam :Contents
      [WriteProg :Seq :ProNam]
   If :PrintProc
      (Sentence "Show Quote :ProNam CmdSepChar "Show
         (Quote :Pronam "1))
   Run Sentence :ProNam :N
End

To Quote :Input
   If NumberP :Input [Output :Input]
   Output Word QuoteChar :Input
End

To QuoteChar
   Output Char 34
End

To CmdSepChar
   ;; The version of Logo this was tested
   ;; on uses the exclamation point to
   ;; separate multiple commands on one line
   Output ExclamationPoint
End

To ExclamationPoint
   Output Char 33
End
```

When a specific letter sequence is given, it is first determined whether this letter sequence has already been seen, that is, whether a program has already been created that can solve the series in question. To do this it consults the global variable :Contents, which is kept up to date with the names of the known procedures. If no program is known (the system doesn't know how to complete the sequence), the knowledge about writing programs is activated by calling

`WriteProg` to write a program that is able to complete the sequence. This program, which can complete the sequence (to any length!), is then invoked using the `Run` command. If the same program is needed later, it can be found in the list `:Contents`, where it is stored using a name that starts with `"Seq` and ends with the letter sequence that specified the problem.

```
To ProgName :Seq
   Output Word "Seq :Seq
End
```

Two Examples:

```
? Sequence "abc 4 "True
to seqabc :n
  seqabc1 :n 0 "a
end
to seqabc1 :n :sofar :lastperiod
  type :lastperiod
  if :sofar > :n [stop]
  seqabc1
    :n
    :sofar + 1
    applyfunctions :lastperiod [[successor 1]]
end
abcd
? Sequence "axdwgv 4 "True
to seqaxdwgv :n
seqaxdwgv1 :n 1 "ax
print "
end
to seqaxdwgv1 :n :sofar :lastperiod
type :lastperiod
if not :sofar < :n [stop]
seqaxdwgv1 :n :sofar + 1 applyfunctions
    :lastperiod [[ascending 3] [descending 1
]]
end
axdwgvju
```

All the programs written by `WriteProg` are constructed as described next. For each sequence, two procedures are written, one that simply handles the basic initializations, and the other that recursively generates the sequence, one period at a time.

The procedure `WriteProg` controls the process of finding and generating the sequence-generating program when `Sequence` cannot find one that has already been built.

(1) `To Seq<sequence> :N`
   The heading for the first procedure.

(2) `Seq<sequence>1 :N 0 "<first-period>`
   This sets up the call to the recursive portion of the code, with the *<first-period>* representing the portion of the sequence that corresponds to the first period of the pattern.

(3) `To Seq<sequence>1 :N :SoFar :LastPeriod`

This is the heading for the lower-level (recursive) procedure that does most of the work.

(4) `Type :LastPeriod`

This prints out either the first part of the sequence or the portion generated by the previous level of recursion.

(5) `If :SoFar > :N [Stop]`

The termination condition for the recursion. The requested number of elements of the series has been printed out.

(6) `Seq<sequence>1 :N :SoFar + 1 ApplyFunctions`
`:LastPeriod <list-of-series-generators>`

The recursion step where the specifications contained in <list-of-series-generators> is applied to the elements of the last period to generate the next period.

```
To WriteProg :Seq :ProNam
   ;; First Figure out the period and the
   ;; series that make up the sequence
   Local "Info
   Make "Info FindPeriodAndSeries :Seq
   Local "Period
   Make "Period First :Info
   Local "SeriesFuncs
   Make "SeriesFuncs ButFirst :Info
   Local "SubProcNam
   Make "SubProcNam Word :ProNam "1
   ;; Write the top level (non-recursive) function
   Make "ProgText [[:N]]
   Make
     "ProgText
     LPut
       (Sentence
         :SubProcNam
         [:N 1]
         Quote FirstN :Period :Seq)
       :ProgText
   Make "ProgText LPut [Print " ] :ProgText
   Define :ProNam :ProgText
   ;; Write the underlying (recursive) procedure
   Make "ProgText [[:N :SoFar :LastPeriod]]
   Make "ProgText LPut [Type :LastPeriod] :ProgText
   Make
     "ProgText
     LPut [If Not :SoFar < :N [Stop]] :ProgText
   Make
     "ProgText
     LPut
       (Sentence
         :SubProcNam
         [:N :SoFar + 1 ApplyFunctions :LastPeriod]
         :SeriesFuncs)
       :ProgText
```

```
    Define :SubProcNam :ProgText
    Make "Contents Sentence :ProNam :Contents
End
```

Determining the Length of the Period

`FindPeriodandSeries` and its related procedures do the real work of figuring out the sequence. The first thing that needs to be done is determining the length of the period (how often the pattern repeats). At the same time, to know what the period is, we need to know what the pattern is so we can know what is repeating. So we proceed by trying out different period lengths dissecting the sequence based on a given period length and see if that results in any patterns appearing. Because both parts of the information are generated hand-in-hand, once we have generated them we keep them both, using what we need at different points in generating the program.

So we proceed in `FindPeriodAndSeries` to generate and test various period lengths.

```
To FindPeriodAndSeries :Sequence
   OutPut FindPerAndSer1 1 :Sequence
End

To FindPerAndSer1 :Period :Sequence
  Local "SearchResult
  If :Period > Count :Sequence [Output [0 []]]
  Make
    "SearchResult
    FindPeriods GroupSeries :Period :Sequence
  If "SearchResult = []
    [Output FindPerAndSer1 :Period + 1 :Sequence]
  Output list :Period :SearchResult
End
```

Example:

```
? Print First FindPeriodAndSeries "ABACAD
2
? Print First FindPeriodAndSeries "ABMCDM
3
? Print First FindPeriodAndSeries "AXUK
0
```

As the last example shows, if there is no periodicity found, a ''0'' is returned as the first part of the result (the period length).

For each period length that is tried out, the sequence is grouped according to that period length into sets of series; these sets are later examined for some type of regularity.

Example:

```
? Print GroupSeries 3 "abacad
ac ba ad
? Print GroupSeries 2 "abacad
aaa bcd
```

```
To GroupSeries :PeriodLength :Sequence
   Output
      GroupSeries1
         :PeriodLength
         :PeriodLength
         :Sequence
End

To GroupSeries1 :NumberLeft :PeriodLength :Sequence
   If Not :NumberLeft > 0 [Output [ ]]
   Output
      FPut
         Group :PeriodLength :Sequence
         GroupSeries1
            :NumberLeft - 1
            :PeriodLength
            ButFirst :Sequence
End

To Group :PeriodLen :Sequence
   If :Sequence = " [Output "]
   Output
      Word
         First :Sequence
         Group
            :PeriodLen
            ButFirstN :PeriodLen :Sequence
End
```

FindPeriods determines for each element of the set of series, whether it represents an ascending or descending sequence and what the spacing is between letters of the sequence. If all series tested do not exhibit regularity in their spacing, the empty list is returned.

```
To FindPeriods :Sequence
   Output FindPeriods1 :Sequence [ ]
End

To FindPeriods1 :Untested :Found
   Local "SeqFcn
   If :Untested = [ ] [Output :Found]
   Make "SeqFcn SequenceFcn First :Untested
   If "SeqFcn = [ ] [Output [ ]]
   Output
      FindPeriods1
         ButFirst :Untested
         LPut :SeqFcn :Found
End
```

Examples:

```
? Print FindPeriods GroupSeries 2 "abacad
[ascending 0] [ascending 1]
? Print FindPeriods [abc ace uxa]
[ascending 1] [ascending 3] [ascending 3]
? Print FindPeriods [aaa abc aha]
[]
? Print FindPeriods [azy adg]
[decending 1] [ascending 3]
```

Both ascending and descending directions are tried on a series in SequenceFcn starting with the maximum width we are willing to try (represented by MaxWidth). This is set to an arbitrary limit of 4 in our examples but can also be set as a global variable by the user. SequenceSpacing tries out all the possible spacings for a given direction and returns False if none works, otherwise it returns the spacing value that did work.

```
To SequenceFcn :Sequence
  Local "SeqSpc
  Make
    "SeqSpc
    SequenceSpacing MaxWidth :Sequence Alphabet
  IfElse :SeqSpc = "False
    [Make
       "SeqSpc
      SequenceSpacing
        MaxWidth
        :Sequence
        Mirror Alphabet
      IfElse :SeqSpc = "False
        [Output []]
        [Output Sentence "Descending :SeqSpc]]
    [Output Sentence "Ascending :SeqSpc]
End

To SequenceSpacing :Spacing :Sequence :Alphabet
  If Not :Spacing > 0 [Output "False]
  If SeqSpacing1 :Spacing :Sequence :Alphabet
    [Output :Spacing]
  Output
    SequenceSpacing
      :Spacing - 1
      :Sequence
      :Alphabet
End

To SeqSpacing1 :Spacing :Sequence :Alphabet
  If EmptyP ButFirst :Sequence [Output "True]
```

```
        If EqualP
           Successor :Spacing First :Sequence :Alphabet
           First ButFirst :Sequence
         [Output
            SeqSpacing1
              :Spacing
              ButFirst :Sequence
              :Alphabet]
        Output "False
   End

   To MaxWidth
     IfElse NameP "MaxWidth
       [Output :MaxWidth]
       [Output 4]
   End
```

Examples:

```
? Print SequenceSpacing 3 "ah
               "abcdefghijklmnopqrstuvwxyz
False

? Print SequenceSpacing 8 "ah
               "abcdefghijklmnopqrstuvwxyz
7
```

Miscellaneous Procedures

```
To ApplyFunctions :Sequence :Functions
  If :Sequence = " [Output "]
  If (Count :Functions) = 1
    (Sentence
       "Output
       First :Functions
       Quote :Sequence)
   Run
     (Sentence
        "Output
        "Word
        First :Functions
        Quote First :Sequence
        Quote
          ApplyFunctions
            ButFirst :Sequence
            ButFirst :Functions)
End

To Ascending :Spacing :Letter
  Output Successor :Spacing :Letter Alphabet
End

To Descending :Spacing :Letter
  Output Successor :Spacing :Letter Mirror Alphabet
End
```

```
To Successor :N :Letter :Sequence
   IfElse :N = 0
      [Output :Letter]
      [Output
         Successor
            :N - 1
            Next :Letter :Sequence
            :Sequence]
End

To Next :Letter :Sequence
   IfElse :Letter = Last :Sequence
      [Output First :Sequence]
      [Output First ButFirst Member :Letter :Sequence]
End
```

Some Final Examples

```
? Sequence "axdwgv 4 "False
axdwgvju
? Sequence "abc 5 "False
abcde
? Sequence "labihkcdgfj 3 "True
to seqlabihkcdgfj :n
seqlabihkcdgfj1 :n 1 "labih
print "
end
to seqlabihkcdgfj1 :n :sofar :lastperiod
type :lastperiod
if not :sofar < :n [stop]
seqlabihkcdgfj1 :n :sofar + 1 applyfunctions
   :lastperiod [[descending 1] [ascending 2]
   [ascending 2] [descending 2] [descending 2]]
end
labihkcdgfjefed
```

27.4. Summary

The program Sequence represents a simple simulation of human problem-solving methods in the context of inductive problem solving. The knowledge of the program consists of the procedures that have been generated (little by little for each specific letter sequence) and a method for generating new procedures.

Letter sequences (as well as natural numbers) are a good example for a domain that is better represented as an algorithm instead of enumerating each element because of the infinite number of elements (or combination of elements).

27.5. Further Possibilities

There are several obvious possible extensions to this program:

- In addition to the `Ascending` and `Descending` successor rules, further rules for recognition could be used, for example, the preceding program could not discover the patterns in these sequences:

ABCDEEDCBA... or

ABBCCCDDDDEEEEEFFFFFF.....

- Other alphabets could be used.

- Digits could be allowed as elements of the sequence.

- Sequences that are structurally the same could be recognized as such and the same procedure could be used to generate or complete them. A simple case of this are sequences that have the same initial series, for example, the two sequences:

ABMCDM... and ABMCDMEFM...

could be recognized as both being sequences generated by `seqabmcdm`.

A more ambitious project would be to detect that

ABMCDMEFM... and HIZJKZLMZ...

are based on the same rules, and with proper parameterization, they could both be represented by the *same, single* "knowledge" procedure.

- Because it is really a simulation of *inductive* thinking, the program could be extended to try to find several possible ways to complete a letter sequence.

Chapter 28:
Production Systems

One psychological model for human reasoning, used to study the structure and limitations of the human "computer," is known as the *production system* model. This model is also used as a way of building computer problem-solving programs. They are also called *rule-based systems*.

Production systems represent a type of programming language; however, the term *production system* can be used for specific systems with a set of primitive operations (in our case `EraseSTM`, `Write`, `Send`, and `Receive`) as well as the systems that use more traditional programming techniques. Production systems have been used for some time to model human problem-solving behavior, since:

- they can be understood as a collection of simple, uniform control structures

- they represent a way procedures are activated and provided with parameters, and how they pass on their results

- they are easy to model (with two memory components, and a pattern-matching method)

The underlying hypothesis for this is that human behavior is controlled, at least in part by simple "if–then" connections. It is not the complexity of the problem-solving process performed by an ant zig-zagging across the sand that results in a complex path being traveled, but instead it is the complexity of the surface of the sand (from the perspective of the ant) [Simon 81]. This hypothesis, that the behavior of a living being is influenced more by the surrounding reality (and less by its inner structure), finds a direct analogy in production systems where the decision about which production fires depends almost exclusively on the data in the short-term memory. In this connection the term *data driven programming* is frequently directly associated with an *environment driven problem solver*.

28.1. What is a Production System?

A *production system* consists of one or more rules called *productions* that have the form:

Condition(s) → Action(s).

The condition(s) refer to the state of the short-term (working) memory, which contains the "active" facts (or "chunks") of information about the state of the "world" relevant to the task at hand. If the condition(s) match(es) the configuration currently in short-term memory, the corresponding action is "triggered."

The actions can be arbitrary procedures in principle, which can change the short-term memory and thereby current view of the "world." When viewed as a special type of programming language, the algorithms for a production system are given by specifying the productions as just described.

A further characteristic of production system is the way in which the collection of condition action pairs is interpreted. Under one method of interpretation all the pairs are placed in a certain order:

$$\text{Condition(s)}_1 \rightarrow \text{Action(s)}_1$$
$$\text{Condition(s)}_2 \rightarrow \text{Action(s)}_2$$
$$\ldots \qquad \ldots$$
$$\ldots \qquad \ldots$$
$$\ldots \qquad \ldots$$
$$\text{Condition(s)}_n \rightarrow \text{Action(s)}_n$$

Allowing such a production system to "run" (in analogy to a program) means to:

- Test whether the condition(s) in the first production is (are) met;
  - If this is the case, then the first production "fires" and the actions of the first production are performed, then the production system starts from the beginning again.
  - If this is not the case, then the second and succeeding productions are handled in the same way as the first.
- If none of the productions' conditions are met, the production system "program" stops.

If one were to implement a production in a procedure, the procedure would have the following overall control structure:

```
To ProductionSystem
   If Condition1 [Action1
                  ProductionSystem
                  Stop]
   If Condition2 [Action2
                  ProductionSystem
                  Stop]
   ...
   If ConditionN [ActionN
                  ProductionSystem
                  Stop]
End
```

If a `Condition` is met, the corresponding `Action` is performed, and the `ProductionSystem` is called again.

The productions of a productions system are often called *rewriting rules* as well, because they transform one sequence of characters into another sequence of characters, which is analogous to the rules of a grammar (see chapter 20). A string that is syntactically just a sequence of characters can be interpreted as knowledge about the "world" when coupled with the semantics of the action component.

What differentiates an algorithm formulated in a production system from one expressed in a normal program is that the decision about what production "fires" and which actions are actually performed are dependent only on the data. The order in which the `Actions` (are permitted to) change the "world" depends less on the order in which they appear in the database, and more on the state of the world that is constantly changing based on the actions of productions.

To understand these systems, it is important to know that two forms of memory are used, which are anthropomorphically called short- and long-term memory (see figure 28–1).

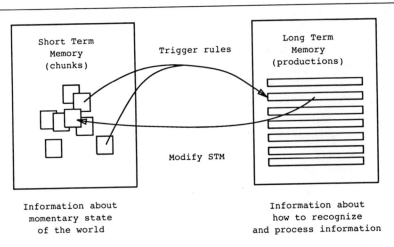

Figure 28–1: Structure of a Production System

The relationships between STM and LTM in a production system have the following dependencies:

- The actions of the production system can change the state of the world.

- Dependent on the state of the world, certain conditions become true, which may trigger further actions.

28.2. The Components of a Production System

The Condition Component

Because the conditions in the productions always refer to the world, which in the simplest case is specified by the global database, "checking the conditions" simply means testing whether certain facts can be asserted with respect to the global database or not; this is best done with *pattern matching* methods (which can be viewed as complex forms of conditions). In our system, we use patterns to specify conditions. The expressive power and the syntax of the pattern matcher used here correspond largely to version 4 of the pattern matcher presented in chapter 19. As with that system, this pattern matcher allows only the specification of constants and variables. The values that are assigned by the matching process are also available in the action portion of the productions.

```
To Match :Pattern :Target
   If :Pattern = [] [Output "True]
   If :Target = [] [Output "False]
   If Match1 First :Pattern First :Target
      [Output Match ButFirst :Pattern ButFirst :Target]
   Output Match :Pattern ButFirst :Target
End

To Match1 :Pattern :Target
   If :Pattern = [] [Output "True]
   If :Target = [] [Output "False]
   If WordP :Pattern
      [Output MatchWord :Pattern :Target]
   If not WordP :Target
      [If Match1 First :Pattern First :Target
         [Output
            Match1 ButFirst :Pattern ButFirst :F]]
   Output "False
End

To MatchWord :Pattern :Target
   If :Pattern = :Target [Output "True]
   If "> = First :Pattern
      [Make ButFirst :Pattern :TargetOutput "True]
   IfElse "< = First :Pattern
      [Output (:Target = Thing ButFirst :Pattern)]
      [Output "False]
End
```

A few examples should show how this works and some of the capabilities allowed:

(1) The pattern elements must be *somewhere* in the list of items specified by Target maintaining the original ordering; they may be interspersed by arbitrary other elements. The comparison proceeds from left to right:

```
? Print Match [A B] [A B]
True
? Print Match [B D] [A B C D]
True
? Print Match [A B D] [A D B C E]
False
```

(2) Variables can be part of the pattern; they begin with a ">" or "<." The ">" prefix means that the rest of the pattern element is a variable name to which the corresponding element from the target should be assigned. The "<" prefix causes the pattern matcher to test whether the next element in the target agrees with the value that has previously been assigned to the corresponding variable name.

```
? Print Match [A >B C] [A 2 C]
True
? Print :B
2
? Print Match [>A B <A C] [A B C A C]
True
? Print :A
A
```

(3) Sublists may be in the pattern as well as in the target; variables can occur at any level of the list hierarchy.

```
? Print Match [A [B C] D] [A 1 [B C] 2 D]
True
? Print Match [>A [B >C] D] [A 1 [B 2] 3 D]
True
? Print :A
A
? Print :C
2
? Print
    Match
       [[Hello >A] [Hello >B]]
       [[Hello Fred] [Hey Joe] [Hello Betty]]
True
? Print :A
Fred
? Print :B
Betty
```

The Action Component

The actions of a production can be arbitrarily complicated and diverse in principle; for simplicity however, we restrict them to four primitive actions:

Write writes new information into short-term memory; the new information is placed at the beginning of short-term memory (a simple list).

EraseSTM erases a piece of information from short-term memory.

Send sends messages (information) to the external environment (e.g., the user).

Receive   receives or accepts information from the external environment and places it at the beginning of short-term memory.

These four actions correspond to the following four LOGO procedures:

```
To Write :Info
  Make "STM FPut :Info :STM
End

To EraseSTM :Info
  Make "STM Remove :Info :STM
End

To Send :Info
  Print []
  (Print ">>>> :Info)
End

To Receive
  Type "<<<<
  Make "STM FPut ReadList :STM
End
```

EraseSTM uses Remove, which is described in appendix III

28.3. Specification of the Syntax for Our Production System

Before we actually describe the interpreter, we need to select the notation and implementation structure for our production system.

A *production system* consists of one or more productions, which we keep as a list:

```
ProductionSystem → [Production1 Production2 ...
... ProductionN]
```

A *Production* consists of a name, the condition (a pattern), and a list of actions to be performed:

```
Production → [Name Condition Action]
```

The *condition*s can be arbitrary patterns, specified as a list suitable for use with Match.

The *action*s are also a list, each element of which is a list whose first element is one of the four basic operations; an optional second element is the information to be written/erased/sent.

The following procedure allows the productions to be input:

```
To DefineProduction
  Type "Name:
  Make "Name ReadList
  If :Name = [] [Stop]
  Make "Name First :Name
```

```
Type "Pattern:
Make "Pattern ReadLines
Type "Actions:
Make "Actions ReadLines
Make "LTM LPut (list :Name :Pattern :Actions) :LTM
DefineProduction
End

To ReadLines
   Local "OneLine
   Make "OneLine ReadList
   If EmptyP :OneLine [Output []]
   Output FPut :OneLine ReadLines
End
```

28.4. An Example

The following three productions illustrate a simple example of a production system. They greet a person with a different level of familiarity based on how well the person is "known" by the system.

```
? DefineProduction
Name: P0
Pattern: Good >Something

Actions: EraseSTM [Good <Something]
Write [Dieter Boecker]
Write [Gerhard Fischer]
Write [Hal Eden]
Send [Good <Something]
Send [My name is production system]
Send [What is your name?]
Receive
```

The production P0 handles the simple case where information such as "Good Morning" is found in short-term memory. If that is the case, this information is first erased from the short-term memory, new information is written into short-term memory, and finally three messages are written out to the external environment. The resulting reply is received and placed into short-term memory.

```
? DefineProduction
Name: P1
Pattern: >Name
>FirstName <Name

Actions: Send [Oh yes, <FirstName , I know you]
EraseSTM [<Name]
EraseSTM [Dieter Boecker]
EraseSTM [Gerhard Fischer]
EraseSTM [Hal Eden]
```

The actions of the production P1 are executed, if a >Name followed by a >FirstName with the same <Name are found in the short-term memory. The basic idea here is that if the name (received by P0) is Boecker, Fischer, or Eden a greeting of the form Oh yes,... can be used. If

the production P1 "fires" (its pattern matches), the information placed in short-term memory by P0 is erased as well. This erasure is important, to keep multiple firings of P1 from occurring.

```
? DefineProduction
Name: P2
Pattern: >Name

Actions: Send [Nice to meet you, Mr./Ms. <Name]
EraseSTM [Dieter Boecker]
EraseSTM [Gerhard Fischer]
EraseSTM [Hal Eden]
EraseSTM [<Name]
```

The pattern of production P2 is - compared to P1 - less specialized; P2 fires when just a >Name is found and a different form of the greeting is used.

In constructing a production system like this one that uses ordering to resolve conflicts when multiple patterns match, it is important to place the more specialized pattern in front of the more general patterns; if, for example, P1 and P2 in the opposite order, P1 would never fire, because P2 would match first, would fire, and as a result would remove the conditions necessary for P1 to fire.

The following two test runs show how the different inputs of the user would proceed.

```
? StartSystem
[Good Afternoon]
...... P0 Fires ......

>>>>Good Afternoon

>>>>My name is production system

>>>>What is your name?
<<<<Fischer

[Fischer]
[Hal Eden]
[Gerhard Fischer]
[Dieter Boecker]
...... P1 Fires ......

>>>>Oh yes, Gerhard , I know you!

? StartSystem
[Good Afternoon]
...... P0 Fires ......

>>>>Good Afternoon

>>>>My name is production system

>>>>What is your name?
<<<<Sandoval

[Sandoval]
[Hal Eden]
[Gerhard Fischer]
[Dieter Boecker]
```

```
...... P2 Fires ......
>>>>Nice to meet you, Mr./Ms. Sandoval!
```

At first both examples proceed in the same way: First the contents of the :STM is printed out in both cases. The trace of the productions shows that P0 fires. Send generates three messages, and the input of the user follows. The production system shows the new state of the STM. Here the paths diverge. Depending on the input either P1 or P2 fires with different messages given by Send.

As the sample runs show, P0 does the job of initializing the :STM with the names of known persons; these could have been specified as the initial contents of :STM.

28.5. The Interpreter

The long- and short- term memories (the production system and the global data base) are implemented as global list variables :LTM and :STM:

```
"LTM is [[P0 [[Good >Something]]
             [[EraseSTM [Good <Something]]
              [Write [Dieter Boecker]]
              [Write [Gerhard Fischer]]
              [Write [Hal Eden]]
              [Send [Good <Something]]
              [Send [My name is production system]]
              [Send [What is your name?]] [Receive]]]
         [P1 [[>Name] [>FirstName <Name]]
             [[Send [Oh yes, <FirstName , I know you!]]
              [EraseSTM [<Name]]
              [EraseSTM [Dieter Boecker]]
              [EraseSTM [Gerhard Fischer]]
              [EraseSTM [Hal Eden]]]]
         [P2 [[>Name]]
             [[Send [Nice to meet you, Mr./Ms. <Name !]]
              [EraseSTM [Dieter Boecker]]
              [EraseSTM [Gerhard Fischer]]
              [EraseSTM [Hal Eden]]
              [EraseSTM [<Name]]]]]]
   "STM is [[Good Afternoon]]
```

Now, to allow the productions to run, an interpreter can be used to compare the contents of the short-term memory with the patterns of the individual productions and, if necessary, execute the actions of the "fired" production. This can be described in the following procedures:

```
To StartSystem
   UseProductions :LTM
End

To UseProductions :Productions
   If :Productions = [] [Stop]
```

```
If Match Condition First :Productions :STM
   [Fire First :Productions
    UseProductions :LTM
    Stop]
   UseProductions ButFirst :Productions
End
```

The procedure StartSystem that was used in the previous example calls the procedure UseProductions with the entire :LTM as an argument.

UseProductions determines for each individual production, whether the condition is met; the first one for which this is the case is allowed to "fire." If no production's condition is met, then the levels of recursion are escaped using TopLevel.

```
To Condition :Production
   Output First ButFirst :Production
End
```

The condition component of a production is the second element.

```
To Action :Production
   Output First ButFirst ButFirst :Production
End
```

The action component of a production is the third element.

```
To Fire :Production
   Print []
   PrintSTM :STM
   Print
      (List "...... First :Production "Fires "......)
   Execute Action :Production
End
```

```
To Execute :ActionList
   If :ActionList = [] [Stop]
   Run ReplaceVars First :ActionList
   Execute ButFirst :ActionList
End
```

```
To PrintSTM :STM
   If :STM = [] [Stop]
   Print (List First :STM)
   PrintSTM ButFirst :STM
End
```

The firing of a production is performed by Fire. First the current contents of short-term memory is presented, then a Trace-like message is printed, giving the name of the production (First :Production) that is being fired, and finally the Actions of the production are performed using Execute.

The procedures that manipulate the "production-system machine," EraseSTM, Write, Send, and Receive are called using the LOGO Run command, after ReplaceVars is used to substitute for variables (recognizable by their "<" prefix) that were set in the matching process.

```
To ReplaceVars :Action
   If EmptyP :Action [Output []]
   If WordP :Action
     [IfElse "< = First :Action
        [Output Thing ButFirst :Action]
        [Output :Action]]
   Output
     FPut
        ReplaceVars First :Action
        ReplaceVars ButFirst :Action
End
```

28.6. More Examples

Addition of Two Natural Numbers

The sum of two natural numbers can be calculated using a successor function, by repeatedly subtracting 1 from the first number and adding 1 to the second number until the first number is 0 (this was discussed in the mathematics section). This basic idea is also used in the following production system with four productions (again we present it in a more readable fashion than it would have to be typed in):

The order of productions is important for this system as well; for example, production **P1** is more specialized than **P2** and must precede it; otherwise it will never fire.

```
"LTM is [[P1 [[X 0] [Y >Y]]
            [[EraseSTM [X 0]]
             [EraseSTM [Y <Y]]
             [Send [result <Y]]]]
        [P2 [[X >X] [Y >Y]]
            [[EraseSTM [Y <Y]]
             [Send [What is the successor of <Y ?]]
             [Receive]]]
        [P3 [[>Y] [X >X]]
            [[EraseSTM [X <X]]
             [EraseSTM [<Y]]
             [Write [Y <Y]]
             [Send [What is the predecessor of <X ?]]
             [Receive]]]
        [P4 [[>X] [Y >Y]]
            [[EraseSTM [<X]]
             [write [X <X]]]]]]
  "STM is [[X 2] [Y 3]]
```

When the STM and LTM are set up as shown, running `StartSystem` gives the following results (the reader is encouraged to examine the system output carefully):

```
? StartSystem
[X 2]
[Y 3]
...... P2 Fires ......
```

```
>>>>What is the successor of 3
<<<<4
[4]
[X 2]
...... P3 Fires ......

>>>>What is the predecessor of 2
<<<<1
[1]
[Y 4]
...... P4 Fires ......

[X 1]
[Y 4]
...... P2 Fires ......

>>>>What is the successor of 4
<<<<5
[5]
[X 1]
...... P3 Fires ......

>>>>What is the predecessor of 1
<<<<0
[0]
[Y 5]
...... P4 Fires ......

[X 0]
[Y 5]
...... P1 Fires ......

>>>>Result 5
```

Moving Objects

Imagine that we have a world with some objects (see figure 28–2) and a one-armed robot that can move these objects around in this world, one at at time. This is similar to the MOVER system described in [Winograd 72]. The use of a *goal-reduction* paradigm [Winston 84] to plan the actions of the robot in moving the Table to a new location XYZ can be formulated in our production system language. Each of the rules can be viewed as a specialist that knows how to do one thing well.

Figure 28–2: A Simple World of Objects

```
Name: P1
Pattern: PutOn >Object >OtherObject
Actions: EraseSTM [PutOn <Object <OtherObject]
         Write [PutAt <Object
             [Location of top of <OtherObject]]
Name: P2
Pattern: PutAt >Object >NewLocation
Actions: EraseSTM [PutAt <Object <NewLocation]
         Write [Goal <Object <NewLocation]
         Write [Grasp <Object]
Name: P3
Pattern: MoveObject >Object
         <Object is on >OtherObject
Actions: EraseSTM [<Object is on <OtherObject]
Name: P4
Pattern: MoveObject >Object
         Goal <Object >NewLocation
Actions: EraseSTM [MoveObject <Object]
         EraseSTM [goal <Object <NewLocation]
         Send [Move hand to <NewLocation]
         Send [Let go]
Name: P5
Pattern: Grasp >Object
         Nothing is on <Object
Actions: EraseSTM [Grasp <Object]
         EraseSTM [Nothing is on <Object]
         Write [MoveObject <Object]
         Send [Move hand to top of <Object]
         Send [Grasp <Object]
Name: P6
Pattern: Grasp >Object
         >obstacle is on <object
Actions: Write [PutOn <obstacle floor]
Name: P7
Pattern: Grasp >Object
Actions: Send [What is on <Object ?]
         Receive
         EraseSTM [Grasp <Object]
         Write [Grasp <Object]
```

The short-term memory initially contains the task of moving Table to location XYZ:

"STM is [[PutAt table xyz]]

Starting the following production system yields the following:

? StartSystem

[PutAt table xyz]
...... P2 Fires ......
[Grasp table]
[goal table xyz]
...... P7 Fires
......
>>>>What is on table ?
<<<<lamp is on table

```
[Grasp table]
[lamp is on table]
[goal table xyz]
...... P6 Fires ......
[PutOn lamp floor]
[Grasp table]
[lamp is on table]
[goal table xyz]
...... P1 Fires ......
[PutAt lamp [Location of top of floor]]
[Grasp table]
[lamp is on table]
[goal table xyz]
...... P2 Fires ......
[Grasp lamp]
[goal lamp [Location of top of floor]]
[Grasp table]
[lamp is on table]
[goal table xyz]
...... P7 Fires ......
>>>>What is on lamp ?
<<<<Nothing is on lamp

[Grasp lamp]
[Nothing is on lamp]
[goal lamp [Location of top of floor]]
[Grasp table]
[lamp is on table]
[goal table xyz]
...... P5 Fires ......
>>>>Move hand to top of lamp

>>>>Grasp lamp

[MoveObject lamp]
[goal lamp [Location of top of floor]]
[Grasp table]
[lamp is on table]
[goal table xyz]
...... P3 Fires ......
[MoveObject lamp]
[goal lamp [Location of top of floor]]
[Grasp table]
[goal table xyz]
...... P4 Fires ......
>>>>Move hand to [Location of top of floor]

>>>>Let go

[Grasp table]
[goal table xyz]
...... P7 Fires ......
>>>>What is on table ?
<<<<Nothing is on table

[Grasp table]
[Nothing is on table]
[goal table xyz]
...... P5 Fires ......
```

```
>>>>Move hand to top of table

>>>>Grasp table

[MoveObject table]
[goal table xyz]
...... P4 Fires ......
>>>>Move hand to xyz

>>>>Let go
```

28.7. Possible Extensions

Adding New Capabilities

With the elements already provided, this system can be extended in much the same way that a procedure-oriented language is. If we need to "define" an elementary action `Replace` (which replaces an element in short-term memory with another item), we can do this by writing a production that "defines" `Replace` with `EraseSTM` and `Write`. This can then be "called" from another production:

```
[P0 Replace >Old >New]]
   [[Erase <Old]
   [Write <New]
   [Erase [Replace <Old <New]]]]
   ...
[PN [... >Old]
   [...
   ...
   [Write [Replace <Old [New Move]]]]]
```

Of course, instead of creating new actions like this, the production system itself can provide this capability. In principle, the production system described in this chapter can (and should) be extended in two ways:

• by extending the pattern matcher,

• by introducing further primitive actions, and

• by allowing priorities to be associated with productions.

The pattern matcher should at least be extended so that the order in which the pattern elements appear is not important. The actions should be extended to include more actions for manipulating :STM (perhaps a `Replace` among others), as well as actions for modifying the production system itself (i.e., the :LTM). Priorities associated with productions can be used to decide which production to use when several productions match :STM. Once this is done, the system is close to a fully integrated, self-sufficient programming system (like LISP for example) with a production system architecture.

A Compiler

Instead of an interpreter, define a *compiler* for executing a production system. By a compiler, we mean a program that transforms a program from one language to an equivalent program in another language (generally with the goal of a more efficient representation or execution). Since the production system can be viewed as a programming language, it can be translated into an equivalent LOGO program. The basic structure of such a program was described on page 311. Write a program that automates this translation.

Chapter 29:
Is it a Mammal?

29.1. The Problem

In this section we describe a program that conducts a simple dialog about the classification of animals. The program should work as follows:

The user thinks of an animal. The program attempts to guess what the animal is. It asks the user questions about the properties of the animal that can be answered with a "yes" or a "no." If the program cannot guess the name of the animal, the user gives the name of the animal and a question (one not already asked by the program) that distinguishes that animal from the one that the program guessed. This question should then be used to differentiate between animals in later attempts.

Sample dialog:

```
? Animals
Do you want to test your knowledge about animals? yes
Think of an animal!
Here we go!

is it a mammal ? yes
Then is it a(n) horse ? no
no ?? What is it then ? elephant
Give me a question that differentiates
a(n) elephant from a(n) horse:
Does it live in India?
And what is the answer in the case
of a(n) elephant yes
Thanks for the information!
Do you want to play again? yes
Think of an animal!
Here we go!
Is it a mammal? yes
Does it live in India ? yes
Then, is it a(n) elephant ? yes
You see, I'm not so dumb!
Do you want to play again? no
See you later!
```

29.2. Objectives

This problem lends itself well to a binary tree data structure because each question generates a yes/no decision branch. The program illustrates some of the problems associated with constructing, traversing, and extending binary trees. This allows us to illustrate one method of handling "knowledge" in a program.

From a slightly different viewpoint, the data structure can also be viewed as a network that discriminates between different concepts and is interpreted by the program at the time of the dialog.

29.3. Implementing the Data Structures

For storing the information gathered by the dialog, a binary tree data structure is used because the questions asked by the program (which were formulated from responses from the user) always represent a binary decision between two possible directions for the dialog. We represent the nodes of the binary tree as a structure made up of three parts (see figure 29–1) The left and right parts contain pointers to the subtrees, whereas the middle part contains the actual data for that node. This information can be either the name of an animal or a question that differentiates between the two subtrees.

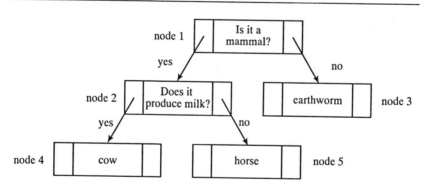

Figure 29–1: Tree Structure

Nodes 1 and 2 contain a question, whereas nodes 3, 4, and 5 contain the name of an animal.

As the example shows, all names of animals are on the leaves of the tree, whereas the questions are on the inner nodes of the tree.

Using the function PutProp described in section 9.2, this tree structure can be implemented as follows:

```
PutProp "Node1 "yes "Node2
PutProp "Node1 "no "Node3
PutProp "Node1 "Info [is it a mammal?]
PutProp "Node2 "Info "horse
PutProp "Node3 "Info "earthworm
```

The procedures YesBranch, NoBranch, Question, Animal, and AnimalP, which use the procedure GetProp (discussed in section III), provide access to the data structure.

```
To YesBranch :Node
   Output GetProp :Node "yes
End

To NoBranch :Node
   Output GetProp :Node "no
End

To Question :Node
   Output GetProp :Node "Info
End

To Animal :Node
   Output GetProp :Node "Info
End

To AnimalP :Node
   Output WordP GetProp :Node "Info
End
```

The procedures Animal and Question are nearly identical since they both access the Info element of the node structure.

29.4. Procedures for the Dialog

```
To Animals
   If Not NameP "DataBase [InitDataBase]
   Type
      [Do you want to test your knowledge about animals?]
   IfElse ReadList = [yes]
      [Play]
      [Print [Don't you like me?]]
End
```

Animals initializes the database with a minimal binary tree, then offers to play the game, and starts the procedure Play.

```
To InitDataBase
   Make "DataBase "available
   PutProp "Node1 "yes "Node2
   PutProp "Node1 "no "Node3
   PutProp "Node1 "Info [Is it a mammal?]
   PutProp "Node2 "Info "horse
   PutProp "Node3 "Info "earthworm
   Make "NumberOfNodes 3
End
```

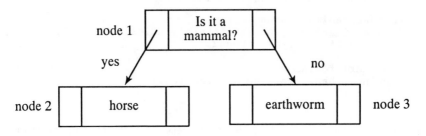

Figure 29-2: Initial State of the Database

InitDataBase initializes the tree as presented in figure 29-2. At the same time, two global variables are created, which have the following meaning:

:DataBase
> is assigned the value "available; this is tested by Animals to see if the database has already been initialized.

:NumberOfNodes
> keeps track of the number of nodes already in the tree; it is initially set to 3 and during the dialog, as the tree is extended, more nodes are added and the value of this variable changes. It is used to generate unique names for the nodes.

```
To Play
   Print [Think of an animal!]
   Print []
   Print [Here we go!]
   Print []
   Search "Node1
   Type [Do you want to play again?]
   IfElse ReadList = [yes]
     [Play]
     [Print [See you later!]]
End
```

The procedure Play handles the startup and closing dialog and calls the procedure Search, which takes care of the main part of the dialog.

```
To Search :Node
   If AnimalP :Node [HandleAnimal :Node
                     Stop]
   Type Question :Node
   IfElse ReadList = [yes]
     [Search YesBranch :node]
     [Search NoBranch :node]
End
```

Search first tests, whether the node contains an animal name, and if so makes a guess. If not, the question is posed to the user, and based on the answer, either the "yes" branch or the "no" branch is searched.

```
To HandleAnimal :Node
    Type (Sentence [Then is it a(n)] Animal :Node "?)
    If ReadList = [yes] [Found
                        Stop]
    GatherInfo :Node
    Print [Thanks for the information!]
    Print []
End
```

HandleAnimal makes the appropriate guess about the animal, and if the guess is correct, it calls the trivial procedure Found and stops. If the animal name that is contained in the node is not the correct guess, then GatherInfo is called to extend the database.

```
To Found
    Print [You see, I'm not so dumb!]
    Repeat 3 [Print []]
End
```

29.5. Extending the Database

```
To GatherInfo :Node
    Type [no ?? What is it then ?]
    Make "NewAnimal First ReadList
    Type
        (Sentence
            [Give me a question that differentiates a(n)]
            :NewAnimal
            [from a(n)]
            Animal :Node
            ": )
    Make "NewQuestion ReadList
    Type
        (Sentence
            [And what is the answer in the case of a(n)]
            :NewAnimal
            "? )
    ModifyTree
        :Node
        GenerateName
        GenerateName
        :NewAnimal
        :NewQuestion
        ReadList
End
```

First, GatherInfo asks the user what the animal was and for a question that would allow it to be differentiated from what was guessed. These are passed on to the procedure ModifyTree along with the names of two new nodes generated by GenerateName

```
To GenerateName
  Make "NumberOfNodes :NumberOfNodes + 1
  Output Word "Node :NumberOfNodes
End

To ModifyTree :Node :Node1 :Node2
               :NewAnimal :NewQuestion :Answer
  IfElse :Answer = [yes]
    [Link :Node :Node2 :Node1]
    [Link :Node :Node1 :Node2]
  PutProp :Node1 "Info Animal :Node
  PutProp :Node2 "Info :NewAnimal
  PutProp :Node "Info :NewQuestion
End
```

ModifyTree modifies the existing tree structure in the following ways:

(1) The two newly generated nodes are connected to the node :Node in the existing tree using Link as specified by :Answer.

```
To Link :node :YesBranch :NoBranch
  PutProp :node "yes :YesBranch
  PutProp :node "no :NoBranch
End
```

(2) The animals are placed in the information fields of the two newly created nodes (the name of the one already known one in :Node1 and the new one in :Node2).

(3) The information field of the node that was previously the "last" node :Node is set to the new question that differentiates between :Node1 and :Node2, replacing the information (the name of the previously known animal).

The results of this addition to the information tree can be seen by comparing figure 29–2 (before) with figure 29–1 (after adding a cow).

29.6. Final Remarks, Further Directions

Even though this program is included in the artificial intelligence section, it is clearly an extremely "dumb" program in comparison to the other ones presented here.

Although the "intelligence" of this program is limited, you should not underestimate the intelligence that is required to play "Twenty Questions" or the old-time TV show "What's My Line." The main difference is that the information used to play these is not built up just during the game but is already in the mind of the guesser. The skillfulness of the guesser depends on the ability to ask questions in such a way that the set of possible answers is divided into two parts of about the same size.

This points to a straightforward extension of the program: It could easily be extended to other domains (e.g., plants, traffic signs, prominent personalities, professions); to do so, any of the `Print` commands that are directly related to animals would have to be modified.

Another possibility, once this has been done, is to have the program use some strategy such as reorganizing the tree, or modifying the way the tree is searched to divide the set of possible answers as described before. If the top-level question were "Is it a plant" and the program only knows about one plant (such that the tree is extremely "imbalanced"), it might be better to ask some other question first (i.e., to "balance" the tree somehow).

Chapter 30:
Who Are the Children of Adam?

30.1. The Problem

This chapter deals with a program that allows the computer to carry on a dialog about family relationships.

This program will be able to:

- Add new people to the ones already known by specifying their family relationships.

- Answer questions regarding the family relationships.

To meet these goals, the program should

- update its database appropriately when a new person is added (even in places not explicitly mentioned

- derive information about concrete family relationships that was not given explicitly using general knowledge about family relationships.

To make the problem manageable, we restrict the kinds of information that our program handles in two ways:

- Each name (each person) occurs only once (e.g., there can only be one "Eve").

- The families are all "good catholic families," that is to say, each person has only one spouse, divorce is not allowed, and all children are legitimate.

The following sample Dialog illustrates the problem:

```
? Dialog
Tell or ask me something: Adam is the husband of Eve
Tell or ask me something: Cain is the son of Eve
Tell or ask me something: Abel is the son of Adam
Tell or ask me something: Is Cain the brother of Abel
True
Tell or ask me something: Who is the brother of Cain
Abel
Tell or ask me something: Who is the mother of Abel
Eve
Tell or ask me something: Who are the children of Adam
Cain Abel
Tell or ask me something: Elizabeth is the wife of Cain
Tell or ask me something: Lisa is the mother of Elizabeth
Tell or ask me something: Elizabeth is the mother of Enoch
```

```
Is Enoch female? no
Tell or ask me something: who is the grandpa of Enoch
Adam
Tell or ask me something: who are the grandkids of Eve
Enoch
Tell or ask me something: Trina is the mother of
Enoch
Enoch already has parents
Tell or ask me something: is Eve the grandfather of
Enoch
The relationship grandfather is unknown
Tell or ask me something: is Eve the grandpa of Enoch
False
Tell or ask me something: is Eve the grandma of Enoch
True
Tell or ask me something: Elizabeth is the father of
Adam
Elizabeth cannot be a father !!!
Tell or ask me something: Abel is The father of Adam
Adam is already one of the parents of Abel
```

30.2. Objectives

This problem illustrates the concepts of a database and interaction with a database well. It also exemplifies some of the problems related to knowledge representation.

Another property of the problem touched on here is that it, more than most of the other problems presented here, forces the designer to reflect on her or his own seemingly reliable thought processes.

The problem shows us that, in spite of the ease with which we as humans can carry on a dialog about family relationships, there are many hidden problems that arise when we try to understand how and why we are able to do so.

30.3. Possible Representations of Family Relationships

One way to represent relationships is by English statements:

• *Adam is the husband of Eve*

• *Cain is the son of Eve*

Figure 30–1 shows this graphically.

If a person is given these two pieces of information about this family he or she can answer these questions:

• *Is Adam the husband of Eve?*

• *Is Cain the son of Eve?*

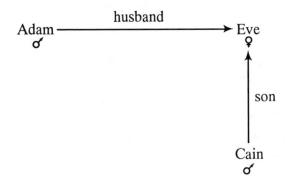

Figure 30-1: The "First" Family

as well as more difficult questions such as:

- *Is Eve the wife of Adam?*
- *Is Eve the mother of Cain?*

"Wife" and "Mother" represent just another perspective on the same facts. A human dialog partner could certainly answer the following questions correctly as well:

- *Is Adam the father of Cain?*
- *Is Cain the son of Adam?*

If the family is extended to include the person "Abel" with the statement:

Adam is the father of Abel

the human dialog partner could also give an affirmative answer to the following questions:

- *Is Adam the father of Abel?*
- *Is Abel the son of Adam?*
- *Is Abel the son of Eve?*
- *Is Eve the mother of Abel?*
- *Is Abel the brother of Cain?*
- *Is Cain the brother of Abel?*

Figure 30-2 illustrates again which relationships between the four people in our dialog can be derived from the three facts explicitly given.

However, the ability of a human to answer all 12 of the preceding questions correctly does not mean that all 12 relationships are explicitly represented

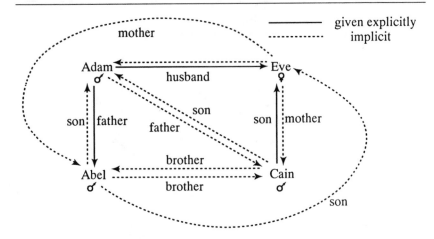

Figure 30–2: Family Relationships between Four Persons

(similar to the way they are in the sketch) mentally; on the contrary, that is extremely unlikely, since even with just 7 people (e.g., grandparents, parents, and one child) there are already 42 relationships that would have to be explicitly represented.

If one accepts this assertion, then the problem of how a person can carry on such a dialog presents itself, and what type of knowledge supports this activity.

The solution to the problem lies in the use of two types of knowledge:

(1) Knowledge about explicitly given facts: *Adam is the husband of Eve,*

(2) Knowledge about how facts can be combined to yield new facts.

If this distinction between knowledge about explicit (static) facts and knowledge about the ways facts can be combined (dynamically) is accepted, then further questions arise:

- Which parts of the knowledge should be represented explicitly?

- Which parts of the knowledge should be represented as rules and procedures for combining other facts?

From a slightly different viewpoint, this question can also be viewed as the question regarding when information is processed:

- Which parts of the knowledge should be processed when they enter into the system (*information processing at read time*), and

- Which parts of the knowledge should be processed only when a question that relates to them arises (*information processing at question time*)?

Both possibilities have their advantages and disadvantages; if a great deal of effort is expended at the time information is placed into the system, then this has the advantage that all the information in the system can be reduced to a canonical form, so that the work that needs to be performed at "question time" is simple. The disadvantage of this method is that much work is done that may never be needed in later dialog.

On the other hand, if all processing is postponed until "question time," it can take a while to come up with an answer (much like a student who does not think about a problem until the teacher asks for the answer).

30.4. The Database

All the knowledge of the system is put into a canonical form; the name of each person in the database is placed on a list and the following information is associated with the name:

- The gender of the person; this is knowledge that a human can usually determine from the first name of a person. If the computer cannot determine the gender of a person from the relationship, such as is the case in our example with Abel:

  Adam is the father of Abel

  it asks for the gender of the person.

- If applicable, the name of the spouse

- If applicable, the names of all the children

The entire database then looks like this:

(1) A list of all the people

(2) A table such as is illustrated in figure 30–3. The cells in the columns "spouse" and "all children" may be empty.

This database is implemented as the global list `:$All`, with the columns `gender`, `spouse`, and `children` represented by associating properties with the names using `PutProp` and `GetProp` (see section 9.2). The list of people is extended using the function `New`:

```
To New :Person
   Make "$All Sentence :$All :Person
End
```

30.5. Manipulating the Database

One of four types of information can cause the system to extend its database:

- the name of a new person; the system asks the gender of this person,

	gender	spouse	all children
person 1			
person 2			
⋮			
person N			

Figure 30–3: The Database of People and their Family Relationships

- Information about a `Marital Re`lationship between two people (`Husband, Hubby, Wife, Spouse`),

- information about a `Parental Re`lationship between two people (`father, mother`),

- information about a `Filial Re`lationship between two people (`son, daughter`).

Adding a New Person

The first of these cases is handled by the procedure `NewPerson`

```
To NewPerson :Person
   If KnownP :Person [Stop]
   Type (Sentence "is :Person "female?)
   IfElse ReadList = [yes]
      [PutProp :Person "Gender "Female]
      [PutProp :Person "Gender "Male]
   New :Person
End

To KnownP :Person
   Output MemberP :Person :$All
End
```

The procedure `KnownP` tests whether a person is already known and thereby avoids duplicate entries and "dumb questions."

If we wanted to give the system somewhat more global knowledge about names to avoid frequent questions about a person's gender, we could create a global list of most common names and their genders that could be consulted first, and only ask the question if the name was not in the list.

Specifying a Marital Relationship

In specifying a `Marital` `Rel`ationship, there are four different cases to be considered (as there are with `Parental` `Rel`ationships and `Filial` `Rel`ationships:

- both persons are already in the database (i.e., known to the system),

- only the first person is known,

- only the second person is known, or

- neither person is known to the system.

```
To MaritalRel :Rel :P1 :P2
   If Not EqualP (Sentence Spouse :P1 Spouse :P2) []
      [Print [Bigamy not allowed!!]
      Stop]
   If And KnownP :P1 KnownP :P2
      [BothKnownMarry :P1 :P2
      Stop]
   If KnownP :P1 [FirstKnownMarry :P1 :P2
      Stop]
   IfElse KnownP :P2
      [FirstKnownMarry :P2 :P1]
      [BothUnknownMarry :Rel :P1 :P2]
End
```

Above all, the system tries to avoid inconsistencies when building the database: It "obeys the law" here by checking whether the "bride" or "groom" is already married and refuses to "perform the ceremony" if this is the case for either one.

```
To BothKnownMarry :P1 :P2
   If (Gender :P1) = Gender :P2
      [Print
         (Sentence :P1 "and :P2 [are both] Gender :P1)
      Stop]
   PutProp :P1 "Spouse :P2
   PutProp :P2 "Spouse :P1
   PutProp
      :P1
      "Children
      Union Children :P1 Children :P2
   PutProp :P2 "Children Children :P1
End

To Gender :Person
   Output GetProp :Person "Gender
End
```

If both people are already known to the system, `BothKnownMarry` is called to make a record of the wedding. The wedding is refused if both people are of the same gender.

If all the tests are passed, the marriage is established. This is nothing more than placing the information that is given explicitly into the database in an explicit form. After that some additional "information processing at read time" is performed: Although nothing has been said explicitly about the `Parental Relationships` between the newlyweds and their respective children, the system performs a "bilateral adoption," merging the two sets of children and associating them with both parents (see figures 30–4 and 30–5).

This situation looks a little different if one of the people is not known by the system.

Before the wedding

	gender	spouse	children
Adam	male		Abel
Eve	female		Cain

After the wedding

	gender	spouse	children
Adam	male	Eve	Abel Cain
Eve	female	Adam	Abel Cain

Figure 30–4: Knowledge about a Family - Table Form

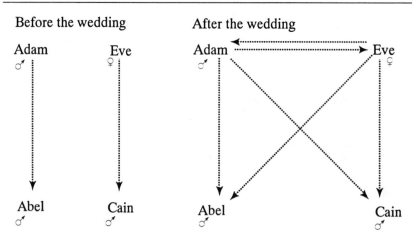

Figure 30–5: Knowledge about a Family - as a Graph

```
To FirstKnownMarry :P1 :P2
  New :P2
  PutProp :P2 "Gender OppositeSex Gender :P1
  PutProp :P2 "Spouse :P1
  PutProp :P1 "Spouse :P2
  PutProp :P2 "Children Children :P1
End

To OppositeSex :Gender
  IfElse :Gender = "Male
    [Output "Female]
    [Output "Male]
End
```

Because :P1 is already known, FirstKnownMarry assumes that the gender of :P2 is the opposite of the gender of :P1. The consummation is even simpler than the first case because the children of :P1 become the children of :P2.

It looks different if two unknown people want to get married. If the stated relationship between the two is Spouse, then the gender of one of them needs to be asked. If the stated relationship is hubby or husband, then this information is used to establish the gender.

```
To BothUnknownMarry :Rel :P1 :P2
  IfElse :Rel = "Spouse
    [NewPerson :P1
     New :P2]
    [New List :P1 :P2]
  If MemberP :Rel [hubby husband groom]
    [PutProp :P1 "Gender "Male]
  If MemberP :Rel [wife bride]
    [PutProp :P1 "Gender "Female]
  PutProp :P2 "Gender OppositeSex Gender :P1
  PutProp :P1 "Spouse :P2
  PutProp :P2 "Spouse :P1
End
```

Having Kids

The task is somewhat more complicated if a FilialRelationship (parent/child) needs to be established between two people.

```
To FilialRel :Rel :Child :Parent
  If And KnownP :Child KnownP :Parent
    [BothKnownKid :Rel :Child :Parent
     Stop]
  If KnownP :Child
    [KidKnown :Rel :Child :Parent
     Stop]
  IfElse KnownP :Parent
    [ParentKnown :Rel :Child :Parent]
    [BothUnknownKid :Rel :Child :Parent]
End
```

If only the parent is known, the gender of the child is determined from the type of the relationship, the child is added to the list of all people, and the child is added to the lists of the parents' children using SetKids.

```
To ParentKnown :Rel :Child :Parent
  IfElse :Rel = "Son
    [PutProp :Child "Gender "Male]
    [PutProp :Child "Gender "Female]
  New :Child
  SetKids :Parent :Child
End

To SetKids :Parent :Child
  PutProp
    :Parent
    "Children
    Union Children :Parent FPut :Child []
  If Not (Spouse :Parent) = []
    [PutProp
       Spouse :Parent
       "Children
       Children :Parent]
End

To Spouse :Person
  Output GetProp :Person "Spouse
End

To Children :Person
  Output GetProp :Person "Children
End
```

The process is simple if both people are not yet known:

```
To BothUnknownKid :Rel :P1 :P2
  NewPerson :P2
  New :P1
  IfElse MemberP :Rel [Father Son]
    [PutProp :P1 "Gender "Male]
    [PutProp :P1 "Gender "Female]
  IfElse MemberP :Rel [Father Mother]
    [PutProp :P1 "Children FPut :P2 []]
    [PutProp :P2 "Children FPut :P1 []]
End
```

The gender of the first person :P1 is derived from the specified relationship; the reason that both Son and Father appear in the list is so that this procedure can also be used by ParentalRel (see following, likewise [Father Mother] in the last If command). The case of a Son or a Daughter is handled in the Else clause.

A third possibility is that only the child is known so far. If this is the case, it can first be checked whether the gender of the child (in the database) and that specified by the relationship agree using GenderMismatchP.

```
To KidKnown :Rel :Child :Parent
  If GenderMismatchP :Rel "Son "Daughter :Child
  [Stop]
  If Count Parents :Child = 2
  [Print FPut :Child [already has parents]]
  If Parents :Child = []
  [NewPerson :Parent
   PutProp :Parent "Children FPut :Child []
   Stop]
  New :Parent
  PutProp
    :Parent
    "Gender
    OppositeSex First Parents :Child
  PutProp First Parents :Child "Spouse :Parent
  PutProp :Parent "Spouse First Parents :Child
  PutProp
    Spouse :Parent
    "Children
    Union Children Spouse :Parent FPut :Child []
  PutProp :Parent "Children Children Spouse :Parent
End

To GenderMismatchP :Rel :A :B :Person
  IfElse
      Or
      And :Rel = :A (Gender :Person) = "Female
      And :Rel = :B (Gender :Person) = "Male
    [Print (Sentence :Person [cannot be a] :Rel "!!! )
     Output "True]
    [Output "False]
End
```

It can also be checked whether two parents are already noted for this person in the database; an error message to this effect is printed out in the second (logical) line of KidKnown.

Furthermore, it is also possible that no parents are known for this person, then we only need to enter the parent in the database with this person as an only child. (third logical line)

If one of the parents is already known, then the rest of the procedure KidKnown comes into play:

• The gender of the new parent is determined

• An explicit marital relationship is created between the two parents (fifth logical line)

• The children of the parents are set up appropriately.

This situation is shown in figure 30–6.

```
Abel is the son of Eve
```

is added explicitly, all the rest of the relationships are derived by the system (including the gender of Eve).

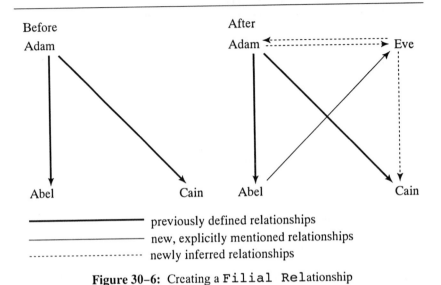

Before	After
Adam	Adam ← - - - - - - - - - - - - → Eve
Abel Cain	Abel Cain

——————————— previously defined relationships
——————————— new, explicitly mentioned relationships
- - - - - - - - - - - - - newly inferred relationships

Figure 30-6: Creating a `Filial Relationship`
with One Unknown Parent and One Known Parent

Determining the parents of a person requires a serial search of all the people stored in the database because that relationship is not stored explicitly. In contrast, `Gender` or `Spouse` are attributes that are stored in the database and do not require such a search.

```
To Parents :Person
   Output Parent1 :Person :$All
End

To Parent1 :Person :All
   If :All = [] [Output []]
   If MemberP :Person Children First :All
     [Output
        FPut First :All Parent1 :Person ButFirst :All]
   Output Parent1 :Person ButFirst :All
End
```

The relationship is similar in complexity when both the child and the parent is already known by the system in other connections.

```
To BothKnownKid :Rel :Child :Parent
   If GenderMismatchP :Rel "Son "Daughter :Child
     [Stop]
```

```
If MemberP :Child Parents :Parent
[Print
    (Sentence
     :Parent
     [is already a child of]
     :Child)
    Stop]
SetKids :Parent :Child
If (Count (Parents :Child)) = 2
    [If (Spouse :Parent) = []
        [BothKnownMarry
            First Parents :Child
            Last Parents :Child]]
End
```

Here, we can first check whether the gender implied by the :Relationship agrees with the gender already in the database.

We can also test whether the person specified as the :Child of the :Parent is not already one the Parents of the :Parent, because this is an impossible relationship.

If both of these tests are negative, the child can be added to the list of children of the parent (and the parent's spouse, if applicable).

If both parents are known, but the "married" relationship has not yet been established, this can also be done.

Setting up a Parental Relationship

Setting up a parental relationship is equivalent to setting up a Filial Relationship—with the roles switched. The difference is that the :Relationship contains implicit information about the gender of the parent (mother, father), whereas specifications of Filial Relationships contain information about the gender of the child (son, daughter). Clearly, this can be handled by the procedure BothUnknownKid, because it was designed to be general enough. There is also strong correlation to the case where both parties are known.

```
To ParentalRel :Rel :Parent :Child
    If And KnownP :Parent KnownP :Child
    [BothKnownPar :Rel :Parent :Child
        Stop]
    If KnownP :Parent
    [ChildUnknown :Rel :Parent :Child
        Stop]
    IfElse KnownP :Child
    [ParentUnknown :Rel :Parent :Child]
    [BothUnknownKid :Rel :Parent :Child]
End
```

The difference between BothKnownPar and BothKnownKid is that here we check whether the :Parent is already one of the Children of :Child, instead of vice versa; the rest is the same.

```
To BothKnownPar :Rel :Parent :Child
   If GenderMismatchP :Rel "Father "Mother :Parent
   [Stop]
   If MemberP :Parent Children :Child
   [Print
       (Sentence
        :Child
        [is already one of the parents of]
        :Parent)
      Stop]
   SetKids :Parent :Child
   If And
       (Count Parents :Child) = 2
       (Spouse :Parent) = []
   [BothKnownMarry
       First Parents :Child
       Last Parents :Child]
End
```

The procedure ChildUnknown is similar to the procedures
ParentKnown, ParentUnknown, and KidKnown.

```
To ChildUnknown :Rel :Parent :Child
   If GenderMismatchP :Rel "Father "Mother :Parent
   [Stop]
   NewPerson :Child
   SetKids :Parent :Child
End
```

```
To ParentUnknown :Rel :Parent :Child
   If (Count Parents :Child) = 2
      [Print FPut :Child [already has parents]]
   IfElse :Rel = "Mother
      [PutProp :Parent "Gender "Female]
      [PutProp :Parent "Gender "Male]
   New :Parent
   If (Parents :Child) = []
      [PutProp :Parent "Children FPut :Child []
       Stop]
   PutProp First Parents :Child "Spouse :Parent
   PutProp :Parent "Spouse First Parents :Child
   PutProp
       Spouse :Parent
       "Children
       Union Children Spouse :Parent FPut :Child []
   PutProp :Parent "Children Children Spouse :Parent
End
```

Retrieving Information about Family Relationships

Compared with the difficulty of adding new information to the database, it is
relatively simple to determine whether a particular relationship exists between
two arbitrary people or not. It is also simple to determine which person (people)
has (have) a particular relationship to a given person. We have already
introduced some simple examples of this with the procedures Children,
Parents, and Spouse.

Here are some more:

```
To Son :Person
  Output Males Children :Person
End

To Daughter :Person
  Output Females Children :Person
End

To Father :Person
  Make "List Males Parents :Person
  IfElse :List = []
    [Output "]
    [Output First :List]
End

To Mother :Person
  Make "List Females Parents :Person
  IfElse :List = []
    [Output "]
    [Output First :List]
End

To Brothers :Person
  Output Males Siblings :Person
End

To Sisters :Person
  Output Females siblings :Person
End

To Siblings :Person
  IfElse Father :Person = "
    [Output Except :Person Children Mother :Person]
    [Output Except :Person Children Father :Person]
End

To Females :People
  Output MaleorFemale :People "Female
End

To Males :People
  Output MaleorFemale :People "Male
End

To MaleorFemale :People :MaleorFemale
  If :People = [] [Output []]
  If (Gender First :People) = :MaleorFemale
    [Output
       Sentence
         First :People
         MaleorFemale ButFirst :People :MaleorFemale]
  Output MaleorFemale ButFirst :People :MaleorFemale
End
```

Even more distant relationships can be determined in a similar way:

```
To GrandMa :Person
  Output Females GrandParents :Person
End

To GrandPa :Person
  Output Males GrandParents :Person
End

To GrandParents :Person
  Output Parents2 Parents :Person
End

To GrandKids :Person
  Output Children1 Children :Person
End

To Children1 :Person
  IfElse :Person = [ ]
    [Output [ ]]
    [Output
        Sentence
          Children First :Person
          Children1 ButFirst :Person]
End

To Parents2 :Person
  If :Person = [] [Output []]
  Output
    Sentence
      Parents First :Person
      Parents2 ButFirst :Person
End
```

Similarly the relationships Aunt, Uncle, Nephew, Niece, Brother-InLaw, SisterInLaw, Cousin, GreatGrandParents, etc. could be formulated. Husband, Hubby, Wife correspond to the procedure Spouse.

The Framework of the Dialog

To make interaction with the database simpler, a small program is needed that makes the dialog between the user and the database easier. Dialog represents such a procedure:

```
To Dialog
  If Not NameP "$All [Make "$All []]
  Make "P1 "
  Make "P2 "
  Make "Rel "
  Type [Tell or ask me something:]
  Make "Input ReadList
  If :Input = [] [Stop]
  If PatternMatch [.P1] :Input
    [NewPerson :P1
     Dialog
     Stop]
```

```
  If PatternMatch [Who . . .Rel . .P1] :Input
     [If ExistP FPut :P1 [] :Rel
        [Print Run Sentence :Rel [:P1]
         Dialog
         Stop]]
  If PatternMatch [Is .P1 . .Rel . .P2] :Input
     [If ExistP List :P1 :P2 :Rel
        [Print
            MemberP
             :P1
               Sentence Run Sentence :Rel [:P2] []
         Dialog
         Stop]]
  If PatternMatch [.P1 . . .Rel . .P2] :Input
     [Run Sentence RelationType :Rel [:Rel :P1 :P2]
      Dialog
      Stop]
  Print []
  Print [I don't understand the input:]
  Print :Input
  Dialog
End
```

Dialog repeatedly ask for input until an empty line is entered.

The structure of the line entered by the user is extracted by the procedure PatternMatch from chapter 19.

The input to Dialog can have the following forms:

• A single word, which is interpreted as the name of a person.

• Who-question can be asked; Find is used to determine the :Relationship and the person, :P1, which are then made into a list and evaluated using Run in order to answer the question.

• Is-questions can be asked; Find is used to determine :Relationship and the two people :P1, and :P2; ElementP then tests whether :P1 is one of the people who have the :Relationship to :P2.

• A :Relationship between two people :P1 and :P2 can be asserted; dependent on the type of the relationship as determined by RelationType, the corresponding procedure MaritalRel, ParentalRel, or FilialRel is executed.

```
  To RelationType :Rel
     If MemberP :Rel [son daughter] [Output "FilialRel]
     If MemberP :Rel [father mother]
        [Output "ParentalRel]
     IfElse MemberP :Rel [spouse husband wife hubby]
        [Output "MaritalRel]
        [Output "UnknownRel]
  End
```

In determining the answers to the "who" and "is" questions, ExistP is used to test whether the :Relationship and the persons are known to the system.

```
To ExistP :People :Rel
  If Not MemberP :Rel Procedures
    [Print
       (Sentence [The relationship] :Rel [is unknown])
     Output "False]
  If Not KnownP First :People
    [Print FPut First :People [is not known]
     Output "False]
  If not KnownP Last :People
    [Print FPut Last :People [is not known]
     Output "False]
  Output "True
End
```

For completeness, we should also mention that the procedures dUnknownRel and Except as well as the global variable "$All are part of the system:

```
To UnknownRel :Rel :P1 :P2
  Print
     (Sentence [The relationship] :Rel [is unknown])
End
```

```
To Except :A :B
  If :B = [] [Output []]
  IfElse :A = First :B
    [Output ButFirst :B]
    [Output FPut First :B Except :A ButFirst :B]
End
```

MemberP and Union are described in appendix III.

Another Dialog example:

```
? Dialog
Tell or ask me something: Dieter is the son of Heinz
is Heinz female? no
Tell or ask me something: Heinz is the mother of Fritz
Heinz cannot be a mother !!!
Tell or ask me something: Heinz is the hubby of Elli
Tell or ask me something: Is Elli the mother of Dieter
True
Tell or ask me something: Marie is the mother of Elli
Tell or ask me something: Luise is the mother of Heinz
Tell or ask me something: Heinrich is the father of
  Heinz
Tell or ask me something: Who is the grandpa of Dieter
Heinrich
Tell or ask me something: Dirk is the son of Friedrich
is Friedrich female? no
Tell or ask me something: Friedrich is the husband of
  Anna
Tell or ask me something: Marie is the wife of Dirk
Tell or ask me something: Who is the grandpa of Elli
Friedrich
Tell or ask me something: Is Dirk the grandpa of
  Dieter
True
```

```
Tell or ask me something: Susanne is the daughter of
Elli
Tell or ask me something: Who are the grandkids of
Dirk
Dieter Susanne
Tell or ask me something: Anne is the daughter of Dirk
Tell or ask me something: Who are the grandkids of
Anna
Elli Anne
```

Possible Extensions

This program (system) can be extended in many different ways; some of these possibilities are presented as short, sometimes open questions:

- The number of relationships could be increased; in addition to fixed relationships such as `Aunt`, `Cousin`, etc., general relationships such as `Ancestor(s)` and `Descendant(s)` could be allowed.

- The input syntax could be made more flexible, such as:

  - The *form* of the input could be made more flexible, such as "Who are the brothers of ..." instead of just `brother`,

  - the number of relationships used to describe a family could be increased; one could allow relationships such as `brother`, `sister`, or `GrandFather` and `GrandMother` as input.

- What changes to the program and database would be necessary to allow divorces or, in general, if we allow deletions from the database (e.g., can a person be both the mother and the aunt of another person)? This amounts to what is known as *nonmonotonic reasoning*; what is true now may not be true later.

- What changes to the program and database would be necessary to allow several people to have the same name (who can only be differentiated based on their different relationships to different people)?

- Testing for contradictions (or illegal relationships) could be improved. In the current version a man can marry his sister or even his grandmother (and thereby become his own grandfather!).

- The ability to answer more general questions could be added, for example: "What relationship exists between the Miller family and the Meyer family?" How could family names be added to the system?

- How can explicit "negative" information be integrated into the system? What could be derived from "Eve is not the grandmother of Adam."

- How could relationships be described by data rather than by programs, so that new relationships could be added by the user using `Dialog`?

There are still a number of further extensions possible, which would allow the program to understand the following story:

The new patient at the asylum was unusually lucid and quite sensible. He knew where he was and explained to the head doctor why he was there: "You see, I married a widow with an adult daughter. Shortly thereafter, my father married my wife's daughter. As a result, my wife became the mother-in-law of her father-in-law, my step-daughter became my step-mother, and my father became my son-in-law.

My step-mother had a son, who was then my step-brother, but he was also my wife's grandson, so I was the grandfather of my step-brother. Now, my wife and I also had a son, so he was my father's brother-in-law, because he was his wife's brother. My step-daughter is her brother's grandmother, because he is also the son of her step-son.

Since I am the step-father of my father, my son is the step-brother of my father, as well the son of my grandmother, because my wife is the daughter-in-law of her daughter. I am the step-father of my step-mother, my father and his wife my step-children, my father and my son are brothers, my wife is my grandmother since she is my step-mother's mother. I am a nephew of my father, and at the same time I am my own grandfather, and that drove me over the edge."

Part 5:
Linguistics

Introduction

Linguistics is the study of the nature and structure of human speech and language. Although linguistics is not currently incorporated into most secondary school curricula, related problems are dealt with to some degree in English and mathematics courses.

Characteristics of Problems from Linguistics

In contrast to problems from mathematics, it can be assumed that the reader has an intuitive understanding of problems that fall into the category of linguistics in the broadest sense. Therefore, errors can be more easily detected than with mathematical problems. An incorrect result in mathematics sometimes requires some careful double-checked, whereas errors in problems from linguistics often can be recognized by simple inspection of the results.

Furthermore, most problems can be introduced with a simple "seed," which can be extended a great deal with respect to scope and difficulty.

One final characteristic is that linguistic problems appear in diverse disciplines; yet they still lend themselves to similar methods of solution. A program that is used to analyze sentences in natural language differs only slightly from compilers or programs that manipulate mathematical formulae. The material from chapter 20 could really be considered as exercises in linguistics, as well.

Further Studies in Linguistics

The material presented here from linguistics makes no claim to generality or completeness but rather should present some basics upon which further study can be based.

- Linguistics can be further studied further as it relates to:
    - recognition, representation, and testing of language structures,
    - differentiation between syntax and semantics,
    - examination of formal languages (from mathematics and computer science) and how they relate to natural languages.
- For solving some problems, certain languages can be designed that could best be described as "minilanguages" (e.g., production systems); these require the definition of suitable primitives that correspond to subproblems of a given problem. With their help, complex problems can be described at different levels of abstraction.

- Linguistic statistics and linguistic games are simple problem domains that illustrate certain simple principles from linguistics.

Another excellent resource for studying linguistics using LOGO is [Goldenberg, Feurzeig 87].

Chapter 31:
Conjugating Verbs

One part of linguistics called *morphology* focuses on how words are formed. The conjugation of verbs in this chapter and the formation of plurals in the next are examples of this area of study.

31.1. The Problem

Let's write a program that conjugates German and French verbs given the infinitive form. It will also "pick-up" and remember irregular verbs. Here are a few examples to illustrate:

```
Enter the verb to be conjugated:
tanzen
ich tanze
du tanzt
er tanzt
wir tanzen
ihr tanzt
sie tanzen

Enter the verb to be conjugated:
chercher
je cherche
tu cherches
il cherche
nous cherchons
vous cherchez
ils cherchent
```

31.2. Objectives

A program for conjugating regular German verbs is so simple to write that it can be done with only a little programming experience.

The program we present here can be extended in a stepwise fashion, so that many verbs can be handled. Designing the program in a modular fashion makes this task easier. Specifying the rules of conjugation forces the explicit formalization of a process, which is acquired in studying a language. If the program conjugates a verb incorrectly, this points out that the information has not been correctly specified.

31.3. A Simple Version of Conjugation of Regular German Verbs

A few procedures suffice to handle the conjugation of regular German verbs in the present tense. Endings and pronouns are represented as lists, which can be combined with the stem to create the various forms.

```
To Endings
  Output [e st t en t en]
End

To Pronouns
  Output [ich du er wir ihr sie]
End

To German
  Print [Enter the verb to be conjugated:]
  Conjugation Stem First ReadList Pronouns Endings
  Print []
  German
End

To Conjugation :Verb :Pronouns :Endings
  Test :Pronouns = []
  IfTrue [Stop]
  Print
    Sentence
      First :Pronouns
      Word :Verb First :Endings
  Conjugation
    :Verb
    ButFirst :Pronouns
    ButFirst :Endings
End

To Stem :Verb
  Output ButLast ButLast :Verb
End
```

Examples

```
? German
Enter the verb to be conjugated:
gehen
ich gehe
du gehst
er geht
wir gehen
ihr geht
sie gehen
Enter the verb to be conjugated:
schwimmen
ich schwimme
du schwimmst
er schwimmt
wir schwimmen
ihr schwimmt
sie schwimmen
```

```
Enter the verb to be conjugated:
wollen
ich wolle
du wollst
er wollt
wir wollen
ihr wollt
sie wollen
```

The verb "wollen" shows that the program makes no exceptions in its present simple form.

31.4. French Verbs

The French language gives us an even richer morphology to deal with, so we use it in this example.

The program presented next solves the following additional problems:

* How to divide a verb into its stem and ending,
* Conjugation of verbs with different endings ("er," "ir," and "re"),
* Exceptions within the individual classes,
* Irregular verbs that cannot be encompassed by any rule.

Each of the different classes and each irregular verb has a procedure associated with it, which contains the information about how to conjugate a corresponding verb. The three classes use the name of their respective ending as the procedure and the information that each procedure returns is a list of the endings for each of the cases. With irregular verbs, the name of the verb is used as the name of the procedure and the resulting "endings" are the conjugation for each of the cases (such that the stem used in forming the results is the empty word). The appropriate procedure name is generated based on the input and then the procedure is invoked using the Run command.

The Program

French defines the dialog framework for the program:

```
To French
  Print [Enter the verb to be conjugated:]
  Make "&Input First ReadList
  Test
    MemberP
      :&Input
      [stop end bye goodbye adieu aurevoir]
  IfTrue [Stop]
  HandleCases :&Input
  Print []
  French
End
```

HandleCases differentiates between regular and irregular verbs and breaks the verb down into its `Stem` and `Ending` and then calls `PrintConj` with the appropriate information.

```
To HandleCases :Verb
  Test MemberP :Verb ExceptionList
  IfTrue [PrintConj FrenchPronouns " Run :Verb]
  IfFalse
    [PrintConj
      FrenchPronouns
      Stem :Verb
      Run Sentence Word Ending :Verb "Ending ":Verb]
End

To Stem :Verb
  Output ButLast ButLast :Verb
End

To Ending :Verb
  Output Word Last ButLast :Verb Last :Verb
End

To FrenchPronouns
  Output [je tu il nous vous ils]
End
```

`ExceptionList` contains the irregular verbs currently known to the program. In order to add new irregular verbs, this procedure needs to be changed and a procedure with the same name as the infinitive form of the new exception needs to be created (see **Irregular Verbs** on page 360).

```
To ExceptionList
  Output
    [avoir etre aller venir pouvoir
     vouloir savoir mourir prendre mettre]
End
```

`PrintConj` first tests whether the stem of the verb must be modified (as is required with dormir, servir, and partir, for example) and whether the verb begins with a vowel or an "h" (to handle the first person singular correctly).

```
To PrintConj :Pronouns :Stem :Endings
  If :Pronouns = [] [Stop]
  IfElse
      And
      MemberP :Stem [dorm serv part]
      MemberP First :Pronouns [je tu il]
    [Print
       Sentence First :Pronouns
         Word ButLast :Stem First :Endings]
    [IfElse
        And
        (First :Pronouns) = "je
        BeginsWithVowel Word :Stem First :Endings
```

```
      [Print
        (Word
          ButLast First :Pronouns
          Apostrophe
          :Stem
          First :Endings)]
      [Print
          Sentence First :Pronouns
            Word :Stem First :Endings]]
    PrintConj
      ButFirst :Pronouns
      :Stem
      ButFirst :Endings
  End

  To BeginsWithVowel :Word
    Output MemberP First :Word [a e i o u h]
  End

  To Apostrophe
    Output Char 39
  End
```

The Three Conjugation Classes with Exception Rules

If it is an "er" verb, we need to test whether the stem ends with a "g" or a "c" so that the first person plural can be modified appropriately (the comma is a replacement representation for the cedilla). The procedure returns a list of the appropriate endings.

```
  To ErEnding :Verb
    Test (Last Stem :Verb) = "g
    IfTrue [Output [e es e eons ez ent]]
    Test (Last Stem :Verb) = "c
    IfTrue [Output [e es e ,ons ez ent]]
    Output [e es e ons ez ent]
  End
```

With "ir" verbs, the exceptions "ouvrir" and "offrir" need to be handled explicitly, as well as those that require that the stem be extended.

```
  To IrEnding :Verb
    Test MemberP :Verb [ouvrir offrir]
    IfTrue [Output [e es e ons ez ent]]
    Test MemberP :Verb ExtendStemList
    IfTrue [Output [is is it issons issez issent]]
    Output [s s t ons ez ent]
  End

  To ExtendStemList
    Output [finir choisir reflechir]
  End
```

With "re" verbs, we test to see whether an extra "s" needs to be inserted for plurals, and whether the "t" needs to be left off in the third person singular of stems that end in "d" (the program does not handle the irregularity that occurs with "vous dites" with the circumflex over the "i").

```
To ReEnding :Verb
   If MemberP :Verb [lire dire]
      [Output [s s t sons sez sent]]
   Output
      (Sentence [s s] ThirdPerson :Verb [ons ez ent])
End

To ThirdPerson :Verb
   If (Last Stem :Verb) = "d [Output Spaces 1]
   Output "t
End
```

Irregular Verbs

With irregular verbs the entire conjugated form is returned instead of just the ending.

```
To Avoir
   Output [ai as a avons avez ont]
End

To Etre
   Output [suis es est sommes etes sont]
End

To Aller
   Output [vais vas va allons allez vont]
End

To Venir
   Output [viens viens vient venons venez viennent]
End

To Pouvoir
   Output [peux peux peut pouvons pouvez peuvent]
End

To Vouloir
   Output [veux veux veut voulons voulez veulent]
End

To Savoir
   Output [sais sais sait savons savez savent]
End

To Mourir
   Output [meurs meurs meurt mourons mourez meurent]
End

To Mettre
   Output [mets mets met mettons mettez mettent]
End

To Prendre
   Output
      [prends prends prend prenons prenez prennent]
End
```

Examples

Normal Conjugation

```
? French
Enter the verb to be conjugated:
fermer
je ferme
tu fermes
il ferme
nous fermons
vous fermez
ils ferment
```

"e" inserted between "g" and "o"

```
Enter the verb to be conjugated:
manger
je mange
tu manges
il mange
nous mangeons
vous mangez
ils mangent
```

using "cedilla" when "c" and "o" occur together

```
Enter the verb to be conjugated:
commencer
je commence
tu commences
il commence
nous commenc,ons
vous commencez
ils commencent
```

extending the stem

```
Enter the verb to be conjugated:
finir
je finis
tu finis
il finit
nous finissons
vous finissez
ils finissent
```

reducing the verb stem

```
Enter the verb to be conjugated:
partir
je pars
tu pars
il part
nous partons
vous partez
ils partent
```

"ir" ending using "re" conjugation

```
Enter the verb to be conjugated:
ouvrir
j'ouvre
tu ouvres
il ouvre
nous ouvrons
vous ouvrez
ils ouvrent
```

Contraction of "je", leaving of the "t" after "d"

```
Enter the verb to be conjugated:
attendre
j'attends
tu attends
il attend
nous attendons
vous attendez
ils attendent
```

Inserting an "s" in forming the plural

```
Enter the verb to be conjugated:
lire
je lis
tu lis
il lit
nous lisons
vous lisez
ils lisent
```

Irregular verb

```
Enter the verb to be conjugated:
avoir
j'ai
tu as
il a
nous avons
vous avez
ils ont
```

Irregular verb, not handled by the system.

```
Enter the verb to be conjugated:
souvenir
je souvens
tu souvens
il souvent
nous souvenons
vous souvenez
ils souvenent
```

31.5. Final Remarks

This program could be used as a "drill" program for a language student, so simply by typing it in and running it would be beneficial to some degree. However, far more is learned by dealing with the issues presented here, by writing the program yourself, even though a large part of a solution is presented here. Becoming immersed in the problem, dealing with the explicit formulation of the declension rules, and being unexpectedly confronted by exceptions are the real goals of this chapter. Thus the completeness of this program is not the most important criterion. A higher value is placed upon its understandability and modifiability of the program and its use to explore properties of natural languages. Some extensions you may want to consider are:

- handling reflexive verbs

- declensions in other tenses

- can some exceptions be generalized from known exceptions: e.g., venir → souvenir.

Chapter 32:
Forming Plurals

32.1. The Problem

This chapter deals with a program that forms the plural for a noun. The following example illustrates the problem:

```
? Plurals
Enter the next word: house
===> houses
Enter the next word: computer
===> computers
Enter the next word: calf
===> calves
Enter the next word: tomato
===> tomatoes
Enter the next word: man
===> men
```

As was done with the conjugation of French verbs, the list of those words that do not follow the rules should be extended incrementally.

32.2. Objectives

Knowledge about forming the plural needs to be formalized and represented algorithmically. Individual cases should be matched with certain rules that characterize certain classes of exceptions, which may contain exceptions as well (see "studio" as an example for nouns that end in "o").

By using the program, inconsistencies can be discovered and the knowledge that was missing from the program can be added.

32.3. Program Construction

The individual classes of exceptions are determined by predicates whose successful evaluation sets in motion the formation of the plural (the architecture of the program resembles a *production system*).

The procedure `Plurals` defines a simple dialog:

```
To Plurals
   Type [Enter the next word:]
   Local "Line
   Make "Line ReadList
```

```
    If EmptyP :Line [Stop]
    Print Sentence "===> FormPlural First :Line
    Print []
    Plurals
End
```

The real work is done by the procedure `FormPlural`. It attempts to determine the class of the specified word. The order in which the individual predicates are called is important. The procedure works from more specific to more general cases, so that the normal case (adding ''s'') is used if no special rule applies.

```
To FormPlural :Word
    If ExceptionP :Word [Output ExceptionPlural :Word]
    If PluralIsSameP :Word [Output :Word]
    If NoPluralP :Word [Output [Word has no plural]]
    If ESPluralP :Word [Output Word :Word "es]
    If UMPluralP :Word [Output UmPlural :Word]
    If FtoVPluralP :Word [Output FtoVPlural :Word]
    If YPluralP :Word [Output Word ButLast :Word "ies]
    Output Word :Word "s
End
```

The exceptions, for which no rule exists, must be listed explicitly.

```
To ExceptionP :Word
    Output MemberP :Word :ExceptionList
End

To ExceptionPlural :Word
    Output
        ExcePlurl
        :Word
        :ExceptionList
        :ExceptionPlurals
End

To ExcePlurl :Word :Exceptions :Plurals
    Test :Word = First :Exceptions
    IfTrue [Output First :Plurals]
    Output
        ExcePlurl
        :Word
        ButFirst :Exceptions
        ButFirst :Plurals
End
```

The lists for this are stored as global variables (and can be extended without difficulty, see section 32.5):

```
"ExceptionList is [foot mouse ox man woman child
appendix goose minimum crisis vertex]
"ExceptionPlurals is [feet mice oxen men women children
appendices geese minima crises vertices]
```

In the next case, the elements of the class are all that need to be specified, because the plural form is defined implicitly (trivially, because the plural is the same as the singular):

```
To PluralIsSameP :Word
  Output
    MemberP
    :Word
    [bison deer grouse moose sheep bantu haddock]
End
```

Those nouns that have no plurals behave in a similar manner.

```
To NoPluralP :Word
  Output
    MemberP
    :Word
    [milk sugar salt meat food knowledge
     news furniture information]
End
```

With the following; classes are implicitly defined by the predicates (that is, as rules), which may also contain exceptions.

```
To ESPluralP :Word
  Test MemberP :Word [studio casino]
  IfTrue [Output "False]
  Output ElementP Last :Word [sxhoz]
End

To UMPluralP :Word
  Output "um = LastTwo :Word
End

To UmPlural :Word
  Output Word ButLast ButLast :Word "a
End

To FtoVPluralP :Word
  Test MemberP :Word [roof chief handkerchief proof]
  IfTrue [Output "False]
  Output Or (Last :Word) = "f (LastTwo :Word) = "fe
End

To FtoVPlural :Word
  Test Last :Word = "f
  IfTrue Output Word ButLast :Word "ves
  Output Word ButLast ButLast :Word "ves
End

To YPluralP :Word
  Output
    And
      (Last :Word) = "y
      Not VowelP Last ButLast :Word
End
```

```
To LastTwo :Word
  Output Word Last ButLast :Word Last :Word
End

To VowelP :Letter
  Output ElementP :Letter [a e i o u]
End
```

32.4. Example

```
? Plurals
Enter the next word: goose
===> geese
Enter the next word: sheep
===> sheep
Enter the next word: milk
===> word has no plural
Enter the next word: box
===> boxes
Enter the next word: chopstick
===> chopsticks
Enter the next word: church
===> churches
Enter the next word: studio
===> studios
Enter the next word: visum
===> visa
Enter the next word: roof
===> roofs
Enter the next word: kid
===> kids
Enter the next word: knife
===> knives
Enter the next word: lady
===> ladies
Enter the next word: toy
===> toys
Enter the next word: mother-in-law
===> mother-in-laws
```

32.5. Final Remarks

The program certainly does not cover the formation of all plurals in English. The error in the last word of the examples make this apparent. Individual problems like this can be handled by extending the exception list.

```
To AddSeveral
  AddException ReadList ReadList
  Print []
  AddSeveral
End
```

```
To AddException :Word :Plural
  Make
    "ExceptionList
    Sentence :ExceptionList :Word
  Make
    "ExceptionPlurals
    Sentence :ExceptionPlurals :Plural
End
```

```
? AddSeveral
mother-in-law
mothers-in-law
? Plurals
Enter the next word: mother-in-law
===> mothers-in-law
```

However, you should understand that successively adding single cases (although it cannot be avoided sometimes) is not the best way to extend a rule system. Instead, you should find a more general case (for this example, words ending in "-in-law") and write a rule to handle it.

Some of the rules are overgeneralized: think about words like "sum," "rum," and "drum." Another point you should note is that the system does not detect when a non-noun or a noun that is already a plural is entered:

```
? Plurals
Enter the next word: doors
===> doorses
Enter the next word: come
===> comes
```

Exercises

(1) Write a rule that handles words ending in "-in-law". Can you generalize this rule even further (what about "editor-in-chief")?

(2) Extend the system so that it detects that a word is already plural. For what words is this particularly difficult?

Chapter 33:
Linguistic Explorations

So far, we have touched on topics from linguistics dealing with the structure of language from the standpoint of grammars (in chapter 20) and morphology in chapters 31 and 32. Another area of linguistics has to do with studying characteristics of the letters used in a language. As we discuss shortly, there are questions that can be asked in this regard from many different fields of study. But first, let's look at some simple experiments that we can perform.

33.1. Removing Vowels and Consonants

As we mentioned in section 11, we might hypothesize that even after certain letters are removed from a sentence it is still possible to reconstruct the original sentence. To verify this hypothesis, we could set up experiments that would require generating paragraphs of text with certain letters removed.

Here are some examples of texts in German, French, and English. We first show how they would appear first with all the vowels removed, then with all the consonants removed.

(1) **Without Vowels**

```
? Print RemoveVowels EnglishSentence
th nmls wr shckd bynd msr t lrn tht vn snwbll cld b glty f sch n
ctn . thr ws cry f ndgntn , nd vryn bgn thnkng t wys f ctchng
snwbll f h shld vr cm bck . lmst mmdtly th ftprnts f pg wr
dscvrd n th grss t lttl dstnc frm th knll . thy cld nly b trcd
fr fw yrds , bt pprd t ld t hl n th hdg . npln snffld dply t thm
nd prnncd thm t b snwbll's . h gv t s hs pnn tht snwbll hd
prbbly cm frm th drctn f fxwd frm .
```

```
? Print RemoveVowels GermanSentence
Bld sllt ch jn blm bssr knnnlrnn . s htt f dm plntn ds klnn
prnzn mmr schn blmn ggbn , shr nfch, s nm nzgn krnz vn
blmmblttrn gfrmt ; s spltn kn grss rll nd strtn nmmdn . s lchttn
ns mrgns m grs f nd rlschn m bnd . br jn n htt ns tgswrzln
gschlgn , s nm smn , wss gtt whr , nd dr kln prnz htt dsn sprss
, dr ndrn sprsslngn ncht glch , shr gn brwcht . ds knnt n n rt
ffnbrtbm sn . br dr strch hrt bld f z wchsn nd bgnn , n blt
nzstzn .
```

```
? Print RemoveVowels FrenchSentence
```
c'st dmnch : drrr ls dcks , l lng d l mr , prs d l gr x mrchndss
, tt tr d l vll l y ds hngrs vds t ds mchns mmbls dns l nr . dns
tts ls msns , ds hmms s rsnt drrr lrs fntrs ; ls nt l tt rnvrs ,
ls fxnt tntt lr mrr t tntt l cl frd pr svr s'l fr b . ls brdls
vrnt lrs prmrs clnts , ds cmpgnrds t ds sldts . dns ls glss , l
clrt ds crgs , n hmm bt d vn dvnt ds fmms gnx . dns ts ls fbrgs
, ntr ls mrs ntrmnbls ds sns , d lngs fls nrs s snt mss n mrch ,
lls vncnt lntmnt sr l cntr d l vll .

(2) Without Consonants

```
? Print RemoveConsonants EnglishSentence
```
e aia ee oe eo eaue o ea a ee oa ou e ui o u a aio ee a a o
iiaio a eeoe ea ii ou a o ai oa i e ou ee oe a ao bieiae e ooi o
a i ee ioee i e a a a ie iae o e o e ou o e ae o a e a u aeae o
ea o a oe i e ee aoeo ue ee a e a ooue e o e oa e ae i a i oiio
a oa a oa oe o e ieio o ooo a

```
? Print RemoveConsonants GermanSentence
```
a oe i ee ue ee eeee e ae au e aee e eie ie ie o ue eee e eiae
au eie eiie a o ueaee eo ie iee eie oe oe u oee ieae ie euee eie
oe i ae au u eoe a ae ae ee eie ae eie ae ue eae au eie ae ei o
oe u e eie i ae iee o e aee oeie i i e eau ueea a oe eie eue a
aeoau ei ae e au oee a au u ae u ea eie uee auee

```
? Print RemoveConsonants FrenchSentence
```
e iae eiee e o e o e a e e e a ae au aaie ou auou e a ie i a e
aa ie e e aie ioie a e oi a oue e aio e oe e ae eiee eu eee i o
a ee eeee i ie ao eu ioi e ao e ie oi ou aoi i ea eau e oe oue a
eu eie ie e aaa e e oa a e eie a a ae e iee u oe oi u i ea e ee
a eou a ou e auou ee e u ieiae e uie e oue ie oie e o ie e ae ee
aae eee u e ee e a ie

33.2. The Procedures

A few simple procedures suffice to transform the sentences as just illustrated.
First, we need to define a predicate, which determines whether a letter is a vowel
or not:

```
To VowelP :Letter
    Output MemberP :Letter [A E I O U]
End
```

The next step consists of defining a procedure that removes the vowels from a
word:

```
To RemoveWordVowels :Word
    Test :Word = "
    IfTrue [Output "]
    Test VowelP First :Word
    IfTrue [Output RemoveWordVowels ButFirst :Word]
    Output
        Word First :Word RemoveWordVowels ButFirst :Word
End
```

Finally, we need a procedure that goes through all the words of a text and invokes RemoveVowels on each of them:

```
To RemoveVowels :List
  If EmptyP :List [Output []]
  Output
    FPut
      RemoveWordVowels First :List
      RemoveVowels ButFirst :List
End
```

If the consonants instead of the vowels need to be removed, a simple change is all that is necessary: In RemoveVowels we simply need to place a Not predicate in front of the call to VowelP (and, of course, change the name of the procedure).

33.3. Text with No Word Breaks and with Incorrect Word Breaks

Another important element of the language involves how the letters are divided into words.[31] The procedure Compress makes the individual words into one long word.

```
To Compress :Text
  Test :Text = []
  IfTrue [Output "]
  Output
    Word (First :Text) (Compress ButFirst :Text)
End
```

? Print Compress EnglishSentence
theanimalswereshockedbeyondmeasuretolearnthatevensnowba
llcouldbeguiltyofsuchanaction.therewasacryofindignation
,andeveryonebeganthinkingoutwaysofcatchingsnowballifhes
houldevercomeback.almostimmediatelythefootprintsofapigw
erediscoveredinthegrassatalittledistancefromtheknoll.th
eycouldonlybetracedforafewards,butappearedtoleadtoahole
inthehedge.napoleonsnuffleddeeplyatthemandpronouncedthe
mtobesnowball's.hegaveitashisopinionthatsnowballhadprob
ablycomefromthedirectionoffoxwoodfarm.

? Print Compress GermanSentence
baldsollteichjeneblumebesserkennenlernen.eshatteaufdemp
lanetendeskleinenprinzenimmerschonblumengegeben,sehrein
fache,auseinemeinzigenkranzvonblumenblaetterngeformt;si
espieltenkeinegrosserolleundstoertenniemanden.sieleucht
eteneinesmorgensimgraseaufunderloschenamabend.aberjenee
inehatteeinestageswurzelngeschlagen,auseinemsamen,weiss
gottwoher,unddderkleineprinzhattediesensspross,deranderen
sproesslingennichtglich,sehrgenauueberwacht.daskonnteei
neneueartaffenbrotbaumsein.aberderstrauchhoertebaldaufz
uwachsenundbegann,eineblueteanzusetzen.

---

[31]Some early written language did not put spaces between words!

? Print Compress FrenchSentence

*c'estdimanche:derrierelesdocks,lelongdelamer,presdelaga
reauxmarchandises,toutautourdelavilleilyadeshangarsvide
setdesmachinesimmobilesdanslenoir.danstouteslesmaisons,
deshommesserasentderrniereleursfenetres;ilsontlateterenv
ersee,ilsfixenttantotleurmiroirettantotlecielfroidpours
avoirs'ilferabeau.lesbordelsouvrentaleurspremiersclient
s,descampagnardsetdessoldats.dansleseglises,alaclartede
scierges,unhommeboitduvindevantdesfemmesagenoux.danstou
slesfaubourgs,entrelesmursinterminablesdesusines,delong
uesfilesnoiressesontmisesenmarche,ellesavancentlentemen
tsurlecentredelaville.*

With the procedure **BreakUp** the compress text is broken up into units again, by inserting arbitrary blank spaces.

```
To BreakUp :Text
   Test :Text = "
   IfTrue [Output [ ]]
   Make "HowMany 1 + Random 10
   Test LongerThan :Text :HowMany
   IfFalse [Output :Text]
   Output
      Sentence
         FirstN :HowMany :Text
         BreakUp ButFirstN :HowMany :Text
End

To LongerThan :Text :HowMany
   If :HowMany = 0 [Output "True]
   If EmptyP (ButFirst :Text) [Output "False]
   Output LongerThan ButFirst :Text :HowMany - 1
End
```

FirstN and **ButFirstN** are described in appendix III. The three texts "broken up"

? Print BreakUp Compress EnglishSentence

*thea nim alswer esh oc ke db ey on dmea s ureto learnth ate vensnowba
llcou ldbeguilty ofsuchan action.t he re wasacryof i ndignat ion,ande
veryonebeg anthin kingoutway sofcatch ings nowballi fheshoulde verco meba
ck.almosti m media telythe f ootpri ntsofapig w eredi sc ov eredinth
egrassa talittl e distancef ro mtheknoll .theyco uldon lybetr acedf or a
few yard s,bu t appe aredt oleadt oaholein thehedge. napoleon snuff
leddeep l y att he mandpr o nou nced themtobe sn owba ll's.he g aveitash
is opinionth atsno w ballha drobab l ycomefr omthedir ectiono ffoxwo
odfarm.*

? Print BreakUp Compress GermanSentence

*b a lds ollteich jene bl umebes ser kenne nlern en.esha tteauf demp lane
tendes klein enprinz enimmersc honblu men gege ben,s ehr einf ache,a use
inemeinz igenkranz vonblu menb laetter ngef ormt;s iespie ltenk
einegrosse rolleund sto erten niem ande n.sieleu chtete nein esmor gensi
mgra seauf underl oschen amaben d. a berj eneeineha tteei nesta geswurz
elngeschl agen ,aus einemsa m en,weis sgott woher,un dderkle inepri nzha
tte dies enspross ,dera nd erensproe sslingenni chtglich, sehrg
enauueberw acht.dask onnteei neneu eartaffe nbrotb aum sein.aberd
erstrauchh oerteb aldaufzu wachsenun dbegann ,eineb luete anzu setzen.*

? Print BreakUp Compress FrenchSentence

c'est diman ch e:derr ier el esdocks ,le lo ngdelamer, pr esde lagarea uxmarc handises ,tou tau tourdelavi llei ly ade shang ar svidesetd esmachin e simmobil e sdan slenoir. danstou teslesm aisons,d eshommess erase ntderrie releurm iroir ettanto tl e cielfr oidpo u rsavo irs'ilfe rab eau.les borde lsouvre ntaleurs premiersc li ents, descampag na rdsetdess oldat s.dansle seglises ,alac lartedesc ier ges,unh o mm eboitduv indevantd es femmesa genoux. dan stou slesfaub our gs , ent reelesmursi nter minablesde susines, delong uesfiles n oirsesses o ntmis esenmarch e,e 1 lesavancen tlent ement surlecen trede lavill e.

33.4. Objectives of these Linguistic Experiments

With just a little programming effort, we have introduced several interesting questions. As we mentioned earlier, these questions are not limited to the field of linguistics but overlap with many other disciplines.

(1) Linguistics

- When letters are moved from words, which words are particularly easy, or hard, to reconstruct (e.g., at one extreme the German word "Ei," when all vowels are removed).

- Is there a difference in the vowel or consonant structure in the three different languages?

- How important is the context in reconstructing the sentences?

- Can the vowel or consonant structure of the text be used to detect incorrectly spelled words and to possibly correct them automatically?

(2) Information Theory

- What is the information content of vowels in contrast to consonants?

- What is the ratio of vowels to consonants in the language?

- What is the average length of words in various languages?

(3) Psychology of Perception

- What role do the perceptive and cognitive processes play in reading?

- What role does context play?

- What role does redundancy play?

- What is the function of the degree of familiarity with the text or with the individual words play?

- What function does reading aloud play?

- Are there several levels of perception (letter, word, sentence)?

(4) Mathematics

- Is the transformation unambiguous (compression and removal of vowels or consonants)?

- Is the transformation unambiguously reversible (see discussion of encryption under "secret codes," following)?

- Can the letter frequencies of an encrypted message be used to aid in its decryption?

(5) Communications Theory

- Can we recover transmissions that are garbled or have lost some information?

- Can we design the communications protocol to contain redundancy so that recovery can be made?

In the following sections, we investigate some of these questions further.

33.5. "Secret Codes"

Let's look at the notion of encryption further. Encryption is the encoding of text in a form that makes it unintelligible but does so in such a way that the original information can be reconstructed (i.e., the transformation needs to be unambiguously reversible). With the previous transformations this was not the case.

One way to do this is using the procedure `Mirror` and `Reverse` discussed in chapter III.

```
? Print Mirror EnglishSentence
mraf doowxof fo noitcerid eht morf emoc ylbaborp dah llabwons taht
noinipo sih sa ti evag eh . s'llabwons eb ot meht decnuonorp dna meht ta
ylpeed delffuns noelopan . egdeh eht ni eloh a ot dael ot deraeppa tub ,
sdray wef a rof decart eb ylno dluoc yeht . llonk eht morf ecnatsid
elttil a ta ssarg eht ni derevocsid erew gip a fo stnirptoof eht
yletaidemmi tsomla . kcab emoc reve dluohs eh fi llabwons gnihctac fo
syaw tuo gnikniht nageb enoyreve dna , noitangidni fo yrc a saw ereht .
noitca na hcus fo ytliug eb dluoc llabwons neve taht nrael ot erusaem
dnoyeb dekcohs erew slamina eht
```

```
? Print Reverse GermanSentence
anzusetzen bluete eine , begann und wachsen zu auf bald hoerte strauch
der aber . sein affenbrotbaum art neue eine konnte das . ueberwacht
genau sehr , glich nicht sproesslingen anderen der , spross diesen hatte
prinz kleine der und , woher gott weiss , samen einem aus , geschlagen
wurzeln tages eines hatte eine jene aber . abend am erloschen und auf
grase im morgens eines leuchteten sie . niemanden stoerten und rolle
grosse keine spielten sie ; geformt blumenblaettern von kranz einzigen
einem aus einfache, sehr , gegeben blumen schon immer prinzen kleinen des
planeten dem auf hatte es . kennenlernen besser blume jene ich sollte
bald
```

Another form of encryption is to replace each letter with another letter in a consistent, reproducible fashion. A popular form of this is known as *rotational substitution*. Using a circular alphabet (much like what was used in chapter 27), the letters are all rotated by a certain amount; a common value here is 13.

```
To Rot13 :Sequence
  Output Rot13R :Sequence Alphabet
End

To Rot13R :Sequence :Alphabet
  If EmptyP :Sequence [Output :Sequence]
  If WordP :Sequence
    [Output
       Word
            Rot13Char First :Sequence :Alphabet
            Rot13R ButFirst :Sequence :Alphabet]
    Output
       Sentence
          Rot13R First :Sequence :Alphabet
          Rot13R ButFirst :Sequence :Alphabet
End

To Rot13Char :Char :Alphabet
  If MemberP :Char :Alphabet
    [Output Successor 13 :Char :Alphabet]
  Output :Char
End
```

Successor and Alphabet were described in chapter progdat.

? Print Rot13 FrenchSentence

p'rfg qvznapur : qreevrer yrf qbpxf , yr ybat qr yn zre , cerf qr yn tner nhk znepunaqvfrf , gbhg nhgbhe qr yn ivyyr vy l n qrf u natnef ivqrf rg qrf znpuvarf vzzbovyrf qnaf yr abve . qnaf gbhgrf yrf znvfbaf , qrf ubzzrf fr enrag qreevrer yrhef srargerf; vyf bag yn grgr erairefrr , vyf sv krag gnagbg yrhe zvebve rg gnagbg yr pvry sebvq cbhe fnibve f'vy sran ornh . yrf obeqryf bhierag n yrhef cerzvref pyvragf , qrf pnzcntaeqf rg qrf fbyqngf . qna f yrf rtyvfrf , n yn pynegr qrf pvretrf , ha ubzzr obvg qh iva qrinag qrf srzzrf n trabhk . qnaf gbhf yrf fnhobhetf , rager yrf zhef vagrezvanoyrf qrf hfvarf , qr ybathrf svyrf abverf fr fbag zvfrf ra znepur , ryyrf ninapraq yragrzrag fhe y r prager qr yn ivyyr .

Exercises

(1) Write the necessary code to *decrypt* the results of Rot13. *Hint: This is a thought problem.*

(2) Generalize the procedures so that the amount of rotation can be specified and may be positive or negative.

33.6. The Original Texts

Here are the texts that were used in the previous sections.

? Print EnglishSentence

the animals were shocked beyond measure to learn that even snowball could be guilty of such an action . there was a cry of indignation , and everyone began thinking out ways of catching snowball if he should ever come back . almost immediately the footprints of a pig were discovered in the grass at a little distance from the knoll . they could only be traced for a few yards , but appeared to lead to a hole in the hedge . napoleon snuffled deeply at them and pronounced them to be snowball's . he gave it as his opinion that snowball had probably come from the direction of foxwood farm .

(from Animal Farm by George Orwell)

? Print GermanSentence

bald sollte ich jene blume besser kennenlernen . es hatte auf dem planeten des kleinen prinzen immer schon blumen gegeben , sehr einfache, aus einem einzigen kranz von blumenblaettern geformt ; sie spielten keine grosse rolle und stoerten niemanden . sie leuchteten eines morgens im grase auf und erloschen am abend . aber jene eine hatte eines tages wurzeln geschlagen , aus einem samen , weiss gott woher , und der kleine prinz hatte diesen spross , der anderen sproesslingen nicht glich , sehr genau ueberwacht . das konnte eine neue art affenbrotbaum sein . aber der strauch hoerte bald auf zu wachsen und begann , eine bluete anzusetzen .

(from the German translation of The Little Prince by Antoine de Saint-Exupery)

Print FrenchSentence

c'est dimanche : derriere les docks , le long de la mer , pres de la gare aux marchandises , tout autour de la ville il y a des hangars vides et des machines immobiles dans le noir . dans toutes les maisons , des hommes se rasent derriere leurs fenetres; ils ont la tete renversee , ils fixent tantot leur miroir et tantot le ciel froid pour savoir s'il fera beau . les bordels ouvrent a leurs premiers clients , des campagnards et des soldats . dans les eglises , a la clarte des cierges , un homme boit du vin devant des femmes a genoux . dans tous les faubourgs , entre les murs interminables des usines , de longues files noires se sont mises en marche , elles avancent lentement sur le centre de la ville .

33.7. Linguistic Statistics

One point made in section 33.4 dealt with information theoretical aspects of linguistics. Let's investigate some of the statistical properties of texts in various languages. The procedures we define here allow absolute and relative frequencies of letters in text to be determined. Because they can be tested on small samples right away, they give some immediate feedback and an opportunity to verify correctness to some degree. The concept of relative frequency and its relationship to the concept of probability can be studied in this context.

33.8. Calculating Absolute Letter Frequency

The crucial step here is the design of a global data structure: We use as many variables as there are letters in the alphabet; in the beginning they all have the value 0 and, as the program is run over some text, each time a certain letter is encountered, the corresponding variable is incremented by 1. The procedure CountWord is used to count the frequency of the letters in a single word.

```
To CountWord :Word
   If :Word = " [Stop]
   Test NameP First :Word
   IfFalse [CountWord ButFirst :Word
      Stop]
   Make First :Word 1 + Thing First :Word
   CountWord ButFirst :Word
End
```

The Test statement is necessary to be able to recognize and skip over letters or digits that we do not wish to count.

The afore-mentioned global names are created in the following way[32]:

```
To Generate
   Generate1 "abcdefghijklmnopqrstuvwxyz
End
```

```
To Generate1 :Letters
   If :Letters = " [Stop]
   Make First :Letters 0
   Generate1 ButFirst :Letters
End
```

Because we want to be able to apply our counting procedure to an entire sentence, let's define a procedure CountSentence:

```
To CountSentence :Sentence
   If :Sentence = [] [Stop]
   CountWord First :Sentence
   CountSentence ButFirst :Sentence
End
```

To facilitate (re)initialization and output of the result we can define the procedures RunCount, PrintStats, and Alphabet:

```
To RunCount :Sentence
   Generate
   CountSentence :Sentence
   PrintStats Alphabet
End
```

---

[32]In most other programming languages that are available, the solution to this problem would use an array, the letter would be used to calculate the index into the array, and the corresponding array element would be incremented by 1.

```
To PrintStats :ABC
  If :ABC = " [Stop]
  Type (Sentence First :ABC "= Thing First :ABC)
  PrintStats ButFirst :ABC
End

To Alphabet
  Output "abcdefghijklmnopqrstuvwxyz
End
```

Examples:

```
? RunCount [the letters in this sentence should be
counted in order to see if this program works]
a = 1     b = 1     c = 2     d = 3     e = 11   f = 1
g = 1     h = 4     i = 5     j = 0     k = 1    l = 2
m = 1     n = 5     o = 6     p = 1     q = 0    r = 6
s = 7     t = 8     u = 2     v = 0     w = 1    x = 0
y = 0     z = 0

? RunCount [this text should serve as a second example]
a = 3     b = 0     c = 1     d = 2     e = 6    f = 0
g = 0     h = 2     i = 1     j = 0     k = 0    l = 2
m = 1     n = 1     o = 2     p = 1     q = 0    r = 1
s = 5     t = 3     u = 1     v = 1     w = 0    x = 2
y = 0     z = 0
```

The following example is a little bit longer to give an indication of which letters are more and less frequent in English:

```
?  RunCount [One of the points made in section 40.3 dealt
with information  theoretical aspects of linguistics. Let
's investigate some of the  statistical properties of
texts in various languages.  The procedures  we define
here allow absolute and relative frequencies of letters
in  text to be determined.  Since they can be tested on
small samples  right away, they give some immediate
feedback and an opportunity to  verify correctness to
some degree.  The concept of relative frequency  and its
relationship to the concept of probability can be studied
in  this context.]
a = 29    b = 7     c = 19    d = 15    e = 70   f = 13
g = 7     h = 13    i = 38    j = 0     k = 1    l = 17
m = 10    n = 30    o = 34    p = 12    q = 2    r = 22
s = 32    t = 53    u = 9     v = 6     w = 4    x = 3
y = 7     z = 0
```

Certainly, we could also use this to count letters in, for example, German text:

```
? RunCount GermanSentence
a = 34    b = 16    c = 11    d = 16    e = 108  f = 7
g = 15    h = 18    i = 28    j = 2     k = 6    l = 22
m = 15    n = 66    o = 16    p = 6     q = 0    r = 31
s = 38    t = 28    u = 22    v = 1     w = 5    x = 0
y = 0     z = 8
```

or in Italian:

```
? RunCount [parlate dell'anno, delle stagioni,  della
settimana e dei giorni. come si divide il  giorni? che
cosa si fa di giorno? e di notte?  quando viene la luce?
e quando dispare? dove si  leva il sole?  e dove
tramonta?  il giorno di  quante ore si compone? e di
quanti minuti si  compone l'ora?]
a = 19    b = 0     c = 6     d = 15    e = 28    f = 1
g = 5     h = 1     i = 29    j = 0     k = 0     l = 15
m = 6     n = 18    o = 23    p = 4     q = 4     r = 9
s = 10    t = 11    u = 6     v = 5     w = 0     x = 0
y = 0     z = 0
```

33.9. Determining Relative Frequency

One reason to generate letter frequencies is to be able to make comparisons of languages based on these statistics. However, comparing the raw data is not really valid because different amounts of text were processed each time. What we need to calculate is the relative frequency of the letters. To make these kinds of comparison easier, we can create new procedure for printing the statistics that gives this information in terms of percentages:

```
To NewPrintStats :ABC :Total :Level
   If :ABC = " [Stop]
   Type
      PadRight
         12
         (Word
            First :ABC
            Spaces 1
            "=
            Spaces 1
            PadLeft 6 Percent Thing First :ABC :Total)
   If (Remainder :Level + 1 5) = 0 [Print "]
   NewPrintStats ButFirst :ABC :Total :Level + 1
   If :Level = 0 [Print "]
End

To Percent :Num :Denom
   Local "Result
   ;; a little trick make sure integer arithmetic is used
   ;; simplifying handling the two digit precision desired
   Make "Result Quotient (Word :Num "0000) :Denom
   Make "WholePart ButLastN 2 :Result
   Make "FractPart LastN 2 :Result
   If :WholePart = " [Make "WholePart "0]
   If :FractPart = 0 [Make "FractPart "00]
   If (Count :FractPart) = 1
      [Make "FractPart Word :FractPart "0]
   Output (Word :WholePart ". :FractPart)
End
```

```
To Total :ABC
  If :ABC = " [Output 0]
  Output (Thing First :ABC) + Total ButFirst :ABC
End

To RunCount :Sentence
  Generate
  CountSentence :Sentence
  NewPrintStats Alphabet Total Alphabet
End
```

ButLastN and LastN are described in appendix III. Example:

```
? RunCountV2 [The frequency of the letters in this
sentence will now be expressed in percentages]
a =   1.44  b =   1.44  c =   4.34  d =   1.44  e =  23.18
f =   2.89  g =   1.44  h =   4.34  i =   5.79  j =   0.00
k =   0.00  l =   4.34  m =   0.00  n =  10.14  o =   2.89
p =   2.89  q =   1.44  r =   5.79  s =   8.69  t =  10.14
u =   1.44  v =   0.00  w =   2.89  x =   1.44  y =   1.44
z =   0.00
```

33.10. Connection to the Concept of Probability

If the procedure RunCount were to be run on several examples of English text, a pattern of "similar" relative frequencies would emerge; this leads us to the assertion that the longer the text sample becomes, the more similar the results should be. This hypothesis cannot be proved with this procedure, and we do not go into the statistical methods that would be necessary to prove it.

If the result does become more similar the longer the text becomes, then it should stabilize at a certain value that we should be able to determine if we had an extremely long text sample.

We could also illustrate the stabilization of the relative frequency in another way: We first count an arbitrary text and calculate and print out the relative frequency (or the percentage, as in our example). The next time we run the procedure on another sample, we keep the results from previous runs and simply add the results from the new text to them. To do this we define the procedure RunCountv3:

```
To RunCountV3
  Print
    (Sentence
      [Previously, ]
      Total Alphabet
      [letters have been evaluated.])
  Type [Do you want to extend these statistics?]
  If Not ReadList = [yes] [Generate]
  Type [Give the text to be evaluated;]
  CountSentence ReadList
```

```
Print
   (Sentence
    [Results for ]
    Total Alphabet
    [letters:])
   Print []
   NewPrintStats Alphabet Total Alphabet
End
```

Examples:

```
? Generate
? RunCountv3
```
Previously,   0 letters have been evaluated.
Do you want to extend these statistics? **yes**
Give the text to be evaluated; **One of the points** made in
section 40.3 dealt with information theoretical aspects of
linguistics. Let 's investigate some of the statistical
properties of texts in various languages. The procedures
we define here allow absolute and relative frequencies of
letters in text to be determined. Since they can be tested
on small samples right away, they give some immediate
feedback and an opportunity to verify   correctness to some
degree. The concept of relative frequency and its
relationship to the concept of   probability can be studied
in this context.
Results for   453 letters:

a =	6.40	b =	1.54	c =	4.19	d =	3.31	e =	15.45
f =	2.86	g =	1.54	h =	2.86	i =	8.38	j =	0.00
k =	0.22	l =	3.75	m =	2.20	n =	6.62	o =	7.50
p =	2.64	q =	0.44	r =	4.85	s =	7.06	t =	11.69
u =	1.98	v =	1.32	w =	0.88	x =	0.66	y =	1.54
z =	0.00								

```
? RunCountv3
```
Previously,   453 letters have been evaluated.
Do you want to extend these statistics? **yes**
Give the text to be evaluated: **The crucial step**

(left out to save space)

a single word.
Results for   768 letters:

a =	7.03	b =	1.69	c =	4.03	d =	3.25	e =	15.88
f =	2.08	g =	1.82	h =	3.77	i =	7.55	j =	0.00
k =	0.13	l =	4.16	m =	1.95	n =	6.64	o =	6.38
p =	2.21	q =	0.39	r =	6.11	s =	6.64	t =	11.06
u =	2.73	v =	1.43	w =	1.04	x =	0.52	y =	1.43
z =	0.00								

```
? Runcountv3
```
Previously,   768 letters have been evaluated.
Do you want to extend these statistics? **yes**
Give the text to be evaluated; **If the procedure RunCount**

(left out to save space)

to prove it.

```
Results for  1081 letters:
a =    6.56  b =    1.66  c =    3.60  d =    3.14  e =   15.72
f =    1.85  g =    1.66  h =    4.34  i =    7.12  j =    0.00
k =    0.9   l =    4.44  m =    2.12  n =    6.10  o =    6.75
p =    2.31  q =    0.37  r =    6.29  s =    7.03  t =   11.28
u =    2.96  v =    1.38  w =    1.29  x =    0.64  y =    1.20
z =    0.00
```

This shows us that, as we increase the number of letters that have been counted, the relative frequency of the individual letters stabilizes and becomes more precise.

After extensive data has been processed, the following values were obtained:

```
a =    7.26  b =    1.55  c =    3.65  d =    2.85  e =   15.81
f =    2.16  g =    1.52  h =    4.60  i =    6.88  j =    0.00
k =    0.22  l =    4.10  m =    2.47  n =    5.93  o =    6.31
p =    1.97  q =    0.38  r =    6.80  s =    6.99  t =   11.17
u =    2.66  v =    1.17  w =    1.48  x =    0.72  y =    1.14
z =    0.11
```

Exercises

(1) Given a piece of text that has been encrypted using rotational substitution with an amount of rotation that is unknown to you, use the letter frequencies determined in the last section to "break the code."

(2) Compare the letter frequency statistics of various languages. Extend these statistics by summarizing them with respect to classes of letters or sounds; such as the classes of vowels, consonants, labial, liquid, nasal, or guttural sounds or letters. For example, for labials and vowels, the procedures would look like this:

```
To LabialPercent
   Output Percent Total "bpmf Total Alphabet
End

To VowelPercent
   Output Percent Total "aeiou Total Alphabet
End
```

And running these on the data from the preceding English text:

```
? Print LabialPercent
8.17
? Print VowelPercent
38.93
```

Compare germanic languages (English, German) and romantic languages (French, Spanish, Italian, even Latin) to see whether they exhibit relationships based on the different types of characteristics.

(3) Use the letter frequency statistics to ensure that the correct number of letter-tiles are provided and that the correct point values are assigned to each letter in your Scrabble™ game.

Part 6:
Games

Introduction

Games have been around for thousands of years—they are inextricably intertwined with the development of our culture. Many of them represent a peaceful measure of strength where the players are constrained by certain rules. It is no wonder that the computer has been such an ideal tool for enriching the world of games. Many see the computer itself as the most interesting toy that humanity has developed. The programmability of the computer, its ability to become a *player* for many games, contributes to this view.

The opportunities for learning provided by games have not been used to the advantage they could have been in the past. Games have the ability to furnish important knowledge and insights, which are also significant for daily life (whether at school, work, or play). Science is nothing more or less than a systematic struggle to find answers to riddles posed by nature.

Games are particularly well suited to our global goals, especially those goals related to learning, for the following reasons:

• You (as an intelligent information-processing system) usually have an intuitive understanding of the problem;

• The problems allow human cognitive processes to be described explicitly and thereby foster a better understanding of them;

• Games illustrate that problems can be of different complexity for humans and machines (for example, recognition of a diagonal controlled by a bishop on a chessboard). This is in part because the human has eyes and ears, which have been optimized for interacting with their environment, and simulation of this on the computer has been much more difficult than partial simulation of the central nervous system thought processes has been;

• They bring the question—often perceived subjectively as an ominous one—of whether computers are able to "think" or not, into sharper focus;

• They allow the threatening aspects of computers to stand out, since they allow us to see the computer at it cleverest.

Games and Problem Solving

An important goal of this book is to support cognitive activities such as problem solving, planning, debugging, etc. directly. We hope to show with this section that games are particularly well suited for these goals. We have consciously steered clear of formal mathematical game theory and instead have attempted to place emphasis on the use of heuristic methods and their realization as a computer program. Among these are:

(1) **Recognition and definition of suitable subproblems.** This is important for any nontrivial problem. Several subproblems can be defined for games (e.g., interaction with the user, selection of a move, checking the validity of a move, determining whether the game has been won or lost) that are valid for almost any game program.

(2) **Finding a suitable representation.** This is an important factor in setting out to write a comprehensible and readable program. We focus on this aspect in the TIC-TAC-TOE game in particular.

(3) **Formulation of strategies.** Many people can play certain games well without being able to describe their decision-making process (see chapter 38). The computer possesses no intuitive understanding. Therefore, strategies such as how to keep spaces from being "captured" in TIC-TAC-TOE must be explicitly formulated, whereas the human player recognizes this kind of threat intuitively.

(4) **Evaluating positions.** Qualities of a certain playing position provide the basis for an evaluation function that can be used to select the best of the possible moves.

(5) **Performing heuristic searches.** Chess is a finite game only from a mathematical standpoint. The actual search tree is so large that normal people and the computer scientist who wants to program the computer must find heuristic search methods to reduce the search tree to a manageable size.

(6) **Definition of alternative systems of rules.** Most games allow an alternative rule system to be used, generally in a straightforward manner. For TIC-TAC-TOE, for example, the game board can be enlarged, say to 4 X 4 or 5 X 5; the first player with three marks in a row loses; use a 3-dimensional playing space; use three different marks and allow them to be removed after they have been played; etc. Games represent the human ability to apply general statements about a subject (the rules of a game) to a specific situation (a specific move or game position). Furthermore, they show that we are able to make use of earlier experiences.

Games and Computers

Simply providing computers as toys will provide entertainment and recreation, much as video games do. This use is fine as far as it goes but does not provide any long-term learning. Imagine applying for a job and indicating that your best "computer experience" was a score of 2,543,255 on Space Invaders. Games can also be used as reinforcement for computer-aided instruction and drill programs, but you are still a passive relationship to the computer.

(1) **Games and Interactive Programming.** Our goal is to have you write the games, to play an active role in designing, developing, and extending them. The cases studied in this book are directed at this kind of use. Games offer the following advantages in this regard:

- They are based on a system of rules, which can be formalized with a reasonable amount of effort.

- They can offer different levels of difficulty; programs can be built incrementally.

- The problems are generally complex enough and require some degree of deliberation; they are not merely exercises in the use of a programming language.

- Errors are easily visible, because you have usually mastered the game and are therefore in the position to be able to identify incorrect or unsatisfactory playing methods.

- If the game program is a good one, you may find it challenging to play against.

- Games are one of the few programs where the "finished product" can also provide a learning environment. A working game can be seen as a "glass box" (instead of a "black box",) which can be studied, understood, modified, and extended. As was mentioned earlier, changing the rules of a game is a good example of this. If you have ever played a video game and thought, "Gee, wouldn't it be neat if it could do this?" yet been unable to do anything with that idea, you will understand the advantages of this approach.

(2) **Games and Artificial Intelligence.** Artificial intelligence has dealt with games since its inception and has investigated many forms of intelligent behavior (e.g., programs that learn, inductive acquisition of underlying rules, etc.) using games. More recently a fundamental change has occurred. Games are now treated as knowledge-based programming (for example, the REVERSI program needs to "know" that capturing pieces is less important than occupying certain positions on the board).

(3) **Games and Intelligent Computer-Aided Learning.** Empirical studies have shown that many people, after reaching a certain level of play in chess, are unable to make any further progress without some

instruction. Games have been embedded into complex systems using techniques from artificial intelligence that include some of the following:

a) An expert system component, which is capable of playing a good game (but not necessarily corresponding to the strategies or knowledge of the user);

b) A user model, which is based on the actions (such as, which errors appear repeatedly) of the particular user.

c) A tutor, which places the expert knowledge into a suitable form so that the user can be given directed advice based on the user's level of knowledge (which is derived from the user model).

(4) Programs like this exist for some of the programs we discuss here, namely WUMPUS (Chapter 36) and HOW THE WEST WAS WON (Chapter 37). Most of the games we discuss could be used in this context as well.

Classification of Games

Games can be classified based on different features (we use the games we discuss as examples):

(1) **Single Person Games.** (These are often called thought problems or puzzles) WUMPUS, as well as LIFE and TOWERS OF HANOI discussed in the computer science section.

(2) **Two Person Games.** REVERSI, TIC-TAC-TOE, HOW THE WEST WAS WON

(3) **Board Games** REVERSI, TIC-TAC-TOE, HOW THE WEST WAS WON

(4) **Card Games.** BLACKJACK

(5) **Games with Complete Strategies.** (Algorithms exist for these games, which give the single best move for a given position) The TOWERS OF HANOI discussed in the computer science section.

(6) **Strategic Games without Complete Strategies.** REVERSI

(7) **Games of Chance with Strategic Elements.** BLACKJACK, WUMPUS, HOW THE WEST WAS WON.

(8) **Inductive Games.** (Not discussed in this book) Rules have to be inferred from individual facts that are discovered while playing.

An interesting task that would be an appropriate extension of what is discussed in this book would be to develop a set of general components for these various classes of games. For example, these could correspond to the following subprocesses:

• The user interface or dialog component

• Uniform representation (such as for the boards for board games)

- Special objects and the predicates and operations defined on them (such as for the concept of "trumps" in card games)

This would create what could be called a "Game Construction Kit," where programming a new game would require less effort because the existing general structures could be specialized for the new game.

Many resources are available if you wish to explore the games microworld further; among these are [Berlekamp, Conway, Guy 82] and the *Mathematical Games* column in Scientific American some of which are assembled in [Gardner 83].

Chapter 34:
TIC-TAC-TOE

34.1. Objectives

The following aspects of problem solving and model formation are discussed and represented in this chapter using the game of TIC-TAC-TOE as a concrete example.

- Choosing an appropriate data structure

- Comparison of external and internal representations of information structures

- Formation of isomorphic though distinct external representations of the same internal representation

- The meaning of heuristics in the context of understanding and controlling complex processes

- The stepwise development of heuristics and the strategies based on them

- The forms, in which knowledge about the problem can be represented in the form of programs, and their significance in comparison to "brute force" methods

34.2. TIC-TAC-TOE

What we do here is describe a program that plays TIC-TAC-TOE "reasonably well." TIC-TAC-TOE is played on a 3 X 3 board, or simply on a piece of paper with two vertical and two horizontal lines forming the 9 squares. The players take turns placing their mark or putting one of their playing pieces on an open square on the board. We use "P" to denote the player and "C" to denote the computer. The goal is to get three of your marks in a row (horizontally, vertically, or diagonally) before the other player does. If the board is filled and neither player has three in a row, then the game ends in a tie (the games "goes to the cat").

The following program output illustrates how the games is played (we have placed the output of successive moves side-by-side to save space):

```
TicTacToe? yes
      1  2  3
   A  .  .  .
   B  .  .  .
   C  .  .  .
```

```
Do you want to go first? yes

Which square? A3                          I choose B2

   1  2  3                                   1  2  3
A  .  .  P                               A  .  .  P
B  .  .  .                               B  .  C  .
C  .  .  .                               C  .  .  .

Which square? C1                          I choose A2

   1  2  3                                   1  2  3
A  .  .  P                               A  .  C  P
B  .  C  .                               B  .  C  .
C  P  .  .                               C  P  .  .

Which square? C2                          I choose C3

   1  2  3                                   1  2  3
A  .  C  P                               A  .  C  P
B  .  C  .                               B  .  C  .
C  P  P  .                               C  P  P  C

Which square? A1                          I choose B1

   1  2  3                                   1  2  3
A  P  C  P                               A  P  C  P
B  .  C  .                               B  C  C  .
C  P  P  C                               C  P  P  C

Which square? B1
This square is already occupied!
Which square? B3

   1  2  3
A  P  C  P
B  C  C  P
C  P  P  C

Since all the squares are filled,
the game is a tie.
```

34.3. Number Scrabble

Let's briefly describe another game that later (in section 34.4) is shown to be isomorphic to TIC-TAC-TOE. With the game called NUMBER SCRABBLE, nine cards are provided marked with the numbers 1 through 9. The players take turns choosing cards, one at a time. The first player who can produce a sum of 15 with exactly three of the cards drawn wins.

Here is an example:

```
? PlayTTT
Tic Tac Toe? no
My numbers:
Your numbers:
Numbers still available: 1 2 3 4 5 6 7 8 9
```

```
Do you want to go first? no
I choose 5
My numbers: 5
Your numbers:
Numbers still available: 1 2 3 4 6 7 8 9

Please choose: 3
My numbers: 5
Your numbers: 3
Numbers still available: 1 2 4 6 7 8 9

I choose 4
My numbers: 5 4
Your numbers: 3
Numbers still available: 1 2 6 7 8 9

Please choose: 6
My numbers: 5 4
Your numbers: 3 6
Numbers still available: 1 2 7 8 9

I choose 2
My numbers: 5 4 2
Your numbers: 3 6
Numbers still available: 1 7 8 9

Please choose: 9
My numbers: 5 4 2
Your numbers: 3 6 9
Numbers still available: 1 7 8

I choose 8
My numbers: 5 4 2 8
Your numbers: 3 6 9
Numbers still available: 1 7

Too bad, you lost!
```

34.4. Internal and External Representations

The external representation is given by the playing board in TIC-TAC-TOE and by the nine numbered cards in NUMBER SCRABBLE. Data structures that are available for the internal representation should be related to the external representation isomorphically, if possible. Furthermore, the internal representation should be such that the most important and most frequent operations are simple to describe and perform. A well-thought-out representation is designed not only to run efficiently on the machine, but also to simplify the construction and therefore the structure of the program.

Matrices, Magic Squares, and Lists

The first data representation that presents itself for TIC-TAC-TOE is a 3 X 3 matrix, where each square is addressed by its row and column index. Such a representation was tacitly assumed in the example.

In TIC-TAC-TOE as in REVERSI (see chapter 35), it is important to be able to determine whether a row is complete or can be completed in the next move or the one after that. The operations to do this with the matrix representation presented before requires a considerable amount of effort. A more suitable representation based on the underlying rules of the game would be a magic square with nine fields. This is constructed so that the sum of any row, column, or diagonal is always 15. Except for simple isomorphisms (rotation, mirroring), the way that the magic square can be constructed is shown in figure 34–1.

Although the underlying structure of the magic square is a matrix, the information that is used for evaluating a move is its "magic" property and the relationship that this creates between the numbers associated with each square.

8	1	6
3	5	7
4	9	2

Figure 34–1: The Magic Square

This representation also shows the reason for the isomorphism between TIC-TAC-TOE and NUMBER SCRABBLE: It is a common basis for the two games.

Human and Machine Information Processing

It can be shown experimentally (along the lines of the discussion in [Simon 81, pages 84-89]) that it is easier for us, as humans, to play TIC-TAC-TOE than NUMBER SCRABBLE. In TIC-TAC-TOE we can easily detect moves that are immediately dangerous or lead directly to a victory. The same information that is readily apparent in TIC-TAC-TOE requires considerable calculation in NUMBER SCRABBLE. The lists that we need, which can be extracted visually from the TIC-TAC-TOE board, are not directly available in NUMBER SCRABBLE, and must be calculated.

In contrast, a computer, which does not have the visual apparatus available, can calculate the necessary lists easily. With the aid of the magic square representation, it is possible to detect squares that can result in win in one or two moves by forming the complement with respect to 15. The implementation described in section 34.7 builds on this list structure (or magic square) in a way similar to NUMBER SCRABBLE.

34.5. Heuristics and Strategy

TIC-TAC-TOE and NUMBER SCRABBLE are "finite" games not only in the mathematical sense (chess, with its 10^{120} possible games is also considered to be a "finite" game), but also in the sense of computer science. This means that a program can be written that plays an optimal game by generating the entire game tree. A quick calculation shows that because there are nine squares and each time a move is made there is one less possible move the next time, there are 9! = 362,880 nodes in the game tree. However, because many of the nodes are really equivalent (except for rotation and mirroring) and many games are finished before the board is full, the actual tree is considerably smaller[33].

Theoretical analysis shows that if TIC-TAC-TOE is played perfectly by both players it always results in a tie. We do not want to concentrate on creating a game that can play TIC-TAC-TOE perfectly. Instead we want to use heuristics and strategies built on top of these heuristics to produce better and better TIC-TAC-TOE playing programs. This approach also allows strategies that are developed in one game to be migrated easily into other games. Furthermore, heuristic methods are not restricted to computer science (they appear predominantly in artificial intelligence, but also in operating systems where they are used to determine which virtual memory page in main memory should be "swapped out"). In general, they play an important role in problem-solving and decision-making processes.

Let's look at some heuristics that the computer can use as a basis for playing the game.

Random Game

The first step in the development is to establish criteria for a legal move; that is, the computer acts as a referee, checking to see that the user makes correct moves, but the moves made by the computer are random, though legal. Even a trivial program like this allows several interesting questions to be studied: What is the probability that the program ends up in a tie if the other player plays perfectly? What kind of crucial mistakes does the computer make when it makes random moves?

Evaluating the squares

After playing a few games you observe that, independent of any particular game situation, not all the squares (or cards) have the same strategic value. This can also be derived from theoretical observations, if the topology of the board or the possible ways of splitting 15 into three summands is studied. Square B2 (card number 5) has a special significance, because it belongs to four rows (there are four of the possible sums that contain 5). In contrast the corner square (the even numbered cards) belongs to 3 rows (are contained in 3 of the possible sums) and the edge squares (the odd numbers except for 5) belong to 2 rows (are contained

---

[33]Another possibility for playing a perfect game is to build a "win-lose" matrix, which can be used to determine the next move.

in 2 of the possible sums). If a mark is placed in the center square, 4 of the 8 possible ways of winning have been blocked. As is done with REVERSI, later, a global evaluation matrix could be used based on these observations.

A Simple Force

A force can be defined in either a positive or a negative way. A player can either be placed in a forced position or can create such a position for the opponent. Creating a force means to move in such a way that you can possibly win in your next move; to be placed in a forced position means that you have to move in a particular way to keep your opponent from winning with the next move[34]. Heuristics based on forces may seem so trivial you may underestimate their importance to the computers ability to play the game. With more complex games (e.g., three-dimensional TIC-TAC-TOE with 4 squares per row) even the human player who concentrates on defense (i.e., who watches primarily for negative forces) can overlook a possibility of winning in the next move.

Double Force

A double force consists of creating two forces by the placement of one piece so that your opponent is powerless to keep you from winning and must concede or allow you to win. The following game shows how the player succeeds in creating *two* double forces, with the computer able to keep only one of them from occurring (the program does not use the complete strategy in this game; a slight change was made to demonstrate the double force).

```
? PlayTTT
TicTacToe? yes

   1  2  3
A  .  .  .
B  .  .  .
C  .  .  .

Do you want to go first? yes
Which square? C1                      I choose B2

   1  2  3                               1  2  3
A  .  .  .                            A  .  .  .
B  .  .  .                            B  .  C  .
C  P  .  .                            C  P  .  .

Which square? A3                      I choose C3

   1  2  3                               1  2  3
A  .  .  P                            A  .  .  P
B  .  C  .                            B  .  C  .
C  P  .  .                            C  P  .  C

Which square? A1                      I choose A2
```

---

[34]The concept of a force plays a role in many games; sometimes it arises in a milder form: The outcome of the game may not hinge on the move, but a game piece, a card, the lead runner, a run, or a game position may be lost.

```
      1   2   3                               1   2   3
A     P   .   P                         A     P   C   P
B     .   C   .                         B     .   C   .
C     P   .   C                         C     P   .   C
```

Which square? **B1**

```
      1   2   3
A     P   C   P
B     P   C   .
C     P   .   C
```

Congratulations, You won

This next game even shows a triple force. If the computer's first move is to B2 and the player chooses an edge square (B1, B3, A2, C2), then the computer is certain to win after three more moves:

```
? PlayTTT
TicTacToe yes

      1   2   3
A     .   .   .
B     .   .   .
C     .   .   .
```

Do you want to go first? **no**
I choose B2   Which square? **B1**

```
      1   2   3                               1   2   3
A     .   .   .                         A     .   .   .
B     .   C   .                         B     P   C   .
C     .   .   .                         C     .   .   .
```

I choose C1   Which square? **A3**

```
      1   2   3                               1   2   3
A     .   .   .                         A     .   .   P
B     P   C   .                         B     P   C   .
C     C   .   .                         C     C   .   .
```

I choose C3   Which square? **A1**

```
      1   2   3                               1   2   3
A     .   .   P                         A     P   .   P
B     P   C   .                         B     P   C   .
C     C   .   C                         C     C   .   C
```

I choose C2

```
      1   2   3
A     P   .   P
B     P   C   .
C     C   C   C
```

Too bad, you lost!

From this result, a generally valid strategy, global strategy can be derived:

If the first player chooses the middle square, then the second player must play on a corner square or lose!

Overall Strategy

The heuristics discussed so far lead to the following strategies for the computers play:

S1:   Move randomly.
S2:   Occupy the middle field if it is empty, otherwise move randomly.
S3:   Occupy the middle field, occupy a free corner, otherwise move randomly.
S4:   See if it is possible to win in the next move, otherwise move as in S3.
S5:   See whether it is possible to win in the next move, respond to a direct threat (a force by your opponent), otherwise move as in S3.
S6:   Try to create a threat two levels away, otherwise move as in S5.
S7:   Try to avoid a thread two levels away, otherwise move as in S6.

If these strategies are made into a program and two programs are allowed to play against each other, you should see how effective these strategies are.

An extended strategy based on S1 to S7 is described in figure 34–2.

The Carry-over to NUMBER SCRABBLE

With the strategies gained from studying TIC-TAC-TOE, it is only necessary to couch these strategies in terms of the language of NUMBER SCRABBLE to be able to play it as well. The easiest way to do this is to base both games on the same internal representation and to formulate the strategies in terms of this representation; this is simple with the magic square representation.

TIC-TAC-TOE	NUMBER SCRABBLE
Occupy middle square	Draw the 5
Occupy a corner square	Draw an available even number
A row with two of the same mark and a free square	Two numbers whose sum's 15-Complement can still be drawn
etc.	etc.

The global strategy mentioned on page 394 would look like this in terms of NUMBER SCRABBLE:

If the first player draws the number 5, then the second player must draw an even number or lose.

Applicability of the Heuristics to Other Games

The heuristics used in TIC-TAC-TOE are applicable to other games with minor changes. When a person learns a new game, this learning process consists largely of incremental acquisition of these strategies. By playing the game and then reflecting critically on these games, the player acquires new strategies and abilities. This occurs when new game situations arise that stimulate the awareness that a particular strategy is appropriate.

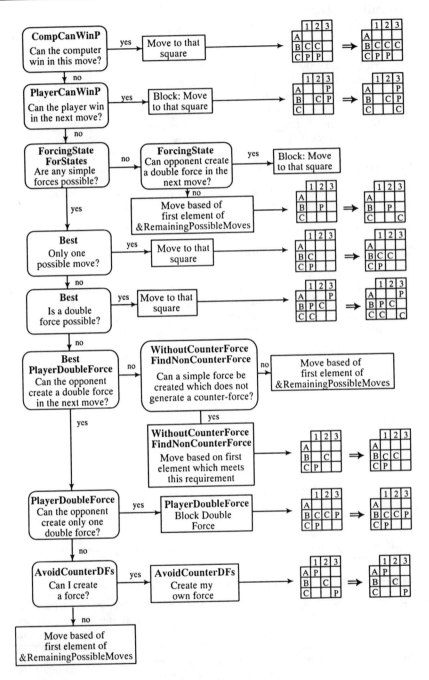

Figure 34–2: The Computer's Strategy

34.6. Implementation

The design criteria are derived from the objectives presented in section 34.1. The program should be able to play both games. Therefore two different external representations for the single internal representation need to be built. These internal data structures should be designed so that the strategies defined in section 34.5 can be defined as procedures without difficulty. In addition, the program's procedures should control and check the interaction for a-two player game (e.g., recognize illegal moves, announce the end of the game, etc.). The individual procedures that are specific to Tɪᴄ-Tᴀᴄ-Tᴏᴇ and Nᴜᴍʙᴇʀ Sᴄʀᴀʙʙʟᴇ should handle the external representation.

The external representation of the two games are united by the common internal representation; numerical values are assigned for the individual fields of the magic square (see the code for the procedure GlobVar on page 398).

34.7. Complete Listing of the Program

The individual procedure divided into groups. To understand what is going on, refer to the complete description of the strategies in figure 34–2.

We should also mention that forces are determined by the differences between combinations of pairs of numbers from the list of available moves and the list of moves already made. Also, the order in which the individual strategies are applied is important.

Overall Control and Global Variables

```
To PlayTTT
   TypeOfGame
   GlobVar
   Begin
   Play
End

To TypeOfGame
   Type "TicTacToe?
   IfElse YesP
      [Make "&TypeOfGame "TicTacToe]
      [Make "&TypeOfGame "NumberScrabble]
End

To GlobVar
   Make "&Player []
   Make "&Computer []
   Make "&RemainingPossibleMoves [5 2 4 6 8 1 3 7 9]
   Make "&Won "False
   Make "&PrintList [1 2 3 4 5 6 7 8 9]
   Make "&1 "A2
   Make "&2 "C3
   Make "&3 "B1
   Make "&4 "C1
```

```
Make "&5 "B2
Make "&6 "A3
Make "&7 "B3
Make "&8 "A1
Make "&9 "C2
Make "A1 8
Make "A2 1
Make "A3 6
Make "B1 3
Make "B2 5
Make "B3 7
Make "C1 4
Make "C2 9
Make "C3 2
End
```

Note: We use the names &1 ... &9 because variable's names can't begin with a digit in our version of LOGO, and for uniformity of access we also use the names &A1 .. &C3.

```
To Begin
  IfElse :&TypeOfGame = "ttt
    [GameBoard]
    [Score]
  Type [Do you want to go first?]
  If Not YesP [Computer]
End

To Play
  Player
  If :&Won [Print [Congratulations, You won]
    Stop]
  If :&RemainingPossibleMoves = [] [TieGame
    Stop]
  Computer
  If :&Won [Print [Too bad, you lost!]
    Stop]
  If :&RemainingPossibleMoves = [] [TieGame
    Stop]
  Play
End

To TieGame
  IfElse :&TypeOfGame = "TicTacToe
    [Print [Since all of the squares are filled]]
    [Print [Since there are no more cards]]
  Print [The game is a tie.]
End
```

The Player's Move

```
To Player
  Make "Move UserMove
  If Not (MemberP :Move :&RemainingPossibleMoves)
    [AlreadyGone
     Player
     Stop]
```

```
   If WinningMoveP :Move (PossiblePairs :&Player)
     [Make "&Won "True]
   MakeMove "&Player :Move
   IfElse :&TypeOfGame = "TicTacToe
     [GameBoard]
     [Score]
End

To UserMove
   IfElse :&TypeOfGame = "TicTacToe
     [Type [Which square?]
      Output Square First ReadList]
     [Type [Please choose:]
      Output First ReadList]
End

To AlreadyGone
   IfElse :&TypeOfGame = "TicTacToe
     [Print [This square is already occupied!]]
     [Print [That card has already been picked]]
End

To MakeMove :WhichPlayer :Move
   Make
     :WhichPlayer
     Sentence Thing :WhichPlayer :Move
   Make
     "&RemainingPossibleMoves
     Remove :Move :&RemainingPossibleMoves
   Make "&PrintList Remove :Move :&PrintList
End

To WinningMoveP :Move :Pairs
   If :Pairs = [] [Output "False]
   If EqualP
     :Move
     Complement15 First :Pairs First ButFirst :Pairs
     [Output "True]
   Output WinningMoveP :Move ButFirst ButFirst :Pairs
End

To PossiblePairs :List
   IfElse 2 > Count :List
     [Output []]
     [Output
        Sentence
          PossiblePairs1
            First :List
            ButFirst :List
          PossiblePairs ButFirst :List]
End
```

```
To PossiblePairs1 :Element :List
  IfElse :List = [ ]
    [Output [ ] ]
    [Output
      (Sentence
        :Element
        First :List
        PossiblePairs1 :Element ButFirst :List)]
End
```

Remove is described in appendix III

External Representation

```
To Square :N
  Output Thing Word "& :N
End
```

```
To Score
  Print Sentence [My numbers:] :&Computer
  Print Sentence [Your numbers:] :&Player
  Print
    Sentence
      [Numbers still available:]
      :&PrintList
  Print [ ]
End
```

```
To GameBoard
  Print [ ]
  Print (Sentence Spaces 2 1 2 3)
  Print (Sentence "A PrtSqr 8 PrtSqr 1 PrtSqr 6)
  Print (Sentence "B PrtSqr 3 PrtSqr 5 PrtSqr 7)
  Print (Sentence "C PrtSqr 4 PrtSqr 9 PrtSqr 2)
  Print [ ]
End
```

```
To PrtSqr :N
  If MemberP :N :&Computer [Output "C]
  IfElse MemberP :N :&Player
    [Output "P]
    [Output ".]
End
```

```
To ChooseMove :N
  IfElse :&TypeOfGame = "ttt
    [Print Sentence [I choose] square :N]
    [Print Sentence [I choose] :N]
  MakeMove "&Computer :N
End
```

Computer's Move—Win or Lose in the Next Move

```
To Computer
  ; Can the computer win in this move?
```

```
Test
   CompCanWinP
     :&RemainingPossibleMoves
     PossiblePairs :&Computer
   IfFalse
     [Test
        PlayerCanWinP
          :&RemainingPossibleMoves
          PossiblePairs :&Player]
   IfFalse [ForcingState]
   IfElse :&TypeOfGame = "ttt
     [GameBoard]
     [Score]
End

To CompCanWinP :List :Pairs
   IfElse WinPossibleP :List :Pairs
     [Make "&Won "True
      Output "True]
     [Output "False]
End

To PlayerCanWinP :List :Pairs
   Output WinPossibleP :List :Pairs
End

To WinPossibleP :List :Pairs
   If (Or (:List = []) (:Pairs = [])) [Output "False]
   If WinningMoveP First :List :Pairs
     [ChooseMove First :List
      Output "True]
   Output WinPossibleP ButFirst :List :Pairs
End
```

Analyze the Forcing State

```
To ForcingState
   ; Are any simple forces possible?
   Local "ForceStates
   Make
      "ForceStates
      ForStates :&RemainingPossibleMoves
   Test :ForceStates = []
   IfFalse [Best :ForceStates
      Stop]
   ; Can the opponent create a double force
   ; in the next move?
   Local "PlyrDblForces
   Make
      "PlyrDblForces
      FindDoubleForces
        :&RemainingPossibleMoves
        :&Player
   IfElse :PlyrDblForces = []
     [ChooseMove First :&RemainingPossibleMoves]
     [ChooseMove First :PlyrDblForces]
End
```

```
To ForStates :List
  If :List = [] [Output []]
  If ForcingMoveP
      First :List
      :&Computer
      Remove
        First :List
        :&RemainingPossibleMoves
    [Output
        FPut First :List ForStates ButFirst :List]
  Output ForStates ButFirst :List
End

To ForcingMoveP :Move :AlreadyMade :StillPossible
  ;; based on the moves :AlreadyMade by a player,
  ;; would :Move force the opponent ?
  If :AlreadyMade = [] [Output "False]
  IfElse
      MemberP
        Complement15 :Move First :AlreadyMade
        :StillPossible
    [Output "True]
    [Output
        ForcingMoveP
          :Move
          ButFirst :AlreadyMade
          :StillPossible]
End

To Complement15 :N1 :N2
  Output 15 - (:N1 + :N2)
End

To Best :Moves
  ; If only one possible move, do it
  If (Count :Moves) = 1
    [ChooseMove First :Moves
     Stop]
  Local "DblForces
  Make "DblForces FindDoubleForces :Moves :&Computer
  ; Is a Double Force Possible?
  IfElse :DblForces = []
    [PlayerDoubleForce
        FindDoubleForces
          :&RemainingPossibleMoves
          :&Player
          :Moves]
    [ChooseMove First :DblForces]
End
```

Determining a Double Force

```
To FindDoubleForces :PossibleMoves :AlreadyMade
  If :PossibleMoves = [] [Output []]
```

```
    IfElse
      DoubleForceP
      First :PossibleMoves
      0
      :AlreadyMade
      Remove
        First :PossibleMoves
        :&RemainingPossibleMoves
    [Output
      Sentence
        First :PossibleMoves
        FindDoubleForces
          ButFirst :PossibleMoves
          :AlreadyMade]
    [Output
      FindDoubleForces
        ButFirst :PossibleMoves
        :AlreadyMade]
  End

To DoubleForceP :Move :Level
            :AlreadyMade :AvailableMoves
  If :AlreadyMade = [] [Output "False]
  If Not
      (MemberP
        Complement15 :Move First :AlreadyMade
        :AvailableMoves)
    [Output
      DoubleForceP
        :Move
        :Level
        ButFirst :AlreadyMade
        :AvailableMoves]
  IfElse :Level = 1
    [Output "True]
    [Output
      DoubleForceP
        :Move
        :Level + 1
        ButFirst :AlreadyMade
        :AvailableMoves]
  End
```

Analysis of the Opponent's Possible Moves

```
To PlayerDoubleForce :OppDoubleForces :MyPossMoves
  If :OppDoubleForces = []
    [WithoutCounterForce :MyPossMoves
    Stop]
  ; Can the opponent create only one double force?
  IfElse (Count :OppDoubleForces) = 1
    [ChooseMove First :OppDoubleForces]
    [AvoidCounterDFs :OppDoubleForces :MyPossMoves]
  End
```

```
To WithoutCounterForce :Moves
  ; Can a simple force be created which does not
  ; generate a counter-force?
  Local "NonCounterForce
  Make "NonCounterForce FindNonCounterForce :Moves
  IfElse :NonCounterForce = []
    [ChooseMove First :Moves]
    [ChooseMove :NonCounterForce]
End

To AvoidCounterDFs :OppDoubleForces :StillPossible
  ; Can I create a force?
  Local "NoCntrDFs
  Make
    "NoCntrDFs
    WithoutCounterDFs :OppDoubleForces :StillPossible
  IfElse :NoCntrDFs = []
    [WithoutCounterForce :StillPossible]
    [WithoutCounterForce :NoCntrDFs]
End

To WithoutCounterDFs :OppDoubleForces :PossMoves
  ;; Find all of :PossMoves which don't generate
  ;; Counter-Double-Forces
  If :PossMoves = [] [Output []]
  IfElse
      MemberP
      ForcingSquare
        First :PossMoves
        :&Computer
        Remove
          First :PossMoves
          :&RemainingPossibleMoves
        :DoubleForces
    [Output
        WithoutCounterDFs
          :DoubleForces
          ButFirst :PossMoves]
    [Output
        Sentence
        First :PossMoves
        WithoutCounterDFs
          :DoubleForces
            ButFirst :PossMoves]
End

To ForcingSquare :Move :AlreadyMade :StillPossible
  ;; Returns the square that the would force the :Move
  Local "Force
  Make "Force Complement15 :Move First :AlreadyMade
```

```
    IfElse (MemberP :Force :StillPossible)
      [Output :Force]
      [Output
         ForcingSquare
            :Move
            ButFirst :AlreadyMade
            :StillPossible]
    End

    To FindNonCounterForce :PossibleMoves
    ;; Does forcing my opponent
    ;; result in a move that forces me?
    If :PossibleMoves = [] [Output []]
    ; does the move I would be forcing.....
    Local "Force
    Make
       "Force
       ForcingSquare
         First :PossibleMoves
         :&Computer
       Remove
          First :PossibleMoves
          :&RemainingPossibleMoves
    ; force the opponent to force me?
    IfElse
       ForcingMoveP
       :Force
       :&Player
       Remove :Force :&RemainingPossibleMoves
      [Output
         FindNonCounterForce ButFirst :PossibleMoves]
      [Output First :PossibleMoves]
    End
```

The procedures MemberP and YesP are described in appendix III.

Chapter 35:
Reversi

35.1. The Problem

In this section we deal with a program that allows the user to play REVERSI against the computer. This program:

- keeps track of the moves of the game
- acts as a referee
- plays REVERSI against the user

35.2. Objectives

REVERSI belongs to the class of strategic board games along with CHESS, GO, and other similar games. It has a long tradition just as these others do, even though it slipped into oblivion and was just recently rediscovered. In spite of (or perhaps because of) the relative simplicity of the game in as far as the rules are concerned, the game has an inviting level of complexity.

REVERSI also acts as an example for the kind of game that has no known winning strategy (such as is known for, say, TIC-TAC-TOE); good REVERSI players rely more on heuristics, or rules-of-thumb, to determine what are good moves or game positions. Often, these have the form "in general, you should watch out that..." and are mostly imprecise, fuzzy, or are given in such a general fashion that they may not apply to specific game positions. REVERSI shares these properties with GO and CHESS; however, in contrast to these, a REVERSI program is a project whose complexity is reasonable for the scope of this book (although it certainly is towards the top end of the range).

35.3. The Rules of the Game

REVERSI is played on a square 8 X 8 board. Each player has an unlimited number of playing pieces available, each with a black side and a white side (we represent the black side with an "X" and the white side with an "O"). The players take turns; one player using the black side of the pieces and the other using the white side of the piece.

The following figure shows the initial board setup:

```
- 1 2 3 4 5 6 7 8 -
A . . . . . . . . A
B . . . . . . . . B
C . . . . . . . . C
D . . . O O . . . D
E . . . X X . . . E
F . . . . . . . . F
G . . . . . . . . G
H . . . . . . . . H
- 1 2 3 4 5 6 7 8 -
```

Now the two players alternately place a piece with their color up; the pieces must be played so that one or more of the opponents pieces are "surrounded" by a previously played piece and the newly played in a horizontal, vertical, or diagonal direction (see the following example); the "surrounded" pieces are then turned over (hence the name REVERSI) and thereby become the same color as those of the moving player.

One possible game position after the first move is the following:

```
- 1 2 3 4 5 6 7 8 -
A . . . . . . . . A
B . . . . . . . . B
C . . . . . . . . C
D . . . O O . . . D
E . . . O X . . . E
F . . O . . . . . F
G . . . . . . . . G
H . . . . . . . . H
- 1 2 3 4 5 6 7 8 -
```

That is, the "white" player played on F3, and turned the piece on E4 over.

If a piece is placed so that it surrounds the opponents pieces in more than one direction, only one of these directions must be selected:

```
- 1 2 3 4 5 6 7 8 -
A . . . . . . . . A
B . . . . . . . . B
C X X X X X . . . C
D . . . X X . . . D
E . . . X X X . . E
F . . O O O O . . F
G . . . . . . . . G
H . . . . . . . . H
- 1 2 3 4 5 6 7 8 -
```

If the white player decides to play on D6, he or she must decide whether the piece on E5 or E6 will be turned over; if the vertical row is selected, the following situation results:

```
- 1 2 3 4 5 6 7 8 -
A . . . . . . . . A
B . . . . . . . . B
C X X X X X . . . C
D . . . X X O . . D
E . . . X X O . . E
F . . O O O O . . F
G . . . . . . . . G
H . . . . . . . . H
- 1 2 3 4 5 6 7 8 -
```

If the player cannot surround any of the opponents pieces, the turn is skipped and it is the other player's turn. Here is an example where neither player can play:

```
- 1 2 3 4 5 6 7 8 -
A . O O O O O O O A
B O O X X X X O O B
C O X O X X O O O C
D O X X O O O O O D
E O X X O O X O O E
F O X O O X O O O F
G O O X X O X O O G
H O O O O O O O O H
- 1 2 3 4 5 6 7 8 -
```

if a move is possible the player must play; it is not permitted to skip a turn by choice.

The game ends if all the spaces are filled, or if neither player can move. The player whose color appears most often on the board is the winner.

35.4. Playing REVERSI Means...

Let's first have a look at the knowledge that is needed to play REVERSI. Later we transform this into programs and data structures.

... Seeing the Possibilities

The first condition for a good game of REVERSI is that the player is able to see all the possible moves that are available. Players, especially beginners, overlook simple things (like good moves, threats from the opponent, ways to block an opponents good move, etc.). This applies in particular to moves dealing with the diagonal rows. The role of seeing the possibilities in playing a good game can be illustrated easily by using symbols for the pieces that are more difficult to distinguish (e.g., "B" and "R" instead of "X" and "O"). Using such a representation leads to possible moves being overlooked more often and results in lower quality play (this is probably the reason that the game uses black and white pieces).

The strong dependence on the abilities provided by the visual system is probably true for other board games such as CHESS and GO as well, although it may not be as apparent.

... Knowing the Best Moves

Even though the end goal of the game is to "capture" the greatest number of pieces possible, a strategy that exclusively maximizes the number of pieces captured at each point in the game is not really optimal and often the opposite is true. An experienced REVERSI player doesn't try to simply maximize the number of pieces captured, especially at the beginning of the game. Instead, each move should be oriented towards a global strategy that could be described as follows:

After playing the game a few times, it appears advantageous to occupy the corner positions of the board, because these cannot be recaptured by the opponent, and they can also be used to capture long rows of pieces towards the end of the game.

The edge squares are similarly favorable. They can only be recaptured by other pieces on the same edge, and they can be used to control considerable area of the board. If this experience (or knowledge) is brought in to play, it should become clear—in some sense working back from the goal—what this implies for the rest of the spaces: It is unfavorable to move to the positions that are next to the corner spaces and, under normal conditions, this should be avoided (these are marked by "x"es in the next figure), because the opponent can only occupy these positions if you have occupied their neighbors (for the relevance of these statements see section 35.4).

```
   -  1  2  3  4  5  6  7  8  -
   A  .  x  .  .  .  .  x  .  A
   B  x  x  .  .  .  .  x  x  B
   C  .  .  .  .  .  .  .  .  C
   D  .  .  .  .  .  .  .  .  D
   E  .  .  .  .  .  .  .  .  E
   F  .  .  .  .  .  .  .  .  F
   G  x  x  .  .  .  .  x  x  G
   H  .  x  .  .  .  .  x  .  H
   -  1  2  3  4  5  6  7  8  -
```

For similar reasons, all the spaces that are next to the edge are also unfavorable, although perhaps not as much so as those next to the corners.

```
-  1  2  3  4  5  6  7  8  -
A  .  .  .  .  .  .  .  .  A
B  .  .  x  x  x  x  .  .  B
C  .  x  .  .  .  .  x  .  C
D  .  x  .  .  .  .  x  .  D
E  .  x  .  .  .  .  x  .  E
F  .  x  .  .  .  .  x  .  F
G  .  .  x  x  x  x  .  .  G
H  .  .  .  .  .  .  .  .  H
-  1  2  3  4  5  6  7  8  -
```

The following figure summarizes the global assessment of the individual spaces:

```
-   1   2    3   4   5   6   7    8  -
A  ++  --    +   +   +   +   --  ++  A
B  --  --    -   -   -   -   --  --  B
C   +   -    +   o   o   +   -    +  C
D   +   -    o   o   o   o   -    +  D
E   +   -    o   X   X   o   -    +  E
F   +   -    +   o   o   +   -    +  F
G  --  --    -   -   -   -   --  --  G
H  ++  --    +   +   +   +   --  ++  H
-   1   2    3   4   5   6   7    8  -
```

For the 12 inner spaces (those that surround the initial pieces) similar observations can be made, although it is not as clear how reliable these assessments are, and in the final analysis they are nothing more than heuristics. The four spaces that are the corners of this inner square (C3, C6, F3, F6) might be viewed as somewhat more favorable, because they are next to the "highly unfavorable" fields B2, B7, G2, and G7.

... Bearing in Mind the Current Situation

The statements we have just made are a characterization of an extremely global playing strategy, which can and must be drastically modified with respect to the current situation. We give some examples in what follows.

The statement that the "corner neighbors" are highly unfavorable is valid only until the corresponding corner space is occupied. If the corner is occupied by one of your own pieces, then it is highly favorable to occupy the neighboring spaces with pieces of your own color, because these cannot be captured by your opponent either. Also the negative value given to the "edge neighbors" needs to be reevaluated once the edge spaces are occupied. Whereas both of these strategies can be easily expressed by a modification of the global assessment, the following considerations make this possibility more difficult.

The global priority, which the moves to the edge spaces have, can be severely restricted by specific situations; here are some examples:

Example 1:

```
- 1 2 3 4 5 6 7 8 -
A . . . O . . . . A
B . . O O . . . . B
C . . X O . . . . C
```

If player X were to move to A3 or A5, this piece (and thereby the edge) would be lost back to player O by a move to A2 or, respectively, A6; It is therefore unfavorable to move to an edge space next to an opponent's piece on an edge space.

Example 2:

```
- 1 2 3 4 5 6 7 8 -
A . . X O X . . . A
B . . X O X . . . B
```

Contrary to the global strategy, it is in no way favorable for Player O to move to A6 and capture A5 in this situation, because this, as well as A4 would certainly be lost when player X moves to A7.

Example 3:

```
- 1 2 3 4 5 6 7 8 -
A . . . . X . . . A
B . . O X X . . . B
C . . X O X . . . C
```

It would also be strongly inadvisable (again contrary to the global assessment) for player X to move to A3, because player O could take over an unthreatenable edge space by moving to A4.

Example 4:

```
- 1 2 3 4 5 6 7 8 -
A . O X X X X X X A
B X . O O O O O X B
C O X O X X O X X C
D O O X X X X X X D
```

This example shows how, towards the end of the game, even the desirable corner space can be an unfavorable move; it is more advantageous for player X to move to B2 and leave A1 to player O than the other way around, because more pieces could be captured. As in CHESS, a beginning, middle, and end game can be distinguished.

35.5. The Program

Before the program is discussed piece by piece, we should note that this program (as many of the others in this book) has gone through many different versions before it reached the form and extent that is shown here. Remember that all the intermediate versions were concrete, manipulable objects that represented gains in knowledge that were important for the development of this program (and for its developers!). The program in its current form was not just pulled out of a mold but has grown bit by bit as the understanding of the problem has grown, representing an empirical effort, underscoring the empirical nature of many areas of computer science.

Do not feel that the kind of results you see here should be the results of a "one-shot effort" but are more the result of a learning process, which is as valuable as any by-product or artifact (such as the program you see here). We encourage you to perhaps tackle parts of the problem without simply using the program "straight from the book," so that you can deal with some of the issues we discuss directly, rather than vicariously. Although the various levels of knowledge within the program are not readily recognizable and the picture that is presented is highly "interwoven" and certainly contains redundancy, it is a good example for another aspect of such programs: The removal of certain parts of the program (knowledge components) does not change the overall operation of the program. The main by-products that should be pointed out are:

- The program can represent the playing board; two players can play against each other; the program takes care of flipping the pieces, and asks which direction is desired when there are several possibilities for capture; it asks who should go first;

- The program takes on the role of the referee; it determines:

  - Whether the game is over (the board is full or no more moves are possible),

  - Who the winner is,

  - Whether the move to a certain square is permitted (the square needs to be empty and there must be some "capture" that can be made from that square),

  - Whether a player's move is permitted;

- The program can take on the role of one of the players.

Of all the programs in this part of the book, REVERSI is by far the most extensive and may be too large for some smaller implementation of LOGO. We have decided to present it in its entirety rather than in a form that would work on smaller system; however, an abbreviated version could be extracted from what is presented here, and although it would not play the game as well, it could be made to run on a smaller system.

Data Structures

Because the individual pieces and squares are accessed frequently, and the order in which they are accessed can be varied (for example, in searching squares for possible moves, examination of horizontal, vertical, and diagonal rows), it is reasonable to represent the playing board as a two-dimensional array or matrix, so that individual squares can be accessed using an index. Because most versions of LOGO do not make this data type available, we simulate it as follows: The eight rows of the board are represented as eight global variables with the names &Board1 through &Board8, each of which contains a list of eight elements each of which represents a square on the board. The last letter of the name, then, is the first index to the element of the array, whereas the procedure Nth is used to extract the appropriate element (based on the second index) from the corresponding list. Using a maxrix representation has the advantage that the data-accessing functions (especially the oft used function Neighbor) can access an arbitrary square in a straightforward way; the neighbors can be accessed by manipulating the index (which is interpreted as a two-digit number between 11 and 88) as follows:

- by adding or subtracting 1 (left of right neighbor)
- by adding or subtracting 10 (neighbor above or below)
- by adding or subtracting 9 (upper left or lower right neighbor)
- by adding or subtracting 11 (lower left or upper right neighbor)

The board is initialized with the beginning board layout and the assessment values of the individual unoccupied squares (see the procedure SetUpSquares). Storing both aspects (occupied squares and the assessment values) into one array is possible because the values of the squares are only needed for unoccupied squares. The following additional global variables (with their respective initial values) are needed.

```
"&InnerPlayable is
     [33 36 63 66 53 46 43 56 64 65 34 35]
"&EdgePlayable is []
```

These two variables contain the coordinates of the inner squares and the edge squares, respectively, that are next to occupied squares and are therefore potentially playable. Both lists are used for calculating possible moves and are updated after each move.

These two variables count the number of pieces "owned" by each player, their values are needed at the end of the game.

```
"&Computer is 2
"&Player is 2
```

This variable is needed to indicate a premature end to the game (both players cannot move).

```
"&CantMove is 0
```

These variables are used to calculate the complementary color of a given color quickly.

```
"X is O
"O is X
```

Procedures

The first procedure we present is `Reversi`; it initializes the global variables we discussed using `GlobVar`, prints out the beginning board, handles the alternating play of the computer and the user, and gives the final result.

```
To Reversi
  GlobVar
  PrintBoard
  Type [Would you like to go first?]
  Local "CurPlyr
  IfElse YesP
    [Make "CurPlyr "Player
     Make "&PlayerColor "o
     Make "&ComputerColor "x]
    [Make "CurPlyr "Computer
     Make "&PlayerColor "x
     Make "&ComputerColor "o]
  PlayGame :CurPlyr
  Print Sentence "Player :&Player
  Print Sentence "Computer :&Computer
  Print
     Sentence "Unoccupied 64 - :&Player - :&Computer
End

To PlayGame :Player
  If Or (:&CantMove = 2) (Thing Word "& :Player) = 0
    [Stop]
  Run
     (Sentence :Player
        (Word char 34 (Thing (Word "& :Player "Color))))
  PlayGame Opponent :Player
End

To Opponent :Player
  Output Thing (Word "& :Player "Opponent)
End

To GlobVar
  Make "O "X
  Make "X "O
  Make "&Dir1 "-11
  Make "&Dir2 "-10
  Make "&Dir3 "-9
  Make "&Dir4 1
  Make "&Dir5 11
  Make "&Dir6 10
  Make "&Dir7 9
  Make "&Dir8 "-1
  Make "&Computer 2
  Make "&Player 2
  Make "&CantMove 0
```

```
      Make "&EdgePlayable []
      Make
         "&InnerPlayable
         [33 36 63 66 53 46 43 56 64 65 34 35]
      Make "&PlayerOpponent "Computer
      Make "&ComputerOpponent "Player
      Make "&PlayerReassess 20
      Make "&ComputerReassess 30
      SetUpSquares
   End

   To PrintBoard
      Print "
      Print (Sentence "- :&Board0 "-)
      Print (Sentence "A Form :&Board1 "A)
      Print (Sentence "B Form :&Board2 "B)
      Print (Sentence "C Form :&Board3 "C)
      Print (Sentence "D Form :&Board4 "D)
      Print (Sentence "E Form :&Board5 "E)
      Print (Sentence "F Form :&Board6 "F)
      Print (Sentence "G Form :&Board7 "G)
      Print (Sentence "H Form :&Board8 "H)
      Print (Sentence "- :&Board0 "-)
      Print "
   End

   To SetUpSquares
      Make "&Board0 [1 2 3 4 5 6 7 8]
      Make "&Board1 [30 1 10 8 8 10 1 30]
      Make "&Board2 [1 1 4 4 4 4 1 1]
      Make "&Board3 [10 4 12 10 10 12 4 10]
      Make "&Board4 [8 4 10 0 0 10 4 8]
      Make "&Board5 [8 4 10 X X 10 4 8]
      Make "&Board6 [10 4 12 10 10 12 4 10]
      Make "&Board7 [1 1 4 4 4 4 1 1]
      Make "&Board8 [30 1 10 8 8 10 1 30]
   End

   To Form :List
      If :List = [] [Output []]
      If NumberP First :List
         [Output FPut ". Form ButFirst :List]
      Output FPut First :List Form ButFirst :List
   End
```

The procedure Player handles the users move:

```
   To Player :Color
      If EmptyP
         (PossMoves
            Sentence :&EdgePlayable :&InnerPlayable
            :Color)
         [Make "&CantMove :&CantMove + 1
          Print [You can't move this turn]
          Stop]
      Type [Your move:]
      Local "Move
      Make "Move First ReadList
```

```
; Make sure user is making a move if s/he can
If :Move = "
   [Print [You must move!]
   Player Stop]
; convert from external index
;   form to internal index form
Make
   "Move
   Word
      First
         ButFirst Member First :Move "A1B2C3D4E5F6G7H8
      Last :Move
; check which row this should affect
Local "DirsOfMove
Make "DirsOfMove PossMoves FPut :Move [] :Color
If :DirsOfMove = []
   [Print [Illegal Move!]
   Player :Color
   Stop]
If (Count :DirsOfMove) > 1
   [Make "DirsOfMove WhichDir :DirsOfMove]
MakeMove
   :Move
   :Color
   First ButFirst First :DirsOfMove
   Last First :DirsOfMove
End
```

We first check to see whether the user has a move, and if not simply specify that. If there is a possible move, the user is prompted for a move, and if no input is given, the user is informed that a move must be made and a recursive call is made. Otherwise the move is converted from external indexing (a letter followed by a digit) to the internal indexing (two digits). Then the variable DirsOfMove is assigned the output of the procedure PossMoves that consists of a list of all the ways this move could affect the play, with each item consisting of a triple of the move, the direction, and the number of pieces affected. The procedure Reassess recomputes the values of the global assessment as needed. If several possible moves are indicated by DirsOfMove, the user is asked (in WhichDir) to choose the direction the move should affect. MakeMove actually makes the move by updating the global data structures to reflect the changes.

The procedure PossMoves uses Poss, FPutIf, and Neighbor to calculate the list of open squares to which legal moves can be made.

```
To PossMoves :Free :Color
   If :Free = [] [Output []]
   Output
      Sentence
         PossMoves1 First :Free :Color 1
         PossMoves ButFirst :Free :Color
End
```

```
To PossMoves1 :OneFree :Color :Dir
  If :Dir > 8 [Output []]
  Output
    FPutIf
      Poss :OneFree :Color :Dir
      PossMoves1 :OneFree :Color :Dir + 1
End

To Poss :FreeSquare :Color :Dir
  Local "Neigh
  Make "Neigh Neighbor :FreeSquare :Dir
  If Not (Get "&Board :Neigh) = (Thing :Color)
    [Output []]
  Output FollowDir Neighbor :Neigh :Dir 1 :Dir :Color
End

To FollowDir :Neigh :Count :Dir :Color
  If (GetSq :Neigh) = Thing :Color
    [Output
        FollowDir
          Neighbor :Neigh :Dir
          :Count + 1
          :Dir
          :Color]
  If (GetSq :Neigh) = :Color
    [Output (Sentence :FreeSquare :Dir :Count)]
  Output []
End

To FPutIf :List1 :List2
  IfElse :List1 = []
    [Output :List2]
    [Output FPut :List1 :List2]
End

To Put :Var :Index :Value
  Make
    Word :Var First :Index
    Replace
      (Thing Word :Var First :Index)
      Last :Index
      :Value
End

To Get :Var :Index
  If LessP :Index 11 [Output "]
  If (Or
      (First :Index) > 8
      (Last :Index) < 1
      (Last :Index) > 8)
    [Output "]
  Output
    Nth Last :Index (Thing Word :Var First :Index)
End
```

```
To Neighbor :Square :Dir
  Output :Square + Thing (Word "&Dir :Dir)
End
```

The following game situations are given as clarification:

```
- 1 2 3 4 5 6 7 8 -
A . . . . . . . . A
B . . . . . . . . B
C . . X . . . . . C
D . . X O O . . . D
E . O O O X . . . E
F . . O . . . . . F
G . . . . . . . . G
H . . . . . . . . H
- 1 2 3 4 5 6 7 8 -
```

```
? Print :&EdgePlayable
51 61 41
? Print :&InnerPlayable
36 66 46 56 64 65 34 35 74 73 72 62 22 23 24 42 32
? Print
  PossMoves Sentence :&EdgePlayable :&InnerPlayable "X
[73 2 2][35 6 1][65 1 1][46 8 2][61 3 1][51 4 3]
```

Each individual element of the list shows one possible move, consisting of the
coordinate of the square to be occupied, the direction in which the opponent's
pieces are to be captured, and the number of pieces that could be captured by
this move. The direction is encoded like this:

1: towards upper left
2: upwards
3: towards upper right
4: to the right
5: towards lower right
6: downwards
7: towards lower left
8: to the left

Neighbor calculates the Neighbor of the :Square in the direction :Dir.
This is the most frequently used function in this program.

```
To Neighbor :Square :Dir
  Output :Square + Thing (Word "&Dir :Dir)
End

To WhichDir :Dirs
  Type "Direction
  Make "Choice ChechDirs First ReadList :Dirs
  If Not :Choice = [] [Output FPut :Choice []]
  Print [This direction isn't appropriate]
  Output WhichDir :Dirs
End
```

```
To ChechDirs :Dir :Dirs
   If :Dirs = [] [Output []]
   If (First ButFirst First :Dirs) = :Dir
      [Output First :Dirs]
   Output Chechdirs :Dir ButFirst :Dirs
End
```

WhichDir and ChechDirs select the triple that represents the move in the direction selected by the user:

```
? Print WhichDir [[63 3 1][63 4 2]]
Direction: 1
This direction isn't appropriate!
Direction: 3
63 3 1
```

```
To Reassess :Move :Number
   If MemberP :Move [11 18 81 88]
      [SetSeveral
          First
             ButFirst
                Member
                   :Move
                   [11 [12 21 22]
                    18 [17 27 28]
                    81 [71 72 82]
                    88 [77 78 87]]
             :Number
          Stop]
   If VertEdgeP :Move
      [IfElse (Last :Move) = 1
          [SetSeveral [32 42 52 62] 8
           Stop]
          [SetSeveral [37 47 57 67] 8
           Stop]]
   If HorizEdgeP :Move
      [IfElse (First :Move) = 1
          [SetSeveral [23 24 25 26] 8]
          [SetSeveral [73 74 75 76] 8]]
End

To HorizEdgeP :Move
   Output MemberP First :Move 18
End

To VertEdgeP :Move
   Output MemberP Last :Move 18
End

To SetSeveral :List :Value
   If :List = [] [Stop]
   If NumberP Get "&Board First :List
      [Put "&Board First :List :Value]
   SetSeveral ButFirst :List :Value
End
```

After certain moves, Reassess changes the global valuations:

- If the move is made to a corner, the valuation for the corresponding neighbors is raised to 20 (if it is the users move) or 30 (if it is the computers move);

- If the move is to a "normal" edge, the valuation of the whole neighboring row or column is raised:

```
To AddNewMoves :Square
   AddNewMoves1 :Square 1
End

To AddNewMoves1 :Square :Dir
   Local "Neigh
   If :Dir > 8 [Stop]
   Make "Neigh Neighbor :Square :Dir
   If NumberP Get "&Board :Neigh
   [If Not
         MemberP
           :Neigh
           (Sentence :&EdgePlayable :&InnerPlayable)
      [IfElse Or HorizEdgeP :Neigh VertEdgeP :Neigh
         [Make
            "&EdgePlayable
            Sentence :Neigh :&EdgePlayable]
         [Make
            "&InnerPlayable
            Sentence :Neigh :&InnerPlayable]]]
   AddNewMoves1 :Square :Dir + 1
End

To MakeMove :Move :Color :Dir :Captured
   Make "&CantMove 0
   Put "&Board :Move :Color
   Make
      Word "& :Player
      (Thing Word "& :Player) + :Captured + 1
   Make
      Word "& Opponent :Player
      (Thing Word "& Opponent :Player) - :Captured
   Reassess
      First :Move
      Thing (Word "& :Player "Reassess)
   MakeMove1 Neighbor :Move :Dir :Color :Dir :Captured
   PrintBoard
   IfElse Or HorizEdgeP :Move VertEdgeP :Move
      [Make "&EdgePlayable Remove :Move :&EdgePlayable]
      [Make
         "&InnerPlayable
         Remove :Move :&InnerPlayable]
   AddNewMoves :Move
End
```

MakeMove modifies the data structures, the playing board, and several global variables:

- The global variables &CantMove is set back to zero, and the move is placed into the game &Board;

- The game situation is recomputed;
  The captured pieces are turned over;

- The game board is printed out;

- The newly occupied square is removed from the edge or inner list of playable squares;

- The list of the playable squares is extended.

The Computer's Move

```
To Computer :Color
  Make "&CompMoves1 [[] [] [] [] [] []]
  If EmptyP
     PossMoves
        (Sentence :&EdgePlayable :&InnerPlayable)
        :Color
    [Print [Sorry, I cannot move.]
     Make "&CantMove :&CantMove + 1
     Stop]
  EvalMoves :Color
  Local "Move
  Make "Move ChooseMoves
  PrintMove :Move
  MakeMove
     First :Move
     :Color
     First ButFirst :Move
     Last :Move
End

To ChooseMoves
  Output ChooseMoves1 1
End

To ChooseMoves1 :Category
  ; this should never happen
  If :Category > 6 [Output []]
  Local "Moves
  Make "Moves Get "&CompMoves 10 + :Category
  If :Moves = [] [Output ChooseMoves1 :Category + 1]
  Output BestMove :Moves
End

To PrintMove :Move
  Type [Computer Move:]
```

```
Print
  Word
    First
      ButFirst
        Member First First :Move  "1A2B3C4D5E6F7G8H
      Last First :Move
End
```

The selection of a move by the computer follows several hierarchically ordered steps. First, using `EdgeMove` any possible moves along the edge (`EdgePlayable`) are looked at to see if a "great" or even "good" move exists. If none such exist, the possible inner squares are searched (`InnerPlayable`) for other moves using `InnerMove`

```
To EvalMoves :Color
  Make "&HaveGreatMove "False
  Make "&HaveGoodMove "False
  If Not :&EdgePlayable = [ ]
    [EdgeMove :&EdgePlayable]
  If Not
    (Or
      :&InnerPlayable = [ ]
      :&HaveGreatMove
      :&HaveGoodMove)
    [InnerMove :&InnerPlayable]
End

To EdgeMove :Free
  If :Free = [ ] [Stop]
  EdgeMove1 First :Free 1
  Edgemove ButFirst :Free
End

To EdgeMove1 :Move :Dir
  Local "ThisMove
  If :Dir > 8 [Stop]
  Make "ThisMove Poss :Move :Color :Dir
  If Not :ThisMove = [ ] [EvalEdgeClasses :ThisMove]
  EdgeMove1 :Move :Dir + 1
End

To EvalEdgeClasses :Move
  If Class1P First :Move First ButFirst :Move
    [Put "&CompMoves 11 FPut :Move Get "&CompMoves 11
    Make "&HaveGreatMove "True]
  If :&HaveGreatMove [Stop]
  If Class2P First :Move
    [Put "&CompMoves 12 FPut :Move Get "&CompMoves 12
    Make "&HaveGoodMove "True]
  If :&HaveGoodMove [Stop]
  IfElse Class4P First :Move First ButFirst :Move
    [Put "&CompMoves 14 FPut :Move Get "&CompMoves 14]
    [Put "&CompMoves 16 FPut :Move Get "&CompMoves 16]
End
```

With `EdgeMove` and `EvalEdgeClasses` all the possible edge moves are placed in four different categories and stored in `&CompMoves1` in the first, second, fourth, or fifth position. We treat the global variable &CompMoves as a two dimensional array (with only one row), so that we can use the same procedures to access it as we do for &Board.

If there are moves in the first two categories, we do not bother to calculate the rest.

```
To BestMove :Moves
  If (Count :Moves) < 2 [Output First :Moves]
  Output
    Compare First :Moves BestMove ButFirst :Moves
End

To Compare :M1 :M2
  IfElse (Value :M1) > (Value :M2)
    [Output :M1]
    [Output :M2]
End

To Value :Move
  Local "Temp
  Make "Temp Get "&Board First :Move
  If Not NumberP :Temp [Make "Temp 0]
  Output (Last :Move) + :Temp
End
```

The best move within a category is determined by adding the valuation for that square and the number of pieces that will be captured by the move. If no move is found in the first two categories, we search for further possibilities in the inner squares using InnerMove and EvalInnerClasses.

```
To InnerMove :Free
  If :Free = [] [Stop]
  InnerMove1 First :Free 1
  InnerMove ButFirst :Free
End

To InnerMove1 :Move :Dir
  If :Dir > 8 [Stop]
  EvalInnerClasses Poss First :Free :Color :Dir
  InnerMove1 :Move :Dir + 1
End

To EvalInnerClasses :Move
  If :Move = [] [Stop]
  IfElse (Value :Move) > 7
    [Put
       "&CompMoves
       13
       FPutIf :Move Get "&CompMoves 13]
    [Put
       "&CompMoves
       15
       FPutIf :Move Get "&CompMoves 15]
End
```

Categorization of the Possible Moves

The possible moves for the computer are placed into categories according to how favorable they are by `EvalEdgeClasses` (for moves on the edge of the board) and `EvalInnerClasses` (for moves elsewhere on the board).

The categories are based on the following conceptual differences:

(1) Moves to a corner square,

(2) Moves to a edge square that will capture pieces on the edge,

(3) Moves to a square that neighbors a corner that will capture inner pieces,

(4) Moves to edge squares not handled by 1 or 2 that capture inner pieces,

(5) Moves to inner squares with a valuation greater than seven. Furthermore, these moves must fulfill predicates that give some indication about whether the corresponding edge can be dominated by the computer.

In `EvalEdgeClasses` the lists of moves from higher categories are checked: Once at least one move has been found in category 1, no moves will be searched in the lower (2-5) categories; likewise, once at least one move has been found in category 2, no moves will be looked for in the lower (3-5) categories. Said another way, once a good move has been found, only moves that are as good or better are sought.

```
To Class1P :Move :Dir
  ; Is it a corner square ?
  If MemberP :Move [11 18 81 88] [Output "True]
  ; Is it a corner neighbor on the edge ?
  If MemberP :Move [21 71 12 82 17 87 28 78]
    [If OnEdgeP :Move :Dir
        [Output Dominate2P :Move :Dir OppositeDir :Dir]]
  Output OnEdgeP :Move :Dir
End

To Dominate2P :Square :Dir :OppDir
  If (GetSq Neighbor :Square :OppDir) = "X
    [Output "True]
  If (GetSq Neighbor :Square :OppDir) = ".
    [Output Dominate3P Neighbor :Square :Dir :Dir]
  Output AllOccuP Neighbor :Square :Dir :Dir
End

To Dominate3P :Square :Dir
  IfElse (GetSq :Square) = "X
    [Output DominateP Neighbor :Square :Dir :Dir]
    [Output Dominate3P Neighbor :Square :Dir :Dir]
End

To AllOccuP :Square :Dir
  If (GetSq :Square) = ". [Output "False]
```

```
IfElse
   Or
      EqualP GetSq :Square "X
      EqualP GetSq :Square "O
   [Output AllOccuP Neighbor :Square :Dir :Dir]
   [Output "True]
End

To GetSq :Index
   Local "Square
   Make "Square Get "&Board :Index
   If NumberP :Square [Output ".]
   Output :Square
End

To DominateP :Square :Dir
   If (GetSq :Square) = "O [Output "False]
   If (GetSq :Square) = ".
   [Output Not (GetSq Neighbor :Square :Dir) = "X]
   IfElse Not (GetSq :Square) = "X
   [Output "true]
   [Output DominateP Neighbor :Square :Dir :Dir]
End

To OnEdgeP :Square :Dir
   If HorizEdgeP :Square [Output MemberP :Dir 48]
   IfElse VertEdgeP :Square
   [Output MemberP :Dir 26]
   [Output "False]
End

To OppositeDir :Dir
   Output First ButFirst Member :Dir "26624884
End
```

Category 1 contains the following kinds of moves:

(1) Moves to a corner;

(2) Moves to squares that are not corner neighbors on the edge (e.g., C1, D1, E1, F1) that capture pieces along the edge (tested by OnEdgeP);

(3) Moves to corner neighbor's that capture pieces along the edge, if the predicate Dominate2P holds for them; Dominate2P distinguishes three cases:

   a) The corner is already occupied by one of the computer's pieces;

   b) The corner is empty, then Dominate3P must be met; Dominate3P is met if, once another piece belonging to the computer (the "counterpiece" that the play is being made on) is found either all the rest of the pieces on that edge are owned by the computer or if an empty square is found, the next one is not occupied by one of the computer's pieces (which is tested by DominateP);

   c) The corner square is occupied by an opponent's piece, in which case the rest of the edge must already be occupied.

```
To Class2P :Square
  Local "Neighbors
  Local "Dir
  If MemberP :Square [21 71 12 82 17 87 28 78]
    [Output "False]
  IfElse HorizEdgeP :Square
    [Make "Dir 4]
    [Make "Dir 2]
  Make
    "Neighbors
    Word
      GetSq Neighbor :Square :Dir
      GetSq Neighbor :Square OppositeDir :Dir
  If :Neighbors = "OO [Output "True]
  If :Neighbors = "..
    [Output
      Not
        MemberP
          "X
          List
            (GetSq
              Neighbor Neighbor :Square :Dir :Dir)
            (GetSq
              Neighbor
                Neighbor :Square OppositeDir :Dir
                OppositeDir :Dir)]
  If AllOccuP Neighbor :Square :Dir :Dir
    [If AllOccuP
        Neighbor :Square OppositeDir :Dir
        OppositeDir :Dir
        [Output "True]]
  Output Dominate1P :Square :Dir
End

To Dominate1P :Square :Dir
  If DominateP Neighbor :Square :Dir :Dir
    [Output
      DominateP
        Neighbor :Square OppositeDir :Dir
        OppositeDir :Dir]
  Output "False
End
```

For *category 2* moves that are on the edge but not corner neighbors, these additional conditions apply:

(1) If both :Neighbors along the edge are occupied by the opponent, the move can be made,

(2) If both :Neighbors are unoccupied, the move may only be made if none of the neighbors "two doors down" in either direction are occupied by the computer's pieces,

(3) In all other cases, the edge must be dominated by the computer in both direction (tested by Dominate1P).

All the "better" moves to the inner squares are placed in *category 3*; these are moves with a valuation higher than seven (as determined by Value.

Category 4 contains all the moves to corner neighbors, as long as the computer dominates that edge in both directions.

```
To Class4P :Square :Dir
  If OnEdgeP :Square :Dir [Output "False]
  If MemberP :Square [12 17 82 87]
    [Output DominatelP :Square 4]
  IfElse MemberP :Square [21 71 28 78]
    [Output DominatelP :Square 6]
    [Output "False]
End
```

Those moves from the inner squares that do not have valuations greater than seven are placed in *category 5.*

The rest of the moves (all the ''bad'' ones from the edge) are placed in *category 6.*

The following figure illustrates graphically how the moves handled by EdgeMove and InnerMove fall into these categories:

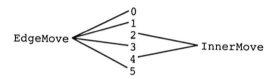

35.6. Final Remarks

The quality of play of this program can be characterized by the following statements:

- It did not lose any of the approximately 50 games played against true novices (people who had never played the game before);

- It lost regularly against practiced REVERSI players when they played seriously;

- It is a worthy opponent for a casual REVERSI player.

The weaknesses of the program lie primarily in that:

- it is not readable,
  only simple game situations are really analyzed, complex dependencies between pieces are not recognized,
  the same strategy is used in all the individual phases of the game (opening, mid-game, end-game); towards the end of the game, the number of captured pieces can be a determining factor in contrast to the beginning of the game.

Exercises

- Add further strategies
- Implement phases of the game
- Modify the rules so that OTHELLO is played instead (more than one direction at a time can be played). How do the strategies need to be modified?

Chapter 36:
Hunting the Wumpus

36.1. The Problem

Let's write a program that makes it possible to play WUMPUS [Yob 75] against the computer. The game can be described as follows:

The Wumpus, a hairy monster who never takes a bath, lives hidden in an underground system of 20 caves interconnected by tunnels. Here is a map of the caves:

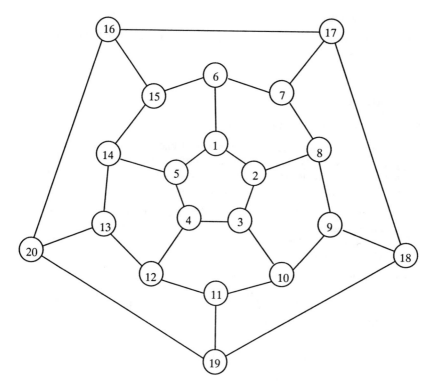

Topologically, this system of caves corresponds to the corners and edges of a dodecahedron. The problem for the player is to track down the Wumpus and shoot him with an arrow without getting gobbled up; the player has 5 arrows in the beginning. The Wumpus is bagged by shooting an arrow from a neighboring cave into the cave that the Wumpus is suspected of hiding in; if the player has no more arrows, she or he is doomed! The player always moves from one cave to a neighboring cave.

In addition to the Wumpus, there are other dangers for the hunter in the system of caves; these are:

- Two caves contain bottomless pits that the hunter should avoid; if you fall in you can never get out.
- In two other caves are enormous bats that will carry the hunter off to some other cave if one of their caves is disturbed; because this could be the cave of the bottomless pit or even that of the Wumpus, there is some small risk if you meet the bats.

Anyway, the hunter is warned ahead of time of these dangers

- The Wumpus can be smelled two caves away (remember, it never takes a bath).
- The squeaking of the bat can be heard from the next cave.
- The pit is identified by the echoing of your footsteps from one cave away.

36.2. Objectives

Here are a few of the interesting aspects of programming the WUMPUS game:

- Because it is a new game and is not well known, you can exercise your creativity by experimenting with various rules; similarly, different interpretations could be placed on the underlying schema (dungeons and dragons, mazes and minotaurs, etc.).
- With such games of chance, simple strategic observations arise that combine logic with probability; for complicated concepts such as "probability" and "risk" simple, intuitive interpretations come from playing the game.
- Especially in the extension of the program presented here in the direction of a WUMPUS expert or even a WUMPUS tutor [Goldstein 82], many interesting problems of knowledge representation and interpretation arise.
- Games like WUMPUS have become popular as video adventure games. This project is a unique venture in building your own video game.

36.3. Examples

The first of these examples is presented without comment. The hunter is about to be consumed by the Wumpus thanks to his own overconfidence.

The second game is interspersed with tactical observations. This should show that a sketch of the cave system with the information that has already been discovered is useful for the determined Wumpus hunter.

```
? Start
*****************************************
You are in cave number: C1
Neighboring caves: C2 C5 C6
You hear a bat squeak!
It smells like a Wumpus here!
Do you want to shoot? no
Which cave do you want to go to? C2

*****************************************
You are in cave number: C2
Neighboring caves: C1 C8 C3
It smells like a Wumpus here!
Do you want to shoot? YES
Into which cave? C3
Missed. You have 4 arrows left.
Shoot again? no
Which cave do you want to go to? C3

*****************************************
You are in cave number: C3
Neighboring caves: C2 C10 C4
It smells like a Wumpus here!
Do you want to shoot? no
Which cave do you want to go to? C4

*****************************************
You are in cave number: C4
You have been eaten by the Wumpus!
```

The second game:

```
? Wumpus
*****************************************
You are in cave number: C20
Neighboring caves: C16 C13 C19
Which cave do you want to go to? C19

*****************************************
You are in cave number: C19
Neighboring caves: C11 C18 C20
Which cave do you want to go to? C18

*****************************************
You are in cave number: C18
Neighboring caves: C17 C19 C9
You hear a bat squeak!
Which cave do you want to go to? C19
```

```
*****************************************
You are in cave number: C19
Neighboring caves: C11 C18 C20
Which cave do you want to go to? C11

*****************************************
You are in cave number: C11
Neighboring caves: C10 C19 C12
You can hear footsteps echoing!
Which cave do you want to go to? C19

*****************************************
You are in cave number: C19
Neighboring caves: C11 C18 C20
Which cave do you want to go to? C20

*****************************************
You are in cave number: C20
Neighboring caves: C16 C13 C19
Which cave do you want to go to? C13

*****************************************
You are in cave number: C13
Neighboring caves: C14 C12 C20
Which cave do you want to go to? C12

*****************************************
You are in cave number: C12
Neighboring caves: C4 C11 C13
Which cave do you want to go to? C11

*****************************************
You are in cave number: C11
Neighboring caves: C10 C19 C12
You can hear footsteps echoing!
```

Apparently this player goes about her work more carefully. As soon as a warning is given she moves backwards, along a known, safe path and tries out another path through the caves. At the same time, she is gathering useful clues: When she was warned of the pit in C11, she knew that it was either in C10 or C12 because she came from C19. During a second approach to C11 via C13, no warning was given, therefore the pit must not be in C12. It can be therefore inferred that C10 contains one of the two bottomless pits.

```
Which cave do you want to go to? C12
*****************************************
You are in cave number: C12
Neighboring caves: C4 C11 C13
Which cave do you want to go to? C4
*****************************************
You are in cave number: C4
Neighboring caves: C3 C12 C5
You hear a bat squeak!
You can hear footsteps echoing!
It smells like a Wumpus here!
Do you want to shoot? no
Which cave do you want to go to? C12
```

```
*******************************************
You are in cave number: C12
Neighboring caves: C4 C11 C13
Which cave do you want to go to? C13

*******************************************
You are in cave number: C13
Neighboring caves: C14 C12 C20
Which cave do you want to go to? C14
```

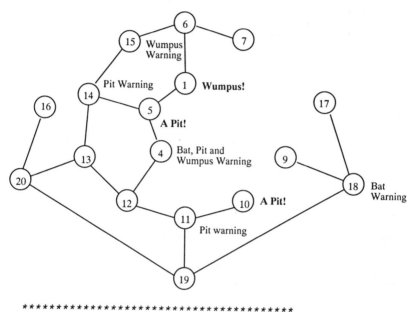

```
*******************************************
You are in cave number: C14
Neighboring caves: C5 C13 C15
You can hear footsteps echoing!
It smells like a Wumpus here!
Do you want to shoot? no
```

Apparently, this hunter is now in an interesting part of the caves, since it seems to be teeming with danger. She is warned about the (second and last) pit in C4 and C14. The only cave that is next to both of these is C5, so it must contain the other bottomless pit.

Even more interesting, to be sure, are warnings given in C4 and C14 about the Wumpus, which must be two caves away. Because no warnings have been given before, the only place that is two caves away that she hasn't been closer than two caves to before is C1. This must be where the Wumpus is! She must be sure to avoid C5 and its bottomless pit on her way there.

Which cave do you want to go to? C15

```
*****************************************
You are in cave number: C15
Neighboring caves: C6 C14 C16
It smells like a Wumpus here!
Do you want to shoot? no
Which cave do you want to go to? C6

*****************************************
You are in cave number: C6
Neighboring caves: C7 C1 C15
It smells like a Wumpus here!
Do you want to shoot? YES
Into which cave? C1

Yes, you got it!!!
```

36.4. Program

Data Structures

The entire system of caves is represented using 20 global variables, whose values are lists of the neighboring caves.

In addition the following global variables that are reinitialized for each game are used:

ArrowCount   The number of remaining arrows (starts at 5)
Pits   A list of the caves that contain the bottomless pits
Wumpus   The Wumpus' cave
YouAreHere   Current location of the hunter
Bats   A list of the bat caves.

Procedures

The procedure Wumpus first initializes the system of caves using DigCaves then uses PlayGame to do the rest of the work.

```
To Wumpus
   DigCaves
   PlayGame
End

To PlayGame
   CreateHazards
   WumpusLoop
   Type [Do you want to play again?]
   IfElse YesP
     [PlayGame]
     [Print "Bye!]
End

To DigCaves
   Make "C1 [C2 C5 C6]
   Make "C2 [C1 C8 C3]
```

```
      Make "C3 [C2 C10 C4]
      Make "C4 [C3 C12 C5]
      Make "C5 [C1 C4 C14]
      Make "C6 [C7 C1 C15]
      Make "C7 [C8 C6 C17]
      Make "C8 [C7 C9 C2]
      Make "C9 [C8 C18 C10]
      Make "C10 [C9 C11 C3]
      Make "C11 [C10 C19 C12]
      Make "C12 [C4 C11 C13]
      Make "C13 [C14 C12 C20]
      Make "C14 [C5 C13 C15]
      Make "C15 [C6 C14 C16]
      Make "C16 [C17 C15 C20]
      Make "C17 [C18 C7 C16]
      Make "C18 [C17 C19 C9]
      Make "C19 [C11 C18 C20]
      Make "C20 [C16 C13 C19]
   End

   To CreateHazards
      Make "Total Random20 6 []
      Make "Bats ButFirst ButFirst ButLast ButLast :Total
      Make "Wumpus First :Total
      Make "YouAreHere First ButFirst :Total
      Make "Pits Sentence Last ButLast :Total Last :Total
      Make "ArrowCount 5
   End

   To Random20 :N :Avoid
      If :N = 0 [Output []]
      Make "Suggestion Word "C Rand20
      If MemberP :Suggestion :Avoid
         [Output Random20 :N :Avoid]
      Output
         FPut
            :Suggestion
            Random20 :N - 1 FPut :Suggestion :Avoid
   End

   To Rand20
      Output 1 + Random 20
   End
```

In CreateHazards a six element list of random caves is generated that is then used to set up the locations of the dangers and the initial position of the hunter.

```
? Print Random20 6 []
C15 C6 C8 C17 C20 C3
? Print Random20 6 []
C2 C18 C4 C19 C20 C8
```

The six elements of this list are assigned to the hazards in the following way:

1st Element: Wumpus

2nd Element: YouAreHere

3rd and 4th Element: `Bats`

5th and 6th Element: The bottomless `Pits`

Finally the number of arrows left (the hazards for the Wumpus, so to speak) is initialized to 5.

```
To WumpusLoop
   PrintStars 40
   Print
      Sentence [You are in cave number:] :YouAreHere
   If InThePitsP [Stop]
   If WumpusHereP [Stop]
   If BatsCaveP [WumpusLoop]
   Print
      Sentence [Neighboring caves:] Thing :YouAreHere
   If WarningsP [Stop]
   Make "YouAreHere NewPlace
   WumpusLoop
End

To PrintStars :N
   Print "
   Repeat :N [Type "*]
   Print "
End

To NewPlace
   Type [Which cave do you want to go to?]
   Make "NewCave First ReadList
   IfElse MemberP :NewCave Thing :YouAreHere
      [Output :NewCave]
      [Print [You can't get there from here!!]
       Output NewPlace]
End
```

The procedure `WumpusLoop` contains the basic game control and recurses repeatedly until one of the four possible fates is met (Wumpus eats hunter, Hunter shoots Wumpus, Hunter falls into the bottomless pit (maybe that one should be an infinite recursion), or the hunter has no more arrows). If any of these cases returns `True`, the recursion stops and the game is over.

These are the basic steps that occur for each move:

- To make the printout more readable, a row of stars is printed out before each move.

- The player (hunter) is told the current location.

- The program checks whether the player has walked into a bottomless pit or into the cave of a bat or the Wumpus; depending on what happens here, normal play will continue, the game is over, or the player is moved to another cave.

```
To InThePitsP
   If MemberP :YouAreHere :Pits
      [Print [You fell into a bottomless pit!]
       Print [The game is over!]
       Output "True]
   Output "False
End

To BatsCaveP
   If Not MemberP :YouAreHere :Bats [Output "False]
   Print [You walked into a bats cave!]
   Print [It carries you off!!]
   Make
      "YouAreHere
      First Random20 1 List :YouAreHere []
   Output "True
End

To WumpusHereP
   If :Wumpus = :YouAreHere
      [Print [You have been eaten by the Wumpus!]
       Output "True]
   Output "False
End
```

• The player is informed what the neighboring caves are:

```
To Vicinity :Caves :N
   If :Caves = [] [Output []]
   If :N = 0 [Output :Caves]
   Output
      (Sentence First :Caves
         Vicinity Thing First :Caves :N - 1
         Vicinity ButFirst :Caves :N)
End
```

• The hunter is warned about the appropriate dangers.

```
To WarningsP
   If MemberP :YouAreHere Vicinity :Bats 1
      [Print [You hear a bat squeak!]]
   If MemberP :YouAreHere Vicinity :Pits 1
      [Print [You can hear footsteps echoing!]]
   If Not
      MemberP :YouAreHere Vicinity FPut :Wumpus [] 2
      [Output "False]
   Print [It smells like a Wumpus here!]
   Type [Do you want to shoot?]
   If YesP [Output ShootP]
   Output "False
End
```

• The player is asked for the next destination and the procedure WumpusLoop is called again.

The list of the endangered caves for all three types of hazards are calculated using Vicinity; caves with a distance of one from C1 are shown by a dot in the following diagram, caves with a distance of two are shown with a small square.

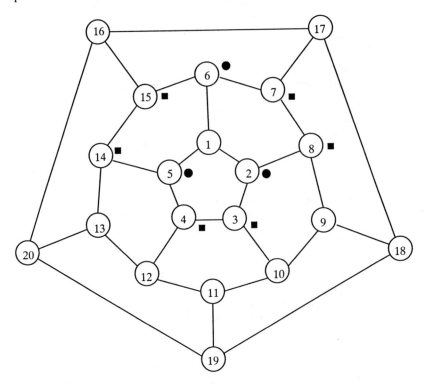

A couple of examples should illustrate how this procedure works:

```
? Print Vicinity [C1] 2
C1 C2 C1 C8 C3 C5 C1 C4 C14 C6 C7 C1 C15
? Print Vicinity [C16] 1
C16 C17 C15 C20
```

If the danger is the bats or pits the warning message is printed out. If the Wumpus is nearby, the player is asked whether she wants to shoot the wumpus, and ShootP is called depending on the answer.

```
To ShootP
   Type [Into which cave?]
   Make "Goal First ReadList
   If Not MemberP :Goal Thing :YouAreHere
     [Print
        Sentence :Goal [is not a neighboring cave!!!]
      Output ShootP]
   If :Wumpus = :Goal
     [Print "
      Print [Yes, you got it!!!]
      Output "True]
```

```
Make "ArrowCount :ArrowCount - 1
If :ArrowCount = 0
   [Print [You have no arrows left!]
    Output "True]
Print
   (Sentence [Missed. You have] :ArrowCount
    [arrows left.])
Type [Shoot again?]
If YesP [Output ShootP]
Output "False
End
```

ShootP asks the hunter (possibly repeatedly) which cave she wants to shoot into, and ends the game by returning the value True if the Wumpus is bagged, or if the hunter is out of arrows.

36.5. Possible Extensions

As already indicated in section 36.2, this game is well suited for experimentation, because there are really no "standard rules" for the game. Some possible modifications are:

- The structure of the labyrinth

- The number of caves

- The number of hazards

- The number of arrows allowed

- The strength of the bow (the arrows could go farther than just one cave)

- The strength of the Wumpus (it could take several shots to bring it down)

- The introduction of different sorts of hazards

- An external representation of the labyrinth

- Allow the wumpus to move.

A large extension to the system would be to attempt to write a program that can play the role of the hunter optimally; there are easily a couple of conceivable versions:

- A version with knowledge about the overall structure of the labyrinth

- A version with no knowledge about the overall structure of the labyrinth

In the last version in particular, the knowledge of a good wumpus hunter would have to be made explicit (see the example in section 36.3). It may not make much sense to have computer play a game against itself: Consider that such a WUMPUS expert could be used as a component of a system to teach the beginning or advanced player how to play the game well.

Chapter 37:
HOW THE WEST WAS WON

37.1. The Problem

This chapter deals with a program that allows the game HOW THE WEST WAS WON [Brown et al. 75] to be played with the computer acting as a player.

The game, whose board layout is shown in figure 37-1, was a computer game developed as part of the PLATO project [Dugdale, Kibbey 77].

The games goes like this: One player moves forward using a stagecoach, and the other with a locomotive. The winner is the one who goes from the starting position (Tombstone) to the ending position (Red Gulch) first. Each move consists of two steps:

- Three random values are generated each from the sets $a = [1 \ 2 \ 3]$, $b = [0 \ 1 \ 2 \ 3 \ 4]$, and $c = [1 \ 2 \ 3 \ 4 \ 5 \ 6 \ 7]$, respectively

- The player whose turn it is combines the three values with two of the three arithmetic operators +, -, *, /, to obtain an arithmetic expression. Each operator can only be used once in each move; the value of the arithmetic expression gives the number of spaces that the player can move if he can calculate the value correctly.

In addition, there are special positions on the game board:

(1) **Cities:** if a player lands directly in a city, he can move ahead to the next city.

(2) **Short Cuts:** if the player lands directly at the entrance to one of these, he can move ahead to the end of that short cut.

(3) **"Bumping":** if a player lands directly on a space already occupied by his opponent, he can send the opponent back (at most) two cities. If a player is in a city, he cannot be "bumped."

The winner is the one who lands directly on final position (70)

37.2. Objectives

Originally this game was a drill program for the four basic arithmetic operations; it can also serve that purpose for us. In addition, however, it is also interesting because its rules are easy to learn, and strategic and probability theoretic

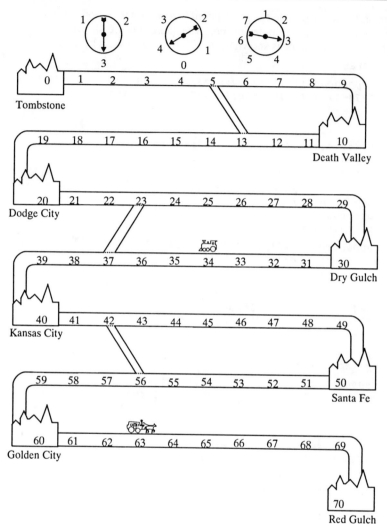

Figure 37–1: HOW THE WEST WAS WON

considerations are combined in an interesting way. An interesting programming technique is the use of the Run command to check the correctness of the arithmetic expression given by the player.

37.3. Example

In the following example the game board is represented by rows of numbers, the cities are located at multiples of ten. The short cuts are shown by arrows; the computer's game piece is shown by a "C" and the player's by a "P".

```
? Start
00000000001111111111222222222233333333333
01234567890123456789012345678901234567890123456789
    -------->             -------------->
P
C
44444444445555555555566666666666
01234567890123456789012345678901234567890F
    -------------->

Do you want to go first? yes
Your numbers: 3 1 2
Construct an expression: 3*2-1
Its value: 5
00000000001111111111222222222233333333333
01234567890123456789012345678901234567890123456789
    -------->             -------------->
                P
C
44444444445555555555566666666666
01234567890123456789012345678901234567890F
    -------------->

My numbers: 3 0 2
My expression: 2+3-0
00000000001111111111222222222233333333333
01234567890123456789012345678901234567890123456789
    -------->             -------------->
P
                C
44444444445555555555566666666666
01234567890123456789012345678901234567890F
    -------------->

Your numbers: 3 1 4
Construct an expression: 3*4-1
Its value: 11
00000000001111111111222222222233333333333
01234567890123456789012345678901234567890123456789
    -------->             -------------->
        P
                C
44444444445555555555566666666666
01234567890123456789012345678901234567890F
    -------------->

My numbers: 3 1 5
My expression: 5+3-1
```

```
00000000001111111111222222222233333333333
01234567890123456789012345678901234567889
--------->               -------------->
         P
                                         C
4444444444555555555556666666666
01234567890123456789012345678901234567889F
-------------->

Your numbers: 2  0  4
Construct an expression: 2*4+0
Its value: 8

00000000001111111111222222222223333333333
01234567890123456789012345678901234567889
--------->               -------------->
         P
                                         C
4444444444555555555556666666666
01234567890123456789012345678901234567889F
-------------->

My numbers: 3  4  7
My expression: 3+7*4

00000000001111111111222222222223333333333
01234567890123456789012345678901234567889
--------->               -------------->
         P
4444444444555555555556666666666
01234567890123456789012345678901234567889F
-------------->
                         C
Your numbers: 1  0  2
Construct an expression: 2-1+0
Its value.0: 1

00000000001111111111222222222223333333333
01234567890123456789012345678901234567889
--------->               -------------->
                                     P
4444444444555555555556666666666
01234567890123456789012345678901234567889F
-------------->
                         C
My numbers: 2  2  4
My expression: 4+2*2

00000000001111111111222222222223333333333
01234567890123456789012345678901234567889
--------->               -------------->
                                     P
4444444444555555555556666666666
01234567890123456789012345678901234567889F
-------------->
```

```
                                   C
Your numbers: 3 0 3
Construct an expression: 3*3+0
Its value: 9

00000000001111111111222222222233333333333
0123456789012345678901234567890123456789
-------->              -------------->
                                         P

444444444455555555556666666666
0123456789012345678901234567890123456789F
-------------->
                                   C
My numbers: 3 1 4
My expression: 4/1-3

00000000001111111111222222222233333333333
0123456789012345678901234567890123456789
-------->              -------------->
                                         P

444444444455555555556666666666
0123456789012345678901234567890123456789F
-------------->
                                   C
I win!
```

37.4. The Program

Data Structures

The data structures of this implementation are rudimentary: The current positions of the computer and player are stored as the property "Position on the names "Player and "Computer; all the rest of the information that could be stored in data structures (primarily the position of the cities, and short cuts) are implicitly represented in the procedures, especially in JumpAhead:

```
To JumpAhead :Position
  If MemberP :Position [10 20 30 40 50 60]
    [Output :Position + 10]
  If MemberP :Position [5 23 42]
    [Output Nth 2 Member :Position [5 13 23 37 42 56]]
  Output :Position
End

? Print JumpAhead 10
20
? Print JumpAhead 13
13
? Print JumpAhead 23
37
```

The use of the procedures FinishedP, CityP, OccupiedP, and BumpBack as well as Modify to check and modify these data structures is described later.

```
To FinishedP :Player
  Output 70 = GetProp :Player "Position
End

To CityP :Position
  Output 0 = Remainder :Position 10
End

To BumpBack :Player
  Local "PP
  Make "PP GetProp :Player "Position
  IfElse :PP < 20
    [PutProp :Player "Position 0]
    [PutProp
       :Player
       "Position
       :PP - 10 - Remainder :PP 10]
End

To OccupiedP :Position :Player
  Output :Position = GetProp :Player "Position
End
```

The procedure BumpBack changes the position of the player by sending him back (at most) two cities.

Procedures

Arithmetic Expressions

In contrast to the original game, we do not allow parentheses in the arithmetic expressions; this makes things a great deal easier. The following table shows the possible combinations of two out of four operators with three numbers.

2nd Operator

		+	-	*	/
	+		X	X	X
1st Operator	-	X		X	X
	*	X	X		X
	/	X	X	X	

By using commutativity and thereby exchanging arguments, the number of possibilities combinations can be reduced from twelve to eight (for example, c+a-b is the same as as a+b-c). For our purposes, these are the possible forms of arithmetic expressions:

a + b * c   a - b * c
a + b - c   a - b / c
a + b / c   a * b - c
a / b - c   a * b / c

With all these combinations of two different operators, the operands could also be exchanged with six different permutations (see `Possibilities`), so that with three numbers and two operators there are altogether at most 6 * 8 = 48 different expressions that can be formed.

In addition to generating the possible operator and argument combinations as described, the corresponding value is calculated by `Possibilities`, `Expression`, and `Eval` (in the first line of `Eval`); should the generated expression contain the division operator, it must also be made sure that the divisor is not zero (this is why the two conditions are placed in `Expression`).

A few of the other complications and restrictions arise because the result of the expression must always be a whole number; for this reason expressions such as 2*3/5 need to be thrown out; this is done by the first couple of tests in `Eval` that make sure that only division without a remainder is being performed. Another restriction is that the value of the generated expression cannot be less than zero (moves must always be forward); this is checked by the last test in `Eval`.

```
? Print Possibilities 3 4 5
23 3+4*5   2 3+4-5   7 3*4-5 23 3+5*4   4 3+5-4
11 3*5-4 19 4+3*5   2 4+3-5   7 4*3-5 19 4+5*3
6  4+5-3 17 4*5-3 17 5+3*4   4 5+3-4 11 5*3-4  1

To Possibilities :A :B :C
   Output
     (Sentence
        Expression :A :B :C
        Expression :A :C :B
        Expression :B :A :C
        Expression :B :C :A
        Expression :C :A :B
        Expression :C :B :A)
End

To Expression :A :B :C
   Local "T1
   Local "T2
   Local "T3
   Make
     "T1
     (Sentence
        Eval "+ "* 0
        Eval "+ "- 0
        Eval "- "* 0
        Eval "* "- 0)
   IfElse :C > 0
     [Make
        "T2
        (Sentence
           Eval "+ "/ 0
           Eval "- "/ 0
           Eval "* "/ 0)]
     [Make "T2 []]
```

```
IfElse :B > 0
   [Make "T3 Eval "/ "- 0]
   [Make "T3 []]
Output (Sentence :T1 :T2 :T3)
End

To Eval :S1 :S2 :Result
Make "Result Run (List :A :S1 :B :S2 :C)
If :S1 = "/
   [If Not Remainder :A :B = 0 [Output []]]
If :S2 = "/
   [IfElse :S1 = "*
      [If Not Remainder (:A * :B) :C = 0
         [Output []]]
      [If Not Remainder :B :C = 0 [Output []]]]
IfElse :Result > 0
   [Output
      Sentence :Result (Word :A :S1 :B :S2 :C)]
   [Output []]
End
```

The procedure RemoveRepeats is used to eliminate all but one of any of a group of expressions that yield the same result.

```
To RemoveRepeats :List
   If :List = [] [Output []]
   If MemberP First :List ButFirst :List
      [Output
         RemoveRepeats ButFirst ButFirst :List]
   Output
      FPut
         First :List
         FPut
            First ButFirst :List
            RemoveRepeats ButFirst ButFirst :List
End
```

To place the list of possible combinations, we can use the procedure WestSort that is similar to the InsertionSort presented in the chapter 18.

```
To WestSort :List
   If (Count :List) = 2 [Output :List]
   Output
      WestInsert
         Sentence First :List First ButFirst :List
         WestSort ButFirst ButFirst :List
End

To WestInsert :List1 :List2
   If :List2 = [] [Output :List1]
   If (First :List1) < (First :List2)
      [Output
         (Sentence
            First :List2
            First ButFirst :List2
            WestInsert :List1 ButFirst ButFirst :List2)]
```

```
      Output Sentence :List1 :List2
   End
```

The Course of the Game

```
To West
  PutProp "Computer "Position 0
  PutProp "Player "Position 0
  GameBoard
  Type [Do you want to go first?]
  IfElse YesP
    [Make "WhoseMove "Player]
    [Make "WhoseMove "Computer]
  OneTurn
End

To OneTurn
  Run
    (List
      :WhoseMove
      1 + Random 3
      Random 5
      1 + Random 7)
  GameBoard
  If FinishedP :WhoseMove
    [IfElse :WhoseMove = "Player
      [Print [You win!]]
      [Print [I win!]]
    Stop]
  TakeTurns
End

To TakeTurns
  Make "WhoseMove Opponent :WhoseMove
  OneTurn
End
```

Start sets up the environment for the game, allows the user to decide who goes first (the computer or the player), and then calls OneTurn to handle the move of the player WhoseMove it is. TakeTurns handles switching whose move it is and invoking OneTurn for the next player.

The Player's Move

```
To Player :A :B :C
  Local "Expr
  Local "Result
  Print (Sentence [Your numbers:] :A :B :C)
  Type [Construct an expression:]
  Make "Expr First ReadList
```

```
IfElse ProperP :Expr
   [IfElse MoveTooLong :Expr
      [Type
          [That move would take you too far, try again]
       Player :A :B :C
       Stop]
      [Type [Its value:]
       Make "Result First ReadList]]
   [Print [Improper expression!]
    Player :A :B :C
    Stop]
   IfElse :Result = Run :Expr
      [Modify "Player :Result]
      [Print [Result is incorrect, Move forfeited!]]
End
```

A good portion of the routines that handle the play of the user function as the referee and test the validity (with respect to the rules) of the expression that the user gives and the correctness of the result. The validity test is handled by ProperP, which uses SameP and LeftOutExprs.

A valid expression must meet several criteria:

- It must contain exactly 5 characters (first condition in ProperP);

- The numbers used must agree with those selected randomly and given to the user (second condition); their order may be different;

- The given combination of numbers and operators must be possible, which is, it must either belong to the set calculated by Expression (that is also used by the computer to figure out all the possible moves) or it must belong to the set calculated by LeftOutExprs. The procedure LeftOutExprs calculates all the expressions that are not considered by the computer because of the commutativity of addition and multiplication.

```
To ProperP :Expr
   If Not (Count :Expr) = 5 [Output "False]
   If Not
       SameP
          (Sentence :A :B :C)
          (Sentence
            First :Expr
            First ButFirst ButFirst :Expr
            Last :Expr)
      [Output "False]
   If (MemberP
         :Expr
         (LeftOutExprs
           First :Expr
           First ButFirst ButFirst :Expr
           Last :Expr))
      [Output "True]
```

```
    Output
      MemberP
        :Expr
        Expression
          First :Expr
          First ButFirst ButFirst :Expr
          Last :Expr
End

To SameP :List1 :List2
  If :List1 = [] [Output :List2 = []]
  Output
    SameP
      ButFirst :List1
      Remove First :List1 :List2
End

To Remove :Element :List
  If :List = [] [Output []]
  If :Element = First :List
    [Output ButFirst :List]
  Output
    Sentence
      First :List
      Remove :Element ButFirst :List
End

To LeftOutExprs :A :B :C :T1 :T2
  Make "T1 (Sentence Eval "- "+ 0 Eval "* "+ 0)
  If :B > 0
    [Make "T2 Sentence Eval "/ "+ 0 Eval "/ "* 0]
  Output Sentence :T1 :T2
End
```

In addition to these criteria, which are independent of the actual game situation, MoveTooLong tests to see whether the actual player position plus the value of the expression is less than 70, so that the move doesn't go off the end of the board.

```
To MoveTooLong :Expr
  Output
    GreaterP
      (GetProp "Player "Position) + Run :Expr
      71
End
```

The move is made by Modify, which also takes care of jumping ahead and bumping the opponent back if necessary.

```
To Modify :Player :Result
  PutProp
    :Player
    "Position
    JumpAhead :Result + GetProp :Player "Position
  If CityP GetProp :Player "Position [Stop]
```

```
      If OccupiedP
         GetProp :Player "Position
         Opponent :Player
         [BumpBack Opponent :Player]
      End

      To Opponent :Player
         IfElse :Player = "Player
         [Output "Computer]
         [Output "Player]
      End
```

The Computer's Moves

```
      To Computer :A :B :C
         Local "Poss
         Print (Sentence [My numbers:] :A :B :C)
         Make
            "Poss
            RemoveLongMoves
               WestSort
                  PossibleGoals
                     RemoveRepeats Possibilities :A :B :C
         If MemberP 70 :Poss
         [Execute Nth 2 Member 70 :Poss
          Stop]
         If MemberP GetProp "Player "Position :Poss
         [Execute
            Nth 2 Member GetProp "Player "Position :Poss
          Stop]
         If :Poss = [] [Print [I can't move!]
                        Stop]
         Execute First ButFirst :Poss
      End
```

When the `Computer` moves, all the possible moves mentioned so far are considered. This list is modified somewhat by `PossibleGoals` and `RemoveLongMoves`.

```
      To PossibleGoals :Poss
         If :Poss = [] [Output []]
         Output
            (Sentence
             JumpAhead
               (GetProp "Computer "Position) + First :Poss
             First ButFirst :Poss
             PossibleGoals ButFirst ButFirst :Poss)
      End

      To RemoveLongMoves :Poss
         ; Remember, this assumes the list is sorted!
         If :Poss = [] [Output []]
         IfElse (First :Poss) > 70
         [Output RemoveLongMoves ButFirst ButFirst :Poss]
         [Output :Poss]
      End
```

Rather than (distance, expression) pairs :Poss contains the field that is reachable by the move next to the expression; also, the moves that would go beyond the end of the board are removed. The computer's strategy consists of a hierarchy of conditions:

- If I can win the game, do that;

- If I can send the opponent back, then do that;

- Otherwise, try to move as far as possible.

```
To Execute :Expr
   Print Sentence [My expression:] :Expr
   Modify "Computer Run FPut :Expr []
End
```

The strategy used by the computer here is not optimal and can therefore be improved; for example, the computer "thoughtlessly" moves to spaces immediately in front of the opponent where the danger of being sent back is higher. How far in front of the opponent is "safe"? This would be a good place to apply some probability theory based on the likelihood that the expressions based on the combinations of randomly selected numbers would yield a certain move. A simulation might be useful to determine what the optimal solution would be.

Printing out the Game Board

```
To GameBoard
   Print "
   Print "00000000001111111111222222222233333333333
   Repeat 4 [Type "0123456789]
   Print "
   Type Spaces 5
   Type "-------->
   Type Spaces 9
   Print "-------------->
   Print1
   Print "444444444455555555556666666666
   Repeat 3 [Type "0123456789]
   Print "F
   Type Spaces 2
   Print "-------------->
   Print2
End

To Print1
   IfElse (GetProp "Player "Position) < 40
     [AheadTo GetProp "Player "Position
      Print "P]
     [Print "]
   IfElse (GetProp "Computer "Position) < 40
     [AheadTo GetProp "Computer "Position
      Print "C]
     [Print "]
End
```

```
To Print2
  IfElse (GetProp "Player "Position) > 39
    [AheadTo (GetProp "Player "Position) - 40
    Print "P]
    [Print "]
  IfElse (GetProp "Computer "Position) > 39
    [AheadTo (GetProp "Computer "Position) - 40
    Print "C]
    [Print "]
End

To AheadTo :N
  Repeat :N [Type Spaces 1]
End
```

These procedures represent a simple solution for presenting the game board and could certainly be improved, This can be done attractively if the full graphics capabilities of your LOGO system are used.

37.5. Final Remarks

Here are a few of the most important possibilities for further work offered by this version of the program:

• Parentheses should be allowed in expressions.

• The output of the game board could be made more readable and attractive.

• The structure of the game board (size, shortcuts, etc) should be selectable or randomly generated according to some rules.

• The computers strategy should be optimized.

• The users playing could be compared to optimal play to build a tutoring capability into the system (see [Burton, Brown 82]).

Chapter 38:

BLACKJACK

38.1. The Problem

BLACKJACK is a card game that is played in most casinos today but is also suitable for playing at home with play money. The program discussed in this section simulates the dealer (an employee of the casino). The rules for BLACKJACK vary a little from country to country as well as from casino to casino. Figure 38–1 shows the BLACKJACK rules from a major Las Vegas casino. These are the rules we use as the basis for our program.

Our program:

- Shuffles the cards,
- Allows the players to place imaginary wagers,
- Deals the cards to the players in accordance with their wishes,
- Gives itself cards according to the dealer's rules,
- Detects situations where doubling is appropriate as well as when the user "busts,"
- Determines whether each player has won or lost, and handles computation of losses or winnings.

Here is a sample run of the program:

```
? Start
Cards are being........shuffled!
How many players? 2

*** *** *** *** *** *** *** *** ***

Player 1 bets: 20
Player 2 bets: 30
Cards for Player 1 : A J --> BJ
Cards for Player 2 : Q 9 --> 19
My exposed card: 4

Cards for Player 2 : Q 9 --> 19
More cards? no

My cards: 7 4 --> 11
I draw again!
My cards: J 7 4 --> 21

        Here is how things stand:
```

Blackjack without face card.

A soft seventeen.

Blackjack with face card.

If you split aces, you get one hit on each.

You may split this hand.

You may double down on this hand.

Blackjack

Blackjack is the casino's most popular card game, adapted from a version of the French game vingt-et-un, or "21".

In Blackjack, or "21," each Player's wager is a bet against the Dealer's hand. The object of this game is in have the total point value of the cards dealt to you exceed the Point value of the Dealer's hand without going over 21. If you go over 21 or "bust," your hand breaks and you automatically lose, even if the Dealer subsequently goes bust. Each card takes the numerical value of the card except for Kings, Queens, and Jacks, which count as 10. The Ace counts either as 1 or 11, whichever you choose.

After you place your wager, the Dealer starts the game by dealing one card to each Player face up and one card to himself/herself faceup. The Dealer then deals a second card to each Player face up but deals his/her second card face down and places the card underneath the first card. If you feel you need additional cards to beat the Dealer, you gesture for each card (called "hits") until you are satisfied with your hand and decide to "stand". After all the Players have completed their hands, the Dealer checks his/her hand. The Dealer must draw a card on any Point total 0f 16 or less and stand on any point total of 17 or more. If a Dealer's point count exceeds 21 he busts and all Players whose point count is 21 or less wins. Otherwise, the Dealer compares his/her hand to each Player's Point total and takes all bets that are less. When your point total is the same as the Dealer's you "push" and the Dealer leaves your wager. All winning bets are paid one-to-one.

SURRENDER

Players have the option of surrendering one-half their original wager only after receiving their first two cards. By surrendering, your cards and half of your wager are taken by the dealer.

BLACKJACK

If your initial two cards total 21, any Ace with a 10, Jack, Queen, or King, you have a Blackjack. If both you and the Dealer have a Blackjack, it is a standoff or "push". A Dealer's Blackjack (two card point total of 21) beats a Player's three card point total of 21. A winning Blackjack is paid 3 to 2.

INSURANCE

If the Dealer's face up card is an Ace, you may elect to take insurance after the initial deal. The insurance bet is a wager that the Dealer has a Blackjack. In other words, you are betting the Dealer's face down card will be a 10, Jack, Queen, or King. You may bet up to one-half of your original bet. Insurance bets pay 2 to 1 if the Dealer has a Blackjack, but lose in all other instances.

SPLITTING PAIRS

If your first two cards have the same numerical value, you may split them into two hands. The bet on the second hand must equal the original bet. Only after the first hand is played and completed may you play on the second hand. A split hand may be split up to a total of four times. If the split pair are Aces you are limited to a one card draw on each hand. If the Dealer gets a Blackjack, you lose the money wagered on the original bet only.

DOUBLING DOWN

After receiving your first two cards, or the first two cards of any split pair (except Blackjack), you may elect to wager an additional amount not to exceed the value of the original bet. With a double down, you are allowed to draw only one additional card. If the Dealer gets a Blackjack, the Dealer collects only the amount of the original wager.

Remember, you should indicate your decision to hit or stand with hand signals. Decisions to split pairs, double down or take insurance should be indicated verbally. The Dealer is the only person allowed to remove or alter the location of the cards. the responsibility for correctly computing the point count of the Player's hand lies solely with the Player. If you're unsure of any betting methods or Player's etiquette, please ask your Dealer. And most importantly, have fun.

Figure 38–1: An Excerpt from a Casino's Gaming Guide, Showing BLACKJACK Rules

```
Player 1 : BJ --> 0 +30 = 30
Player 2 : 19 --> 0 -30 = -30
Dealer: 21 --> 0
Play again? yes

*** *** *** *** *** *** *** *** ***

Player 1 bets: 60
Player 2 bets: 20
Cards for Player 1 : J A --> BJ
Cards for Player 2 : 8 8 --> 16
My exposed card: Q

Cards for Player 2 : 8 8 --> 16
More cards? no

My cards: K Q --> 20

    Here is how things stand:

Player 1 : BJ --> 30 +90 = 120
Player 2 : 16 --> -30 -20 = -50
Dealer: 20 --> -70
Play again? yes
*** *** *** *** *** *** *** *** ***

Player 1 bets: 100
Player 2 bets: 10
Cards for Player 1 : K 4 --> 14
Cards for Player 2 : 7 10 --> 17
My exposed card: 3

Cards for Player 1 : K 4 --> 14
More cards? yes
Cards for Player 1 : 10 K 4 --> busts

Cards for Player 2 : 7 10 --> 17
More cards? no

My cards: 6 3 --> 9
I draw again!
My cards: 3 6 3 --> 12
I draw again!
My cards: 8 3 6 3 --> 20

    Here is how things stand:

Player 1 : busts --> 120 -100 = 20
Player 2 : 17 --> -50 -10 = -60
Dealer: 20 --> 40
Play again? no
```

38.2. Objectives

The goals we pursue in this case study are:

(1) to render a complex but comprehendable rule system as a program,

(2) to discuss some of the basic rules of casino games and probability theory

(3) present a subject that on the, one the hand, is easy to understand but, on the other hand, cannot be analyzed to the point that permits a computer simulation of human insight.

38.3. The Dialog for BLACKJACK

BLACKJACK programs exist not only for almost all computers, but also for video games. As with all our examples, we are less interested in providing a finished product to play with than with the design and implementation of the program itself, and providing a framework that you can build upon. This program should describe the individual processes of BLACKJACK as realistically as possible. In order to make things as straightforward as possible in this initial system, we do not support splitting.

Data Structures

Our data structure is constructed so that each player is represented by a list with four elements, with the dealer represented as Player 0.

The four elements have the following meaning:

- The first element contains the players hand,
- The second element contains the numerical value of the hand (with special notations for special situations),
- The third element contains the current bet,
- The fourth element contains the total winnings (or losses) up to this point.

The individual elements are accessed with the aid of the following procedures:

```
To GetHand :Player
   Output First GetAll :Player
End

To PutHand :Player :Hand
   PutAll :Player FPut :Hand ButFirst GetAll :Player
End

To GetValue :Player
   Output First ButFirst GetAll :Player
End

To PutValue :Player :Value
   PutAll
     :Player
     FPut
       First GetAll :Player
       FPut :Value ButFirst ButFirst GetAll :Player
End
```

Here are some examples using the preceding information to illustrate how these functions work.

```
? Print GetHand 1
K 8
? PutHand 1 "K
? Print GetAll 1
[K K 8] [18] 100 10
? Print GetValue 2
BJ
? PutHand 2 Sentence "A GetHand 2
? Print GetAll 2
[A A J] [BJ] 15 -45
? Print GetAll 3
[Q 9] [19] 20 -40
```

The rest of the data access functions:

```
To GetBet :Player
   Output Last ButLast GetAll :Player
End

To PutBet :Player :Bet
  PutAll
    :Player
    LPut
      Last GetAll :Player
      LPut :Bet ButLast ButLast GetAll :Player
End

To GetAccount :Player
  Output Last GetAll :Player
End

To PutAccount :Player :Money
  PutAll
    :Player
    Sentence ButLast GetAll :Player :Money
End

To GetAll :Player
  Output Thing Word "&Player. :Player
End

To PutAll :Player :Info
  Make Word "&Player. :Player :Info
End
```

Cards sets up an additional global variable &Cards that contains a list that represents the deck of cards. This deck is shuffled at the beginning of and appropriate during the game.

```
To Cards
  Output
    [2  4  5  10 7  6  3  K  8  A  J  Q  9
     3  2  4  6  5  7  J  A  8  Q  9  K  10
     4  2  3  7  5  6  8  10 K  9  J  A  Q
     2  3  10 4  6  7  5  Q  J  A  K  8  9]
End
```

```
To Shuffle
  Make "&Cards Cards
  Type [Cards are being]
  Repeat Random 10
    [Type ".
    Make
      "&Cards
      Insert
        First :&Cards
        ButFirst :&Cards
        1 + Random 52]
  Print "Shuffled!
End
```

Playing the Game

A game begins with a call to the procedure BlackJack:

```
To BlackJack
  Shuffle
  Type [How many players?]
  Make "&NumberOfPlayers First ReadList
  Loop
    "I
    0
    :&NumberOfPlayers
    [PutAll :I [[] [0] 0 0]]
  PlayGame
End
```

```
To PlayGame
  Print "
  Print [*** *** *** *** *** *** *** *** ***]
  Print "
  If (Count :&Cards) < (:&NumberOfPlayers * 4)
    [Shuffle]
  Loop "I 0 :&NumberOfPlayers [DBInit :I]
  Loop "I 1 :&NumberOfPlayers [PlaceBet :I]
  Loop "I 1 :&NumberOfPlayers [Deal2Cards :I]
  DealerDraws
  Loop "I 1 :&NumberOfPlayers [Hit :I]
  If (not AllBust :&NumberOfPlayers) [DealerPlays]
  Standings :&NumberOfPlayers
  Type [Play again?]
  If YesP [PlayGame]
End
```

The first part of BlackJack sets the system up, shuffles the cards, asks how many players are playing, etc., and then calls PlayGame, which takes care of each round of play. Before the cards are dealt, PlayGame checks to see whether there are at least four times as many cards as there are players (if not the deck is shuffled). The players are then asked to place their bets, the first two cards are dealt, and then the dealer deals its exposed card. After that each player is asked if she or he wants anymore cards (Hit) until she or he says "no" or until she or he "busts." If not all of the players have "gone bust," the dealer plays, and then the results are tabulated. Finally the players (collectively) are asked if they want to play another hand.

The procedure DBInit serves to initialize a hand for a new game (it is called repeatedly to initialize all the hands):

```
To DBInit :I
   PutHand :I []
   PutValue :I [0]
End
```

The procedure PlaceBet is called until the player places a bet of at least 10 dollars:

```
To PlaceBet :Player
   Type (Sentence "Player :Player "bets)
   Make "Answer First ReadList
   If Or (:Answer = 0) Not (Remainder :Answer 10) = 0
     [PlaceBet :Player
      Stop]
   PutBet :Player :Answer
End
```

Deal2Cards gives the player two cards, using TakeCard to remove a card from the deck.

```
To Deal2Cards :I
   PutHand
     :I
     (Sentence
       GetHand :I
       First :&Cards
       First ButFirst :&Cards)
   TakeCard
   TakeCard
   PutValue :I ValueOf GetHand :I
   PrintHand :I
End

To TakeCard
   Make "&Cards ButFirst :&Cards
End
```

ValueOf ascertains the numerical value of a hand, detecting BLACKJACK (BJ), when the player "busts," and when doubling is allowed.

```
To ValueOf :Hand
   If HaveBJP :Hand [Output [BJ]]
   Make "Hand HandleBustDoubling Values :Hand
   IfElse :Hand = []
     [Output [busts]]
     [Output :Hand]
End

To HaveBJP :Hand
   If Not (Count :Hand) = 2 [Output "False]
```

```
If MemberP "A :Hand
  [Output
    Or
      (MemberP Last :Hand [10 J Q K])
      (MemberP First :Hand [10 J Q K])]
  Output "False
End

To Values :Cards
  If :Cards = [] [Output [0]]
  If (First :Cards) = "A
    [Output
      Sentence
        (SumList 11 Values ButFirst :Cards)
        (SumList 1 Values ButFirst :Cards)]
  IfElse MemberP First :Cards [J Q K]
    [Output SumList 10 Values ButFirst :Cards]
    [Output
      SumList First :Cards Values ButFirst :Cards]
End

To SumList :Number :List
  If :List = [] [Output []]
  Output
    FPut
      (:Number + First :List)
      (SumList :Number ButFirst :List)
End

To HandleBust&Doubling :Hand
  If :Hand = [] [Output []]
  If Or
      (MemberP First :Hand ButFirst :Hand)
      (21 < First :Hand)
    [Output HandleBust&Doubling ButFirst :Hand]
  Output
    FPut
      First :Hand
      HandleBust&Doubling ButFirst :Hand
End
```

PrintHand prints out the players hand and the value(s) associated with it:

```
To PrintHand :I
  Print
    (Sentence
      [Cards for Player]
      :I
      "
      GetHand :I
      "-->
      GetValue :I)
End
```

At this point in the play, all the players have their first two cards. Then the dealer draws:

```
To DealerDraws
   PutHand 0 Sentence First :&Cards GetHand 0
   Print Sentence [My exposed card:] GetHand 0
   TakeCard
End
```

Now the second phase of the game begins with each player accepting cards as desired:

```
To Hit :I
   Print "
   If HaveBJP GetHand :I [Stop]
   PrintHand :I
   If DoubleP :I [PlayDouble :I Stop]
   MoreCards
End

To MoreCards
   Type [More cards?]
   If Not YesP [Stop]
   Deal1Card :I
   If MemberP First GetValue :I [busts 21] [Stop]
   MoreCards
End
```

During the second phase in addition to checking for a BLACKJACK, the opportunity for a doubling needs to be detected. As was already mentioned, we have left out handling splits in the interest of clarity.

```
To PlayDouble :I
   Deal1Card :I
   PutBet :I 2 * GetBet :I
   PutValue :I ValueOf GetHand :I
End

To DoubleP :I
   If Not
       Or
          MemberP First GetValue :I [9 10 11]
          MemberP Last GetValue :I [9 10 11]
      [Output "False]
   Type [Do you want to double?]
   Output YesP
End
```

Deal1Card deals exactly one more card and changes the data structures appropriately:

```
To Deal1Card :I
   PutHand :I Sentence First :&Cards GetHand :I
   TakeCard
   PutValue :I ValueOf GetHand :I
   PrintHand :I
End
```

AllBust checks to see whether all the players have already "gone bust," in which case the dealer does not need to play, because the house has already won:

```
To AllBust :N
  If :N = 0 [Output "True]
  IfElse (GetValue :N) = [busts]
    [Output AllBust :N - 1]
    [Output "False]
End
```

If any of the players are still "alive," the dealer needs to draw according to specific rules; this is handled in GoOnP:

```
To DealerPlays
  Print "
  PutHand 0 Sentence First :&Cards GetHand 0
  PutValue 0 ValueOf GetHand 0
  Print
    (Sentence
      [My cards:]
      GetHand 0
      "-->
      GetValue 0)
  IfElse GoOnP GetValue 0
    [Print [I draw again!]]
    [Stop]
  TakeCard
  DealerPlays
End

To GoOnP :Values
  IfElse NumberP First :Values
    [Output (First :Values) < 17]
    [Output "False]
End
```

The rest of the procedures take care of the standings, calculate the winnings and losses, and update each player's accounts:

```
To Standings :N
  Print "
  Print [   Here is how things stand:]
  Print "
  Loop "I 1 :N
    [Print
      (Sentence "Player :I ": (First GetValue :I)
      "--> GetAccount :I ComputeScore :I "=
      GetAccount :I)]
  Print
    (Sentence "Dealer: First GetValue 0 "-->
      GetAccount 0)
End

To ComputeScore :I
  If HaveBJP GetHand :I
    [PutBet :I (GetBet :I) + (Quotient GetBet :I 2)]
```

```
    If SmallerP First GetValue 0 First GetValue :I
      [Rearrange 0 :I GetBet :I
       Output Word "+ GetBet :I]
    If Not (GetValue 0) = [busts]
      [If (First GetValue 0) = First GetValue :I
        [Output "+0]]
    Rearrange :I 0 GetBet :I
    Output word "- GetBet :I
  End

  To Rearrange :I :J :E
    PutAccount :I (GetAccount :I) - :E
    PutAccount :J (GetAccount :J) + :E
  End

  To SmallerP :A :B
    If And NumberP :A NumberP :B [Output :A < :B]
    If :A = "busts [Output Not :B = "busts]
    IfElse NumberP :A
      [Output :B = "BJ]
      [Output "False]
  End
```

The **Loop** construct is defined on page 233.

The procedures **MemberP** and **YesP** are described in Appendix III.

38.4. Possible Extensions

Splitting

The program could be extended to handle splitting. One approach would be to modify the data structures in such a way that a fictitious player (e.g., **&Player.3A**) is created whenever a player splits. In addition, the **Standings** would have to be changed to handle the accounting correctly. Special cases have to be handled as well, so that after a player has split, he cannot split again or double.

Playing Strategies

BLACKJACK is one casino game in which the player's strategy can have some effect on the odds of winning. This can best be illustrated by comparing it to ROULETTE.

Comparison with ROULETTE. In ROULETTE bets are placed on the *layout*, and then the winning wager is decided by selecting one of the possible 38 numbers (1-36, 0 and 00). The *layout* is organized such that the numbers 1-36 are in 12 rows and 3 columns, with 0 and 00 at one end.

Here are most of the wagers that can be made (with sample payoffs from one Las Vegas casino):

- Single number bet ("straight-up"); pays 35 to 1.

- Double number bet ("split") for two adjacent numbers; pays 17 to 1.
  Three number bet for three numbers in a row of the layout; pays 11 to 1.
  Four number bet ("corner bet") for four adjectent numbers; pays 8 to 1.
  Five number bet for 0, 00, 1, 2, or 3; pays 6 to 1.
  Six number bet for two adjacent rows; pays 5 to 1.
  Twelve number bet ("dozens") for first, second, or third dozen of 36 numbers; pays 2 to 1.
  Column bet for 12 numbers in a single column; pays 2 to 1.
  18 number bet for first or second half of 36 numbers; pays 1 to 1;
  Red or black bet (the numbers 1-36 are either red or black, 0 and 00 are green); pays 1 to 1.

- Odd of even bet for odd or even of the 36 numbers; pays 1 to 1.

The selection of the winning number is made by spinning a ball in a counter-clockwise direction on the wheel, which is rotating in a clockwise direction. The ball eventually comes to rest in one of the pockets on the wheel, indicating the winning number.

In ROULETTE, the player has no possible decisions aside from the amount of the bet and the chances of winning. Furthermore, ROULETTE is a game in which successive plays are independent from one another (assuming that the table is working properly and does not favor any particular choices). Without too much mathematical effort, it can be shown that the player has a disadvantage of slightly more than 5% (exactly 2/38 × 100). This is because the wheel has 38 compartments (i.e., the odds are 37 to 1 on a single number bet) whereas the payoff is 35 to 1.

This disadvantage cannot be eliminated by any strategy on the part of the player, not even by doubling a red or black bet each time based on the assumption that after multiple "reds" eventually a "black" must occur. The player cannot double his bets as often as he/she wants because casinos have a maximum limit on bets for each table.

Basic Strategy for BLACKJACK. In contrast to ROULETTE, the player has a number of choices in BLACKJACK, for example:

- *When should I stand and when should I ask for another hit? This is an interesting question for all card values between 12 and 20, because on the one hand, another card could improve the score, increasing the chances of beating the dealer, but on the other hand, it could cause the player to go "bust."*

- *When should I double, split, or take insurance?*

- *How should I react differently when I have a "soft" hand (where one of my cards is an Ace, such that I can count it as 1 or 11 without busting) as opposed to a "hard" hand (all other cases)?*

These choices make an analysis of BLACKJACK according to the laws of probability difficult and allow the probabilities to be calculated in only the simplest cases.

Here are some possible strategies that could be followed by the player:

(1) *As long as I have less than 12, I can draw without thinking, because there is no way to "bust." If I have a "soft" hand, I can safely stretch the limit up 17 (half-way between 12 and 22), gaining some advantage while still remaining safe.*

Strategy 1: Stand on "hard" hands of 12 or greater and "soft" hands of 17 or greater.

[Thorp 62] shows that the house's advantage over the player using this strategy is somewhere in the range of 5 to 8%. The player would be better off at the ROULETTE table!

(2) *Based on the observation that most casinos are not exactly begging on the streets: Isn't it reasonable to play according to the rules of the dealer?*

Strategy 2: Play according to the rules of the dealer!

A little study shows that with strategy 2, a player is clearly at a disadvantage. The house profits from the rule that, when both the player and the dealer "bust", the player loses (which is definitely in favor of the house). Calculations in [Thorp 62] show that this disadvantage amounts to 8.04%. This is reduced because the player wins 1.5 times the bet for having BLACKJACK. This is an advantage of 2.34%, so the player remains at a 5.73% disadvantage.

(3) [Thorp 62; Uston 81] describe strategies that were derived with the aid of computer simulations (in one case, the computer program played several million games). These strategies consist of two parts:

  a) **Strategy 3:** The "basic strategy" that determines what one should do in one of the preceding situations is based on the dealer's exposed card;

  b) **Strategy 3a:** An "extended strategy" that is based on the fact that BLACKJACK is a game in which the individual events are dependent on each other (the probabilities are dependent on which cards remain in the deck).

Thorp and Uston's "basic strategy" is based on the idea that the dealer's exposed card was a valuable piece of information for the player. The basic idea is that a 2, 3, 4, 5, or 6 are bad and a 7, 8, 9, 10, or an Ace are good for the dealer. This is because the dealer must draw up to 17, and the number of cards with a value of 10 (tens and all picture cards) make up almost a third (exactly 16/52). If the dealer has a bad card exposed, then the player should avoid going bust. Instead, he should double or split if his cards permit.

With this basic strategy, BLACKJACK is a fair game; that is, the player does not have an advantage or a disadvantage over the casino.

The advanced strategies involve keeping track of how many of certain types of cards have been played (e.g., 5's and Aces), and result in a slight advantage for the player.

Using Strategies in a BLACKJACK Program. In addition to using the strategies just discussed as a player, you could also extend the program to on the role of several players that play different strategies. To do this `Hit` would have to be changed so that the decision about whether to take any more cards would be performed according to the strategies rather than by asking the user.

This could then be used to run a simulation by removing the dialog portion and working on the efficiency of the program (since LOGO, as an interpreted language, is only minimally suited for simulations). Appropriate statistics would have to be maintained to evaluate the strategies.

Other Ideas

You may also want to experiment with the user interface utilizing the graphics facilities of your LOGO implementation.

You could also re-write the program so that different sets of rules could be selected by the user (whether doubling is allowed, when splitting is allowed, how many decks are used, etc.)

The program could be extended to include help facilities to let the player ask what moves are allowed according to rules in effect. A strategy tutor could be developed, as well, to help the player learn to use a particular strategy well.

Part 7:
New Developments in
Computers and Education

Introduction

In this last part of the book, we would like to give the reader an overview of new developments in computers and education that have grown out of the LOGO culture. We are strongly convinced that the ideas originally explored in the LOGO culture have had a major impact on many developments—in most cases not as the sole source of a new idea or a new development, but as a major contributing factor.

If we ask "Where does the MACINTOSH come from?," it does not seem unreasonable to give some credit to the LOGO culture. Alan Kay's [Kay 77] ideas about a DYNABOOK had some of the same objectives as the work with LOGO: to make computation a generally accessible medium. Schoolchildren were perceived as being able to provide the best testbed for these ideas. Personal computers with bit-mapped screens and mice (e.g., the ALTO machine) provided the hardware base, and SMALLTALK was developed as the communication media for the envisioned DYNABOOK. These developments (with some intermediate systems, e.g. Xerox's STAR and Apple's LISA) led to the MACINTOSH, which by itself influenced the design of many other systems.

In this part, we first discuss new developments in the LOGO culture itself and then broaden our discussion to new approaches in computers and education, drawing in part from our own research work of the last decade.

Chapter 39:
Extensions to the Programming Language LOGO

Combining Programming and Word Processing. Word processing has provided major success models for the use of computers. It seems a natural conclusion to combine LOGO with text-processing capabilities—a goal of the LOGOWRITER system. Additional design goals of this recent system (which is in widespread use now) were to lower the threshold of getting acquainted with computers and to be able to mix text and graphics. The programming itself can be applied to the text editor, providing the capability for customizable tools.

Object-Oriented Programming. A major (if not the major) new paradigm in programming that emerged over the last 15 years has been object-oriented programming (see chapter 40). Pioneered by SMALLTALK, it has now become an integral part of many programming formalisms (e.g., the extension of C to C++ or the CLOS system that extends COMMON LISP). In the LOGO culture there have been several early efforts to extend it in an object-oriented direction; for example, by providing multiple turtles, `Forward 100` (which implicitly assumed a command send to the *one* turtle in the system) needed to be expressed now by `Turtle4 Forward 100`, meaning that the message `Forward 100` was send to the object `Turtle4`.

Multiprocessing and Parallel Processing. The one goal of the LOGO culture "to make computation more accessible to *more* people" was always accompanied by the complementary goal "to make *more, qualitatively-different* computational worlds accessible to people." Inspired by the turtle and by the apparent success of video games, animation was considered to be a requirement to many new interest worlds.

This requirement (based on these educational concerns) led to new hardware development (pioneered by the Texas Instruments "Sprite" controller) to support multiple turtles that, once set in motion, kept moving without further program invention.

This new environment allowed the exploration of a new programming construct called the *demon*. Demons support interrupt driven programming, meaning a specified instruction is activated whenever a certain event occurs. Demons are usually created using a primitive When, for example,

```
When MouseClickP [ReverseDirection]
```

would make the turtle reverse direction whenever the mouse is clicked.

MULTILOGO [Resnick 88] takes these developments further and extends LOGO with new metaphors and constructs for modeling concurrency providing control

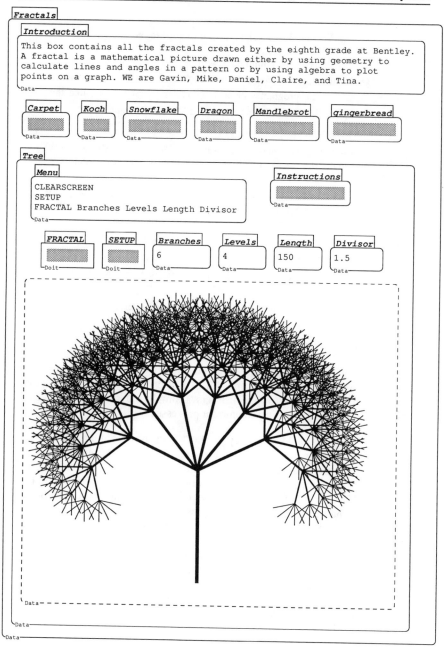

Figure 39–1: BOXER—an Example of a Reconstructable Medium

Figure 39-2: Description of Figure 39-1

This "fractals" box is the community working environment of a group of eighth grade students and their teacher. Each of the subboxes contains a fractal demonstration program with instructions and explanations, like the "tree" box. The figure illustrates a number of BOXER characteristics:

(1) Spatial arrangement of text and boxes within boxes.

(2) Control of detail: One may use mouse-click commands to shrink boxes (greyed in the figure), expand them, or expand once again to "zoom in," filling the screen.

(3) Data boxes: These are variables, chunks of text, menus (point and click) or entire environments. Editing variables directly changes them; if a program changes a variable, that change is also directly visible.

(4) Doit boxes: These are programs. One may use BOXER's hierarchical structure to organize them.

(5) Box labels: Any box may be labeled, which makes them computationally accessible by name.

(6) Graphics data boxes: These contain graphics and interactive ("touch" sensitive) computational objects, like extended LOGO turtles.

---

over real-time activities (such as animation and robotics). Contrary to other developments in parallel programming, MULTILOGO is not primarily concerned with speed but is an effort to give learners a simple but powerful model for thinking about and programming concurrent processes.

BOXER; Because of the long history of LOGO, its roots are in the teletype interfaces. The communication between users and computer is linear (e.g., users type something and the computer responds to it). New technological developments (e.g., bitmap displays, pointing devices, and sufficient computational power) enable a new style of computation. BOXER [diSessa, Abelson 86] is based on two basic principles: the spatial metaphor and naive realism. All computational objects in BOXER are represented as boxes, which are regions on the screen. *Naive realism* characterizes the idea that the computational world should be represented on the screen. Another important design goal of BOXER was that it could be used as a reconstructable medium that would allow people of all levels of competence to customize tools and building blocks they had obtained from others. Figure 39-1 shows an example of a screen image from BOXER.

Chapter 40:
Object-Oriented Programming in LOGO

The purpose of this chapter is to provide some motivating examples and to explore some of the background and rationale for object-oriented programming. The examples we present use OBJECTLOGO [Davidson 86], an object-oriented version of LOGO.

Object-oriented programming is a new paradigm that has grown out of knowledge representation research in the field of artificial intelligence and programming languages research in the field of computer science. Object-oriented programming was pioneered by the development of the simulation programming language SIMULA 67 at the Norwegian Computing Center, and was later incorporated into the SMALLTALK programming environment [Goldberg 81; Goldberg 84] developed by the Learning Research Group of Xerox Palo Alto Research Center [Kay 77].

Modelling A World with Multiple Turtles and Multiple Classes of Objects

In conventional turtle geometry [Abelson, diSessa 80] there existed one turtle. In order to direct the turtle to draw a square, the following program could be written:

```
To Square :Size
   Repeat 4 [Forward :Size Right 90]
End
```

Interesting questions arise when we extend this world to allow:

- multiple turtles

- other objects (in addition to turtles) that understand the message Forward (e.g., ships, airplanes, etc.).

Multiple Turtles.

To allow for multiple turtles, LOGO could be extended in a number of ways:

- A command TalkTo could be introduced to tell the LOGO system which turtle the user would like to interact with (e.g., the following set of commands first sends Turtle1 forward 100 units and then makes Turtle2 change directions):

```
? TalkTo "Turtle1
? Forward 100
? TalkTo "Turtle2
? Right 180
```

- The forward command could be extended with a second argument indicating to the system the object to whom the command should be sent:

```
? Forward 100 "Turtle1
```

Multiple Types of Objects.

Beyond the extension of allowing multiple turtles, we might want to have multiple classes of objects where each class of objects has a different understanding of the Forward command. Let's assume that we have ships, cars, and airplanes defined as classes of objects, and their respective Forward commands are named TurtleForward, ShipForward, Car-Forward, and AirplaneForward.

In order to decode the LOGO command

```
? Forward 100 "Car1
```

properly (namely that :Car1 should go forward according to its understanding of Forward), we could write the following definition of Forward:

```
To Forward :Amount :Object
   If (TypeP :Object "turtle) [TurtleForward :amount]
   If (TypeP :Object "ship) [ShipForward :Amount]
   If (TypeP :Object "airplane)
     [AirplaneForward :Amount]
   If (TypeP :Object "car) [CarForward :Amount]
End
```

The typing scheme could be implemented as follows:

```
To NewCar :Name
   PutProp :Name "Type "car
End
```

or, in a more general form:

```
To New :Type :Name
   PutProp :Name "Type :Type
End
```

These procedures could be used to access the typing information:

```
To TypeP :Object :Type
   Output EqualP TypeOf :Object :Type
End
To TypeOf :Object
   Output GetProp :Object "Type
End
```

Car1 could be then be created with:

```
? NewCar "Car1
```

or, using the more general form:

```
? New "Car "Car1
```

One problem with this approach is that whenever a new type of object is created that understands some type of Forward command, the procedure Forward needs to be changed to add the functionality. Another approach would be to use the data-driven programming technique shown in chapter 28:

```
To Forward  :Amount :Object
    Run Sentence Word TypeOf :Object "Forward :Amount
End
```

Object-Oriented Programming versus Procedural Programming

Object-oriented programming takes a different global approach and global view towards the problem of modelling the world and factoring the knowledge of the world. Procedural languages (such as LOGO) factor knowledge around the concept of the procedure:

```
              Real Numbers      Vectors

   Whole Numbers                      Matricies
                        Plus
      Coordinates                     Strings

          Fractions          Sets

              Complex Numbers
```

Object-oriented programming languages (such as SMALLTALK) factor knowledge around the concept of the object:

```
              ButFirst      Count

      Sentence                     MemberP
                      List
        Replace                    Sort

          Delete          Reverse

              First
```

Inheritance in Object-Oriented Programming.

Another important aspect of object-oriented programming is the introduction of *inheritance mechanisms*. Many disciplines have benefited from the introduction of classification schemes where more general properties are positioned at higher levels of classification. For example, in biology there is an entire classification system for living organisms: kingdom, phylum, division, subphylum, superclass, class, order family, genus, species, subspecies, variety. We can create similar classification systems for objects within our object-oriented systems:

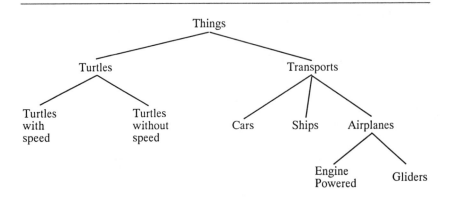

By creating such a classification scheme for programming objects, it is then often possible to extend the system by:

- creating a new object that inherits most of its properties from an existing object

- adding any new properties that are unique to the new object.

Of course, that same new object could have been built from scratch, duplicating the effort needed to create the object that it could have inherited from. Object-oriented programming does not answer all the questions about managing objects; however, it does provide mechanisms for the programmer to do so.

Why do we need object-oriented programming?

The general paradigm of programming in procedure- and operation-oriented languages is based on a single unified intelligent agent (the program) that can deal with all aspects of a given problem. However, as programs become more complex, it is more difficult to manage all this intelligence, even though procedures help us "divide and conquer." A new paradigm based on a "society of communicating experts," where knowledge is distributed over that society as a whole, is an alternative approach supported by object-oriented systems. Each part of the system ("member of the society") embodies expertise regarding some part of the problem being solved, instead of restricting decomposition to only the procedural aspects of the problem. This may be a better framework for understanding parallel processes and communication between independent systems.

Programming in object-oriented paradigm.

The central idea of object-oriented programming is factorization of knowledge based on the behavior of objects. This focus on objects with behavioral traits that can be inherited leads to a new approach. The main steps of such an approach are [Hewitt 77, page 325; Goldberg, Kay 77, page 3]:

(1) Describe all objects taking part in the system.

(2) Group these objects into classes based on common properties.

(3) Describe behavioral properties of each class.

(4) Create appropriate instances.

These recommendations apply to a project as a whole, extending the principles mentioned in chapter 4 to a more global view of the project.

An Example: the Moving Camera Revisited

The moving camera and the world of objects presented in chapter 24 lend themselves well to representation in an object-oriented system. We only sketch out the basics of a solution, but the framework provided is easily extensible.

Let's start out by following the steps outlined in the last section:

Describe all objects taking part in the system.

- camera
- pyramid
- cubes
- lines
- squares
- triangles

Group these objects into classes based on common properties.

- objects with position
  - camera
  - pyramid
  - cube
  - lines
  - squares

- triangles
- movable objects
    - camera
    - later perhaps pyramids and cubes, too
- graphic objects—sometimes composed of other graphics objects
    - lines
    - squares
    - rectangles
    - triangles
    - pyramids
    - cubes
    - (perhaps cameras as well?)
- objects that can "see"
    - camera

Describe behavioral properties of each class.

- objects with position
    - have some way of keeping track of their position and orientation.
- movable objects
    - change position(translation)
    - roll (z axis rotation)
    - pitch (x axis rotation)
    - yaw (y axis rotation)
- graphic objects
    - draw self (which may include drawing component objects)
    - scale (change size)
- objects that see
    - project an image on focal plane
    - erase view
    - change focal length (zooming)

This is what part of the object hierarchy for this project would look like:

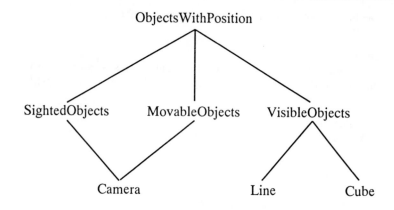

With that as a basis, we can start to specify some of the OBJECTLOGO code necessary to implement this. First, let's look at some of the primitives available to us in OBJECTLOGO

Object-oriented Programming in OBJECTLOGO

Object-Logo provides the following primitive language constructs to support object-oriented programming:

- **KindOf**
This creates a class that inherits from another class. For example:
```
Make "SportsCar KindOf :Car
```

- **SomeThing**
Something creates an class that inherits only from the root class Logo. This is equivalent to:
```
KindOf Logo
```

- **Ask**
Invokes the specified LOGO code in the context of a particular object. This can be procedure definition, command execution, or the evaluation of an operation. You could write the procedures described in the last section in the following way:
```
Make "Car SomeThing
Ask :Car [To Forward :Amount]
.
.
End
```

- **OneOf**
Creates an object as an instance of a class.

```
Make "Carl OneOf :Car
Ask :Carl [Forward 100]
```

- **Self**
  Within the scope of an object, this operation returns the object itself.

- **Have**
  Creates a name within the scope of an object. This is essentially an instance variable; that is, each instance of this type of object will have its own version of this variable.

- **HaveMake**
  Like **Have** but also assigns a value.

- **Exist**
  This procedure is called when an instance is created using **OneOf**. It can be defined in the class to allow for specific operations to be performed when a new object is created.

- **Usual.<procedure>**
  Used within a <procedure> to gain access to the inherited behavior of that object for that procedure. For example, in **Exist** it is common to write:

```
To Exist
  ;perform the inherited initialization
  Usual.Exist
  .          ;perform initialization
  .          ;specific to this class
  .
End
```

Programming Our Example in OBJECTLOGO Let's start with the root of our hierarchy; creating a class; ObjectWithPosition:

```
;;;;;;;;;;;;;;;;;;;;;;;;;;;;;;;;;;;;;;;;;;;;
;;; Objects with position, orientation
;;;     position and orientation are all represented
;;;     by a transformation matrix
;;;;;;;;;;;;;;;;;;;;;;;;;;;;;;;;;;;;;;;;;;;;
Make "ObjectWithPosition SomeThing
```

Next, we tell :ObjectWithPosition to react to the initialization message, Exist:

```
Ask :ObjectWithPosition [To Exist]
  Usual.Exist
  HaveMake
    "MyOrientation
    Extract :InitList "Orientation :IdentityTm
End
```

This procedure first uses Usual.Exist to inherit initialization behavior from the system, then creates an instance variable :MyOrientation, where the current transformation matrix for the object is stored. This can be specified in the initialization list given to the `OneOf` message when an instance is created; otherwise it is given the default value of the identity transformation matrix, `:IdentityTm`.

```
Make "IdentityTM ListToArray [1 0 0
                              0 1 0
                              0 0 1
                              0 0 0]
```

The other main classes can be derived from this `ObjectWithPosition`:

```
Make "MovableObject :ObjectWithPosition
```

`MovableObjects` can be *moved* or translated in space, so we define the procedure `Translate` for this:

```
Ask :MovableObject [To Translate :X :Y :Z]
   Make
      "MyOrientation TranslateTM :X :Y :Z :MyOrientation
   End
```

For now this suffices to demonstrate the system; you can add the ability to rotate these objects later.

Next, let's look at objects that are visible graphic objects:

```
Make "VisibleObject KindOf :ObjectWithPosition
```

Our strategy here is to allow *VisibleObjects* to be composed of other objects (e.g., a cube might be composed of 12 lines), so we need an instance variable to keep track of the component parts.

```
Ask :VisibleObject [To Exist]
   Usual.Exist
   HaveMake "Components []
   End
```

A `VisibleObject` needs to know how show itself to a ''sighted'' object. To do this, it needs to take into account its own location (stored in its own instance variable `MyOrientation`), as well the position of any object that it is a component of (passed down in the parameter `:Transformation`.

If this object has components, each one of those objects is asked to show itself (`MapAsk` is similar to `MapCar` and `MapC` discussed in chapter 23). If the object has no components, then it asks itself to `ShowImage`.

```
Ask :VisibleObject [To ShowSelf :ToObject :Transformation]
   Local "NewTranformation
   Make
      "NewTransformation
      TMProduct :Transformation :MyOrientation
   MapAsk
      (Sentence [ShowSelf] :ToObject :NewTransformation)
      :Components
```

```
          If EmptyP :Components
          [(AskInvoke
             Self
             "ShowImage
             :ToObject
             :NewTransformation)]
End
```

Objects that have no component parts have to be able to show an image of what they look like. Here we define a "dummy" procedure that gets called if a subclass object forgets to define how to draw itself.

```
Ask :VisibleObject
    [To ShowImage :ToObject :Transformation]
    ; This should be defined in each
    ; class (e.g., line, square, circle)
    ; if not, this one gets called
    (Print [ShowImage not defined for object] self)
End
```

And now, here is the class of objects that can "see" the world.

```
Make "SightedObject SomeThing
```

A SightedObject shows what it sees by drawing it on a graphics window. On initialization, it creates this window and an invisible turtle to do the drawing on that window.

```
Ask :SightedObject [To Exist]
    Usual.Exist
    HaveMake "FocalLength 100
    ;; these are the interface to the Macintosh
    ;; Window system each instance can show a
    ;; different view on a different window.
    HaveMake "MyWindow OneOf TurtleWindow
    HaveMake
        "MyTurtle
        (OneOf Turtle "MyWindow :MyWindow "ShownP "False)
End

Ask :SightedObject [To Erase]
    Ask :MyWindow [ClearScreen]
End
```

ProjectLine is used by the VisibleObject to show its picture to the SightedObject

```
Ask :SightedObject [To ProjectLine :P1 :P2]
    Local "TransP1
    Local "TransP2
    Make
        "TransP1
        TMPointProduct :P1 TMProduct :MyOrientation :NegateTM
    Make
        "TransP2
        TMPointProduct :P2 TMProduct :MyOrientation :NegateTM
```

```
Ask :MyTurtle [PenUp]
Ask Self [ProjectPoint :TransP1]
Ask :MyTurtle [PenDown]
Ask Self [ProjectPoint :TransP2]
End

Ask :SightedObject [To ProjectPoint :Point]
  Local "X
  Local "Y
  Local "Z
  Make "X First :Point
  Make "Y Nth 2 :Point
  Make "Z Nth 3 :Point
  IfElse :Z = 0 [Ask :MyTurtle [SetXY 0 0]]
                [(AskInvoke
                    :MyTurtle
                    "SetXY
                    :FocalLength * :X / :Z
                    :FocalLength * :Y / :Z)]
End
```

Now we can start to get more specific. A camera is both a `MovableObject` and a `SightedObject` (and later you can even make it a `VisibleObject`, if you wish). This demonstrates the use of multiple inheritance.

```
Make "Camera (KindOf  :MovableObject :SightedObject)
```

The first `VisibleObject` we introduce is a simple line:

```
Make "Line (KindOf :VisibleObject)
Ask :Line [To Exist]
  Usual.Exist
  HaveMake
    "MyStartPoint
    Extract "StartPoint :InitList [0 0 0]
  HaveMake
    "MyEndPoint
    Extract "EndPoint :InitList [1 1 1]
End
```

And the `ShowImage` procedure for a `Line`:

```
Ask :Line [To ShowImage :ToObject :Transformation]
  Local "NewTransformation
  Make
    "NewTransformation
    TMProduct :Transformation :MyOrientation
  Local "TransformedPoint1
  Local "TransformedPoint2
```

```
Make
  "TransformedPoint1
  TMPointProduct :MyStartPoint :Transformation
Make
  "TransformedPoint2
  TMPointProduct :MyEndPoint :Transformation
Ask
  :ToObject
  [ProjectLine :TransformedPoint1 :TransformedPoint2]
End
```

Notice that we define a procedure ShowImage that is specific to Lines and this overrides the default one defined in VisibleObject.

Cubes are VisibleObjects that are composed of 12 lines.

```
Make "Cube (KindOf :VisibleObject)

Ask :Cube [To Exist]
  Usual.Exist
  HaveMake "Size Extract "Size :InitList 1
  Make
    "MyOrientation
    ScaleTM
        :Size
        :Size
        :Size
        Extract
          "Orientation
          :InitList
          :IdentityTM
  Make
    "Components
    MakeLines [[0 0 0] [0 0 1]
               [0 0 1] [0 1 1]
               [0 1 1] [0 1 0]
               [0 1 0] [0 0 0]
               [1 0 0] [1 0 1]
               [1 0 1] [1 1 1]
               [1 1 1] [1 1 0]
               [1 1 0] [1 0 0]
               [0 0 0] [1 0 0]
               [0 0 1] [1 0 1]
               [0 1 1] [1 1 1]
               [0 1 0] [1 1 0]]
End

To MakeLines :List
  If EmptyP :List [Output []]
  Output
    FPut
      (OneOf
          :Line
          "StartPoint First :List
          "EndPoint Nth 2 :List)
      MakeLines ButFirst ButFirst :List
End
```

Now we are ready to: *create appropriate instances.*

```
Make "Cube1 (OneOf :Cube)
Make
  "Camera1
  (OneOf :Camera "Orientation TranslateTM 0 0 -5 :IdentityTM)
```

The image of the single cube can be displayed on the camera using:

```
? Ask :Cube1 (List "ShowSelf :Camera1)
```

Although this sketch of our system lacks some of the functionality of the one presented in chapter 24, it would not be difficult to extend it. More importantly, it would be reasonable to add functionality to this system in ways that would have been difficult before. You could add many different types of objects, organized into a world. The camera's "picture" could then be generated by Asking each object in the world to ShowSelf to the camera. Multiple cameras could be used to show different views in different windows. The cameras themselves could be made into visible objects by having :Camera inherit from :VisibleObject and then defining a DrawImage procedure. The graphics objects could also be made movable by adjustments in their inheritance. Two cameras could be coupled together in such a way that their two images would create a stereoscopic view.

Conclusions

This short excursion into the world of object-oriented programming can provide only a glimpse at a computational approach whose relevance is being recognized more and more. Object-oriented programming formalisms have been added to and integrated into procedural languages (e.g., CLOS [Keene 89] as an extension to COMMON LISP and C++ or OBJECTIVE C as extensions to C) and SMALLTALK becomes increasingly popular. There are many more interesting concepts associated with object-oriented programming (e.g., inheritance, message passing, etc. [Stefik, Bobrow 86]). The LOGO community has explored some of these ideas in a variety of different contexts and demonstrated that these concepts are valuable and understandable for the nonexpert computer user. It is a challenge for the future to develop interest worlds particularly suited and centered around an object-oriented approach.

Chapter 41:
New Approaches to Using Computers in Education

Human Problem-Domain Communication and Construction Kits. LOGO was originally developed to enhance general intellectual skills that can be developed in computational environments. But the LOGO culture was more successful in building interest worlds (e.g., Turtle Geometry) on top of the general LOGO programming environment, allowing learners to explore at their desire and their interest a specific cluster of ideas. These interest worlds enable learners to perceive the communication with the computer at the problem-domain level, allowing them to concentrate on the problems of their domain and to ignore the fact that they are using a computer tool.

To support communication at the domain level, concepts of the problem domain must be represented in the system. *Construction kits* make abstractions of the problem domain directly available to the user. They can be combined to achieve the user's task. Construction kits provide syntactic support for this combination process and for the visualization of the results.

Human problem-domain communication requires environments that support design methodologies whose main purpose is not the generation of new, independent programs, but the comprehension, integration, modification, and explanation of existing ones. Just as one relies on already established theorems in a new mathematical proof, new systems should be built as much as possible using existing parts.

The Pinball and Music Construction Kits (two interesting programs for the Apple MacIntosh from Electronic Arts; see figures 41–1 and 41–2) provide domain-level building blocks (bumpers, flippers; staves, piano keyboard, notes, sharps, etc.) to build artifacts in the two domains of pinball machines and musical composition. Users can interact with the system in terms already familiar to them; they need not learn abstractions peculiar to a computer system.

These systems come close (within their scope) to the notion of human problem-domain communication. Users familiar with the problem domains but inexperienced with computers have few problems using these systems, whereas computer experts unfamiliar with the problem domains are unable to exploit the power of these systems. Most people consider it a difficult (if not impossible) task to achieve the same results using only the basic Macintosh system without the construction kits. Using the construction kits, subjects have a sense of accomplishment because they can create their own impressive version of something that works, yet is not difficult to make. Persons using the systems do *programming*, but the programming consists of constructing artifacts in the domain and not of writing statements of a general-purpose programming language.

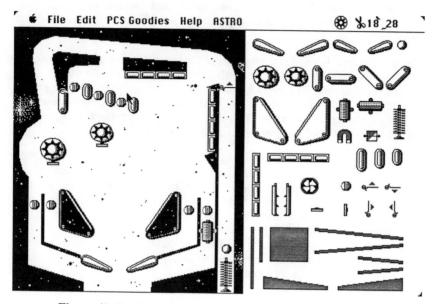

Figure 41–1: Screen image from the Pinball Construction Kit

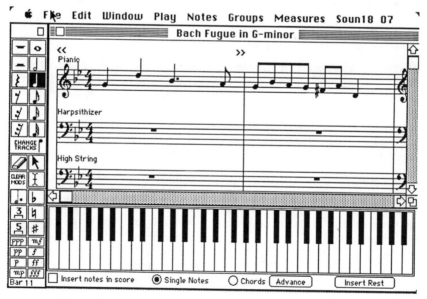

Figure 41–2: Screen image from the Music Construction Kit

Evaluating the Pinball and Music Construction kits as prototypical examples against the objective to support human problem-domain communication, several shortcomings can be identified.

The two systems do eliminate programming errors below the domain level, but they do not assist the user in constructing interesting and useful artifacts in the application domains. The pinball construction kit allows users to build sets in which balls get stuck in certain corners and certain devices may not be reachable [Hutchins, Hollan, Norman 86]. To assist users in constructing truly interesting objects, more powerful environments are needed.

Design Environments. In contrast to simple software construction kits (e.g., the Pinball and Music Construction Kits described previously), which present the designer with the available parts and operations for putting them together and allows the resulting system to be run, *design environments* give additional support. They incorporate knowledge about which components fit together and how they do so, and they may serve as a critic that recognizes errors or inefficient or useless structures. They are able to deal with multiple representations of the design including drafts, program code, and graphical representations. Design environments constrain the problem space, leaving beginners with fewer choices by providing defaults and grouping the available functions.

Design environments considerably reduce the amount of knowledge a designer has to acquire before useful work can be done. This is especially important if the design environment contains many special purpose components and if each of them is used rarely, even by a full-time designer.

JANUS: an Example of a Design Environment for Architectural Design. JANUS [Fischer, McCall, Morch 89] allows designers to construct artifacts in the domain of architectural design and at the same time informs them about principles of design and their underlying rationale by integrating two design activities: construction and argumentation. *Construction* is supported by a knowledge-based graphical design environment (see figure 41–3) and *argumentation* is supported by a hypertext system (see figure 41–4).

JANUS provides a set of domain-specific building blocks and has knowledge about how to combine them into useful designs. With this knowledge it "looks over the shoulder" of users carrying out a specific design. If it discovers a shortcoming in the users' designs, it provides a critique, suggestions, and explanations and assists users in improving their designs. JANUS is not an expert system that dominates the process by generating new designs from high-level goals or resolving design conflicts automatically. Users control the behavior of the system at all times (e.g., the critiquing can be "turned on and off"), and if users disagree with JANUS, they can modify its knowledge base.

Critics in JANUS are procedures for detecting nonsatisficing partial designs. JANUS' concept for integrating the constructive and argumentative component originated from the observation that the critiques are a limited type of

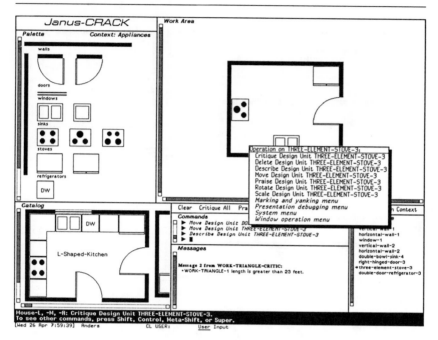

Figure 41–3: JANUS Construction Interface

The interface of JANUS's construction component is based on the world model. Design units are selected from the Palette and moved into the work area. Operations on design units are available through menus. The screen image shown displays a message from the WORK-TRIANGLE-CRITIC.

---

argumentation. The construction actions can be seen as attempts to resolve design issues. For example, when a designer is positioning the sink in the kitchen, the issue being resolved is "Where should the sink be located?"

The knowledge-based critiquing mechanism in JANUS bridges the gap between construction and argumentation. This means that critiquing and argumentation can be coupled by using JANUS' critics to provide the designer with immediate entry into the place in the hypertext network containing the argumentation relevant to the current construction task. Such a combined system provides argumentative information for construction effectively, efficiently, and designers do not have to realize before hand that information will be required, anticipate what information is in the system, or know how to retrieve it.

Integrating Construction and Argumentation. The constructive part of JANUS supports the building of an artifact either "from scratch" or by

---

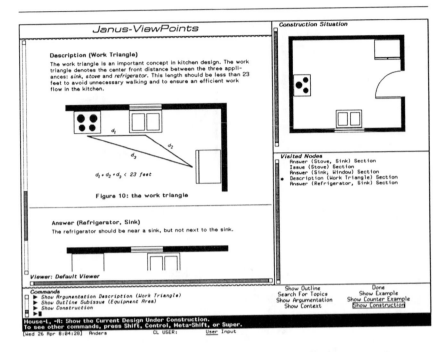

JANUS's argumentation component uses the Symbolics Document Examiner as a delivery interface. The construction situation can be displayed in one of the panes to allow users to inspect the constructive and argumentative context simultaneously.

Figure 41–4: JANUS argumentation interface

modifying an existing design. To construct from scratch, the designer chooses building blocks from a design units "Palette" and positions them in the "Work area" (see figure 41–3).

To construct by modifying an existing design, the designer uses the "CATALOG" (lower left in figure 41–3), which contains several example designs. The designer can browse through this catalog of examples until an interesting one is found. This design can then be selected and brought into the "Work Area," where it can be modified.

The CATALOG contains both "good" designs and "poor" designs. The former satisfy all the rules of kitchen design and will not generate a critique. People who want to design without having to bother with knowing the underlying principles might want to select one of these, because minor modifications of them will probably result in few or no suggestions from the critics. The "poor" designs in the CATALOG support learning the design principles. By bringing these into the "Work Area," users can subject them to critiquing and thereby illustrate those principles of kitchen design that are known to the system.

The "good" designs in the CATALOG can also be used to learn design principles and explore their argumentative background. This can be done by bringing them into the "Work Area," then using the "Praise all" command. This command causes the system to display all the rules that the selected example satisfies. This positive feedback also provides entry points into the hypertext argumentation.

When users enter the *argumentative part* of JANUS, they are brought into a section of the issue base relevant to their current construction situation. Their point of entry into the hypertext network should contain the information required to understand the issue of interest. But argumentation on an issue can be large and complex so they can use this initial display of relevant information as a starting place for a navigational journey through the issue base, following links that will lead them to additional information. Upon completion of the examination of the argumentative information the designer can return to construction and complete the current task.

Critics as Hypertext Activation Agents. JANUS' knowledge-based critics serve as the mechanism to link construction with argumentation. They "watch over the shoulders" of designers, displaying their critique in the "Messages" pane (center bottom in figure 41–3) when design principles are violated. In doing so, they also identify the argumentative context that is appropriate to the current construction situation.

For example, when a designer has designed the kitchen shown in figure 41–3, the "Work-Triangle-Critic" fires and detects that the work triangle is too large. To see the arguments surrounding this issue, the designer has only to click on the text of this criticism with the mouse. The argumentative context shown in figure 41–4 is then displayed.

High-Functionality Computer Systems. Representing the abstractions of many problem domains in a computer system leads to high-functionality computer systems that contain substrates of components and parts for the design of artifacts in a variety of domains. Some of today's systems (e.g., LISP machines or operating systems) contain tens of thousands of functions and require thousands of pages of description. Systems with such a rich functionality offer power as well as problems. Users of these systems can no longer be experts with respect to all existing tools—especially in a dynamic environment where new tools are being continuously added. High-functionality computer systems create a "tool-mastery" burden that must not outweigh the advantages of tools. Modern LOGO systems suffer from the same problem (e.g., the number of primitives ranges between 250 and 800). These systems raise the ceiling, but what happens to the threshold?

Architectures for Learning Environments. A goal of the LOGO culture has been to create systems with "no threshold and no ceiling," characterizing the challenge of preserving the ease of use while increasing the power. Using skiing as a success model, we have designed a framework for acquiring complex skills through *increasingly complex microworlds* [Burton, Brown, Fischer 84; Wenger 87]. The increasingly complex microworlds paradigm formalizes the notion of a succession of microworlds where the modifications at each step are driven by the learners' goals and by the recommendations of a coach. Learners start with a simplified world, and new dimensions of complexity are added as needed. Simplifications may cause inappropriate generalizations on the parts of the learner. The challenge is to create environments that make errors constructive by generating enough feedback for the learner to recognize, understand, and correct them.

The increasingly complex microworlds philosophy allows systems to be built so that:

- They have a low threshold (i.e., it is easy to get started) and a high ceiling (i.e., the possibilities offered by the system grow with the experience of the user).

- They present the user with challenging but attainable goals.

- They provide transient objects (e.g., short skis used in the graduated length method).

- They provide protective shields (i.e., eliminate the danger of making irreversible mistakes) and scaffolding, including the gradual removal of support until the users can operate on their own ("crutches" should not be left around for too long).

- They assist users in the *stepwise extension* of their view of the system by making sure that basic concepts are well understood and by not introducing too many new features at once.

- They eliminate prerequisite skills (e.g., ski lifts allow the user to practice skiing instead of uphill climbing; construction kits eliminate low-level system building work and support human problem-domain communication) and give the user access to new environments.

Figure 41–5 illustrates the increasingly complex microworld structure behind the organization of this book.

Resolving the Dichotomy between Open Learning Environments and Teacher-Driven Tutoring Systems. The goal of the LOGO culture was always to provide an open-ended learning environment—in sharp distinction to the computer-assisted instruction systems that provided little flexibility for learners to follow their interests. In the past these two approaches were regarded primarily as a dichotomy. But progress has been made from both ends to turn this dichotomy more into a continuum. The unstructured environments based on the LOGO language were enriched by interest worlds that support human problem-domain communication for a particular and bounded set of ideas. Computer-assisted instruction has incorporated artificial intelligence techniques

- Step 1: learn some technical details (e.g., use of mouse and keyboard, logging on and off, accessing and storing files) using the user's manual for your LOGO version

- Step 2: learn the existing building blocks (e.g., some of the built-in functions) by investigating their behavior (in direct execution mode)

- Step 3: learn to combine them (e.g., the syntax of a programming language) by defining your own procedures

- Step 4: learn to understand existing solutions to problems

- Step 5: solve problems given to you

- Step 6: solve your *own* problems

Figure 41–5: The Increasingly Complex Microworld
Structures Underlying this Book

This microworld structure is based on the "no threshold and no ceiling" principle. It changes from a teacher- and system-driven oriented approach in the early phases to a student- or learner-driven approach in the later phases.

to provide more flexibility and a deeper understanding of the learners' goals, their existing knowledge, and their performance and difficulties carrying out a specific task. The need to support additional learning environments also arises because high-functionality computer systems cannot be completely mastered, and the support of strategies such as *incremental learning* and *learning on demand* have become a necessity rather than remaining a luxury.

Incremental learning. Not even experts can completely master complex, high-functionality systems. Support for incremental learning is required. Incremental learning eliminates suboptimal behavior (thereby increasing efficiency), enlarges possibilities (thereby increasing functionality), supports learning on demand by presentation of new information when it is relevant, uses models of the user to make systems more responsive to the needs of individuals, and tailors explanations to the user's conceptualization of the task.

Learning on demand. The major justification for learning on demand is that education is a distributed, lifelong process of learning material as it is needed. Learning on demand has been successful in human societies or organizations when learners are afforded the luxury of a personal coach or critic. Aided by a human coach or critic, learners can articulate their problems in an infinite variety of ways.

On a broad scale, learning on demand is neither practical nor economical without computers. Learning on demand should include "learning to learn," showing the user how to locate and use information resources. It should not be restricted just to learning procedures but should help to restructure the user's conceptual model of the domain. It should not only provide access to factual information but also assist the user in understanding when that knowledge can be applied.

Learning on demand is a guided discovery approach to learning. It is initiated when the user wants to do something, not learn about everything. Learning on demand affords that learning occurs because knowledge is actively used rather than passively perceived. At least one condition under which knowledge can be applied is learned and it can make a crucial difference in motivating learning.

The demand to learn more can originate with the user. It can be triggered by a discrepancy between an intended product and the actual product produced. Experimentation with a system may turn up interesting phenomena that users find worth exploring further. The demand to learn cannot originate with users when they are unaware that additional functionality exists in the system. The system has to take the initiative. A coach or a critic is needed who is capable of diagnosing the cause of a student's misunderstanding and then judiciously deciding, on its own, when to interrupt and what to say. Interrupting too often can destroy motivation, but too few interruptions result in learning experiences being missed or floundering by the user.

Chapter 42:
New Approaches for Education, Psychology, and Epistemology

> *"Wheel chairs are tools that enable us to get around.*
> *They are liberating, not confining."* -- A Paralyzed Person

Empowerment and Prosthesis. Sylvia Weir [Weir 87] has done interesting research in the LOGO culture by developing theories and creating environments that reveal hidden strengths of learners (e.g., matching the preferences of visualizers) and liberate the intellect of individuals with severe physical handicaps. She has used the computer as an information prosthesis device aiding handicapped persons by providing these persons with opportunities for personal development not otherwise accessible to them. Her case studies describe success stories working with autistic children and children who suffer from cerebral palsy. It is important to point out that her work grew out of the LOGO culture not because of specific features of the programming language LOGO, but because of the larger questions asked by this culture. Educational concerns were the motivators and incubators for these ideas, not the computer aids that computer experts wanted to produce or that the computer industry found most amenable to their purposes.

Cognitive Artifacts. External devices, ranging from prosthetics to tools, play an essential role in human activities. Although we know a lot about artifacts that enhance physical capabilities, little is known about how artifacts enhance cognitive capabilities, in part because the necessary technology is only now beginning to emerge. The LOGO culture has made major contributions towards the design and development of cognitive artifacts. Research in this area has followed a three-pronged approach: development of theory (see [Papert 80], empirical studies (primarily case studies in naturalistic settings), and engineering construction (e.g., the programming language LOGO, the turtle, LEGO-LOGO, etc.). The development of theory is aimed at explaining

- how human cognition results from an interplay between mental processes and external computational and memory aids and

- learning as an active reconstruction process rather than as a transmission of knowledge.

The empirical research examines the roles of artifacts and how people perform tasks. The engineering construction allows testing of the ideas in natural settings. Among the properties to be investigated are appropriate representations, how the human and artificial capabilities can complement each other, and the nature of the interaction between the artifact and the person.

Cognitive artifacts can amplify and augment human problem solving and decision making. They range from simple tools (e.g., spelling correctors, hand-held calculators) to sophisticated tools (e.g., knowledge-based design environments). They offer interesting opportunities and challenges; they can be used to

- eliminate or augment prerequisite skills (e.g., a knowledge-based design environment such as JANUS allows non-experts to engage in architectural design),

- eliminate cognitive shortcomings (e.g., spelling problems for dislexic individuals),

- allow creation of exciting environments (e.g., the different interest worlds developed in the LOGO culture), and

- train new skills (e.g., debugging, estimation instead of precise computation).

Studying Appropriate Impacts of Technology: As we discussed in the previous section, artifacts can have different impacts on the nature of tasks. Further study is needed to determine what approaches are most appropriate in particular environments and settings. The following list enumerates some possible ways these artifacts might be used:

- *Approach 1:* leave things unchanged (i.e., ignore the existence of hand held calculators, spelling programs, etc.);

- *Approach 2:* enhance the acquisition of the traditional skill, (e.g., by providing more exciting environments; e.g., equip a hand-held calculator with interesting games that support the acquisition of arithmetic skills) or by lowering the threshold through an increasingly complex microworld architecture (e.g., the graduated length method in skiing [Burton, Brown, Fischer 84]);

- *Approach 3:* learn the traditional skill, but after having mastered it, support tools can be used in executing it (i.e., allow people to use hand-held calculators after they are proficient in arithmetic);

- *Approach 4:* reevaluate which skills should be learned (e.g., replace elaborate arithmetic skills with estimation skills, replace shoelaces with hook-and-loop fastener);

- *Approach 5:* encourage the use of understanding and insight instead of requiring the use of formal relationships; artifacts can be used to provide representations that are closer to our understanding of the world (e.g., by supporting human problem-domain communication or visualization techniques);

- *Approach 6:* decouple secondary effects: Sometimes, access to a skill is lost, not because the ability to perform those skills is lacking, but due to impairment or absence of prerequisite skills. For example, vision-impaired individuals do not necessarily lack the ability to learn how to drive an automobile, but without clear vision, (safe) driving cannot be learned. In most cases, eyeglasses can allow the secondary-level skill to be developed by mitigating the effects of the missing skill. In the same way that glasses are used to decouple the secondary effect (not being able to drive) from the primary cause (vision impairment), skills that were previously inaccessible can be developed by using cognitive artifacts to eliminate cognitive shortcomings.

Constructionism: Extending the Construction Kit Metaphor into the Physical World. Papert [Papert 80] defines constructionism as follows:

> Constructionism is a synthesis of the constructivist theory of developmental psychology (as developed by Jean Piaget) and the opportunities offered by technology to base education for science and mathematics on activities in which students work towards the construction of an intelligible entity rather than on the acquisition of knowledge and facts without a context in which they can be immediately used and understood.

To support constructionism and the philosophy that learners should make rather than be provided with the objects they study, the active approach of constructing artifacts with LOGO was coupled with doing the same with technical construction kits. The MIT group has developed LEGO-LOGO as an integrated environment that combines ideas from mathematics, architecture, engineering, computer science and social studies. In our own work, we have developed similar ideas working with Fischer-Technik and LOGO [Fischer, Boecker 83]. LEGO-LOGO creates a "science-land", in which learners cannot just learn about science, but they can *do* science. The LEGO-LOGO world extends the turtle world by providing artifacts that, through sensors and motors, are more integrated into the real world, allowing the learner to study a variety of problems in robotics and control theory.

Human-Centered Computing. The texture of the computer tools of the future will depend on the people who design and use them. To the extent that artistic, musical, and literary people are computer-literate and make use of the new medium, the medium itself will reflect the wide range of human experience. To the extent that the educational system isolates such people from computers, the medium lacks those qualities. Historical evidence shows that computer professionals have not been the leading figures in bringing innovative uses of computers to the population at large. Only after personal computing (e.g., in the SMALLTALK culture) was developed by the Dynabook effort, the computer professionals recognized that bit-map screens, windows, mice, object-oriented programming, and graphics were useful to their work as well. What the Dynabook was for the seventies, the "Vivarium" [Brand 87] may be for the nineties, a project whose goals are to do for the next generation of humanizing computer use what the Dynabook did for the first—to be a "forcing function for technology that should have been worked 15 years ago."

Twenty years ago, the LOGO culture has pioneered the idea that "normal" people, even schoolchildren, could not only use computer but program computers. Eliminating the boundary between "using computers" and "programming computers" has become a major goal for many research efforts.

We need more than a driver education approach to computer literacy. Reducing people's competence in using computers to drive application programs without allowing them to tailor a system to their wants is as absurd as requiring essays to be formed out of paragraphs that are already written.

The goals of the efforts to create truly "convivial tools" have been best articulated by Ivan Illich [Illich 73] in his book "Tools for Conviviality":

> "Tools are intrinsic to social relationships. An individual relates himself in action to his society through the use of tools which he actively masters, or by which he is passively acted on. To the degree that he masters his tools, he can invest the world with his meaning; to the degree that he is mastered by his tools, the shape of the tool determines his own self-image. Convivial tools are those that give each person who uses them the greatest opportunity to enrich the environment with the fruits of his or her vision. Tools foster conviviality to the extent to which they can be easily used, by anybody, as often or as seldom as desired, for the accomplishment of a purpose chosen by the user."

Appendix I
LOGO Versions

Over the last 10 years, many different versions of LOGO have come into existence (see the discussion in chapter 39). The programs (as they appear in the text) have been written and tested using a modified version of LINCOLN–SUDBURY REGIONAL HIGH SCHOOL / BOSTON CHILDREN'S MUSEUM LOGO under UNIX™ and OBJECTLOGO on the MACINTOSH.

We do not intend for this section to be an exhaustive description of all the differences between all the LOGO systems available. Our goal is to present some differences that exist to give you an indication of things to look out for. [Harvey 85; Harvey 86; Harvey 87b; Friendly 88] contain excellent discussions of this topic.

The various programming environments for LOGO differ from each other even more than the various versions of the language. Therefore, we have intentionally omitted information that deals with details related to the programming environment (e.g., how to load LOGO, how to type a LOGO command, how to use the LOGO editor to modify procedures, how to **Save** the work on a disk file, and how to **Load** it back in at another time, etc.). We recommend that you consult the manual for your LOGO system for this information.

I.1. Syntax differences between LOGO versions

Autoquoting

Some systems allow you to leave the quote-mark off of words in certain situations:

```
? PrintOut MyProc
```

In this case, `MyProc` is not evaluated but is used as a literal name. This is known as "autoquoting." Although this has the advantage that typing is simpler when a listing of a procedure is needed, it has the disadvantage that when something other than a literal is intended, it cannot be specified without the use of the `Run` command. In some versions of LOGO, the primitive `Procedures` returns a list of all procedures. If you want to print out all the procedures in the workspace in a system that does not do autoquoting, this works:

```
? PrintOut Procedures
```

But, if autoquoting is performed, the definition of `Procedures` is printed instead.

If Commands

The syntax for constructs like the If command may vary. Whereas the systems we use in our examples have an If syntax that is no different than is used with other procedures, giving it a uniform syntax, some versions use special keywords to serve as mnemonic cues to someone writing (or reading) a program. For example:

- Keyword version:

      If :Word = "abc <u>Then</u> Output "def

  (The underlining is for emphasis only).

- Nonkeyword version:

      If :Word = "abc [Output "def]

The difference is even more noticeable with an if-else construct:

- Keyword version:

      If :Word = "abc <u>Then</u> Output "def <u>Else</u> Output "ghi

- Nonkeyword version:

      IfElse :Word = "abc [Output "def] [Output "ghi]

- Some nonkeyword versions treat If as having 2 or 3 arguments:

      If :Word = "abc [Output "def] [Output "ghi]

Special Treatment of Certain Characters

Some versions treat characters such as "(", ")", "[", "]", "=", "+", etc. as special characters called *delimiters*. These special characters do not require "white space" to separate them from neighboring words. As a matter of fact they can signal that the previous character was the end of a word. For example:

    "a=First Word

would be treated as

    "a = First Word

where other systems might consider this to be the two elements, the word a=first and the procedure name Word. In general, it is a good practice to put the spaces around these characters anyway, but what about the converse problem, when we **do** want to include these characters (or white space) in a word? Each system seems to have its own way of handling this: LINCOLN–SUDBURY REGIONAL HIGH SCHOOL / BOSTON CHILDREN'S MUSEUM LOGO uses the backslash ("\") to escape any special meaning of the next character, so "this\ \= would be the word this =. OBJECTLOGO uses pairs of the "|" character to delimit portions of literals containing special characters: We would write the last example:"|this =|. The best approach is to read your user's manual to find out how special characters are handled.

What is in a Name (Procedures and Variables)

A related topic concerns the use of nonalphabetic characters in the names of procedures and variables. The rules here vary from system to system:

* Almost no restrictions (except for delimiters)

* allow only letters

* allow only letters and digits but must start with a letter

* allow only letters and digits but must contain at least one letter

Sometimes the rules are different for procedure names than for variable names. The rationale for this may be based on parsing considerations: If the name of a procedure is allowed to be a number, then a number cannot always be taken at face value; it may be the name of a procedure to be executed instead of a literal value. Some funny things can be done[35]:

```
To 345
   Output 543
End

? Print 1 + 345
544
```

With names, however, the "`:`" usually provides a syntactic cue to distinguish between the number as a number and the number as a name:

```
Make "345 543
Print 345 + 1
345
Print :345 + 1
544
```

Once again, our recommendation to you if you wish to use special characters in names is to study your user's manual for your LOGO system.

Conventions for Naming Predicates

Some systems use the convention that the final letter of a predicate is the letter "P," whereas others use a final "?". For example: `NameP` vs. `Name?`.

I.2. Differences in Environment or Semantics

Redefinition of Primitives

In many versions of LOGO, you are not allowed to redefine the primitives provided by your system. In general, it is not a good idea to do this. Imagine the chaos that might ensue if you were to redefine `EqualP` in such a manner

---

[35]Some systems **do** allow this.

that things that should be equal weren't and vice versa! However, there are times when such an ability would be useful. In chapter 18 we resorted to defining and using the procedure MyGreaterP to keep track of how many times comparisons were made. It would have been simpler to write our own version of GreaterP, including the counting logic in it.

Using the Trace Command

The trace facility is extremely useful in debugging. For some systems, the Trace command has no inputs and turns on tracing for all user-defined procedures. In large programs, this creates a great deal of information, sometimes scrolling by on the screen so quickly that it is of little use (unless your system has scrollable windows, such that you can look back at what has scrolled off the top). In this situation it is better to isolate your problem (if possible) to portions of your program that can be traced easily.

Other systems require you to give an input to the Trace command, which specifies the procedure(s) to be traced. This allows you to do selective tracing, which limits substantially the amount of information printed out. If you need to trace all procedures, the Procedures operation (if available) outputs a list of all user-defined procedures; this can be used as input to Trace to achieve the same result as with systems whose Trace command takes no inputs.

In general, primitives or procedures that have been compiled do not show up on traces.

Some systems print out the values of inputs on entry into a procedure and the value output by an operation on exit from a procedure. This is very useful because it not only tells what procedures are called but it also gives a picture of the state of the computation at that point.

Indentation of the tracing information according to the level of the procedure nesting is also a useful feature of many systems as it gives you a better idea of where in the procedure tree you are at any given time.

Your system may also provide other debugging tools (such as a Step) command) to help you with pinpointing problems. Study your user's manual for what facilities are available and how to use them.

Purely Function Based vs. Command / Operation Based

Systems such as EXPERLOGO take an approach that removes the distinction between commands and operations discussed in section 2.3. All procedures are functions returning values, and the Output command is needed at the end of a function because it automatically outputs the last value it computed.

Number Limitations, Conversions

Some LOGO systems depend solely on the numeric capabilities of their computer's processor for numeric computation and are thereby limited to some computer-dependent value of how large a number can be. If the limits are exceeded some systems will merely complain (or worse, simply continue with their computation, using a bad value). Other systems will convert to floating point representation if an integer value becomes too large, taking advantage of the larger magnitude allowed by floating point numbers, while losing some precision.

Other systems utilize the symbolic capabilities of the computer to perform arbitrary precision integer arithmetic similar to what is done with LongSum in chapter 6. Although this is slower in general, for all practical purposes it allows integers to become as large as needed. A hybrid approach used by OBJECTLOGO uses the faster numeric capability for numbers that are small enough, then switches to the arbitrary precision format (rather than floating point) when the integer value becomes too large.

I.3. Lexical vs. Dynamic Scope

OBJECTLOGO makes a departure from traditional LOGOs in its use of *lexical* scope instead of dynamic scope. As described in section scope, dynamic scope allows procedures that have been invoked (directly or indirectly) by a given procedure to access that procedure's local variables unless there is some intervening definition that "intercepts" that reference. Lexical scope does not allow this; the only type of *nonlocal* reference is a *global* reference.

This can can problems in defining the tools described in chapter 23 such as For or WhileDo that need access to local variables from the calling procedures without having those values passed explicitly. OBJECTLOGO does provide a command, InsideAny, to circumvent lexical scoping.

Appendix II
LOGO Primitives Used in this Book

Here is a summary of the LOGO primitives used in this book. Each entry uses the following format:

PrimitiveName (Primitive type)	Synopsis of use Abbreviation or alternate name *An example of its use* Explanatory text See Also: `Cross references to other primitives`

| And
(predicate) | And *Boolean1 Boolean2*
Both *Boolean1 Boolean2*

`If And :Number < 8 :Number > 3`
`   [Print`
`      [The number is between`
`         4 and 7 (inclusive)]]`

Outputs `"True` if (and only if) both inputs are `"True`

See Also: `Or` |
| ASCII
(operation) | ASCII *Character*

`? Print ASCII "a`
`97`

Outputs the number that is the internal numeric (ASCII[36] and is a standard way of encoding characters as numbers.) representation of the character given as input

See Also: `Char` |

---

[36]ASCII stands for American Standard Code for Information Interchange

ButFirst	ButFirst *WordOrList*
(operation)	BF *WordOrList*

```
? Print ButFirst "house
ouse
? Print ButFirst [Jan Jerry Julia]
Jerry Julia
```

Requires a word or a list as input and outputs the word (resp. the list) without its first element (i.e., the word without its first character; resp. the list without its first element). If a list is given, the result is always a list, even if it only consists of one word.

See Also: `First, Last, ButLast`

ButLast	ButLast *WordOrList*
(operation)	BL *WordOrList*

```
? Print ButLast "house
hous
? Print ButLast [Jan Jerry Julia]
Jan Jerry
```

Requires a word or a list as input and outputs the word (resp. the list) without its last element (i.e., the word without its last character; resp. the list without its last word). If a list is given, the result is always a list, even if it only consists of one word.

See Also: `ButFirst, First, Last`

Char	Char *Number*
(operation)	

```
? Char 97
a
```

Outputs a word composed of the character that has the ASCII code given by the input

See Also: `ASCII`

Cos	Cos *Degrees*
(operation)	

```
? Print Cos 0
1.0
```

Outputs the cosine of the angle given as input. The angle is specified as a number representing degrees.

See Also: `Sin`

Count (operation)	Count *Sequence*

```
? Print Count "abcde
5
? Print Count [ab cd ef]
3
```

Outputs the number of elements contained in the input sequence. If the input is a word, it counts the number of letters in the word. If the input is a list, it counts the number of elements (words or lists) at the top level of that list

Difference (operation)	Difference *Number1 Number2* (infix) *Number1 - Number2*

```
? Print 5 - 3
2
```

Outputs the result from subtracting the second number from the first.

See Also: Sum, Product, Quotient, Remainder

EmptyP (predicate)	EmptyP *Sequence*

```
? Print EmptyP []
True
? Print EmptyP "
True
? Print EmptyP [a b c]
False
? Print EmptyP "abc
False
```

Outputs "True if the input sequence is empty (the empty word or the empty list).

EqualP (predicate)	EqualP *Object1 Object2* Is *Object1 Object2* (infix) *Object1 = Object2*

```
? Print (ButFirst [a]) = []
True
```

Outputs "True if the two inputs are equal.

EraseName
(command)

EraseName *Name*

```
? PrintOutName Names
a is [a b c]
b is [d e f]
? EraseName "a
? PrintOutName Names
b is [d e f]
```

The name specified by the input is removed from the workspace. This may be Erase in some versions, or may not exist in other versions

See Also: PrintOutName

First
(operation)

First *WordOrList*

```
? Print First "house
h
? Print First [Jan Jerry Julia]
Jan
```

The input to First must be a word or a list; the output is the first element of the input (i.e., the first character of the word or the first element of the list).

See Also: Last, ButFirst, ButLast

Forward
(command)

Forward *Amount*
FD *Amount*

```
? Repeat 3 [Forward 100 Left 60]
```

Moves the graphics turtle forward the amount indicated in the current direction.

See Also: Left, Right, SetXY

| FPut
(operation) | FPut *Element Seqeunce* |

? **Print FPut "Jan [Jerry Julia]**
Jan Jerry Julia

FPut requires two inputs. The first input—a word—is inserted as the new first element or the the second input, which must be a sequence.

See Also: **Sentence, List, LPut**

GreaterP
(predicate)

GreaterP *Number1 Number2*
(infix) *Number1 > Number2*

If :Val > 5 [Print [Number to large!]]

Outputs "**True** if the first input is numerically larger than the second input. Both inputs must be numbers.

See Also: **LessP, EqualP**

If
(command)

If *Condition CommandList*

? **If 4 > 3 [Print [What do you know!]]**
What do you know!

```
To Abs :Number
 If (First :Number) = "-
  [Output ButFirst :Number]
 Output :Number
End
```

If executes the command list if the first input is "**True**.

See Also: **IfElse**

IfElse
(command)

IfElse *Condition CommandList1 CommandList2*

```
? IfElse 4 > 3
        [Print [What do you know!]]
        [Print [Somethings rotten in Logo]]
What do you know!

To Abs :Number
 IfElse (First :Number) = "-
 [Output ButFirst :Number]
 [Output :Number]
End
```

If executes the first command list if the first input is "True; otherwise it executes the second command list.

See Also: If

IfFalse
(command)

IfFalse *CommandList*

```
? Test 4 > 3
? IfFalse Print [What do you know!]
What do you know!

To Abs :Number
 Test First :Number = "-
 IfTrue Output ButFirst :Number
 IfFalse Output :Number
End
```

IfFalse checks whether the flag (set by Test) is set to False. If so, the command list is executed.

See Also: Test, IfTrue

IfTrue
(command)

IfTrue *CommandList*

```
? Test 4 > 3
? IfTrue Print "Aha!
Aha!

To Abs :Number
 Test First :Number = "-
 IfTrue Output ButFirst :Number
 IfFalse Output :Number
End
```

IfTrue checks whether the flag (set by Test) is set to True. If so, the command list is executed.

See Also: Test, IfFalse

Last (operation)	Last *WordOrList*

```
? Print Last "house
e
? Print Last [Jan Jerry Julia]
Julia
```

The input to Last must be a word or a list; its output is the last element of the input (i.e., the last character of the word; resp. the last element of the list).

See Also: First, ButFirst, ButLast

Left (command)	Left *Degrees* LT *Degrees*

See Entry for Forward

Changes the heading (direction of travel) of the graphics turtle by the number of degrees indicated to the left.

See Also: Forward, Right

LessP (predicate)	LessP *Number1 Number2* (infix) *Number1 < Number2*

```
If LessP :Value 3
    [Print [The number is too small]]
```

Outputs "True if the first input is numerically smaller than the second input. Both inputs must be numbers.

See Also: GreaterP, EqualP

ListP (predicate)	ListP *Input*

```
? Print ListP 1234
False
? Print ListP Sentence "Handy "Dan
True
```

The input is checked to see whether it is a List. If so it outputs True otherwise False.

See Also: WordP, Sentence

Make (command)	Make *Word Value* ``` ? Make "Number 10 ? Print :Number 10 ``` Make requires two Inputs. The first input must be a word and then becomes the name of a variable; the second input can be any object and that object becomes the value contained by the variable. See Also: Thing
MemberP (predicate)	MemberP *Element Sequence* ``` ? Print MemberP "a "sample True ? Print MemberP "abc [xyz abc def] False ``` Outputs "True if the element is one of the elements of the sequence
NameP (predicate)	NameP *Word* ``` ? NameP "Variable False ? Make "Variable [] ? NameP "Variable True ``` Outputs "True if the word is the name of a variable. See Also: Make
Not (predicate)	Not *Boolean* ``` ? Print Not "True False ``` Outputs "True if the input is "False and vice versa. See Also: And, Or

Nth (operation)	Nth *Index Sequence* Item *Index Sequence* ```? Print Nth 3 [ab cd ef gh]``` *ef* Outputs the item from the sequence whose position is indicated by the index.

Or
(predicate)
	Or *Predicate1 Predicate2*
	
	```? Print Or (1=2) (1+1=3)```
	False
	```? Print Or```
	``` (Wordp [Handy Dan])```
	``` (Listp [Handy Dan])```
	True
	
	Or requires two inputs, which are either "True or "False. The output is "True, if at least one input is "True, otherwise the output is "False. Several inputs may be given by surrounding the Or and its inputs with parentheses.
	
	See Also: And, Not

Output
(command)
	Output *Value*
	OP *Value*
	
	```To Add1 :Number```
	``` Output :Number + 1```
	```End```
	
	```? Print Add1 10```
	11
	
	The command Output ends the execution of a procedure and makes its input the output of the procedure. Procedures with Output have the characteristics of operations.
	
	See Also: Stop

Print   Print *Input*
(command)   PR *Input*

```
? Print "house
house
? Print [This is a sentence]
This is a sentence
```

The input to `Print` is printed followed by a linefeed.
Several inputs may be given, if `Print` and its inputs are
grouped with parentheses.

PrintOut   PrintOut *ProcedureName*
(command)

```
? PrintOut Add1
To Add1  :Number
  Output :Number + 1
End
```

A procedure, which has been defined in the workspace, is
displayed on the terminal screen, without using the LOGO
Editor.

See Also: `Erase`

PrintOutName   PrintOutName *Name*
(command)

```
? PrintOutName Names
a is [a b c]
b is [d e f]
? EraseName "a
? PrintOutName Names
b is [d e f]
```

The name(s) specified by the input is (are) printed out.
This may be `PrintOut` in some versions, or may not
exist in other versions

See Also: `EraseName`

Product   Product *Number1 Number2*
(operation)   (infix) *Number1 * Number2*

```
? Print 5 * 3
15
```

Outputs the result of multiplying number1 by number2.

See Also: `Quotient`, `Sum`, `Difference`,
`Remainder`

Quotient (operation)	Quotient *Number1 Number2*
	(infix) *Number1 / Number2*
	
	`? Print 15 / 3`
	`5`
	
	Outputs the result of dividing number1 by number2. If both inputs are integers, the result is the truncated integer dividend. If one input is floating point, the result is a floating point number.
	
	See Also: `Product, Sum, Difference, Remainder`

Random (operation)	Random *Number*
	
	`? Print Random 50`
	`31 (a number between 0 and 49 inclusive)`
	
	Outputs a (pseudo) random number less than the indicated number.

ReadList (operation)	ReadList
	RL
	
	`To SpeakTo`
	`  Print [ Say something to me!]`
	`  Print ReadList`
	`  SpeakTo`
	`End`
	
	`ReadList` waits for keyboard input and furnishes the subsequent input characters (up to the `Return`) as output in form of a sentence.

Remainder (operation)	Remainder *Integer1 Integer2*
	(infix) *Integer1 \ Integer2*
	
	`? Print Remainder 19 5`
	`4`
	
	Outputs the remainder resulting from dividing integer1 by integer2
	
	See Also: `Quotient, Sum, Difference, Product`

Repeat
(command)

Repeat *Number CommandList*

```
? Repeat 3 [Print "Hello]
Hello
Hello
Hello
```

Performs the command list the specified number of times.

See Also:

Right
(command)

Right *Degrees*
Rt *Degrees*

Analagous to use of Left in example
of Forward

Changes the heading (direction of travel) of the graphics
turtle by the number of degrees indicated to the right.

See Also:

Run
(command or
operation)

Run *RunList*

```
? Run [Print "Harry]
Harry
? Run Sentence "Show Word "Mag "Nitude
To Abs :Number
  Test First :Number = "-
  IfTrue Output ButFirst :Number
  IfFalse Output :Number
End
```

Run requires a sentence as input and executes the contents
of this sentence, as if it were given directly from the
Keyboard. If the executed sentence has the characteristics
of an operation, then its output is ''passed through'' and
becomes the output of Run.

Sentence (operation)	Sentence *WordOrSentence1 WordOrSentence2*

```
? Print Sentence "Handy "Dan
Handy Dan
? Print Sentence "This [is a sentence]
This is a sentence
```

Two words or sentences are joined into one sentence and output. Several inputs may be given, if the Sentence and its inputs are grouped with parentheses.

See Also: Word, FPut

SetXY (command)	SetXY *XPosition YPosition*

See chapter 24

Moves the mouse to the indicated X and Y position.

Show (command)	Show *Input*

```
? Show FPut "a []
[a]
```

Show is similar to Print because it prints its input on the terminal screen or window. However, Show prints the enclosing bracket on lists whereas Print does not.

See Also: Print, Type

Sin (operation)	Sin *Degrees*

```
? Print Sin 0
0.0
```

Outputs the sine of the angle given as input. The angle is specified as a number representing degrees.

See Also: Cos

Stop
(command)

Stop

```
To Shorten :In
  Test :In = "
  IfTrue Stop
  Print :In
  Shorten ButLast :In
End
```

Stop ends the execution of a procedure, without giving back a value to the calling procedure (as Output does). Procedures with Stop have the characteristics of commands.

See Also: Output

Sum
(operation)

Sum *Number1 Number2*
(infix) *Number1 + Number2*

```
? Print Sum 1 99
100
```

Outputs the result of adding the two numbers together.

See Also: Difference, Product, Quotient, Remainder

Test
(command)

Test *Predicate*

```
? Test 4 > 3
? IfTrue Print "AHA!
AHA!
```

```
To Abs :Number
  Test First :Number = "-
  IfTrue Output ButFirst :Number
  IfFalse Output :Number
End
```

Test sets the flag to True or False, according to whether the condition after Test is met or not. The flag remains unchanged up to next Test-Command and can be checked with IfTrue and IfFalse.

See Also: IfTrue, IfFalse

Thing
(operation)
	Thing *VariableName*
	
	`? Make "Number 10`
	`? Print Thing "Number`
	`10`
	`? Print :Number`
	`10`
	
	`Thing` needs the name of a variable as its input and outputs the value that has been assigned to that variable (with `Make`) value.
	
	See Also: `Make`

TopLevel
(command)
	TopLevel
	Top
	
	`If :Divisor = 0`
	`    [Print [You can't divide by zero]`
	`    TopLevel]`
	
	Returns control to the top level LOGO interperter.

Trace (command)	System Dependent `See your User's Manual` Used to initiate tracing. See discussion in Appendix I.

Type
(command)
	Type *Input*
	
	`? Type "This`
	`This?`
	
	Similar to `Print` except that no newline is printed after the information is printed on the terminal screen or window.
	
	See Also: `Print, Show`

UnTrace (command)	System Dependent `See your User's Manual` Used to turn off tracing. See discussion in Appendix I.

Word
(operation)

Word *Word1 Word2*

```
? Print Word "Handy "Dan
HandyDan
```

The two inputs (which must be words) are joined into one and the resulting word is output. Several inputs may be given, if Word and its inputs are grouped with parentheses.

See Also: Sentence

WordP
(predicate)

WordP *Input*

```
? Print WordP "house
True
? Print WordP [ house ]
false
```

The Input is checked to see whether it is a word. If it is, the output of WordP is True; otherwise the output is False.

See Also: ListP

Appendix III
Utility Procedures

You may find that there are a number of procedures that are not defined in advance in the version of LOGO you are using, but would be useful as building blocks in various programs. This appendix is a compilation of some procedures that we feel fit into this category.

III.1. Arithmetic

Exp is an operation that raises its first input to the power specified by the second input and returns the result.

```
To Exp :Basis :Expo
  Test :Expo = 0
  IfTrue [Output 1]
  Output :Basis * Exp :Basis Sub1 :Expo
End
```

Abs computes the magnitude of a number:

```
To Abs :Number
  Test (First :Number) = "-
  IfTrue [Output ButFirst :Number]
  Output :Number
End

? Print Abs -5
5
```

Minimum and Maximum compare two numbers returning the one that is smaller (respectively, larger).

```
To Minimum :A :B
  IfElse GreaterP :A :B
    [Output :B]
    [Output :A]
End

To Maximum :A :B
  IfElse LessP :A :B
    [Output :B]
    [Output :A]
End
```

III.2. Formatting

With many problems, you need to print the results out in clearly arranged form (see, for example, printing the table of statistics in chapter 33). `Spaces` produces an arbitrary number of space characters. `BlankLines` prints out the specified number of empty lines.

```
To Spaces :N
  Test :N = 0
  IfTrue [Output " ]
  Output Word Char 32 Spaces :N - 1
End

To BlankLines :N
  Test :N = 0
  IfTrue [Stop]
  Print "
  BlankLines :N - 1
End
```

In `Spaces`, a space character is generated using `Char 32` (`Char` is described in appendix I.3, and `32` is the ASCII code of the space character).

`PadLeft` and `PadRight` help with producing columns of data by creating words of at least the specified length by adding spaces to one end or the other of a word.

```
To PadLeft :N :Word
  Local "Length
  Make "Length Count :Word
  If :Length < :N
    [Output Word Spaces :N - :Length :Word]
  Output :Word
End

To PadRight :N :Word
  Local "Length
  Make "Length Count :Word
  If :Length < :N
    [Output Word :Word Spaces :N - :Length]
  Output :Word
End

? Print (Word ". PadLeft 5 "a ".)
.    a.
? Print (Word ". PadRight 5 "a ".)
.a    .
```

III.3. Data Structures

`PutProp` stores a value (the third input) on the property list of a name (the first input) under a specified property (the second input). `GetProp` retrieves the value from the property (the second input) of the specified name (the first input):

```
To Putprop :Object :Property :Value
   Make (Word :Object "& :Property) :Value
End

To Getprop :Object :Property
   Output Thing (Word :Object "& :Property)
End
```

This version of PutProp generates global variables of the form:

```
"bill&age is 27
"bill&profession is "teacher
```

III.4. Program Modifications

This group of procedures, which we discussed in section 10.1, could form the basis for a package that could be used as an editing system.

```
To Change :Pname :Old :New
   Define :Pname ModifyProcedure Text :Pname :Old :New
End

To ModifyProcedure :Text :W1 :W2
   Test :Text = [ ]
   IfTrue [Output [ ]]
   Output
     Put
       ModifyLine First :Text :W1 :W2
       ModifyProcedure ButFirst :Text :W1 :W2
End

To ModifyLine :Line :W1 :W2
   Test :Line = [ ]
   IfTrue [Output [ ]]
   Test (First :Line) = :W1
   IfTrue
     [Output
       Fput
         :W2
         ModifyLine ButFirst :Line :W1 :W2]
   Output
     Fput
       First :Line
       ModifyLine ButFirst :Line :W1 :W2
End
```

The last procedure can be use independently from the two others. With it, all occurrences of a word in an arbitrarily long sentence can be replaced by another word.

```
? Print ModifyLine [every cow has horns] "cow "bull
every bull has horns
```

III.5. General Procedures

The procedures given in this section have proven to be building blocks that can be used for varied programs. It is not necessary to describe their applicability further.

EmptyP test whether a sequence contains no elements.

```
To EmptyP :Item
   Output Or :Item = " :Item = [ ]
End
```

Count determines the number of elements in a sequence (letters in a word, words in a sentence, or elements in a list);

```
To Count :Sequence
   Test EmptyP :Sequence
   IfTrue [Output 0]
   Output (Count ButFirst :Sequence) + 1
End
```

SentenceCount determined the number of letters in a sentence.

```
To SentenceCount :Sentence
   Test EmptyP :Sentence
   IfTrue [Output 0]
   Output
     (Count First :Sentence)
     +
     (Count ButFirst :Sentence)
End
```

```
? Print Count "house
5
? Print Count [this is a sentence]
4
? Print Count [this [is a] list]
3
? Print SentenceSize [The house burned]
14
```

The oft-used Mirror procedure creates a mirror image of a word or list

```
To Mirror :Sequence
   IfElse WordP :Sequence
     [Output MirrorWord :Sequence]
     [Output MirrorList :Sequence]
End
```

```
To MirrorWord :Word
   Test EmptyP :Word
   IfTrue [Output :Word]
   Output Word MirrorWord ButFirst :Word First :Word
End
```

```
To MirrorList :List
  Test EmptyP :List
  IfTrue [Output :List]
  Output
    LPut Mirror First :List MirrorList ButFirst :List
End
```

The procedure Reverse works just like Mirror for words, but for lists the order of the elements is reversed, but the elements themselves are remain unchanged.

```
? Print Mirror "abc
cba
? Print Mirror [this is a sentence]
ecnetnes a si siht
? Print Mirror [this [is a] list]
tsil [a si] siht
? Print Reverse "abc
cba
? Print Reverse [this is a sentence]
sentence a is this
? Print Reverse [this [is a] list]
list [is a] this
```

The procedure Remove removes the first instance of an element from a sequence:

```
To Remove :Element :Sequence
  IfElse WordP :Sequence
    [Output RemoveFromWord :Element :Sequence]
    [Output RemoveFromList :Element :Sequence]
End

To RemoveFromWord :Letter :Word
  If EmptyP :Word [Output :Word]
  If :Letter = First :Word [Output ButFirst :Word]
  Output
    Word
      First :Word
      RemoveFromWord :Letter ButFirst :Word
End

To RemoveFromList :Element :List
  If EmptyP :List [Output :List]
  If :Element = First :List [Output ButFirst :List]
  Output
    FPut
      First :List
      RemoveFromList :Element ButFirst :List
End

? Print Remove "b "abcabc
acabc
? Print Remove [ab] [a [a] ab [ab] c]
a [a] ab c
```

`RemoveAll` removes all instances of an element from a sequence:

```
To RemoveAll :Element :Sequence
  IfElse WordP :Sequence
    [Output RemoveAllFromWord :Element :Sequence]
    [Output RemoveAllFromList :Element :Sequence]
End

To RemoveAllFromWord :Letter :Word
  If EmptyP :Word [Output :Word]
  If :Letter = First :Word
    [Output RemoveAllFromWord :Letter ButFirst :Word]
  Output
    Word
       First :Word
       RemoveAllFromWord :Letter ButFirst :Word
End

To RemoveAllFromList :Element :List
  If EmptyP :List [Output :List]
  If :Element = First :List
    [Output RemoveAllFromList :Element ButFirst :List]
  Output
    FPut
       First :List
       RemoveAllFromList :Element ButFirst :List
End

? Print RemoveAll "b "abcabc
acac
? Print RemoveAll [ab] [a [a] ab [ab] c [ab]]
a [a] ab c
```

`Insert` inserts an element into a list at the specified position:

```
To Insert :Element :List :Pos
  IfElse WordP :List
    [Output InsertWord :Element :List :Pos]
    [Output InsertList :Element :List :Pos]
End

To InsertWord :Letter :Word :Pos
  IfElse :Pos = 1
    [Output Word :Letter :Word]
    [Output
       Word
          First :Word
          InsertWord :Letter ButFirst :Word :Pos - 1]
End

To InsertList :Element :List :Pos
  IfElse :Pos = 1
    [Output FPut :Element :List]
    [Output
       FPut
          First :List
          InsertList :Element ButFirst :List :Pos - 1]
End
```

```
? Print Insert "a "defg 2
daefg
? Print Insert "a [d e f g] 2
d a e f g
? Print Insert [a] [d e f g] 2
d [a] e f g
```

The procedures FirstN, LastN, ButFirstN, and ButLastN generalize the LOGO primitives First, Last, ButFirst, and ButLast.

```
To FirstN :N :List
   IfElse WordP :List
      [Output FirstNWord :N :List]
      [Output FirstNList :N :List]
End

To FirstNWord :N :Word
   If :N = 0 [Output "]
   Output
      Word First :Word FirstNWord :N - 1 ButFirst :Word
End

To FirstNList :N :List
   If :N = 0 [Output [ ]]
   Output
      FPut First :List FirstNList :N - 1 ButFirst :List
End

To ButFirstN :N :List
   If :N = 0 [Output :List]
   If EmptyP :List [Output :List]
   Output ButFirstN :N - 1 ButFirst :List
End

To LastN :N :List
   IfElse WordP :List
      [Output LastNWord :N :List]
      [Output LastNList :N :List]
End

To LastNWord :N :Word
   If :N = 0 [Output "]
   Output
      Word LastNWord :N - 1 ButLast :Word Last :Word
End

To LastNList :N :List
   If :N = 0 [Output [ ]]
   Output
      LPut Last :List LastNList :N - 1 ButLast :List
End

To ButLastN :N :List
   If :N = 0 [Output :List]
   If EmptyP :List [output :List]
   Output ButLastN :N - 1 ButLast :List
End
```

The procedure Nth allows an arbitrary element to be extracted from a sequence.

```
To Nth :N :List
   If EmptyP :List [Output "]
   If :N = 1 [Output First :List]
   Output Nth :N - 1 ButFirst :List
End
```

The procedures UpToChar and AfterChar also "divide-up" a word, but instead of this being specified as position number, it is based on finding the first match of a letter.

```
To UpToChar :N :S
   If (First :S) = :N [Output "]
   Output Word First :S UpToChar :N ButFirst :S
End
```

```
To AfterChar :N :S
   If (Last :S) = :N [Output "]
   Output Word AfterChar :N ButLast :S Last :S
End
```

III.6. Set Operations

The predicate MemberP tests whether a letter (word) is contained in the given word (list).

```
To MemberP :Element :Set
   Test EmptyP :Set
   IfTrue [Output "False]
   Test :Element = First :Set
   IfTrue [Output "True]
   Output MemberP :Element ButFirst :Set
End
```

SetDifference returns all the elements in the first set not contained in the second set (we use the name SetDifference to avoid conflict with the primitive for subtraction Difference):

```
To SetDifference :A :B
   If :A = [ ] Output [ ]
   If MemberP First :A :B
      [Output SetDifference ButFirst :A :B]
   Output FPut First :A SetDifference ButFirst :A :B
End
```

Union creates the union of two sets represented by lists(all elements of both sets combined with duplicates removed):

```
To Union :A :B
   If :B = [ ] [Output :A]
   If MemberP Last :B :A [Output Union :A ButLast :B]
   Output LPut Last :B Union :A ButLast :B
End
```

`Intersection` returns all elements that are members of both sets.

```
To Intersection :List1 :List2
  ;; this doe not really enforce the "no duplicates"
  ;; rule for sets; if there matching duplicates in
  ;; the inputs, there will be duplicates in the result
  Test :List1 = [ ]
  IfTrue [Output [ ]]
  Test MemberP (First :List1) :List2
  IfTrue
    [Output
       FPut
         (First :List1)
         (Intersection
            (ButFirst :List1)
            (Remove (First :List1) :List2))]
  Output Intersection (ButFirst :List1) :List2
End
```

Examples:

```
? MemberP [50] [[[100] [50]] [[50] [0]] [[10] [0]]]
True
? Print
    Difference
        [[100] [60] [55] [52]] [[60] [10] [20] [10]]
[100] [55] [52]
? Print Union
    [[100] [50] [55] [20] [10]]
    [[100] [90] [50] [40] [20] [15]]
[[100] [50] [55] [20] [10] [40] [15]]
? Print Intersection
    [[100] [50] [55] [50] [20] [10]]
    [[100] [90] [50] [40] [20] [15]]
[100] [50] [20]
```

`YesP` can be used to read a yes-or-no response from the user; it returns `"True` if the response is a positive one, and `"False` otherwise.

```
To YesP
  Output MemberP First ReadList [y yes oui 1 + si]
End
```

This can easily be extended with other words and phrases to be accepted as affirmative responses.

Appendix IV
Conventions Used in this Book

The following conventions are used throughout the text :

- Interactive examples use the convention that words in *this font* are words printed out by the computer and words in **this font** are things that were typed into the computer, for example:

```
Welcome to Logo
? "word
You don't say what to do with "word.
```

- When presenting the entire text of a procedure we use the following font/indentation scheme.

```
To Compute :Input1 :Input2 ...
   One
      Logo
         Line
   Second Line
   If You Can Read "This
      [You understand our indentation
         Don't You]
End
```

- Even though some versions of LOGO require continuation characters to allow command lines to be spread over several text lines, or special notation to allow several commands on one line or in a run list, we have not included these elements, because they are implementation dependent. We have attempted to use an indentation scheme that makes the procedures more readable. We have also used a MixedCase convention for names, because there are studies that have shown mixed-case text to be more readable . For the same reason, we have used the full names of primitives (e.g., `Print` instead of `Pr`, `ButFirst` instead of `BF`).

- We make the assumption that the *case* of the letters in words does not matter: Just as many systems will understand `butfirst`, `BUTFIRST`, `ButFirst`, or `BUtfiRSt`, we feel that the default behaviour should be that comparisons of `"this`, `"THIS`, and `"tHiS` would treat them as all being equal. If there is a need to make distinctions based on case (say, you want to write a program that checks your capitalization), there should be a mechanism to specify this. Most systems do not allow this; OBJECTLOGO does ignore case when comparing words, but there is no easy way to indicate that comparisons should be case sensitive. One of the modifications we made to the LINCOLN–SUDBURY REGIONAL HIGH

SCHOOL / BOSTON CHILDREN'S MUSEUM LOGO we used was to map all strings to lowercase; this was not the proper way to handle the problem either. If you are working on a system other than OBJECTLOGO, you should determine how it handles case and make the appropriate adjustments in the programs.

- Comments in the LOGO programs begin with a ";" and continue through the end of line.

- The names of predicates end with a "P".

- We do not use quotes for numbers (e.g., `Print` 5), but inputs to `Edit`, `Show`, `Text`, etc. are quoted (i.e., the systems we use don't do autoquoting).

Appendix V
Additional Resources

It is our hope that this book provides you with a starting point for exploring interactive problem solving. To continue this journey, the resources mentioned here may be useful.

Supplementary Materials on Diskette

The focus of our book has been on problem solving, not on technical skills, such as typing. Whereas it may be important to develop such skills, more often than not those skills develop naturally as an outgrowth of being immersed in some other activity like writing or problem solving. In keeping with this, we have made the text of the LOGO procedures shown in this book available on diskette.

These supplementary materials are made available to be used as a starting point for further study. The procedures may still contain some "bugs" but we feel that their presence provides an opportunity for you to grapple with them and thereby better understand the material.

The materials are available on 3 forms of media (3.5 inch MacIntosh diskettes, 3.5 inch IBM diskettes, and 5.25 inch IBM diskettes). However, the contents of all of the diskettes are the same; we have made no adaptations for various versions of LOGO. They all are basically as presented in this book (LCSI-Family syntax) but they are not formatted (indented, etc.) in the same way. Unless you use the same LOGO system that we used to test the programs, you will probably have to change them to make them work on your system. For some of the chapters, a `TestSuite` procedure containing most of the examples of test runs from the chapter is provided to help with this process. We have tried to avoid elements that we knew were specific to our versions of LOGO, but we may have missed some. If you do find specific problems, we would like to know about them; just write to us in care of the publisher.

A mail-in card has been included with this book if you wish to order these materials. If it is missing, you can obtain ordering information from:

Lawrence Erlbaum Associates, Inc., Publishers
365 Broadway
Hillsdale, NJ 07642
(201) 666-4110

Organizations

Here are the names and addresses of a couple of organizations that provide valuable resources for the LOGO educator and user.

SIGLogo
International Society for Technology in Education (ISTE)
University of Oregon
1787 Agate St
Eugene, OR 97403-9905
(503) 346-4414

Curriculum Instruction Division
Learning and Instruction Division
AI & ED SIG
American Educational Research Association (AERA)
1230 17th ST NW
Washington DC 20036-3078
(202) 223-9485

British Logo Users Group (BLUG)
P. O. Box 43
Houghton on the Hill
Leicestershire, England
LE7 9GX

Publications

Logo Exchange
Sharon Yoder, Ed.
ISTE
University of Oregon
1787 Agate St
Eugene, OR 97403-9905
(503) 346-4414

Interactive Learning Environments
Eliot Soloway, Ed.
Ablex Publishers
355 Chestnut St.
Norwood, NJ 07648
(201) 767-8450

Cognitive Science
Martin Ringle, Ed.
Ablex Publishers
355 Chestnut St.
Norwood, NJ 07648
(201) 767-8450

Logos
British Logo Users Group
P. O. Box 43
Houghton on the Hill
Leicestershire, England
LE7 9GX

Star Logo
Logotron, Ltd
Dale's Brewery
Gwydir St
Cambridge, England
CB1 2LJ
0223 323 656

Terrapin Times
Dorothy Fitch, Ed.
Terrapin Software
400 Riverside St
Portland, ME 04103
(207) 878-8200

Classroom Computer Learning
Peter Lee Publications
Dayton OH
(513) 294-5785
New York, NY
(212) 947-2300
Los Angeles, CA
(415) 457-4333

Children's Environment Quarterly
Lawrence Erlbaum Associates, Inc., Publishers
365 Broadway
Hillsdale, NJ 07642

LOGO Systems

We provide this information only as a service to the reader. This is not a complete listing of products and companies. Inclusion in this list does not constitute an endorsement of the company or their products.

ObjectLogo (MacIntosh)
Paradigm Software
P.O. Box 2995
Cambridge, MA 02238
(617) 576-7675

LogoWriter (IBM/Tandy, AppleIIe, IIGS, Commodore 64, IBM PCjr)
LCSI LogoII (Apple 128)
Logo Computer Systems, Inc.
P.O. Box 162
Higate Springs, VT 05460
(800) 321-LOGO (5646)

Logo PLUS (128K Apple)
Terrapin Logo (64K Apple)
Commodore Logo (64/128)
Terrapin Logo (512K MacIntosh)
PC Logo (128K IBM)
Also: Curriculum Materials, Robotic Kits
Terrapin Software, Inc.
400 Riverside Street
Portland, ME 04103
(207) 878-8200

ExperLogo (MacIntosh)
Expertelligence Inc.
5638 Hollister Ave.
Suite 302
Goleta, CA 93117

Index

\ 9

Index of Procedures

This is a compilation of all the procedures defined in this book, as well as all LOGO primitives discussed. If a procedure is used in this book, it should be referenced here; if it is not, we goofed!

References

[Abelson 82]
H. Abelson, *Apple Logo*, McGraw-Hill, New York, 1982.

[Abelson, diSessa 80]
H. Abelson, A. diSessa, *Turtle Geometry: Computer as a Medium for Exploring Mathematics*, The MIT Press, Cambridge, MA, 1980.

[American Heritage Dictionary 82]
W. Morris (ed.), *American Heritage Dictionary*, Houghton Mifflin, Boston, MA, 1982.

[Berlekamp, Conway, Guy 82]
E.R. Berlekamp, J.H. Conway, R.K. Guy, *What is Life?*, in *Winning Ways for your mathematical plays—Games in Particular*, Academic Press, London - New York, 1982, pp. 817-849, ch. 25.

[Boecker, Fischer, Plehnert 86]
H.-D. Boecker, G. Fischer, M. Plehnert, *Interaktives Problemloesen mit LOGO -- Vol. 1: Einfuehrung in das interaktive Programmieren*, IWT-Verlag GmbH, W. Germany, 1986.

[Boecker, Fischer, Plehnert 87]
H.-D. Boecker, G. Fischer, M. Plehnert, *Interaktives Problemloesen mit LOGO -- Vol. 5: Spiele*, IWT-Verlag GmbH, W. Germany, 1987.

[Boecker, Fischer, Schollwoeck 86a]
H.-D. Boecker, G. Fischer, U. Schollwoeck, *Interaktives Problemloesen mit LOGO -- Vol. 2: Mathematik*, IWT-Verlag GmbH, W. Germany, 1986.

[Boecker, Fischer, Schollwoeck 86b]
H.-D. Boecker, G. Fischer, U. Schollwoeck, *Interaktives Problemloesen mit LOGO -- Vol. 3: Informatik*, IWT-Verlag GmbH, W. Germany, 1986.

[Boecker, Fischer, Schollwoeck 87]
H.-D. Boecker, G. Fischer, U. Schollwoeck, *Interaktives Problemloesen mit LOGO -- Vol. 4: Kuenstliche Intelligenz und Sprache*, IWT-Verlag GmbH, W. Germany, 1987.

[Brand 87]
S. Brand, *The Media Lab*, Viking Penguin Inc., New York, 1987.

[Brown et al. 75]
J.S. Brown, R. Burton, M. Miller, J. de Kleer, S. Purcell, C. Hausmann, R. Bobrow, *Steps Toward a Theoretical Foundation for a Complex Knowledge-Based CAI*, Report 3135, BBN, August 1975.

[Burton, Brown 82]
R.R. Burton, J.S. Brown, *An Investigation of Computer Coaching for Informal Learning Activities*, in D.H. Sleeman, J.S. Brown (eds.), *Intelligent Tutoring Systems*, Academic Press, London - New York, 1982, pp. 79-98, ch. 4.

[Burton, Brown, Fischer 84]
R.R. Burton, J.S. Brown, G. Fischer, *Analysis of Skiing as a Success Model of Instruction: Manipulating the Learning Environment to Enhance Skill Acquisition*, in B. Rogoff, J. Lave (eds.), *Everyday Cognition: Its Development in Social Context*, Harvard University Press, Cambridge, MA - London, 1984, pp. 139-150.

[Davidson 86]
L.J. Davidson, G.C. Forrester, S. Hain, B. Harvey, J.A. Jones, P.G. Lewis, *ObjectLogo*, Coral Software Corp., Cambridge, MA, 1986.

[diSessa, Abelson 86]
A. diSessa, H. Abelson, *Boxer: A Reconstructible Computational Medium*, Communications of ACM, Vol. 29, No. 9, September 1986, pp. 859-868.

[Dugdale, Kibbey 77]
S. Dugdale, D. Kibbey, *Elementary Mathematics with PLATO*, University of Illinois (Computer-based Education Research Laboratory, Urbana, IL, 1977.

[Falbel 89]
A. Falbel, *FRISKOLEN 70: An Ethnographically Informed Inquiry Into the Social Context of Learning*, Unpublished Ph.D. Dissertation, Media Arts and Sciences, Massachusetts Institute of Technology, June 1989.

[Feurzeig et al. 69]
W. Feurzeig, et al., *Programming Languages as a Conceptual Framework for Teaching Mathematics*, Report 1989, BBN, Boston, MA, 1969.

[Fischer 81]
G. Fischer, *Computer als konviviale Werkzeuge*, Proceedings der Jahrestagung der Gesellschaft fuer Informatik (Muenchen), Springer-Verlag, Gesellschaft fuer Informatik, Berlin - Heidelberg - New York, 1981, pp. 407-417.

[Fischer, Boecker 83]
G. Fischer, H.-D. Boecker, *The Nature of Design Processes and how Computer Systems can Support them*, Integrated Interactive Computing Systems, Proceedings of the European Conference on Integrated Interactive Computer Systems (ECICS 82), P. Degano, E. Sandewall (eds.), North-Holland, 1983, pp. 73-88.

[Fischer, McCall, Morch 89]
G. Fischer, R. McCall, A. Morch, *Design Environments for Constructive and Argumentative Design*, Human Factors in Computing Systems, CHI'89 Conference Proceedings (Austin, TX), ACM, New York, May 1989, pp. 269-275.

[Foley, Dam 82]
J.D. Foley, A. van Dam, *Fundamentals of Interactive Computer Graphics*, Addison-Wesley Publishing Company, Reading, MA, 1982.

[Friendly 88]
M. Friendly, *Advanced LOGO*, Lawrence Erlbaum Associates, Hillsdale, NJ, 1988.

[Gardner 70]
M. Gardner, *The fantastic combinations of John Conway's new solitaire game "life"*, Scientific American, Vol. 223, No. 4, October 1970, pp. 120-123.

[Gardner 83]
M. Gardner, *Wheels, Life, and Other Mathematical Amusements*, W.H. Freeman, New York and San Francisco, 1983.

[Goldberg 81]
A. Goldberg, *Smalltalk*, BYTE, Special Issue, Vol. 6, No. 8, 1981.

[Goldberg 84]
A. Goldberg, *Smalltalk-80, The Interactive Programming Environment*, Addison-Wesley Publishing Company, Reading, MA, 1984.

[Goldberg, Kay 77]
A. Goldberg, A. Kay, *Teaching Smalltalk*, Technical Report SSL-77-2, Xerox Palo Alto Research Center, Palo Alto, CA, 1977.

[Goldenberg, Feurzeig 87]
E.P. Goldenberg, W. Feurzeig, *Exploring Language with Logo*, The MIT Press, Cambridge, MA, 1987.

[Goldstein 82]
I.P. Goldstein, *The Genetic Graph: A Representation for the Evolution of Procedural Knowledge*, in D.H. Sleeman, J.S. Brown (eds.), *Intelligent Tutoring Systems*, Academic Press, London - New York, 1982, pp. 51-77, ch. 3.

[Guy 81]
R.K. Guy, *Unsolved Problems in Number Theory*, Springer-Verlag, Berlin - Heidelberg - New York, 1981.

[Harvey 85]
B. Harvey, *Computer Science Logo Style: Intermediate Programming*, The MIT Press, Cambridge, MA, Vol. 1, 1985.

[Harvey 86]
B. Harvey, *Computer Science Logo Style: Projects, Styles, and Techniques*, The MIT Press, Cambridge, MA, Vol. 2, 1986.

[Harvey 87a]
B. Harvey, *Computer Science Logo Style: Advanced Topics*, The MIT Press, Cambridge, MA, Vol. 3, 1987.

[Harvey 87b]
B. Harvey, *Versions of Logo*, Classroom Computer Learning, Vol. 7, No. 7, April 1987.

[Hewitt 77]
C. Hewitt, *Viewing Control Structures as Patterns of Passing Messages*, Artificial Intelligence, Vol. 8, 1977, pp. 323-364.

[Hurley 85]
J.P. Hurley, *Logo Physics*, Holt, Rinehart and Winston, New York, 1985.

[Hutchins, Hollan, Norman 86]
E.L. Hutchins, J.D. Hollan, D.A. Norman, *Direct Manipulation Interfaces*, in D.A. Norman, S.W. Draper (eds.), *User Centered System Design, New Perspectives on Human-Computer Interaction*, Lawrence Erlbaum Associates, Hillsdale, NJ, 1986, pp. 87-124, ch. 5.

[Illich 73]
I. Illich, *Tools for Conviviality*, Harper and Row, New York, 1973.

[Kay 77]
A.C. Kay, *Microelectronics and the Personal Computer*, Scientific American, 1977, pp. 231-244.

[Keene 89]
S.E. Keene, *Object-Oriented Programming in Common Lisp: A Programmer's Guide to CLOS*, Addison-Wesley Publishing Company, 1989.

[Knuth 69]
D.E. Knuth, *The Art of Computer Programming. Vol. 1: Fundamental Algorithms*, Addison-Wesley Publishing Company, Reading, MA, Menlo Park, CA, Addison-Wesley-Series in Computer Science and Information Processing, 1969.

[Lifeline 73]
Lifeline; a quarterly newletter for enthusiasts of John Conway's game of Life, 1971-1973.

[Papert 80]
S. Papert, *Mindstorms: Children, Computers and Powerful Ideas*, Basic Books, New York, 1980.

[Papert 86]
S. Papert, *Constructionism: A New Opportunity for Elementary Science Education*, Proposal to The National Science Foundation, MIT - The Media Laboratory, Cambridge, MA, 1986.

[Polya 45]
G. Polya, *How to Solve it?*, PUP, Princeton, NJ, 1945.

[Poundstone 85]
W. Poundstone, *The Recursive Universe: Cosmic Complexity and the limits of Scientific Knowledge*, William Morrow and Company, Inc, New York, 1985.

[Resnick 88]
M. Resnick, *MultiLogo: A Study of Children and Concurrent Programming*, Master's Thesis, MIT, Cambridge, MA, 1988.

[Simon 81]
H.A. Simon, *The Sciences of the Artificial*, The MIT Press, Cambridge, MA, 1981.

[Stefik, Bobrow 86]
M.J. Stefik, D.G. Bobrow, *Object-Oriented Programming: Themes and Variations*, AI Magazine, Vol. 6, No. 4, Winter 1986.

[Thorp 62]
E.O. Thorp, *Beat the dealer: a winning strategy for the game of twenty-one; a scientific analysis of the world-wide game known variously as blackjack, twenty-one, vingt-et-un, pontoon, or Van John.*, Blaisdell Pub. Co., New York, NY, 1962.

[Ulam 64]
S. Ulam, *Problems in Modern Mathematics*, John Wiley, New York, 1964.

[Uston 81]
K. Uston, *Million Dollar Blackjack*, Gambling Times Inc., Hollywood, CA, 1981.

[Watt 83]
D. Watt, *Learning with Logo*, McGraw-Hill, New York, 1983.

[Weir 87]
S. Weir, *Cultivating Minds*, Harper and Row, New York, 1987.

[Weizenbaum 65]
J. Weizenbaum, *ELIZA—A Computer Program for the Study of Natural Language Communication between Man and Machine*, Communications of the ACM, Vol. 9, No. 1, January 1965.

[Wenger 87]
E. Wenger, *Artificial Intelligence and Tutoring Systems*, Morgan Kaufmann Publishers, Los Altos, CA, 1987.

[Winograd 72]
T. Winograd, *Understanding Natural Language*, Academic Press, New York, 1972.

[Winston 84]
P.H. Winston, *Artificial Intelligence*, Addison-Wesley Publishing Company, Reading, MA, 1984.

[Woods 70]
W.A. Woods, *Transition Network Grammars fo Natural Language Analysis*, Communications of the ACM, Vol. 13, No. 10, October 1970.

[Yarbrough 76]
L.D. Yarbrough, *Input/Output: Notorius 196! (a letter to the editor)*, Creative Computing, Vol. 2, No. 1, January 1976.

[Yob 75]
G. Yob, *Hunt the Wumpus*, Creative Computing, September/October 1975, pp. 51-54.